Library of
Davidson College

Allocation under Uncertainty

OTHER INTERNATIONAL ECONOMIC ASSOCIATION PUBLICATIONS

LATIN AMERICA IN THE INTERNATIONAL ECONOMY
MODELS OF ECONOMIC GROWTH
SCIENCE AND TECHNOLOGY IN ECONOMIC GROWTH
TRANSPORT AND THE URBAN ENVIRONMENT
THE ECONOMICS OF HEALTH AND MEDICAL CARE
THE MANAGEMENT OF WATER QUALITY AND THE ENVIRONMENT
AGRICULTURAL POLICY IN DEVELOPING COUNTRIES

Allocation under Uncertainty: Equilibrium and Optimality

Proceedings from a Workshop sponsored
by the International Economic Association

EDITED BY
JACQUES H. DRÈZE

with the assistance of F. Delbaen, L. Gevers
R. Guesnerie and D. Sondermann

A HALSTED PRESS BOOK

JOHN WILEY & SONS
New York – Toronto

© The International Economic Association 1974

All rights reserved. No part of this publication may be reproduced or transmitted, in any form or by any means, without permission.

First published in the United Kingdom 1974 by
THE MACMILLAN PRESS LTD

Published in the U.S.A. and Canada by Halsted Press, a Division of John Wiley & Sons, Inc., New York

Library of Congress Cataloging in Publication Data

Main entry under title:

Allocation under uncertainty: equilibrium and optimality.

"A Halsted Press book."
1. Risk—Congresses. 2. Equilibrium (Economics)—Congresses. 3. Saving and investment—Congresses. I. Drèze, Jacques H., ed. II. International Economic Association.
HB615.A68   332.6   73-1908
ISBN 0-470-22166-6

Printed in Great Britain

Contents

Acknowledgements vii
List of Participants ix
Preface and Introduction xi

PART ONE: INDIVIDUAL DECISIONS

1 Axiomatic Theories of Choice, Cardinal Utility and Subjective Probability: a review   *Jacques H. Drèze*   3
2 Two-Period Models of Consumption Decisions Under Uncertainty: a survey   *Agnar Sandmo*   24
3 Optimum Accumulation Under Uncertainty: the Case of Stationary Returns to Investment   *James A. Mirrlees*   36

PART TWO: GENERAL EQUILIBRIUM

4 Allocation Under Uncertainty: a survey   *Roger Guesnerie and Thierry de Montbrial*   53
5 Optimality of Equilibrium of Plans, Prices and Price Expectations   *Roger Guesnerie and Jean-Yves Jaffray*   71

PART THREE: INDIVIDUAL RISKS IN LARGE MARKETS

6 Optimum Allocation of Risk in a Market With Many Traders   *Yaffa Caspi*   89
7 Stochastic Preferences and General Equilibrium Theory   *Freddy Delbaen*   98
8 The Allocation of Individual Risks in Large Markets   *Edmond Malinvaud*   110

PART FOUR: OPTIMUM INVESTMENT WITH ASSET MARKETS

9 Investment Under Private Ownership: Optimality, Equilibrium and Stability   *Jacques H. Drèze*   129
10 Competitive Equilibrium of the Stock Exchange and Pareto Efficiency   *Louis Gevers*   167
11 Discount Rates for Public Investment Under Uncertainty   *Agnar Sandmo*   192

PART FIVE: SHORT-RUN EQUILIBRIUM WITH MONEY

12 On the Short-Run Equilibrium in a Monetary 213
    Economy   *Jean-Michel Grandmont*
13 Temporary Competitive Equilibrium Under Uncertainty 229
    Dieter Sondermann
14 Continuity of the Expected Utility   *Freddy Delbaen* 254

Acknowledgements

This volume contains one section of the studies which were prepared for the Workshop in Economic Theory organised by the International Economic Association in Bergen in 1971. The Association owes its gratitude to the Ford Foundation at whose suggestion the Workshop was undertaken and who were almost entirely responsible for its financing. In addition the Association is indebted to the Director of the Course, Professor James A. Mirrlees, and to his co-Directors, Professor Jacques Drèze, the Editor of this volume, and Professor Edmond Malinvaud. Thanks are also due to the Norwegian School of Economics and Business Administration, Bergen, which made available accommodation and library facilities, and in particular to Dr Agnar Sandmo who was in charge of the local secretariat and organisation.

List of Participants

J. A. Mirrlees, Oxford, England, Director
J. H. Drèze, CORE, Louvain, Belgium, Co-director (first two weeks)
E. Malinvaud, INSEE, Paris, France, Co-director (last two weeks)
A. Sandmo, Norwegian School of Economics and Business Administration, Bergen, Norway, Local Organiser

M. G. Allingham, University of Essex, England
C. Berthomieu, University of Nice, France
Mrs. Y. Caspi, Hebrew University, Jerusalem, Israel
P. Champsaur, INSEE, Paris, France
A. Chekhutov, Association of Soviet Economic Scientific Institutions, Moscow, U.S.S.R.
F. Delbaen, University of Brussels, Belgium
L. Eekhoudt, University of Mons, Belgium
J. Flemming, Nuffield College, Oxford, England
L. Gevers, CORE, Louvain, Belgium
J.-M. Grandmont, CEPREMAP, Paris, France
R. Guesnerie, CEPREMAP, Paris, France
P. J. Hammond, Nuffield College, Oxford, England
M. Jones-Lee, University of York, England
S. Littlechild, Graduate Centre for Management Studies, Birmingham, England
M. Marchand, University of Mons, Belgium
T. de Montbrial, Ecole Polytechnique and Commissariat du Plan, Paris, France
P. van Rompuy, University of Leuven, Belgium
P. Ruys, University of Tilburg, Netherlands
U. Schlieper, University of Saarland, Germany
C. Seidl, University of Vienna, Austria
C.-H. Sivan, University of Stockholm, Sweden
D. Sondermann, University of Saarland, Germany
D. Soskice, University College, Oxford, England
L. Tomasini, Einaudi Institute, Turin, Italy

Preface and Introduction

Jacques H. Drèze
CENTER FOR OPERATIONS RESEARCH AND ECONOMETRICS, LOUVAIN

The workshop organised by the International Economic Association and held in Bergen, 18 July–14 August 1971, differed in several respects from the well-known Symposia regularly sponsored by the Association. These Symposia have typically brought together, for a week, a group of senior economists interested in a specific topic. The topic is chosen first, the participants are then selected (by invitation) from among leading authorities on that topic. The proceedings consist mostly of original research papers and give a comprehensive picture of the state of research in a given area.

The Bergen workshop was organised in a different spirit. The purpose was to promote the professional development of young economists engaged in teaching or research at European universities. Although initially approached to organise an advanced summer course in economic theory, the directors of the workshop – James A. Mirrlees, Edmond Malinvaud and myself – preferred to entrust all teaching to the participants themselves. The announcement of the workshop indicated that participants would be expected to prepare, circulate and present both a research paper and a survey paper. The survey papers were meant to serve as a form of systematic teaching and also to provide a common, broad background against which the more specific research contributions could be evaluated. The announcement further stated that the work would be concentrated in two or three areas of economic theory, to be selected on the basis of interests expressed by participants, and invited young European economists to apply for participation.

When the twenty-five participants were selected, from a group of some seventy qualified applicants, it turned out that 'uncertainty' provided a central theme around which the workshop could most conveniently be organised. It was also decided to devote the first week (out of four) of the workshop to the general theory of resource allocation under uncertainty. The ten papers prepared for that first week (four survey papers and six research papers) form the basic material in the present volume. Although no systematic publication of proceedings had been planned, it was felt that these papers constituted a sufficiently articulate presentation of the current state of theorising to justify collecting them in a volume. It was also felt that the educational purpose of the workshop would be enhanced if these papers were carefully revised (or even rewritten, in some cases) in the light of the discussions at the workshop.

Four papers not presented during the first week of the workshop were added to the volume, namely Chapters 3, 8, 9 and 14. The chapter by Mirrlees on Optimum Accumulation (Savings) is a revised version of the first part of a paper which he presented during the third week of the workshop. It forms a natural complement to Sandmo's paper in Part 1, and was included for that reason.

Chapters 8 and 9 reproduce papers, by Malinvaud and myself respectively, that were not presented, but were circulated and discussed informally at the workshop. They were included so as to render Parts 2 and 3 more complete and self-contained.

Chapter 14 consists of a technical note, written during the workshop, which generalises some results in Chapter 13.

The final responsibility for organising the first week of the workshop, and for editing this volume, was mine. But I received substantial assistance in both tasks from Freddy Delbaen, Louis Gevers, Roger Guesnerie and Dieter Sondermann. During the spring of 1971, all four of them were in residence at the Center for Operations Research and Econometrics in Louvain, and we worked as a team in selecting topics, discussing the contents of survey papers and editing research papers. This close cooperation was continued during and after the workshop; all the papers in this volume have been read by at least one of them, and many have been substantially improved as a consequence. Most of the credit for the success of the first week of the workshop, and for whatever merits the present volume may possess, belongs to these four talented and congenial young economists.

The papers were read by Mrs. Alan Kirman, who patiently amended our style and grammar; she deserves much gratitude from the readers, as well as from the authors, of this volume.

The manuscript was prepared for the printer by Mrs. Jacques Vincent, who had already typed and retyped several papers and who handled competently the administrative tasks connected with editing this volume. Mrs. Jean Verkaeren and Mrs. Vincent proof-read the whole volume and collated the references. I wish to thank them for their valuable assistance.

Thanks are due to the Center for Operations Research and Econometrics, which covered secretarial costs, and to the Fonds de la Recherche Fondamentale Collective, Brussels, for general support of research in this area, and specific support of the work of Gevers and Sondermann (under contracts No. 611 and No. 968).

Preface and Introduction

Thanks are also due to the editors and publishers of the *Journal of Economic Theory* and of the *International Economic Review* for permission to reprint Chapters 8 and 11 respectively.

The contents of this volume can be described concisely with reference to subject matters. The book presents extensions to a world of uncertainty of the general theory of resource allocation. Consumption decisions are treated in Part 1; production and investment decisions are treated in Part 4; general equilibrium is treated in Part 2; equilibrium on insurance markets is treated in Part 3, and monetary equilibrium (with a fixed money supply) in Part 5.

Such a description does not bring out the methodological interrelationships among the various parts, and does not point to the methodological difficulties that remain to be overcome in the search for a more operational theory. I will accordingly organise along methodological lines a systematic summary of the volume, which may serve as a guide for exploring its contents.

The economic theory of resource allocation was initially developed for a given environment, defined by (i) a set of commodities, with the total resources (quantities of these commodities) initially available; (ii) a set of consumers, with their consumption sets and preferences; (iii) a set of producers, with their production sets. The theory has been concerned with allocations (i.e. feasible productions and consumptions) endowed with an optimality property (typically, the Pareto optimality property) or with an equilibrium property (typically, the property of 'equilibrium relative to a price system', or the property of 'competitive equilibrium'). The theory has consisted in finding conditions (about the initial resources, the consumer preferences and the technology) that imply the existence of such allocations or permit certain characterisations of these allocations (for instance, under minimal assumptions, an equilibrium relative to a price system is a Pareto optimum; under convexity assumptions, the converse proposition holds).

In a world of uncertainty, the environment is not given but depends upon uncertain events: research introduces new commodities and new technological possibilities, resources are discovered or accidentally destroyed, consumer tastes are affected by physical and psychological developments, the yield of production processes is affected by meteorological and random circumstances, and so on. It has become natural to describe uncertainty in economics by a set of alternative, mutually exclusive environments, or 'states of the environment', among which 'nature' will choose. This is a more basic starting point than 'derived' descriptions of the prevailing uncertainties – for instance, descriptions in terms of probability distributions of environmental characteristics, or in terms of uncertainty about economic variables (prices, production rates ...). This remark seems obvious today; it was not so obvious twenty years ago, when Arrow [1] and Savage [6] simultaneously showed how states of the environment (states of nature) provided an operational way of describing uncertainty situations in economics or in decision theory.[1]

The theory of resource allocation under uncertainty expounded in this volume relies upon the description just mentioned. It rests fundamentally upon a simple proposition: the results obtained for a given environment can be generalised to an uncertain environment, if a commodity is defined not only by its physical properties (including the time and place at which it is available) but also by an event conditional upon which it is available. That is, 'commodities' become 'contingent claims' or 'real insurance contracts'. The dimension of the commodity space rises to the product of the number of physical commodities by the cardinality of the set of events.

Initial resources, preferences and technology are defined in the enlarged commodity space. Allocations specify consumptions and productions for every event. Under this extension, the theory of optimality and equilibrium developed for a certain environment remains valid without modification; all that needs to be added is an appropriate reinterpretation.

This generalisation is spelled out with some detail in Part 2 of the present volume. The survey paper by Guesnerie and de Montbrial (Chapter 4) contains basic material that cannot be summarised further. These authors review the description of uncertainty by means of states of nature, and the implied reinterpretation of general equilibrium theory. They trace the consequences of the reinterpretation, for the significance of the optimality concept and of the convexity assumptions on preferences and production sets. They also indicate the important role that securities can play in the allocation of risk-bearing.

This last point – the role of securities – is treated more extensively by Guesnerie and Jaffray (Chapter 5), whose paper surveys previous work by Arrow [1] and Radner [5] and spells out in detail the link between the general equilibrium model of Part 2 and the more specialised models of Parts 4 and 5.

In an economy with a numeraire or with 'money', a contract promising delivery of one unit of a given physical commodity, conditionally on a given event, may be decomposed into a first contract promising a certain amount of 'money', conditional on that event;

[1] For a similar remark, in the introduction to another Proceedings volume published for the International Economic Association, see Borch [3], pp. xiv–xv.

Preface and Introduction

and a second contract stipulating the exchange of that amount of money against one unit of the given commodity (again conditionally on the event). The first contract is an insurance contract; more generally, collections of insurance contracts on alternative events define 'securities' or 'assets'. Insurance contracts and assets provide the basic opportunities for transferring risks among individuals. The models presented by Guesnerie and Jaffray bring out precisely the extent and limitations of these opportunities. They also reveal that correct expectations of future spot prices are required for an efficient allocation of risks among individuals to result from insurance contracts alone. The models of Part 4 explore situations where the existing assets offer insufficient insurance opportunities. The models of Part 5 study the more realistic 'temporary equilibria' that emerge from subjective (not necessarily correct) price expectations.

The survey papers in Part 2 thus present the basic model within which the economic theory of resource allocation under uncertainty is currently being developed. The model is elegant and powerful; it is also abstract and idealised. The remainder of the volume illustrates both the strength and the weaknesses of the general model.

In Parts 1 and 3 to 5, more specific allocation problems are considered. For some of these (Parts 3 and 4), the model of Part 2 provides the general framework which is indispensable for a proper formulation and clear understanding of the issues at hand. For other problems (Parts 1 and 5), progress seems to have been achieved by ignoring the general framework rather than by exploiting it; at least, such has been the case up to this time.

Ultimately, all risks are borne by the individual economic agents, the consumers. Optimal allocations will be defined with reference to consumer preferences among uncertain prospects. Equilibrium allocations will be determined by consumer choices among such prospects. In either case, consistent individual preferences among uncertain prospects will be the starting point of the theory.

The axiomatic theory of consistent decisions under uncertainty presented by Savage [6] provides a natural and general starting point for research on the economics of uncertainty. That theory is reviewed in Chapter 1, where objections, merits and limitations are also evaluated. The description of uncertain prospects by means of the consequences associated with alternative states of nature provides a simple link with the general equilibrium model – a link which is also brought out in Chapter 1.

The main result of the theory is the 'moral expectation theorem': there exists a subjective probability measure on the states of nature and a cardinal utility function for consequences, such that decisions are ordered by their expected utility. This result provides a rationale for models where uncertainty is described by probability distributions of economic variables (like prices, incomes, yields, etc.).

The most important decisions made by consumers bear upon the allocation of their resources among immediate consumption on the one hand and provision for future consumption – through a portfolio of insurance contracts and assets – on the other hand. This problem has been studied by some authors within a two-period model (the present and the future), by other authors within an infinite time-horizon model. In both cases, consumers are assumed to allocate their resources so as to maximise the expected utility of present and future consumption, when future income and/or the yield of assets are uncertain.

In Chapter 2, Sandmo reviews the two-period models. He first discusses the impact of uncertainty about future resources on current consumption. Risk aversion in itself does not determine whether increased uncertainty about future income leads to increased savings, but decreasing absolute risk aversion (properly defined, in the two-period case) has that implication. The impact of increased uncertainty about asset yields is less determinate, in particular because it works differently for lenders and for borrowers. Several other specific issues are also reviewed (for instance, the conditions under which the demand for risky assets increases with income, or under which consumption and portfolio decisions are separable.)

The infinite-horizon models are covered by Mirrlees in Chapter 3. After reviewing various problems and various types of uncertainties, he concentrates on a model with a single, risky asset and no income uncertainty. Both a discrete–time formulation and a continuous–time formulation are presented, with stochastic independence over time of the uncertain yields. Mirrlees introduces a new existence theorem for optimal policies and observes that uncertainty may affect saving either positively or negatively, depending upon the utility function. However, if there is no impatience, a positive impact of uncertainty on saving obtains in the discrete model with homogeneous utility and emerges from a heuristic argument in the continuous model.

The studies collected in Part 1 of the volume fit the consumers into the general model. It should, however, be clear from the foregoing that consumer decisions are analysed at a partial equilibrium level: the budget sets (incomes, asset prices, yield distributions) are exogenously given. In contrast, Parts 3 to 5 deal with general equilibrium analysis, and specialise the basic model of Part 2 in three distinct ways.

Part 3 proceeds from the distinction between risks which are socially relevant and risks which affect the individuals but disappear at the social level by the operation of the law of large numbers.

Preface and Introduction

In Chapter 6, Mrs. Caspi considers an exchange economy involving a single physical commodity but a set of alternative states of nature. Consumers are assumed to be risk averse and to have a common subjective probability measure over the states (but different utility functions for consumption). Their endowments depend upon the state that obtains. When society's endowment is the same in two states, then Pareto optimality requires that every individual consumption also be the same in both states.[1] Mrs. Caspi considers 'replica economies', with a basic set of consumers 'replicated' r times; two 'replicated' consumers (two consumers 'of the same type') have identical tastes; their endowments are identically but independently distributed. Competitive allocations assign identical (and perfectly correlated) consumptions to consumers of the same type. When the number of independent replicas tends to infinity, the consumption of every individual tends to the expected value of his endowment.

Delbaen (Chapter 7) specifically considers uncertainty about consumer tastes. His paper surveys alternative approaches to the definition of random preferences; he adopts the approach developed by Hildenbrand [4] in order to introduce random preferences into equilibrium analysis. This paper uses deeper mathematical reasoning than most other chapters in this volume, but careful definitions make it largely self-contained, and the basic ideas are simple and elegant. Consumer preferences depend upon the state of nature (once again, this approach is more basic than the alternative based upon choice probabilities). Consequently, individual and aggregate demand functions also depend upon the state of nature. Delbaen introduces the concept of 'asymptotically independent' consumers – a generalisation of the stochastic independence assumption used by Hildenbrand [4]. As the number of asymptotically independent consumers tends to infinity, the random fluctuations of aggregate demand per capita tend to zero (at all prices).

This neat application of the law of large numbers underlies the broader analysis of Malinvaud in Chapter 8. The framework of his analysis is the general model of Part 2, with production and an arbitrary set of commodities. The consumers and producers are replicated, in the same way as in Mrs. Caspi's paper. An assumption of asymptotic independence, similar to that of Delbaen, is introduced within each type. A Pareto optimum for this economy is also an equilibrium relative to a price system. Because the random fluctuations of aggregate demand per capita tend to zero as the number of replicas goes to infinity, they will be ignored – and the Pareto optimum will be sustained by a price system for the physical commodities that does not depend upon the state of nature. As

[1] This result was first presented by Borch [2].

Malinvaud ingeniously shows, it follows that firms should, under the assumption of his model, maximise the expected value of their profits. It also follows that a Pareto optimal allocation of risks among consumers can be achieved by a system of actuarially fair insurance of individual risks. These two statements are intuitively plausible; they provide the strongest form of conclusion applicable to socially irrelevant risks.

In contrast, the papers of Part 4 are directly concerned with socially relevant risks and more specifically with the decisions to engage, or not to engage, in various types of risky activities. That is, one is not only concerned with allocating among individuals the bearing of existing risks but also with influencing, through economic activities, the global risks to be borne. The activities under consideration are the production and investment activities of firms and public institutions. The three papers in Part 4 are concerned with the optimality of production and investment decisions.

Chapters 9 and 10 use the same model, which aims at capturing the essential operating features of private ownership economies. There is a single physical commodity, but there are two time periods and the state of nature in the second period is unknown. Firms transform current inputs into vectors of future outputs that depend upon the state of nature. They have access to activities with different state distributions of output (e.g. safe investments with moderate yields in all states versus risky investments with either high or negative yields depending upon the state). They must choose among these activities and there is no provision for insurance of the resulting risks. These firms are owned by individuals (consumers), and there exists a possibility of redistributing among individuals the ownership shares in the firms (e.g. through a stock market). The future consumption opportunities of each individual depend upon the (uncertain) yield of the investments chosen by the firms in which he owns shares. One wishes to characterise Pareto optimal programs (investment decisions for the firms and portfolios of shares for the consumers), and to investigate the prospects for decentralising decisions (e.g. with investment decisions taken within the firms and shares of ownership traded among individuals).

Drèze (Chapter 9) shows that the set of feasible allocations for such an economy is not convex, even when all production and consumption sets are convex. Accordingly, one can only hope to characterise locally optimal programs; no test for global optimality of a program is available. He next shows that, under a given distribution of ownership shares among consumers, the problems of reaching Pareto optimal production and investment decisions within a single firm is formally identical to the problem of finding a Pareto optimal allocation in an economy with public goods.[1] Under given production and investment decisions in all firms, a Pareto optimal distribution of ownership shares among individuals is an equilibrium relative to a price system on the stock market.

A local optimum is characterised by Pareto optimality of the production and investment plans of all firms, the distribution of ownership shares among consumers being given; and by Pareto optimality of the distribution of shares among individuals, the production plans being given. The paper gives some examples of local optima that are stable but globally inefficient. Drèze considers finally sequences of decentralised decisions. Each firm in turn revises its production plan, whereupon the consumers exchange shares. The process is repeated until no further exchanges result. If each decision of the sequence is Pareto optimal (for a single firm, given the distribution of shares and the plans of other firms; or for the consumers exchanging shares, given the production plans), then the sequence will converge to a local optimum (or a set of local optima). That is, sequences of 'myopic optima' converge to local optima. Procedures for generating such sequences are discussed.

The main difficulty here lies with the Pareto optimality of production decisions within a firm. The analogy with the public goods problem reveals the nature of that difficulty. Information about the preferences of consumers (shareholders) among state distributions of output must be collected and aggregated. Gevers (Chapter 10) investigates the prospects for reaching Pareto optimal decisions within a firm through majority voting by shareholders, in an economy with a stock market. These prospects are almost non-existent. There are two reasons for this negative conclusion. One reason is that shareholders, when voting about production and investment plans, will be concerned simultaneously about the implications of the decision for (i) their own (state distribution of) consumption, if they continue to hold an unchanged share in the firm; and (ii) the market value of the firm on the stock market, hence the possibility of realising capital gains. The first concern is conducive to Pareto optimality, the second is not. Another reason is that majority voting will generally not perform the type of aggregation of individual preferences required for Pareto optimality. Gevers considers the alternative of delegating decisions to management and reaches equally pessimistic conclusions. He finally considers uncertainty about future prices in a multi-commodity model and reaches the same conclusions once more.

These two chapters raise serious doubts about the ability of

[1] An alternative, and more general, development of this point is given in the first part of the paper by Gevers, Chapter 10.

existing institutions in market economies to bring about efficient production and investment decisions, when socially relevant risks are at stake.

If each firm has access to a single activity, and must accordingly decide about the level but not the nature of its production and investment, then absence of increasing returns is sufficient to preserve convexity of the set of feasible allocations. If, furthermore, one is interested in decisions of public institutions, then the problems raised by Gevers about control by majority voting or managerial dictatorship do not arise. The prospects for Pareto optimality of decentralised investment decisions might accordingly be restored. They are explored by Sandmo in Chapter 11.

Sandmo's main concern is to derive operational rules for Pareto optimality of public investment, in 'mixed economies' where a private and a public sector coexist – that is, where the same activities are carried out (possibly at different levels) in both the private sector and the public sector. He considers two institutional frameworks, one with private firms organised as joint-stock corporations whose shares are traded on the stock market, the other with a private sector consisting of unincorporated firms owned by single individuals.

In the previous literature on this problem, some authors have taken the view that the public sector as a whole is pooling risks (across activities and/or across individuals) and could therefore ignore the 'risk margins' prevailing in the private sector. Other authors have taken the view that the public sector should react to the riskiness of investments in the same way as the private sector, when similar activities are at stake.

Sandmo's analysis confirms the latter view, for the case of a 'mixed economy'. In the simpler framework corresponding to private production by corporate firms, the stock market provides opportunities for pooling risks in the private sector, and the market 'risk margins' represent a social evaluation of the risk associated with each type of investment (market imperfections aside). In the alternative framework of unincorporated private firms, public investments should still be geared to the risk margins prevailing in the private sector, but market data no longer contain the information required to that effect.

When we turn to Part 5, the concern shifts from characterisation and implementation of optimal allocations to existence of equilibrium allocations. At the same time, an important step is taken in the direction of descriptive realism. I will first describe the model used by Grandmont in Chapter 12, then indicate the generalisations of that model introduced by Sondermann in Chapter 13.

Grandmont studies an exchange economy where money is the

Preface and Introduction

only store of value. There is an arbitrary set of physical commodities. Although there is in principle an infinity of time periods (1, ... t, $t+1$, ...), only two periods, t and $t+1$, are considered explicitly. At the beginning of period t, each trader owns a certain quantity of money, which he has carried over from period $t-1$, and certain quantities of the physical commodities, his initial resources for period t. An exchange market for physical commodities and money is organised. After the exchanges are completed, each trader will consume in period t the quantities of physical commodities, and carry over into period $t+1$ the quantity of money, which he then owns.

Grandmont assumes that (i) each trader has consistent preferences among vectors specifying his consumption in periods t and $t+1$, and (ii) each trader acts (in period t) as if he were to spend in period $t+1$ all the money carried over from t. The trader is assumed to maximise the expected utility of consumption in periods t and $t+1$; the maximisation is with respect to consumption at t (given the prices of consumption goods at t); the expectation is with respect to prices prevailing in period $t+1$ (initial resources accruing at $t+1$ are assumed known at t). Consumption at $t+1$ will be optimal, given past consumptions, over the budget set defined by initial resources at $t+1$, money carried over from t and the prices effectively prevailing at $t+1$. Expectations about future prices are assumed representable by a probability density that depends continuously upon current prices.

Does there exist a price system for physical commodities at t which equates supply and demand for money as well as for all physical commodities? Grandmont shows that standard assumptions (including continuity and convexity of preferences) are not sufficient to prove an existence theorem. For instance, if all traders are convinced that prices at $t+1$ will be the same as prices at t, if initial resources at $t+1$ are the same as initial resources at t, and if all traders display a preference for present consumption, then the money market cannot be in equilibrium. An additional assumption is needed to prove the existence theorem. Grandmont assumes that the range of the probability density for prices at $t+1$ remains bounded, no matter what prices prevail at t. In particular, this assumption rules out unit elasticity of price expectations. However, it suffices to introduce this assumption for a single consumer, and the existence theorem follows.

The analysis of Grandmont is readily extended to an arbitrary finite, or to an infinite, number of periods, when the traders' price expectations are certain. The case of stochastic expectation is more complicated but it is likely that the main conclusions would continue to hold.[1]

---

[1] Grandmont's paper contains an interesting discussion of homogeneity of the demand functions and 'money illusion'.

Sondermann's paper (Chapter 13) retains the basic feature of Grandmont's model (two periods, expected utility maximisation, continuous bounded price expectations) but extends the model in two directions. First, he introduces production and storage of physical commodities. Second, he introduces a multiplicity of assets.

Production and storage activities are carried out by a set of firms; their outputs at t depend upon past decisions; they can transform inputs at t into outputs at $t+1$. There is no technological uncertainty; still, because prices at $t+1$ are not known with certainty, the producers take decisions under uncertainty (about the value of their output). Shares of ownership in the firms constitute assets that may be held (in addition to money) by the consumers and by the firms. The market prices of these assets in period t are determined simultaneously with commodity prices. Asset prices in period $t+1$ are unknown, so that price expectations are defined (for consumers and for firms) over commodity prices and asset prices.

Sondermann assumes that each firm acts (in choosing inputs and a portfolio of outputs) as if it were maximising the expected utility of its market value at $t+1$. The market value is defined as the value of output plus the value of the portfolio of assets, at $t+1$ prices. The expectation is with respect to those prices. The utility function of each firm is taken as given; it is assumed concave, thus allowing for maximisation of expected value as a limiting case. As Sondermann points out, this is a behaviouristic assumption for which no normative justification is given. The assumption eliminates the difficulties, stressed by Drèze and Gevers, which would arise if production decisions were guided by the interests of shareholders.[1]

Under convexity of the production sets, continuity of the price expectations of the firms, and assumptions similar to those of Grandmont for consumers, Sondermann proves the existence of a price system for physical commodities and assets at t, which equates supply and demand for all physical commodities, for assets and for money.

Sondermann's paper starts with the presentation of a 'general structure for temporary equilibrium analysis', of which the model reviewed here is a specific application. The discussion of the general structure contains a proposition about the continuity of expected utility, which was generalised during the Bergen workshop by Delbaen. That generalisation is reproduced here as Chapter 14.

The models of Part 5 are concerned with the existence of price equilibria, under specific assumptions about the way in which uncertainty about the future is perceived by the economic agents. It was stressed, at the beginning of this summary, that the description of

[1] The stage seems to be set, however, for merging the two approaches.

uncertainty, in terms of probability distributions for such economic variables as prices, is not the most basic one (probability distributions of prices are not a primitive concept for economic analysis); yet, that description may well be the most fruitful one, in our present state of knowledge, to study such problems as monetary equilibrium. The equilibria obtained by Grandmont and Sondermann do not have the optimality properties of the equilibria defined in Parts 2 to 4; but they exist under more realistic assumptions.

It was generally felt by participants at the workshop, at the end of the first week, that the analysis of optimality in Parts 2 and 4 rested on assumptions about (market) opportunities for pooling risks, or implied information and motivation structures for guiding decisions, that have no observable counterpart in existing economies. The more realistic models of temporary equilibrium analysis, which extend the approach introduced by Hicks in *Value and Capital*, were felt to offer the more promising avenue for further research.

These conclusions are undoubtedly well founded. Still, I feel inclined to stress the complementarity, rather than the antagonism, which exists between the two approaches. In the search for optimal ways of allocating resources under uncertainty, realism dictates the recognition of constraints that preclude the attainment of Pareto optimal allocations, so that the search becomes concerned with constrained Pareto optima. Temporary equilibria have an optimality property under rather extreme constraints on the set of attainable allocations. Realism again dictates that all the existing opportunities for pooling risks be recognised in the analysis of short-run equilibrium. The single preoccupation of increased realism thus seems to pull the two approaches towards each other; hopefully, the sets of models used within the first and the second approach will soon intersect. The quality of the work presented during the whole Bergen workshop seems to justify this hope, which is reflected in the title chosen for the proceedings volume.

J. H. D.

Louvain, June 1972

REFERENCES

[1] K. J. Arrow, 'Le rôle des valeurs boursières pour la répartition la meilleure des risques', in *Econométrie*, Colloque International XL, CNRS (Paris, 1953), pp. 41–7; translated as 'The Role of Securities in the Optimal Allocation of Risk-Bearing', *Review of Economic Studies*, vol. XXXI (1964), pp. 91–6.
[2] K. Borch, 'The Safety Loading of Reinsurance Premiums', *Skandinavisk Aktuarietidskrift*, vol. XLIII (1960), pp. 163–84.
[3] K. Borch and J. Mossin (eds.), *Risk and Uncertainty*, Proceedings of an I.E.A. Conference (London: Macmillan, 1968).

[4] W. Hildenbrand, 'Random Preferences and Equilibrium Analysis', *Journal of Economic Theory*, vol. III (1971), pp. 414–29.
[5] R. Radner, 'Existence of Equilibrium of Plans, Prices and Price Expectations in a Sequence of Markets', *Econometrica*, vol. XL (1972), pp. 289–303.
[6] L. J. Savage, *The Foundations of Statistics* (New York: Wiley, 1954).

Part 1

Individual Decisions

1 Axiomatic Theories of Choice, Cardinal Utility and Subjective Probability: a review

Jacques H. Drèze[1]
CORE, LOUVAIN

Most of the papers collected in this volume rely, explicitly or implicitly, upon (i) a formal description of uncertainty situations in terms of the concepts of events, acts and consequences; and (ii) an axiomatic theory of individual choices, which justifies the representation of preferences among acts by their expected utility.

The purpose of this introductory essay is to review these concepts and axioms against the background of their economic applications. The essay is not a systematic exposition of the theory (results will be stated without proofs); neither is it a survey of contributions to the theory (only a few key references will be used). Rather, it is a *review* of the main properties of the concepts and of the axiomatic theory, with a discussion of their usefulness and limitations in economic applications.[2]

Section I provides an element of historical perspective. Section II reviews the concepts of events, acts and consequences. Section III reviews the axioms of a normative theory of individual choice under uncertainty and their main implication (the moral expectation theorem). Section IV reviews some objections that have been raised against the normative appeal of the axioms. Section V is devoted to a general discussion of the usefulness and limitations of the theory. Section VI relates the concepts of the general theory to those underlying economic applications presented elsewhere in this volume.

I. HISTORICAL PERSPECTIVE

On 13 May 1952, the participants in a symposium on 'Foundations and Applications of the Theory of Risk-Bearing' [11] held in Paris

---

[1] I am grateful to Louis-André Gérard Varet, Louis Gevers, Roger Guesnerie, Agnar Sandmo and Dieter Sondermann for their comments on a first draft of this paper.

[2] Participants in the conference had been urged to become acquainted beforehand with the theory of individual choice under uncertainty, as exposed for instance by Savage [29] or Arrow [4]; and with the model of allocation of resources under uncertainty introduced by Arrow [3] and Debreu [5].

heard successively L. J. Savage present 'An Axiomatisation of Reasonable Behavior in the Face of Uncertainty' [31] and K. Arrow analyse 'The Role of Securities in the Optimal Allocation of Risk-Bearing' [3]. These two papers have influenced deeply the development of the theory of resource allocation under uncertainty. In order to appreciate the significance of these two papers, one must look back at the state of the theory of risk-bearing prior to the 1952 symposium in Paris.

Those who have the privilege of youth and who received their training in this field after these two papers were published,[1] can still get a picture of the previous state of affairs from the survey paper published by Arrow in 1951 [2]. Actually, that paper presents, in an orderly manner, a spectrum of approaches and results that could, at that time, be grasped only by those who had fully mastered a highly diversified literature.

Arrow surveys the status of theories 'explaining how individuals choose among alternate courses of actions when the consequences of their actions are incompletely known to them' ([2], p. 1). It is noteworthy that he proceeds from the following premise ([2], p. 9): 'It is understood that in economic situations the consequences about which uncertainty exists are commodity bundles or money payments over future dates.' His survey deals successively with two topics: the description of uncertain consequences, and the ordering of courses of actions (whose uncertain consequences have been described in some way).

With reference to the *description of the consequences* resulting from a given course of action, the major distinction is between 'those [descriptions] which use exclusively the language of probability distributions and those which call for some other principle, either to replace or to supplement' ([2], p. 8). The first category is further subdivided according to the chosen interpretation of probability (see Savage [29], p. 3, for a concise description of alternative approaches). The second category reflects the views of scholars of no lesser standing than the economists Keynes, Knight and Shackle, the statisticians Neyman, Pearson and Wald.

With reference to the *ordering of courses of action*, sharper issues arise when the problem has been recognised as that of ordering probability distributions of consequences. In the 1930s and early 1940s, economists like Hicks [18], Marschak [23] and Tintner [34]

---

[1] The proceedings of the Conference appeared (in French) in November 1953; Savage's contribution was fully developed in his book, *The Foundations of Statistics* [29] which appeared in 1954; Arrow's paper did not become available in English until 1963, but the material in his paper is covered and extended by Debreu in chapter 7 of the *Theory of Value* [5], which appeared in 1959.

were debating whether the ordering of such distributions could be based on their means and standard deviations alone (as in [18]), or on these two and other parameters as well (as in [23]), or should more generally be represented by a 'risk preference functional' (as in [34]).

An axiomatic approach to the ordering of probability distributions, recognising explicitly the 'mutually exclusive' nature of alternative consequences, had been introduced by Ramsey [28]. This approach was revived in successively clearer and simpler terms by von Neumann and Morgenstern [25] and Marschak [24], gaining increasing recognition for the existence of a utility function which permits the representation of an ordering among probability distributions of consequences by the mathematical expectation of the utility of these consequences.

Still, by 1951, this approach was far from being generally accepted (see, for instance, the various papers by Allais in [11] and elsewhere); and its applicability was limited to those situations where the probability distribution of consequences was somehow given. The main suggestions contained in Arrow's survey, insofar as other situations are concerned, came from the minimax school of Wald [35] (extended to 'minimax regret' by Savage [30]) and from the specific theory of Shackle [33]. The shortcomings of these approaches are exposed by Arrow.[1]

The defects of this state of affairs were numerous. The lack of agreement among specialists was rather confusing for the beginning student. There was no general conceptual framework, within which one could identify the difficulties specific to certain classes of problems, and assess the significance of specific results.

The most useful theoretical contribution seemed to be that of von Neumann and Morgenstern – yet it was still surrounded by rather obscure discussions. Its applicability seemed restricted to situations where probabilities reflecting the beliefs of the decision-maker could be objectively defined; its relation to the neo-classical theories of consumer choice and of the firm had not been spelled out; and its exposition in terms of 'consequences' identified with wealth was a continuous source of misunderstandings.[2] The need for a more general theory was thus acute.

[1] Arrow's survey devotes a few pages to the work of de Finetti, Ramsey, Rubin and Chernoff on axiomatic theories of '*a priori* probabilities'. However, little emphasis is placed on these developments, the significance of which was by no means evident at that time.

[2] This is perhaps best evidenced by the famous article of Friedman and Savage [12], where a single function is assumed to describe satisfactorily the utility of wealth to both a consumer and his heirs; and by the attention paid to the reinterpretation by Markowitz [22] of the Friedman-Savage analysis.

II. THE CONCEPTUAL FRAMEWORK

It is by now standard practice to describe a problem of individual decision under uncertainty (or a 'game against nature') in terms of a matrix where:

(i) the rows correspond to alternative, mutually exclusive courses of action open to the decision-maker;
(ii) the columns correspond to alternative, mutually exclusive courses of future events;
(iii) the entries of the matrix correspond to the consequences for the decision-maker resulting from a given course of action under a specific course of events.

Such a description aims at starting from primitive concepts, endowed with an operational meaning in terms of observable phenomena. Thus, the uncertainty is traced back to its source (the future course of events), instead of being described in derived terms – a probability distribution, for instance. And the consequences need not be commodity bundles or money payments; their description may encompass any relevant consideration – from which, possibly, a consumption vector or budget constraint may eventually result.

The trilogy of rows, columns and entries of the matrix, corresponding to 'what the decision-maker does, what nature does, what happens to the decision-maker' admits of a natural abstract representation in terms of two sets. Denoting a course of action by a, a course of future events by s, one then considers the set A of elements $a, a', \ldots$ and the set S of elements $s, s', \ldots$;[1] every entry of the matrix may then be denoted by an ordered pair (a, s). This formal structure is fully adequate as a starting point of the theory. In the same way as 'the currently prevalent axiomatic treatment of probability as a branch of measure theory seems designed to keep the technical development of the theory from being bogged down in the difficulties of the 'foundations' ([2] p. 406) so the exclusive reliance upon the sets A, S and their cartesian product $A \times S$ makes it possible to develop the theory of choice under uncertainty without facing explicitly any difficulties of interpretation.

Expositors of the theory discuss concisely the interpretation of the basic concepts. Thus, Savage ([29], p. 9) proposes 'the following nomenclature ... as brief, suggestive, and in reasonable harmony with the usages of statistics and ordinary discourse:

---

[1] The words 'course of action', 'action' and 'act' are here treated as synonyms; the same remark applies to 'course of future events', 'state of the world' and 'state'.

Axiomatic Theories

the *world*: the object about which the person is concerned;
a *state* (of the world): a description of the world, leaving no relevant aspect undescribed;
the *true* state (of the world): the state that does in fact obtain, i.e. the true description of the world.'

He then completes his set of definitions as follows:

an *event*: a set of states;
a *consequence*: anything that may happen to the person;
an *act*: a function attaching a consequence to each state of the world.[1]

The primitive concepts are thus states and consequences. The formal theory is based upon a set of states S, a set of events (to be denoted $E, E', \ldots$) given by the σ-algebra of S, a set of consequences C and a set of acts given by the mappings of S into C. To consider every such mapping as an act means, of course, to consider hypothetical acts, which do not correspond to courses of action effectively open to the decision-maker.[2]

Some of these hypothetical acts (e.g. constant acts) are needed in the construction of the theory.

The cardinality of the sets S and C has important technical implications. S must be at least denumerably infinite. On the other hand, the theory is easier to develop for acts with only a finite number of distinct consequences.

Before turning to the axioms, three properties of the concepts of events, acts and consequences should be stressed. These properties define the class of decision situations which the theory aims at encompassing; the reasonableness of the axioms should be appraised with reference to those situations only.

(1) *About Events*

Events must be defined with *interpersonal objectivity* and their occurrence must lie *beyond the control of the decision-maker*. These two aspects are covered by the interpretation of events as circumstances upon which bets can be placed, since the very idea of a bet[3] presupposes that (i) it can be ascertained with interpersonal objectivity who has won the bet, and (ii) neither party to the bet can unilaterally enforce his winning.

---

[1] This definition is motivated as follows: 'If two different acts had the same consequences in every state of the world, there would from the present point of view be no point in considering them two different acts at all. An act may therefore be identified with its possible consequences' ([29], p. 14).

[2] For instance, many consumers could buy a lottery ticket giving them a very small chance of winning a million dollars, but very few have access to a course of action giving them the certainty of winning that amount.

[3] As distinct from a 'challenge'.

The relevance of these remarks for economic applications is the following: (i) uncertainty of the decision-maker about his own tastes at a future date cannot be described through distinct events corresponding to distinct preference structures, since this would violate the condition of interpersonal objectivity;[1] (ii) 'moral hazards', that is, uncertainties that lie (at least in part) under the control of the decision-maker, cannot be described through events either.[2]

(2) *About Consequences*

'In the description of a consequence is included all that the agent values' ([4], p. 45); accordingly, commodity bundles will generally prove inadequate to define consequences. To quote Savage:

> Before going on a picnic with friends, a person decides to buy a bathing suit or a tennis racket. . . . The possession of the tennis racket and the possession of the bathing suit are to be regarded as acts, not consequences. . . . The consequences relevant to the decision are such as these: a refreshing swim with friends, sitting on a shadeless beach twiddling a brand new tennis racket while one's friends swim, etc. . . .([29], p. 25).

Even in those cases where commodity bundles prove adequate to define consequences, a careful definition of commodities may be required. Thus, a person buying 6 eggs, some of which may conceivably be bad, is in fact buying x good eggs and $6-x$ bad eggs, where x is an *unknown* integer, $0 \le x \le 6$. This purchase may be described by a point in the two-dimensional space of 'good' and 'bad' eggs, the location of the point being a function of the state of the world (x).[3]

(3) *About Constant Acts*

The assumption that every consequence can be attained in any state (which implies the existence of constant acts) precludes the explicit consideration of events that are of significant value to the decision-maker; thus, a person's death is clearly a circumstance on which bets can be placed (e.g. through a life-insurance contract), but it is also a

[1] With reference to the economics of insurance, a contract specifying that 'I shall receive a certain capital if I develop a taste for Bourbon whisky' would be viewed by the company as equivalent to a sure promise of that capital, since the event mentioned in the contract is not amenable to their verification.

[2] With reference to the economics of insurance again, 'moral hazards' (e.g. arson) occur when the person's actions (as opposed to his tastes) escape verification.

[3] Whereas '6 good eggs' is arithmetically equal to two times '3 good eggs' the same property of addition does not hold for '6 eggs, some of which are good', unless specific assumptions about the determinants of the quality of the eggs are added.

Axiomatic Theories

'vital' element in the description of consequences. In defining constant acts, a consequence like 'being alive, poor and healthy' should be attainable in the event that the decision-maker dies – which stretches the imagination of mere mortals a bit too far, in my opinion. It thus seems best to exclude such circumstances from explicit consideration.[1]

These properties being understood, it should be clear that the basic concepts offer a medium for the description of problems of decision under uncertainty, which is far more general and flexible than previously available alternatives. To some extent, the gain in clarity and generality is comparable to that achieved by relying upon the formal concept of probability space as the starting point of probability theory. The general conceptual framework can always be particularised to handle specific problems – but the nature of the particular assumptions is then easily assessed.

III. AXIOMS OF A NORMATIVE THEORY

Consistency of preferences is traditionally identified with the existence of a simple ordering among the objects of choice; that is, of preferences which are complete and transitive. The preference relation itself is a primitive concept.

To assume that a preference relation is a simple ordering is to assume that the decision-maker behaves neither like Buridan's ass, who died of starvation half-way between a bale of hay and a pail of water, because he could not decide which, his hunger or his thirst, he should satisfy first; nor like Grimm's Hans in Glück, who received a precious gift, then made a series of exchanges, each of which looked favourable to him, and eventually reverted to his initial position.

In the theory of choice under uncertainty reviewed here, the assumption that there exists a simple ordering is successively applied to

(i) acts;
(ii) acts, conditionally on events;
(iii) consequences;
(iv) events.

Using the symbol $\gtrsim$ to mean 'preferred or indifferent', the first assumption reads:
For all $a, a', a'' \in A$:

    (i) either $a \gtrsim a'$ or $a' \gtrsim a$;
    (ii) $a \gtrsim a'$ and $a' \gtrsim a'' \Rightarrow a \gtrsim a''$.

[1] See, however, page 19 (note 1).

Some definitions are needed to state the other three assumptions. It will be said that 'a' is not preferred to a, given E (or conditionally on E)' if and only if $b \gtrsim b'$ whenever:

$$\left.\begin{array}{l} c(a, s) = c(b, s) \\ c(a', s) = c(b', s) \end{array}\right\} \forall s \in E; \quad c(b, s) = c(b', s) \forall s \in \tilde{E}.^{1}$$

To assume that conditional preference, given an arbitrary event E, is well defined (is a simple ordering) is to say that the consequences $c(b, s) = c(b', s)$, $s \in \tilde{E}$, are irrelevant to the choice between b and b': if two acts have identical consequences under a certain event ($\tilde{E}$), then the choice between them should proceed as if that event did not exist as a possibility; that is, the choice should not depend in any way upon the nature of these identical consequences. The justification for this assumption (sometimes called 'Sure Thing Principle', as in [29], and sometimes called 'Strong Independence Axiom', as in [24]) is that an event E and its complement $\tilde{E}$ are mutually exclusive, so that the attractiveness of the consequences associated with E should be assessed independently of those consequences associated with $\tilde{E}$. The logic of this reasoning seems compelling, even though the implications of the assumption are very strong, as one may realise with the help of an example introduced in the next section.

With conditional preferences well defined, one may define the 'nullity' (subjective impossibility) of an event E either by the condition '$a \gtrsim a'$ given E for all $a, a' \in A$' or by the condition '$a \gtrsim a'$ given $\tilde{E}$ if, and only if, $a \gtrsim a'$'. A preference relation among consequences is then easily defined as follows: $\bar{c} \gtrsim \bar{c}'$ if, and only if, $a \gtrsim a'$ given E whenever $c(a, s) = \bar{c}$, $c(a', s) = \bar{c}'$ for all $s \in E$, E being non-null (but otherwise arbitary). To assume that this relation is well defined (is a simple ordering) is to assume that consequences are so defined that preferences among them are never modified by knowledge of the event that obtains.

Finally, if $\bar{c}$ and $\bar{c}'$ are two consequences such that $\bar{c} \gtrsim \bar{c}'$, the event E is said to be 'revealed at least as likely' as the event E' if, and only if,

$a \gtrsim a'$ whenever:
$c(a, s) = \bar{c}, s \in E; \quad c(a, s) = \bar{c}', s \in \tilde{E};$
$c(a', s) = \bar{c}, s \in E'; \quad c(a', s) = \bar{c}', s \in \tilde{E}'.$

This definition states that if a person prefers to stake a prize on E rather than on E', then we may infer that the person regards the occurrence of E as more likely than the occurrence of E'. To assume that this relation is well defined (is a simple ordering among events) is to assume that which one of two events a person prefers to stake a

[1] $\tilde{E}$ denotes the complement of E (in S).

Axiomatic Theories

prize on, does not depend upon the nature of the prize.[1] Within the conceptual framework of the theory, it seems hard to object to this assumption, even though the implications of the assumption are very strong, as one may realise with the help of an example introduced in the next section.

The four assumptions just reviewed may be summarised by saying that a consistent decision-maker is assumed always to be able to compare (transitively) the attractiveness of acts, of hypothetical acts and of consequences as well as the likelihood of events. These requirements are minimal, in the sense that no consistency of behaviour may be expected if any one of them is violated; but they are very strong, in the sense that all kinds of comparisons are assumed possible, many of which may be quite remote from the range of experience of the decision-maker. This is also the reason why the axioms have more normative appeal than descriptive realism; few people would insist on maintaining, consciously, choices that violate them, but their spontaneous behaviour may frequently fail to display such rigorous consistency.

In order to avoid the trivial case of generalised indifference, it is further assumed that one does not have $c \gtrsim c'$ for all c, c'.

In the theory of consumer choice under certainty, one typically starts with an assumption of simple ordering among commodity bundles.[2] Specific theorems in economics rely upon assumptions about preferences that have no counterpart in the general theory reviewed here; such is the case for the assumptions of desirability and convexity frequently made about preferences among vectors in Euclidian space. There is, however, another assumption which plays an important role in many economic models, and which has a counterpart in the theory of decision under uncertainty; namely, the assumption of continuity. The intuitive concept of continuity of preference is that consequences which are 'close' to each other in some real (physical) sense must also be 'close' to each other in terms of preferences: $c \not\lesssim \bar{c}$ implies $c' \not\lesssim \bar{c}$ for all c' sufficiently close to c (in terms of Euclidian distance).

Continuity of preferences is necessary (and almost sufficient) for the representation of preferences by a continuous real-valued function.

Continuity is frequently described as a 'technical' assumption, to distinguish its nature from the 'logical' assumption of consistency

---

[1] Remember that a 'prize' is a consequence, and consequences are defined so comprehensively that preferences among them are never modified by knowledge of the event that obtains.
[2] Some results of economic interest do not require the assumption of complete preferences; see, e.g. [32].

(identified with the existence of a simple ordering). A certain structure must be placed on the objects of choice in order for the technical assumption of continuity to be meaningful. In general, no particular structure applies to the sets A, C or S. But a rich structure can be created by assuming that non-null events can be partitioned at will into other non-null events (for instance, by means of such random mechanisms as dice or coins). This possibility is introduced by means of the assumption of *atomlessness* (if E is non-null, E contains E' less likely than E and non-null). Sequences of non-null events, each of which is contained in, and is less likely than, the preceding one (i.e. monotonic decreasing sequences) are then used to introduce a *continuity* assumption which has the desired implications for representation of preferences by real-valued functions.[1] Atomlessness and continuity are 'technical' assumptions, that bear upon the structure of events as well as upon preferences; and insofar as they bear upon preferences, they reflect 'convenience' rather than logical necessity. Thus, Arrow [4] refers to a simple ordering among objects of choice as being 'the hallmark of rationality' (p. 47), and to the axiom of continuity as being 'the harmless simplification almost inevitable in the formalisation of any real-life problem' (p. 48).

From the assumptions reviewed so far, one deduces the celebrated 'moral expectation theorem' for acts with finitely many distinct consequences,[2] namely:

– there exists a (countably-additive) probability measure P,
– there exists a real-valued function of consequences U, defined up to a linear transformation,

such that

if $c(a, s) = c_i$ for all $s \in E_i$, $c(a', s) = c_i'$ for all $s \in E_i'$,
$a \lesssim a'$ if, and only if, $\sum_i P(E_i) U(c_i) \leq \sum_i P(E_i') U(c_i')$.

The theorem states that the orderings of consequences and events are representable, respectively, by a cardinal utility function and by a probability measure, in such a way that the ordering among acts is representable by their expected utility. In particular, the ordering among acts can be constructed by first constructing independently P and U, and then computing expected utilities.[3]

---

[1] For precise statements of these assumptions, see [4], pp. 48 and 77.
[2] An additional assumption of 'dominance', namely: '$a \lesssim c(a', s)$ given E for every $s \in E$ implies $a \lesssim a'$ given E', is required to extend the theorem to acts with infinitely many distinct consequences.
[3] An example of these constructions, which may serve as a useful revision of the theory, is given in [26].

Axiomatic Theories

By way of concluding this section, I will illustrate by a simple example how the utility of *information about events* can be inferred from the expected utility of acts. Consider the events E and E', with $P(E) = \frac{1}{2}$, $P(E') = \frac{1}{4}$, $P(E \cap E') = \frac{1}{8}$. Let the act a have two possible consequences, c and c', with

$U(c) = 1$, $U(c') = -1$ and
$c(a, s) = c$ for all $s \in E \cap \tilde{E}'$ and for all $s \in \tilde{E} \cap E'$
$c(a, s) = c'$ otherwise.

Clearly, the expected utility of a is zero, with conditional expectations of $\frac{1}{2}$ given E and $-\frac{1}{2}$ given $\tilde{E}$. Let, finally, the act a' be such that $c(a', s) = c$ for all s such that $c(a, s) = c'$, $c(a', s) = c'$ for all s such that $c(a, s) = c$. Again, the expected utility of a' is equal to 0, with conditional expectations of $-\frac{1}{2}$ given E and $\frac{1}{2}$ given $\tilde{E}$.

If the decision-maker is offered the choice between a and a', he will be indifferent between these two acts, and his expected utility will be equal to 0. Should he know whether E is true or not, he could choose a if E is true, a' if E is not true, with an expected utility of $\frac{1}{2}$ in either case. Hence, information about E would have a utility value of $\frac{1}{2}$.

IV. OBJECTIONS TO THE NORMATIVE APPEAL OF THE AXIOMS

Although objections to the descriptive realism of the theory have been numerous, objections to its normative appeal have been addressed almost exclusively to the assumption regarding conditional preference. The objections have been sustained by examples of simple choice situations, where violations of the axioms of conditional preference are frequently observed among rankings of acts elicited through casual or systematic questionnaires. Two clever examples, due respectively to Maurice Allais and Daniel Ellsberg, will be reproduced here.

The example of Allais consists of four acts, the consequences of which depend upon the drawing of a ball from an urn containing 100 numbered balls. These consequences consist of prizes, expressed say in thousands of dollars, and described in Table 1.1.

TABLE 1.1

NUMBER ON BALL DRAWN AT RANDOM

Acts	0	1–10	11–99
a	50	50	50
a'	0	250	50
b	50	50	0
b'	0	250	0

Many people report the ranking $a \not\lesssim a' \not\lesssim b' \not\lesssim b$: the certainty of 50 thousand dollars is preferred to a lottery offering 89 chances in a hundred of 50 thousand and 10 chances in a hundred of 250 thousand; but a lottery offering 10 chances in a hundred of 250 thousand is preferred to a lottery offering 11 chances in a hundred of 50. On the other hand, the axiom of conditional preference requires: $a \not\lesssim a'$ if, and only if, $b \not\lesssim b'$, since the identical consequences associated, by either a and a' or b and b', with the event '11–99' should not affect the rankings within these two pairs of acts.

The example of Ellsberg consists of four acts, the consequences of which depend upon the drawing of a ball from an urn containing 90 coloured balls. It is specified that 30 balls are red, the other 60 being either black or white; the number of black (white) balls is *not* specified. Accordingly only the events 'red' and 'black *or* white' have objectively defined numerical probabilities. The Acts are described in Table 1.2.

TABLE 1.2
COLOUR OF BALL DRAWN AT RANDOM

Acts	Red	Black	White
a	50	0	0
a'	0	50	0
b	50	0	50
b'	0	50	50

Many people report the ranking $b' \not\lesssim b \not\lesssim a \not\lesssim a'$, which violates the axiom of conditional preference. Reportedly, a is better than a' because a entails an 'objective' probability of $\frac{1}{3}$ of winning the prize, whereas no 'objective' probability of gain is offered by a'. A similar argument applies to $b' \not\lesssim b$.

These two examples rely upon an illusory complementarity operating across mutually exclusive events. In the example of Allais, the consequence associated with the event '11–99' looks 'complementary' to the other consequences in the case of act a, but not in the case of act b. The illusory nature of this 'complementarity' is perhaps best evidenced by the fact that a person insisting on the preferences '$a \not\lesssim a'$, $a' \not\lesssim a$ given 0–11' would prefer to a an act a^0 whereby the person would first be informed whether the event '11–99' obtains; if it obtains, the person receives 50; otherwise, the person may choose between a and a' (and would choose a'). The ranking would then be $a^0 \not\lesssim a \not\lesssim a'$ – but a^0 (with the assumed strategy) is *identical* to a'!

In the example of Ellsberg, the event 'white' looks complementary to the event 'black' in the case of act b', but not in the case of act a'. To bring out the illusory nature of that complementarity, it is helpful

Axiomatic Theories

to consider also an act a^0 promising 50 if the ball is *white*, zero otherwise. One then typically finds that persons preferring a to a' are indifferent between a' and a^0. It may then be remarked that a 50-50 chance of either a' or a^0 entails an objective probability of $\frac{1}{3}$ of winning the prize, *irrespective* of the number of black (white) balls, and should be indifferent to a; thus (in an obvious notation): $a \lesssim a' \sim a^0 \sim (a', a^0; \frac{1}{2}; \frac{1}{2}) \sim a$, which brings out the contradiction quite explicitly.

In both examples, the root of the difficulty is that a decision-maker must decide upon his preferences between a and a' conditionally on a certain event (0–11 in Table 1.1, red or black in Table 1.2); once that ranking is ascertained, consistent choices follow. The temptation to avoid facing squarely the issue of conditional preference is cleverly exploited in constructing the examples. I feel strongly that they belong to the family of 'optical illusions', their main purpose being to remind us of the strength of the assumptions of consistency and of the usefulness of decomposing logically complex choice situations into their elementary components.

Finally, I would like to mention another example, which was constructed during the Bergen Conference. Four acts are involved, with consequences depending upon the toss of a coin. Some consequences are monetary prizes ($\lessgtr 0$), others are tickets for a concert (the person is assumed to be fond of classical music, and equally eager to attend either one of two concerts planned for the same evening). Several participants at the conference mentioned the ranking $a' \lesssim a \lesssim b \lesssim b'$.

Table 1.3
OUTCOME OF COIN TOSS

Acts	Heads	Tails
a	$1,000	hear Beethoven's Ninth Symphony (concert A)
a'	$1,000	hear Mozart's *Requiem* (concert B)
b	$-1,000	Concert A
b'	$-1,000	Concert B

One may try to reconcile this understandable ranking with the axiom of conditional preference by claiming that 'concert A' or 'concert B' are not consequences, whereas 'attending concert · in an elated mood', and 'attending concert · in a depressed mood' are consequences. This reinterpretation raises, however, a subtle issue of dependence of the consequences upon the *acts*. Alternatively (or consequently?) one may recognise this type of situation as a limitation to the realm of applicability of the theory – a limitation, however, that may be regarded as innocuous from the viewpoint of economics.

V. MERITS AND LIMITATIONS OF THE THEORY

In this section, I will propose an evaluation of the merits and limitations of the theory under review from the successive viewpoints of its relevance, usefulness, generality and integration with other theories. In each case, merits and limitations will be mentioned successively, in that order. I will then conclude with an overall evaluation.

(1) *Relevance*

(i) *The theory has strong normative appeal.* The normative appeal of a theory may be measured by the acceptability of its premises and the strength of the conclusions derived from them. As indicated in section IV, I personally regard the axioms of the theory under review as perfectly acceptable. It seems generally agreed that the moral expectation theorem is a strong conclusion based upon these premises. Yet, my interest in the theory derives, in large part, from a slightly different consideration.

Scientists should not attempt, in a professional capacity, to prescribe values or norms of behaviour; but they should explain how, and under what conditions, scientific methods can be brought to bear upon realistic problems. If we accept the view that the values and judgements of a person are eminently relevant to his own decisions, then it seems clear that a consistent assessment of these values and judgements is a necessary condition for scientific reasoning to be brought to bear on his decision problems; and the theory under review has the great merit of telling us that the condition is also sufficient.

To be more specific: whether a person wants to accept a bet involving one chance in eleven of losing 50 thousand dollars, and ten chances in eleven of winning 200 thousand dollars, seems to be for that person to decide; but if a scientist is to use that person's choice in this simple situation to prescribe solutions in more complex situations, then it is a minimal requirement that the choice be unambiguous; (unstable or) intransitive preferences do not meet that minimal requirement; consequently, persons with (unstable or) intransitive preferences not only risk having unfair bets placed against them, they also deprive themselves of the potential assistance of scientists in solving decision problems.

In other words, a person who does not accept the axioms of simple ordering for conditional acts, consequences and events, should not expect any assistance from scientific methods in handling decision problems.

(ii) *The theory has doubtful descriptive realism.* Three remarks will be made in this respect:

Axiomatic Theories

(i) casual empiricism suggests that spontaneous behaviour of reasonable persons may fail to satisfy the axioms of the theory;

(ii) the formalisation of even the simplest decision problems proves amazingly intricate, and this casts doubts upon the possibility of using the theory as a model within which future choices could be predicted on the basis of past observations;

(iii) it may still be true (but remains to be demonstrated?) that economic theories based upon the behavioural assumption of expected utility maximisation will have implications that are borne out by empirical tests, and have predictive power.

(2) *Usefulness*
(i) *The theory is of substantial theoretical usefulness.* A normative theory of decision can be helpful in two ways:

(i) in resolving logical difficulties connected with the statement of problems and criteria for solving them;

(ii) in bringing powerful scientific methods to bear upon the solution of decision problems.

On both counts, the theory under review is extremely helpful.

(i) The description of decision problems in terms of acts, events and consequences, is 'far more general and flexible than previously available alternatives' (*supra*, p. 9). The maximisation of expected utility is a generally applicable decision criterion, which resolves logical difficulties previously regarded as serious.

(ii) The theory brings the powerful mathematical theory of probability to bear upon decision problems. Since a decision-maker's judgements about the likelihood of events are summarised in a probability measure, the rules of conditional probability and Bayes' theorem can be used to incorporate new information.[1]

(ii) *The theory is of limited practical usefulness.* The practical usefulness of the theory is subject to limitations stemming from three problems, which the theory, as such, leaves entirely open, namely:

(i) the calibration of probabilities;
(ii) the calibration of utilities;
(iii) the discovery of an optimal act from a given set.

[1] Arrow remarks ([4], p. 46): 'The influence of experience on beliefs is of the utmost importance for a rational theory of behaviour under uncertainty, and failure to account for it must be taken as a strong objection to theories such as Shackle's [33]'.

Experiments dealing with individual ability to make realistic probability assessments point strongly towards systematic biases [27]. This is not surprising, since hardly anybody has ever been trained in assessing probabilities; and it is by no means clear how such training could be effective. As for individual ability to calibrate utilities, very little is known on that score.

The third problem is the subject-matter of optimisation theory, operations research and statistical decision theory. The class of decision problems under uncertainty which can be handled formally is still very limited, and problems of sequential decision raise very serious difficulties.[1]

(3) *Generality*

(i) *The theory has almost complete formal and logical generality.* The formal generality of the theory derives from its ability to encompass situations that were previously distinguished as calling for distinct formalisms – for instance, situations of 'risk' where the relative frequencies in repeated observations invited the formalism of probability, as opposed to situations of 'uncertainty' where the absence of such observations precluded the use of that formalism.

The logical generality of the theory derives from its main conclusion, which justifies the use of expected utility as a single decision criterion. This result provides a single answer to a variety of questions with which economists and statisticians were concerned, and to which they were tempted to offer distinct answers (ranging from 'risk preference functional' to minimax solutions).

Although this view is not generally accepted, I personally understand the expected utility criterion to be applicable to (non-cooperative) games of strategy as well. If the pure strategies of the opponent(s) are treated as events and if the pay-off of the game is understood to be expressed in utility terms, then one may regard the specific object of the theory of games as being the assessment of the probabilities of events, the ultimate decision criterion being the maximisation of expected utility (under due recognition for the influence of strategy choices on the probabilities of the events).

(ii) *The applicability of the theory is limited by its conceptual structure*. It was emphasised in section II that events and consequences had to be defined in such a way that:

(i) every consequence can be attained in any state;
(ii) the occurrence of any event can be verified with interpersonal objectivity and lies beyond the control of the decision-maker.

As was noted there, these conditions preclude explicit consideration of events which are themselves of value to the decision-maker

[1] On this topic, see the last section of [9].

(e.g. his own death), or which have a dimension of 'moral hazard'. This is a serious limitation for economic applications.[1]

(4) *Integration with Other Theories*
(i) *Economics, statistics and decision theory.* A major merit of the theory under review lies in the provision of an integrated framework within which the disciplines of economics, statistics and decision theory can be developed jointly. Uncertainty in economics can best be described through events and consequences. Utility analysis is only natural for economists. The existence of a probability measure on events provides the bridge with statistical theory, whereby empirical information can be used to revise previous judgements. A systematic development of statistical procedures, designed to facilitate such revisions, is currently under way, and goes under the name of 'Bayesian statistics'.[2]

(ii) *Individual versus group decisions.* The theory under review is presented with reference to a single decision-maker. Yet it must be recognised that many, if not most, decision problems of interest to social scientists call for group decisions. In economics, the abstract 'consumer' is typically a family, and most families consist of more than a single person; the abstract 'producer' is typically a firm, grouping many individuals; and problems of 'social choice' arise specifically from the presence of several decision-makers, with distinct values and judgements, and typically with conflicting interests. Savage ([29], p. 154) also advances the view that '... *statistics proper* can perhaps be defined as the art of dealing with vagueness and *with interpersonal difference* in decision situation'. One is thus naturally led to wonder about the integration of the theory with other work dealing explicitly with group decisions.

The most important theorem on group decisions in economics is Arrow's impossibility theorem [1], which has drawn attention to the difficulties inherent in group decisions based on ordinal preferences (rankings) of the members. Cardinal preferences (a utility function defined up to a linear transformation) open a natural avenue to overcome these difficulties. When there is unanimous agreement about the probabilities, reasonable axioms proposed by Harsanyi [17] lead to a group utility function, which is a weighted average of individual utility functions. In the absence of agreement about the

[1] I have shown elsewhere [7] that such situations could be encompassed in a generalised theory, at the cost of considerable formal complexity, and within the limitations of a serious identification problem.

[2] An additional axiom is required to validate these procedures, namely an axiom which states that the probability of any event E, *after* making an observation x, is equal to the prior probability of E conditionally on x (that is the probability of E given x *before* making the observation).

probabilities, a group probability measure may be defined as a weighted average of the individual measures, but Madansky [21] has shown that the weights must be revised in the light of new information. And Zeckhauser has proved another important impossibility theorem: there does not exist, in general, a group utility function which aggregates individual utilities, and a group probability measure which aggregates individual probability measures, in such a way that admissible group decisions maximise the expectation of the group utility (in terms of the group probabilities). Further results on this problem have been established by Wilson [36].[1]

(5) *Overall Evaluation*

If one refers to the earlier situation, as outlined in section I, the merits of the theory under review are substantial, and generally outweigh its limitations. In my opinion, the theory provides a starting point for research on the economics of uncertainty that is both natural and satisfactory. Specific applications may call for further specifications or for specific extensions; and one should remain conscious of the doubtful descriptive realism of the theory. But that being understood, it seems fruitful to investigate economic models relying, explicitly or implicitly, upon the axioms or conclusions of the theory.

VI. LINK WITH ECONOMIC APPLICATIONS

Several chapters of this book [15, 16, 14, 10] proceed from a description of uncertainty in terms of events and states of the world. In these models, decisions about production and allocation of commodities are evaluated from the viewpoint of consumer preferences. Given a list of commodities and a list of possible states, a consumption plan for a consumer is a vector specifying his consumption of every commodity in every state. Such a consumption plan corresponds to an act in the terminology used here. Thus, acts are functions from the state of the world to the commodity space. Does it follow that points in the commodity space define consequences? It was noted on p. 8 above that 'commodity bundles will generally prove inadequate to

---

[1] When the group decisions concern the production and allocations of commodities, Pareto-optimal decisions can be sustained by a price system for contingent claims to commodities (see [15] below). These prices admit of an expected utility interpretation: under appropriate normalisation, undiscounted prices for a numeraire commodity have all the properties of a probability measure on the events; prices for other commodities, expressed in terms of the numeraire conditionally on any given event, measure the utility of these commodities (see [15] and [8]). In this sense, efficient group decisions sustained by a price system admit of an expected utility interpretation.

define consequences'. This is also the reason why it is *not* assumed in these papers that preferences among consumption vectors are independent of the state that obtains. It is thus natural to think about consequences as being elements of the Cartesian product of the state space and the commodity space.[1]

These papers rely upon the assumption of a simple ordering among acts. Typically, assumptions of continuity and convexity are made about this ordering. As was explained in section III, continuity of preferences among acts with values in a Euclidian space is a rather different assumption from the monotone continuity axiom of the theory of subjective probability, and convexity assumptions have no place in the general theory.

Under continuity, the simple ordering of acts is representable by a continuous real-valued function, defined up to a *monotonic* transformation. Values of that function correspond to expected utilities of the acts in the general theory. Under the assumption of conditional preference, the simple ordering of acts with finitely many consequences is representable by an *additive* function, that is by a sum, over the states, of continuous real-valued functions of the consumption in those states. (Of course, the additive property is not preserved by non-linear transformations.) Each such function then corresponds to the product of the probability of the state by the utility of the consequences attained in that state. The assumption of conditional preference, which is equally justified in these models as in the general theory, is not introduced explicitly so long as it is not required to establish general results.

A discussion of the convexity assumption, and of its relation to risk aversion when points in the commodity space define consequences, is given by Arrow in section IV of [3].

Delbaen's chapter on stochastic preferences [6] deserves a special mention. At first sight, it might appear that stochastic preferences among the objects of choice are the very negation of consistent preferences, i.e. of a simple ordering of the objects of choice. Earlier work on this subject (by Georgescu–Roegen [13] or Luce [20] for instance) seemed to proceed in that spirit. But the same remark does not apply to the approach introduced by Hildenbrand [19] and followed by Delbaen. Indeed, the work of these authors seems better described in terms of consequences belonging to the Cartesian product of a state-space and a commodity-space – a formal structure already discussed above. The new element seems to be that the relevant state-space is specific to each consumer, so that states are implicitly defined by uncertainty about consumer tastes. Given the state, commodity vectors are ordered consistently.

[1] That is also the approach followed in [7].

REFERENCES

[1] K. J. Arrow, *Social Choice and Individual Values* (New York: Wiley, 1951).
[2] K. J. Arrow, 'Alternative Approaches to the Theory of Choice in Risk-Taking Situations', *Econometrica*, vol. XIX (1951), pp. 404–37.
[3] K. J. Arrow, 'Le rôle des valeurs boursières pour la répartition la meilleure des risques', pp. 41–7 in [11], translated as 'The Role of Securities in the Optimal Allocation of Risk-Bearing', *Review of Economic Studies*, vol. XXXI (1964), pp. 91–6.
[4] K. J. Arrow, 'Exposition of the Theory of Choice under Uncertainty', pp. 44–89 in *Essays in the Theory of Risk-Bearing*, by K. J. Arrow (Amsterdam: North-Holland, 1970).
[5] G. Debreu, *Theory of Value* (New York: Wiley, 1959).
[6] F. Delbaen, 'Stochastic Preferences and General Equilibrium Theory', chapter 7 *infra*.
[7] J. H. Drèze, 'Fondements logiques de la probabilité subjective et de l'utilité', in *La Décision* (Paris: CRNS, 1961), pp. 73–87.
[8] J. H. Drèze, 'Market Allocation under Uncertainty', *European Economic Review*, vol. II (1971), pp. 133–65.
[9] J. H. Drèze, 'Econometrics and Decision Theory', *Econometrica*, vol. XL (1972), pp. 1–17.
[10] J. H. Drèze, 'Investment under Private Ownership: Optimality, Equilibrium and Stability', chapter 9 *infra*.
[11] *Econométrie*, Colloque International XL (Paris: CRNS, 1953).
[12] M. Friedman, and L. J. Savage, 'The Utility Analysis of Choices Involving Risk', *Journal of Political Economy*, vol. LVI (1948), pp. 279–304.
[13] N. Georgescu-Roegen, 'Threshold in Choice and the Theory of Demand', *Econometrica*, vol. XXVI (1958), pp. 157–68.
[14] L. Gevers, 'Competitive Equilibrium of the Stock Exchange and Pareto Efficiency', chapter 10 *infra*.
[15] R. Guesnerie, and T. de Montbrial, 'Allocation under Uncertainty: a survey', chapter 4 *infra*.
[16] R. Guesnerie, and J. Y. Jaffray, 'Optimality of Equilibrium of Plans, Prices and Price Expectations', chapter 5 *infra*.
[17] J. Harsanyi, 'Cardinal Welfare, Individualistic Ethics and Interpersonal Comparisons of Utility', *Journal of Political Economy*, vol. LXIII (1955), pp. 309–21.
[18] J. R. Hicks, 'The Theory of Uncertainty and Profit', *Economica*, vol. XI (1931), pp. 170–89.
[19] W. Hildenbrand, 'Random Preferences and Equilibrium Analysis', *Journal of Economic Theory*, vol. III (1971), pp. 414–29.
[20] R. D. Luce, *Individual Choice Behavior* (New York: Wiley, 1959).
[21] A. Madansky, 'Externally Bayesian Groups', Memorandum RM-4141-PR, The Rand Corporation, November 1964.
[22] M. Markowitz, 'The Utility of Wealth', *Journal of Political Economy*, vol. LX (1952), pp. 151–8.
[23] J. Marschak, 'Money and the Theory of Assets', *Econometrica*, vol. VI (1938), pp. 311–25.
[24] J. Marschak, 'Rational Behaviour, Uncertain Prospects, and Measurable Utility', *Econometrica*, vol. XVIII (1950), pp. 111–41.
[25] J. von Neumann, and O. Morgenstern, *Theory of Games and Economic Behavior* (Princeton: Princeton University Press, 1953).
[26] J. Pratt, H. Raiffa and R. Schlaifer, 'The Foundations of Decision under

Uncertainty: An Elementary Exposition', *Journal of the American Statistical Association*, vol. LIX (1964), pp. 353–75.
[27] H. Raiffa, 'Assessments of Probabilities', mimeographed, 1969.
[28] F. P. Ramsey, 'Truth and Probability', in *The Foundations of Mathematics and Other Logical Essays* (London: Routledge and Kegan Paul, 1931), pp. 156–98.
[29] L. J. Savage, *The Foundations of Statistics* (New York: Wiley, 1954).
[30] L. J. Savage, 'The Theory of Statistical Decision', *Journal of the American Statistical Association*, vol. XLVI (1951), pp. 55–67.
[31] L. J. Savage, 'Une axiomatisation du comportement raisonnable face à l'incertitude', pp. 29–34 in [13].
[32] D. Schmeidler, 'Competitive Equilibria in Markets with a Continuum of Traders and Incomplete Preferences', *Econometrica*, vol. XXXVII (1969), pp. 578–85.
[33] G. L. S. Shackle, *Expectation in Economics* (Cambridge: Cambridge University Press, 1952).
[34] G. Tintner, 'The Theory of Choice under Subjective Risk and Uncertainty', *Econometrica*, vol. IX (1941), pp. 298–304.
[35] A. Wald, *Statistical Decision Functions* (New York: Wiley, 1950). (2nd ed., Bronx, N.Y., Chelsea, Publ. Co., 1971.)
[36] R. Wilson, 'On the Theory of Syndicates', *Econometrica*, vol. XXXVI (1968), pp. 119–32.

2 Two-Period Models of Consumption Decisions Under Uncertainty: a survey

Agnar Sandmo[1]
NORWEGIAN SCHOOL OF ECONOMICS AND BUSINESS ADMINISTRATION, BERGEN

I. INTRODUCTION

One of the classical formulations of the theory of choice between saving and consumption is that of Irving Fisher, whose work culminated in his book *The Theory of Interest* [8]. In the two-period model introduced by him the individual consumer has a preference ordering over present and future consumption, and is able to lend and borrow in a perfect capital market at a given rate of interest. Especially after its reconsideration by Hirshleifer [10] the model has become very popular and has found many applications in theoretical work. In its simplest version, this model postulates a consumer with exogenously given amounts of income in the two periods and no opportunities for real investment; it is then used to analyse the dependence of consumption on the rate of interest and on (lifetime) income. In the absence of uncertainty, and with amounts consumed as the only arguments in the utility function, there is clearly no basis for portfolio choices; the consumer invests total savings in the highest-yielding asset available, and he is never a borrower in one asset and a lender in another. The general equilibrium implication of this model is evidently that the rate of return must be the same on all assets, which thereby become perfect substitutes for each other.

In another version of the model the consumer also has opportunities for real investment. He is seen as the 'owner' of one or more production functions, giving amounts available for future consumption as functions of present inputs of capital. In the simplest case, where there is only one type of capital and one production function, the most striking aspect of the optimal solution is that the level of investment is independent of preferences. Optimality in fact calls for equating the marginal productivity of real investment to the rate of interest, thereby maximising the present value of lifetime income

[1] This paper was presented to the European Research Workshop in Economic Theory, July 1971. I am indebted to several participants in the workshop, to Hayne Leland and above all to Jacques Drèze for interesting and useful suggestions.

available for consumption. The optimal consumption program is then found by maximising utility under the budget constraint implied by this level of investment. The resulting independence between saving and investment decisions is frequently referred to as the separation theorem.[1]

This is the framework into which uncertainty is introduced in the models to be surveyed here. The other main building block of these models is portfolio theory, particularly in the version given by Arrow [2, 3]. Instead of relying on quadratic utility functions and mean-variance analysis, which had dominated portfolio theory since the influential pioneering works of Markowitz [14] and Tobin [23], Arrow deduced properties of demand functions for assets from a model in which the investor maximises the expected utility of wealth, utility being a concave function of wealth. He demonstrated that the basic comparative static results depended on the nature of some theoretically and intuitively appealing measures of the strength of the investor's risk aversion; these measures have also been analysed by Pratt [17]

It is clearly unsatisfactory to have two essentially different theories to explain the division of total wealth between consumption and saving on the one hand, and the composition of the savings portfolio on the other. This is so not only for more or less aesthetic reasons, but because there are interesting questions that can only be put to, and answered by, models in which the saving-consumption decision is seen as one made under conditions of uncertainty, and/or in which the size and the composition of the savings portfolio are simultaneously determined. The following survey is organised around some of these questions which, to me at least, seem to be the more interesting ones.

II. THE EFFECT OF UNCERTAINTY ON THE CONSUMPTION-SAVING DECISION

One of the more basic questions that one can ask of a model of consumption decisions under uncertainty, is how uncertainty *per se* affects the consumer's allocation of present resources between present consumption and saving for an uncertain future. It might perhaps be thought that the existence of risk aversion, in itself, would

---

[1] A related separation theorem for the case of uncertain rates of return on assets is discussed in section IV below. In pure portfolio theory there is another theorem which is referred to by this name; for certain classes of utility functions, only the division of wealth between safe and risky assets depends on the level of wealth, whilst the share of each asset in the total portfolio of risky assets is independent of wealth. See [4].

be sufficient to yield the result that increased uncertainty about the future leads to a decrease of present consumption (and so to an increase of saving). This conjecture, however, turns out to be false.

Closely related approaches to this problem can be found in the papers by Leland [11] and Sandmo [21]. The main simplification of these articles is that there is no portfolio choice, so that the only decision to be made relates to the choice between saving and consumption. The consumer's preferences can be represented by a cardinal utility function $U(C_1, C_2)$, assumed to be continuous and differentiable where required. The amounts of income in the two periods are Y_1 and Y_2. These are exogenously given, Y_1 with certainty, Y_2 as a random variable. If the sure rate of interest in the perfect capital market is denoted by r, the budget constraint for the two periods can be written as

$$C_2 = (Y_1 - C_1)(1 + r) + Y_2. \tag{2.1}$$

The consumer maximises expected utility,

$$E[U(C_1, (Y_1 - C_1)(1 + r) + Y_2)],$$

with respect to C_1. This yields the first-order condition

$$E[U_1 - (1 + r)U_2] = 0. \tag{2.2}$$

(Subscripts are used throughout to denote partial derivatives.) We assume that the second-order condition for a maximum is satisfied.

As posed by Leland and Sandmo the problem is now: what is the effect on present consumption of a change in the probability distribution of future income such that it becomes 'more risky'? An increase in risk is defined by Leland as an increase in the variance of Y_2 with the mean constant; Sandmo defines it as a multiplicative shift in the distribution of Y_2 combined with an additive shift to keep the mean constant.

Additional assumptions on attitudes to risk are required to obtain a conclusion on the direction of the response of consumption to an increase in risk. To obtain such assumptions one can define the (absolute) *risk aversion function* as

$$R_A(C_1, C_2) = -\frac{U_{22}}{U_2}. \tag{2.3}$$

This is a generalisation of the concept introduced by Arrow and Pratt. This risk aversion function can be defined as twice the risk premium per unit of variance for infinitesimal risks; a formal derivation can be found in Sandmo [20].

Leland's hypothesis on the risk aversion function is that when C_2 increases and C_1 is simultaneously decreased to keep utility constant, the function will decrease, with the implication that the risk premium for infinitesimal gambles on C_2 will fall. Sandmo [21] assumes that the risk aversion function is decreasing in C_2 and increasing in C_1. Using these hypotheses and their respective definitions of increased riskiness, both authors are led to the conclusion that increased riskiness about future income will increase saving (reduce consumption).[1]

While the analysis summarised above is concerned solely with uncertainty about future income, Sandmo [21] also considers the case of an uncertain rate of return to savings, with the symbols used above it is now assumed that $Y_2 = 0$[2] and that r is a random variable. He finds that the effect of increased 'capital risk' is more complicated than the effect of 'income risk'. There is first a 'substitution effect' which tends to reduce saving, granted only that the consumer is risk averse. However, there is also an 'income effect' which tends to increase saving, given the assumptions about the risk aversion function referred to above. The combined outcome is therefore indeterminate.

A weakness of the formulations of Leland and Sandmo may be that their definitions of increased risk are somewhat arbitrary. One would prefer to derive these definitions from a more basic criterion, stating when one probability distribution is more risky than another. This problem has been studied by Rothschild and Stiglitz [18a]. Let X and Y be two random variables with identical mean values. Then consider the following four specifications of the statement, 'Y is more risky than X': (1) Risk averters prefer X to Y; (2) Y has the same distribution as X plus noise; (3) the density of Y is more spread out than that of X; (4) Y has a greater variance than X. Rothschild and Stiglitz demonstrate that the first three specifications are equivalent in the sense that they induce the same partial ordering on the random variables; this ordering is weaker than the one induced by (4). They further argue that this ordering is the most reasonable definition of increased risk.

Although it seems to be clear that Rothschild and Stiglitz have provided a more fundamental criterion of increased riskiness, it is not entirely clear whether this should lead to a substantial revision of the results in the literature referred to above. As an example of the application of their criterion Rothschild and Stiglitz [18b] consider

---

[1] With additive utility, assumed, e.g., by Sandmo [19] and Mirman [15], the argument is much simplified.

[2] This is the case where future income is all capital income, so that $C_1 < Y_1$. This is a restriction on the sign of the 'income effect' discussed below. However, the general case is easily established from equation (12) in the article (Sandmo [21], p. 357). Under the assumption made, the sign of the 'income effect' on saving is that of $(Y_1 - C_1)$.

a two-period consumption model with additive utility and constant *relative* risk aversion (i.e. $-U_{22}C_2/U_2 =$ constant). They demonstrate that increased uncertainty about the rate of return will increase, leave constant or decrease saving, depending upon whether relative risk aversion is greater than, equal to, or less than 1. However, the same result was derived by Sandmo [21], using his less general criterion of increased riskiness.[1] This particular case is therefore one in which the result is not very sensitive to the choice of a definition of increased riskiness.

The models surveyed so far are all one-asset models. Sandmo [20] considers the effect of increased risk in a model with two assets, one of which has a random rate of return. He finds that the effect of increased risk is in the same direction as an adverse change in the expected rate of return. This means that for lenders, increased risk works in the same direction as a fall in the expected rate of return, while for borrowers (in the risky asset) it works as an increase in the expected rate. The effects of changes in expected rates are, however, theoretically indeterminate both for lenders and borrowers, so that the result is, in itself, not very strong. But it is of interest to note that the conclusion is in line with the widespread intuitive view that an increase in risk is of the same nature as an unfavourable change in the (expected) rate of return. This view again lies behind some of the recommendations to adjust interest rates to take account of uncertainty in investment planning, particularly in some of the older literature on this topic.

In the contributions reviewed above, the standard of comparison between two prospects is always the expected values of the random variables. It is argued by Drèze and Modigliani [6][2] that this is an unsatisfactory procedure, their main argument being that the expected values of yield and future income are unobservable magnitudes *ex ante*. They therefore introduce two alternative reference criteria based on (1) constant market value, and (2) constant expected utility. Let (Y_2, r) denote an uncertain prospect, and let (Y_2^*, r^*) be a sure prospect serving as a reference criterion. In the cases discussed above Y_2^* and r^* are simply equal to the expected values. Now imagine that there exist markets in which one can insure future incomes[3] and stock markets for assets with uncertain rates of return,

[1] Sandmo derived this result in commenting on the article by Levhari and Srinivasan [13] where an equivalent result is proved in a multi-period model.

[2] This paper includes the essential results of an earlier contribution by the same authors [5].

[3] The paper contains a theory of occupational choice in which the differences of occupations lie only in the time profiles and riskiness of earnings. Thus two occupations identical in these respects would be perfect substitutes for the consumer.

Two-Period Models

as well as a loan market where the rate of return (the rate of interest) is certain. The reference criterion for constant market value is then:

Y_2^* and r^* are such that
(1) an uncertain future income commands the same present value on the (insurance) market as the sure income Y_2^*;
(2) an asset with uncertain yield commands the same price on the (stock) market as an asset with the sure yield r^*.

The reference criterion for constant expected utility can be formulated as follows:

Y_2^* and r^* are a solution to the implicit equation:
$$\operatorname*{Max}_{C_1} \int U(C_1, (Y_1 - C_1)(1+r) + Y_2) \, d\phi(Y_2, r) =$$
$$\operatorname*{Max}_{C_1} U(C_1, (Y_1 - C_1)(1 + r^*) + Y_2^*).$$

Drèze and Modigliani prove two theorems relating the optimal consumption under the uncertain prospect (Y_2, r) – call it $\hat{C}_1$ – respectively to:

(1) the consumption that would be optimal if the uncertain prospect were exchanged against the sure prospect (Y_2^*, r^*) of equal market value – call that consumption C_1^*;
(2) the consumption that would be optimal if the uncertain prospect were exchanged against a sure prospect (Y_2^0, r^*) of equal expected utility, with r^* denoting again a sure market rate – call that consumption C_1^0.

The first theorem states that $\hat{C}_1 \gtreqless C_1^*$ depending upon whether

$$\partial^2 \left(\frac{U_1}{U_2} \right) / \partial C_2^2 \gtreqless 0 \tag{2.4}$$

(at $\hat{C}_1$ and identically in C_2). This condition reflects purely ordinal properties of the utility function, and none of the three possibilities can be ruled out on *a priori* grounds.

The second theorem states that $C_1 \gtreqless C_1^0$ depending upon whether absolute risk aversion $(-U_{22}/U_2)$ increases, remains constant or decreases with C_2 for movements along budget lines with slope $-(1+r^*)$.[1] Accordingly, under decreasing absolute risk aversion, consumption is reduced by uncertainty at least to the level where it

[1] Leland's assumption that risk aversion decreases with C_2 for movements along indifference surfaces is locally equivalent to the condition here. Sandmo's assumption that risk aversion decreases with C_2 and increases with C_1 implies decreasing risk aversion here; in fact this assumption is asymptotically equivalent to that of Drèze and Modigliani, if the latter is assumed to hold for all $r > -1$.

would settle if a maximal insurance premium were paid to dispose of the uncertainty, and possibly below. When the uncertainty concerns Y_2 alone (r^* given), then clearly $Y_2^0 < E[Y_2]$, and the conclusion of Leland and Sandmo is confirmed, even strengthened.

Summing up the results surveyed in this section, it is probably fair to say that the conclusion which can claim the widest support is that, on what seem to be plausible assumptions, uncertainty about future income tends to increase saving. Uncertainty about the rate(s) of return, however, has no clearcut effect on saving, even in the simple case with only one asset. There may be good intuitive reasons for the lack of unambiguous results on this point. Under uncertainty about income, increased saving raises the expected value of future consumption, while leaving the variance (and higher moments) unaffected. Hence the consumer reacts to increased riskiness by raising his level of saving, so that the increased variance of future consumption is compensated for by a higher expected value. But under uncertainty about the rate of return this is only part of the story, since increases in saving will now increase both the mean and the variance of future consumption; hence the consumer might reasonably react to increased risk, either by saving more, or by saving less.

III. INTEGRATED CONSUMPTION-PORTFOLIO ANALYSIS

Apart from the effect of increases in risk, the comparative statics of the one-asset model are straightforward and not very exciting. The analysis is more interesting for models incorporating portfolio choice. We shall therefore begin by writing down a rather general version of this model. We shall assume that incomes in both periods are certain and that there exists an asset with a sure rate of return r. The amount invested in this asset is denoted by m. In addition there are n risky assets; the amount invested in the i'th asset is a_i and its return is x_i.

The budget constraint for the first period is

$$C_1 + m + \sum_i a_i = Y_1. \tag{3.1}$$

For the second period we have that

$$C_2 = Y_2 + m(1+r) + \sum_i a_i(1+x_i), \tag{3.2}$$

or, by substituting from (3.1)

$$C_2 = Y_2 + (Y_1 - C_1)(1+r) + \sum_i a_i(x_i - r). \tag{3.3}$$

Two-Period Models

The consumer maximises expected utility subject to (3.3); we can then write the problem as

$$\underset{C_1, a_1, \ldots, a_n}{\text{Max}} \quad E[U(C_1, Y_2 + (Y_1 - C_1)(1+r) + \sum_i a_i(x_i - r))]. \tag{3.4}$$

The first-order conditions are then

$$E[U_1 - (1+r)U_2] = 0. \tag{3.5}$$

$$E[U_2(x_i - r)] = 0. \quad i = 1, \ldots, n. \tag{3.6}$$

These conditions may be rewritten as

$$\frac{E[U_1]}{E[U_2]} = 1 + r \tag{3.7}$$

$$\frac{E[U_2 x_i]}{E[U_2]} = r. \quad i = 1, \ldots, n. \tag{3.8}$$

(3.7) is the equivalent in this model of the well-known 'rule' of Fisher [8]: equality between the marginal rate of time preference and the 'sure' rate of interest. (3.8) says that the rate of return on a risky asset, weighted by the marginal utility of future consumption, should be equal for all risky assets and equal to the rate of return on the safe asset.[1]

This model can now be analysed by comparative static tools to obtain predictions about the consumer's reactions to changes in income, the rate of interest (r), and the expected returns on the risky asset. This has been done by Sandmo [20] for the case of only one risky asset.

As is the case in demand theory generally, the sign of the income derivatives are indeterminate *a priori*. In this model, however, one might pose the following interesting question: Suppose that $0 < \partial C_1 / \partial Y_1 < 1$, so that both consumption and saving increase with income. Does it then follow that the demand for the risky asset also increases with income? Arrow [2] showed that in the pure portfolio model the assumption of decreasing absolute risk aversion implies that the risky asset is a normal good. Sandmo assumes that risk aversion is decreasing in C_2 and increasing in C_1; this is, however, insufficient to determine the sign of $\partial a / \partial Y_1$. But in the interesting special case of an additive utility function, where the risk aversion function no longer depends on C_1, the analogue of Arrow's result can be derived quite easily.

---

[1] Sufficient conditions for the existence of solutions to the portfolio problem have been obtained by Leland [12]; he shows that if all assets have finite expected returns, an optimal solution exists if the marginal utility of wealth tends to zero as wealth approaches infinity.

The effects on consumption of changes in (expected) rates of return turn out to be quite complex – with one exception. With complete certainty there is an appealing result for the effect of an interest rate change on consumption; the substitution effect is always negative, whilst the income effect is positive for lenders ($Y_1 - C_1 > 0$), and negative for borrowers ($Y_1 - C_1 < 0$). Sandmo shows that this result carries over to the two-asset model if the rate of interest and the expected rate of return on the risky asset change by the same magnitude, provided only that the consumer is risk averse ($U_{22} < 0$).

IV. SEPARATION OF CONSUMPTION AND PORTFOLIO DECISIONS

Once the integration of consumption and portfolio decisions has been achieved it is natural to ask whether, after all, there do exist conditions under which consumption and portfolio decisions can be in some sense separated. No doubt the 'pure' models will still be with us; it is therefore of considerable interest to investigate the conditions, if any, under which separate treatment can be rigorously justified. This problem has been studied by Drèze and Modigliani [6]. We shall describe their main result in terms of the model outlined in the previous section, which is actually somewhat simpler than the one used in their paper. The difference lies only in the absence in this model of insurance markets for future earnings, which is not of much importance for this particular problem.

The first theorem of Drèze and Modigliani [6] is directly applicable to this model and tells us that consumption, as determined by (3.7)–(3.8), will exceed, be equal to or fall short of the consumption that would result if there were no risky assets depending upon whether

$$\partial^2 \left(\frac{U_1}{U_2}\right) / \partial C_2^2$$

is positive, zero or negative. In particular, if

$$\partial^2 \left(\frac{U_1}{U_2}\right) / \partial C_2^2 = 0,$$

then optimal consumption is independent of the optimal portfolio and of the investment opportunities in risky assets. This has the following implications:

(i) For given market prices the impact of uncertainty on consumption decisions is *nil*; the riskiness of assets may affect their market value and thereby consumption, but no additional effects on C_1 need to be considered.

(ii) Consumption and portfolio decisions may be separated in the sense that C_1 may be chosen prior to, and independently of, the optimal portfolio, and will be a function of income and the sure rate of interest alone.

(iii) The optimal consumption is independent of the consumer's risk aversion and is entirely determined by the ordinal properties of the utility function. The optimal portfolio, on the other hand, is determined by the risk aversion function, $-U_{22}/U_2$, and depends upon C_1 only through C_1's influence on that function.

The class of utility functions which satisfies this property – i.e. for which the marginal rate of substitution is a linear function of C_2 for given C_1 – is given by

$$U(C_1, C_2) = F[g(C_1) + h(C_1)C_2], \; F' > 0, \; h > 0, \; g' \geqq 0, \; h' \geqq 0, \tag{4.1}$$

a special case of which is

$$U(C_1, C_2) = F(C_1^\alpha C_2^\beta), \; F' > 0, \; \alpha > 0, \; \beta > 0. \tag{4.2}$$

The example (4.2) has a wider interest. Pestieau [16] has shown in a three-period model that if a suitably generalised version of (2.4) holds with equality, and if one makes the additional assumption that the indifference surface is homothetic, this implies that the utility function belongs to the class (4.2). The homotheticity assumption was made explicitly by Friedman [9] in the theoretical formulation of his permanent income hypothesis; one can then infer that since he implicitly assumes that saving and portfolio decisions can be separated, the preference ordering underlying the permanent income hypothesis can be represented by the class of utility functions (4.2).

V. CONCLUDING REMARKS

What is there to be learnt from these models? It will not have escaped the reader that the number of testable propositions which can be derived from the theory seems rather modest, although it is probably true that the situation is no worse in this respect than in other branches of economic theory, e.g. the classical theory of demand. However, even though some of the results mentioned above may be difficult to test empirically at the present stage of our knowledge, they may still be important in contributing to a deeper insight into some important economic phenomena.

It should also be stressed that no attempt has been made here to apply the model to more specific problems of greater relevance for public policy. Models like these might be used to study the relationship between taxation and risk-taking; the literature on this important topic, as surveyed by Allingham [1], has largely ignored the intertemporal aspect of the problem. The extension by Sandmo [20] seems to indicate that this may be a serious limitation of the discussion. Another example of application is to the term structure of interest rates, where interesting results have been obtained by Stiglitz [22].

One might raise the question of the justification of two-period models when multi-period models are available. If one is interested in the sequential nature of decision-making, two-period models are clearly inadequate. But the literature surveyed here is not concerned with that problem; it analyses the impact of uncertainty about the future on *current* decisions. When that is the focus of the analysis one would not expect the implications of two-period and multi-period models to be qualitatively different; this argument has received some interesting support by Fama [7]. The main advantage of two-period models is that they need not be based on the very restrictive assumptions about preferences which have characterised the multi-period models; in that way they may contribute to a better understanding of the economic implications of those assumptions.

REFERENCES

[1] M. G. Allingham, 'Risk-Taking and Taxation: A Survey', mimeo, 1971. Prepared for the IEA Workshop in Economic Theory, Bergen, 1971.
[2] K. J. Arrow, *Aspects of the Theory of Risk-Bearing* (Helsinki: Academic Bookstore, 1965).
[3] K. J. Arrow, *Essays in the Theory of Risk-Bearing* (Amsterdam: North-Holland, 1970).
[4] D. Cass, and J. E. Stiglitz, 'The Structure of Investor Preferences and Asset Returns, and Separability in Portfolio Allocation: A Contribution to the Pure Theory of Mutual Funds', *Journal of Economic Theory*, vol. II (1970), pp. 122–60.
[5] J. H. Drèze, and F. Modigliani, 'Épargne et consommation en avenir aléatoire', *Cahiers du Séminaire d'Économétrie*, vol. IX (1966), pp. 7–33.
[6] J. H. Drèze, and F. Modigliani, 'Consumption Decisions under Uncertainty', *Journal of Economic Theory*, vol. V (1972), pp. 308–35.
[7] E. F. Fama, 'Multiperiod Consumption-Investment Decisions', *American Economic Review*, vol. LX (1970), pp. 163–74.
[8] I. Fisher, *The Theory of Interest* (New York: Kelley, 1930).
[9] M. Friedman, *A Theory of the Consumption Function* (Princeton: Princeton University Press, 1957).
[10] J. Hirshleifer, 'On the Theory of Optimal Investment Decision', *Journal of Political Economy*, vol. LXVI (1958), pp. 329–52.
[11] H. E. Leland, 'Saving and Uncertainty: The Precautionary Demand for Saving', *Quarterly Journal of Economics*, vol. LXXXII (1968), pp. 465–73.

[12] H. E. Leland, 'On the Existence of Optimal Policies under Uncertainty', *Journal of Economic Theory*, vol. IV (1972), pp. 35–44.
[13] D. Levhari, and T. N. Srinivasan, 'Optimal Savings under Uncertainty', *Review of Economic Studies*, vol. XXXVI (1969), pp. 153–63.
[14] H. M. Markowitz, *Portfolio Selection* (New York: Wiley, 1959).
[15] L. J. Mirman, 'Uncertainty and Optimal Consumption Decisions', *Econometrica*, vol. XXXIX (1971), pp. 179–85.
[16] P. Pestieau, 'Épargne et consommation dans l'incertitude: un modèle à trois périodes', *Recherches Économiques de Louvain*, vol. XXXV (1969), pp. 63–88.
[17] J. W. Pratt, 'Risk Aversion in the Small and in the Large', *Econometrica*, vol. XXXII (1964), pp. 122–36.
[18a] M. Rothschild, and J. E. Stiglitz, 'Increasing Risk I–II', *Journal of Economic Theory*, vol. II (1970), pp. 225–43; [18b] vol. III (1971), pp. 66–84.
[19] A. Sandmo, 'Portfolio Choice in a Theory of Saving', *Swedish Journal of Economics*, vol. LXX (1968), pp. 106–22.
[20] A. Sandmo, 'Capital Risk, Consumption, and Portfolio Choice', *Econometrica*, vol. XXXVII (1969), pp. 586–99.
[21] A. Sandmo, 'The Effect of Uncertainty on Saving Decisions', *Review of Economic Studies*, vol. XXXVII (1970), pp. 353–60.
[22] J. E. Stiglitz, 'A Consumption-Oriented Theory of the Demand for Financial Assets and the Term Structure of Interest Rates', *Review of Economic Studies*, vol. XXXVII (1970), pp. 321–51.
[23] J. Tobin, 'Liquidity Preference as Behavior Towards Risk', *Review of Economic Studies*, vol. XXV (1958), pp. 65–86.

3 Optimum Accumulation Under Uncertainty: the Case of Stationary Returns to Investment

James A. Mirrlees[1]
NUFFIELD COLLEGE, OXFORD

In the theory of optimum growth it has been found that models with discrete time are easier to treat rigorously than models with continuous time. But continuous-time models often have the advantage of providing simpler results. I shall illustrate this tension in the present paper by discussing the model for optimum growth under uncertainty that has received most attention in the literature (Phelps [6], Levhari and Srinivasan [4], Hahn [2], Hakansson [3], Brock and Mirman [1]). An existence theorem will be proved for the discrete-time case. By a heuristic argument, I obtain an equation for the optimum under continuous-time which makes possible results about the effects of uncertainty on the optimum policy more general than are available in discrete time. These latter results are somewhat surprising. By way of prelude I outline the reasons for research into optimum growth under uncertainty, and offer a classification of models. The model discussed in this paper is less appealing than some others; but it seems to be the easiest one.

I. PROBLEMS

Models of intertemporal optimisation are fascinating and potentially useful. They may be considered relevant to the saving, portfolio and insurance behaviour of the consumer, or to the optimal choice of national economic policy. I shall restrict myself to models without a finite time-horizon: these have always seemed to offer the possibility of simpler formulations and results, and locate the question of suitable terminal conditions appropriately in the case of the national economy. Such models may be used to illuminate, for example, the following kinds of problem:

(i) As is well known, the usual first-order, or 'competitive', conditions for optimality, are not sufficient for optimality in such

[1] This is a revised version of the first part of 'Optimum Growth and Uncertainty', May 1972 version. The first three sections formed part of a paper prepared for the Bergen workshop. Section IV was developed during the workshop.

models. These conditions, which I shall refer to as the 'local optimality conditions', are derived from the argument that variations from the optimal path that affect only a finite number of periods (or length of time) should not increase our valuation of the economy. It is possible that satisfaction of these conditions, even for all time, is consistent with a dynamically inefficient development of the economy; so that, roughly speaking, capital is accumulated at a wastefully rapid rate. An apparent solution is to calculate the initial shadow prices for the optimal path and allow competition or its equivalent to determine the path (with the possibility of occasional recalculation of the true optimum as a check). Other methods of attempting to realise an optimal development of the economy through the operation of a price system may also suggest themselves. One must enquire whether similar procedures are possible in models with uncertainty.

(ii) A deterministic model for the economy may be proposed, such that policies optimal relative to the model can be computed. A better model might have stochastic components, to allow for real uncertainty about technology, say, and the specification errors of the original model. One would like to have methods for computing optimal policies in such a stochastic model (subject to the questions raised below). This is likely to present more difficulties than the computation of optimal policies for the deterministic model.

(iii) The question arises, granted that the stochastic specification of the model provides a more accurate description of the economy than the deterministic version, whether it makes any great difference. Would the gains for a planned economy from following the optimal policy for the stochastic model be sufficiently substantial to justify the further study of such models? Would they predict substantially different behaviour by a consumer?

(iv) It may also be of interest to discuss the qualitative effect on optimal policies of the introduction of uncertainty. One may ask whether the stochastic specification leads to more or less saving. Since certain proposals to allow for uncertainty crudely, e.g. by introducing a finite time-horizon, may have clear and unambiguous qualitative effects on the optimal policy, results of this kind may provide a useful check on the value of such proposals, even when the more precise checks suggested in (iii) are difficult or impossible. In a similar spirit, it may be possible to suggest by this means certain comments on the value of current institutional structures.

(v) It has proved possible, in some deterministic models, to give a rather simple characterisation of the steady state towards which the optimal path tends. Detailed knowledge of the optimal path is not a prerequisite for the steady-state computation. It is therefore interesting to ask whether any similar characterisation of the steady state (supposing one exists) is available for stochastic models.

These examples do not exhaust the lines that have been pursued, but they may suggest some of the reasons why such models should be studied. It needs to be said, however, that not all the problems mentioned look promising once some initial analysis has been done; and in most of the cases that would be likely to interest the economist, the analysis runs a serious risk of becoming excessively complicated, and computation may be definitely hard.

II. UNCERTAINTIES

I think it is convenient to classify the kinds of uncertainty that one might attempt to capture in stochastic models of the economy or the consumer, into

(i) preference uncertainty;
(ii) income uncertainty;
(iii) uncertainty about present technology;
(iv) uncertainty about future technology.

These uncertainties can be specified by fixed random variables or, in a more Bayesian way, so as to capture the real-time accumulation and interpretation of information, including that accruing as a result of economic policies deliberately pursued.

In category (i), I include such considerations as imperfect knowledge of one's own future preferences, and comparison of present and future consumption when the nature of the consumption experience is uncertain; and also the uncertainty of governments and planners regarding the preferences of future governments and planners. One might think that these considerations would not be worth including explicitly in a model, being unlikely significantly to influence current policies. But the subject remains to be explored.

In category (ii) I include sources of uncertainty that are unaffected by current portfolio and investment policies. This might be true to some extent of the availability of foreign aid, or of agricultural output in any economy where buffer stocks are the only relevant form of accumulation; but the main case is that of the single consumer with uncertain income, fixed or related to labour done.

It is convenient to distinguish from income uncertainty imperfect knowledge of returns to investment. For a consumer, this uncertainty may relate simply to the rate of interest at which he can borrow and lend. In the case of an economy, we are uncertain about the precise technology that is available and will be available. It is simplest to assume that knowledge about technology is fixed: this is done in models of category (iii). In any case, it seems natural to regard our knowledge of future technology as being conditional upon our knowledge of current technology. Even if we knew the present technology with certainty, we should be uncertain about the course of future technology. Uncertainty about the currently available technology exists as well. In the case of category (iv), uncertainty about future technology, we should regard it as a reason for making uncertainties about production possibilities increase with time.

Of these different kinds of models, category (ii) seems to me to promise the most valuable applications, since optimal inventories depend essentially on uncertainty. Not much work has been done on the natural economic formulations. (But cf. Yaari [7], [8]). Category (iv) offers a number of intriguing problems, to which I hope to return on another occasion. But most work has been done on category (iii), specifically on the model for which, with

$$\left. \begin{array}{c} k_t = \text{capital at time } t; \\ c_t = \text{consumption at time } t; \\ X_1, X_2, \ldots, X_t, \ldots \text{ independent and identically} \\ \text{distributed random variables, with mean } m; \end{array} \right\} \quad (2.1)$$

$$k_{t+1} = X_t(k_t - c_t) \qquad (t = 1, 2, \ldots). \tag{2.2}$$

k_1 is given, and k_t is constrained to be non-negative for all t. It is desired to maximise

$$E[\sum_1^\infty R^{t-1} u(c_t)]. \tag{2.3}$$

c_t is chosen when k_t is known, but the values of $X_t, X_{t+1}, \ldots$ are not. u is assumed to be continuous, strictly concave, and increasing, with $u'(0) = \infty$. R is positive, and usually ≤ 1.

III. THE DISCRETE-TIME MODEL

I shall first prove an existence theorem for this problem. The technique has not been applied to the model previously, but it is quite simple. I need to assume (what can be readily checked for particular utility functions u) that

$$\sum_1^\infty R^{t-1} u(m^t k) \text{ converges for all } k > 0; \tag{3.1}$$

and also that a particular feasible path (c_t') exists such that for some number M,

$$\sum_1^T R^{t-1} Eu(c_t') \geq M \qquad (T = 1, 2, \ldots). \tag{3.2}$$

(3.1) implies that $E[\sum_1^T R^{t-1} u(c_t)]$ is bounded above for given initial capital stock, since

$$Eu(c_t) \leq u(Ec_t) \leq u(m^{t-1} k_1),$$

where the last step is implied by

$$c_t \leq k_t \leq X_{t-1} k_{t-1} \leq \ldots \leq X_{t-1} X_{t-2} \ldots X_1 k_1.$$

Indeed, we can claim more, for, by the argument just used,

$$\sum R^{t-1} E[u(c_t) - u(m^{t-1} k_1)] \tag{3.3}$$

is a series of nonpositive terms, and therefore converges (possibly to $-\infty$) for all feasible paths. It follows, using (3.1), that $\sum_1^\infty R^{t-1} Eu(c_t)$ converges, or diverges to $-\infty$. By assumption (3.2), the series converges to a finite number for some path, and we are therefore entitled to introduce the definition

$$W(k_1) = \mathrm{Sup}\{\sum_1^\infty R^{t-1} Eu(c_t)\} \tag{3.4}$$

where the supremum is taken over all feasible paths with initial capital k_1.

By Bellman's familiar 'dynamic programming' argument, we have

$$W(k_1) = \sup_{0 \leq c \leq k_1} \{u(c) + REW(X_1(k_1 - c))\}. \tag{3.5}$$

I show that the supremum is actually achieved, by proving that it is the supremum of a continuous function. u is a continuous function of c by assumption. It is quite easy to show, directly from the definition (3.4), that $EW(X, k)$ is a concave function of k, and therefore continuous for $k > 0$. Continuity at $k = 0$ is proved by a routine argument.[1] Since a continuous function achieves its supremum on any closed interval, the supremum is achieved, and we have found c_1^* such that

$$W(k_1) = u(c_1^*) + REW(X_1(k_1 - c_1^*)). \tag{3.6}$$

If we apply the formula (3.6) iteratively, we obtain the series for W:

$$W(k_1) = \sum_1^T R^{t-1} E[u(c_t^*)] + R^T EW(k^*_{T+1}). \tag{3.7}$$

[1] See the appendix to this chapter (p. 49).

As before, we have $k^*_{T+1} \leq X_T X_{T-1} \ldots X_1 k_1$. Using the concavity of W, we deduce that

$$R^T E W(k^*_{T+1}) \leq R^T W(m^T k_1)$$

$$\leq \sum_{T+1}^{\infty} R^{t-1} u(m^{t-1} k_1), \qquad (3.8)$$

by the argument used before (3.3). Assumption (3.1) guarantees that this last expression tends to zero as $T \to \infty$. Therefore, given any positive number ϵ, we can find T_1 such that

$$W(k_1) \leq \sum_{1}^{T} R^{t-1} E[u(c_t^*)] + \epsilon \qquad (T \geq T_1). \qquad (3.9)$$

If we successively let $T \to \infty$ and $\epsilon \to 0$, we have

$$W(k_1) \leq \sum_{1}^{\infty} R^{t-1} E[u(c_t^*)]. \qquad (3.10)$$

By the definition of W, this inequality can be replaced by equality; and we have proved

Theorem 1. If (3.1) and (3.2) hold, an optimum path exists. The optimum policy $c(k)$ and the maximum value $W(k)$ satisfy the relations

$$W(k) = u(c(k)) + REW(X[k - c(k)]), \qquad (3.11)$$

$$c(k) \text{ maximises } u(c) + REW(X(k - c)). \qquad (3.12)$$

This is quite a useful existence theorem for the problem,[1] and substantially more convenient than the Levhari–Srinivasan results, which are readily applicable only to homogeneous utility functions.[2] It should be noticed that the assumption of independence among the random variables X_t can be weakened, and a corresponding theorem obtained for yet more general cases. The argument throws no light on the possibility of nonexistence, however. One would not expect that these conditions are necessary for existence. However, it is

---

[1] (3.2) is automatically satisfied if u is bounded below and $R<1$, since $Eu(c_t) \leq u(m^{t-1} k_1)$.

If u is bounded above, it may as well have sup $u=0$. Then (3.1) is implied by (3.2); for $\Sigma R^{t-1} u(m^{t-1} k_1)$ is a series of negative terms, bounded below by $\Sigma R^{t-1} Eu(c_t)$.

(3.2) is most conveniently checked by considering a path generated by a constant saving ratio: $c_t = ak_t$.

[2] Phelps, who first obtained the solution (3.16) for the case of homogeneous utility, obtained it as the limit of policies optimal for finite time-horizons, and did not study the problem without time-horizon directly. Hakansson, in his analysis, merely satisfies the relations (3.11) and (3.12); but that does not, strictly speaking, prove anything.

likely that in some sense they are not far from being necessary. The following conjecture suggests itself:

Problem: Is it the case that no optimum exists if $R^T u(m^T k_1)$ tends to either $+\infty$ or $-\infty$ as T tends to ∞?

(3.11) and (3.12) do not look easy to solve, but there is one solvable case – as Phelps found – the case of homogeneous utility:

$$u(c) = -\frac{1}{n} c^{-n} \qquad (3.13)$$

(As usual, it is convenient to have $u(c) = \log c$ correspond to $n=0$, since in all cases, then, $u'(c) = c^{-n-1}$.) Under assumption (3.13), the following argument shows that optimum consumption must be proportional to k, and the maximum valuation homogeneous of degree $-n$ in k. An increase in capital stock by a factor λ allows any feasible path to be increased by the same factor λ, thus multiplying total utility by λ^{-n}. Therefore if (c_t^*) was the optimal path from initial capital k_1, (λc_t^*) must be the optimum path from initial λk_1. Thus c_1^* is homogeneous of degree 1 in k_1; i.e.

$$c(k) = \gamma k. \qquad (3.14)$$

Similarly,
$$W(k) = -w \cdot k^{-n}, \qquad (3.15)$$
for some number w.

If we substitute (3.14) and (3.15) in (3.11), we obtain

$$w = \frac{1}{n} \gamma^{-n} + Rw(1-\gamma)^{-n} E(X^{-n}),$$

γ maximises $-\frac{1}{n}\gamma^{-n} - Rw(1-\gamma)^{-n} E(X^{-n}),$

which together imply that

$$\gamma = 1 - [RE(X^{-n})]^{1/(n+1)}. \qquad (3.16)$$

This calculation proves that (3.16) gives the optimum policy, provided that conditions (3.1) and (3.2) are satisfied. It is clear at once from the special form of u that (3.1) is satisfied if and only if

$$Rm^{-n} < 1. \qquad (3.17)$$

To discover when (3.2) is satisfied, consider the consumption policy $c = ak$ and the path generated by it. It is immediately seen that $c_t = a(1-a)^{t-1} X_{t-1} X_{t-2} \ldots X_1 k_1$. Therefore this path satisfies (3.2) if $R(1-a)^{-n} E(X^{-n}) < 1$. An a for which this is so can always be found when

$$RE(X^{-n}) < 1. \qquad (3.18)$$

Optimum Accumulation Under Uncertainty

Thus we can apply our existence theorem if both (3.17) and (3.18) hold. If $n>0$, $E(X^{-n}) \geq m^{-n}$, and (3.18) therefore implies (3.17). If $0 \geq n > -1$, $E(X^{-n}) \leq m^{-n}$, and (3.17) implies (3.18). We can summarise these results in

Theorem 2. In the case of homogeneous utility, an optimum path exists provided that

$$n>0 \text{ and } RE(X^{-n})<1; \text{ or } 0 \geq n > -1 \text{ and } Rm^{-n}<1.$$

In either case, the optimum policy is given by

$$\frac{c}{k} = 1 - [RE(X^{-n})]^{\frac{1}{n+1}}.$$

Corollary. The optimum level of saving is in this case greater than under perfect certainty (i.e. the case $X=m$ with probability 1) if $n>0$, and less than under perfect certainty if $n<0$.

The corollary follows by comparing $E(X^{-n})$ with m^{-n}. Notice that if there is no utility-discounting (i.e. no impatience) and a positive expected rate of return ($m>1$), n must be positive if we are to apply the theorem, and in that case uncertainty about the rate of return is a reason for saving more than would otherwise have been saved.

This second theorem refers only to a rather special case, and may be misleading, since it is almost certainly not the case that the qualitative effect of uncertainty on the saving decision depends only on the elasticity of marginal utility (the relative risk aversion index). But in the continuous-time model, we shall be able to go further.

Two properties of $c(k)$ can be obtained easily, but they are not particularly surprising. Assuming differentiability of everything, we obtain from the first theorem:

$$W(k) = u(c(k)) + REW(X[k - c(k)]) \tag{3.19}$$

$$u'(c(k)) = RE[XW'(X[k - c(k)])]. \tag{3.20}$$

Differentiating (3.19) with respect to k, and using (3.20), we have

$$W'(k) = RE[XW'(X[k - c(k)])] \tag{3.21}$$

$$= u(c(k)), \quad \text{by (3.20).} \tag{3.22}$$

Since W is concave, $W'(k)$ is a decreasing function of k, and $E[XW'(X[k - c(k)])]$ is a decreasing function of $k - c$. Therefore

$$0 < c'(k) < 1. \tag{3.23}$$

The second inequality follows from the remark that, if $k - c(k)$ were nonincreasing in k, (3.20) could not hold. Notice that differentiability of c would follow from twice-differentiability of W, but that is hard to verify.

The model suggests two further remarks:

(1) *Competitive Realisation*

Competitive equilibrium in this model would imply that

$$u'(c_t) = E[X_t u'(c_{t+1})]. \tag{3.24}$$

(3.24) expresses indifference between an increment to consumption now and an increment to capital, which then becomes an increment to consumption next period. It is easily verified that (3.24) is implied by (3.19) and (3.20). Suppose that $c_1{}^*$ (the optimum consumption level) were in fact the level of consumption in the first period. It is then possible for (3.24) to be satisfied for $t=1$ without c_2 being generated by the optimum policy in the next period. In other words, intertemporal equilibrium combined with the correct initial policy is not sufficient to guarantee optimality – very far from it. Notice that none of the qualitative properties of optimal policies that have been derived above can be deduced from (3.24) alone. It is rather hard to see how competitive equilibrium can be used to help generate an optimum path. It seems to be necessary to generate correct expectations about prices at the end of some period – which would be hard.

(2) *The Importance of Uncertainty*

If uncertainty is not too great, and X has a nicely behaved distribution, we may be able to evaluate (3.16) by using a Taylor expansion around $X = m$. In this way one obtains

$$\frac{c}{k} = 1 - (Rm^{-n})^{\frac{1}{n+1}} \left[1 + \frac{1}{2}n(n+1)\left(\frac{\sigma}{m}\right)^2 + \ldots \right] \tag{3.25}$$

where σ is the standard deviation of X. In realistic cases, σ/m could well be quite small, and its square much smaller. Thus, in response to problem (iii) of section I, there may be good grounds for regarding the effort of deriving, or at least applying, (3.16) as unwarranted, *ex post*. The form of (3.25) is to be expected on the basis of Malinvaud's 'second-order certainty equivalence' (cf. Malinvaud [5]).

IV. THE CONTINUOUS-TIME MODEL

The awkwardness of the functional equations that determine the optimal policy in Theorem 1 arises from the discrete-time formulation of the model. I shall now show that an interesting continuous-time version is possible. The production constraint in discrete-time was:

Optimum Accumulation Under Uncertainty

$$k_{t+1} = X_t(k_t - c_t), \ k_t \geq 0. \tag{2.2}$$

$X_1, X_2, \ldots$ are independent and identically distributed random variables. From (2.2),

$$k_t = X_{t-1}X_{t-2}\ldots X_0 k_0 - X_{t-1}c_{t-1} - X_{t-1}X_{t-2}c_{t-2} - \ldots$$
$$\ldots X_{t-1}X_{t-2}\ldots X_0 c_0.$$

If the technology were 'really' continuous-time, we should want to write

$$k_t = A_t k_0 - \int_0^t \frac{A_t}{A_s} c_s \, ds, \tag{2.2'}$$

where A_t is a stochastic process with $A_0 = 1$. Here $\dfrac{c}{A}$ is constant from 0 to 1, and again from 1 to 2, and so on. It is natural to think of (2.2) as the continuous-time model (2.2'), subject to the constraint that consumption be fixed in advance for a year at a time. If the unit of time can be chosen arbitrarily, (A_t) is a process with independent multiplicative increments (so that $\log A_t$ is distributed according to a Lévy-stable distribution). Let us write $E(A_t) = e^{gt}$.

We may consider the maximisation of

$$E \int_0^\infty e^{-rt} u(c_t) dt, \tag{2.3'}$$

subject to (2.2') with $k_t \geq 0$ for all t, but with c_t restricted only to be continuous, and chosen with the knowledge of A_t. In the first instance, let us put $r = 0$.

If it is assumed that u is bounded above (with sup $u = 0$), and that, for all $k > 0$, there exists $a > 0$ such that

$$\int_0^\infty Eu(ae^{-at}A_t)dt > -\infty, \tag{3.2'}$$

theorem 1 of section II suggests, by analogy with the discrete-time case, that an optimum exists, maximising (3.2') subject to (2.2'). Clearly the condition that $k_t \geq 0$ for all t is equivalent to the requirement that

$$\int_0^\infty A_t^{-1} c_t dt \leq k_0.$$

Define, then, the function $W(\,.\,)$ by

$$W(k) = \text{Sup}\left\{ E\int_0^\infty u(c_s)ds : \int_0^\infty A_s^{-1} c_s dt \leq k \right\} \tag{3.4'}$$

$$= E\int_0^\infty u(c_t^*)dt,$$

where (c_t^*) is the optimum policy, with $k_0 = k$.

Following the dynamic programming argument, we notice that

$$W(k) = \text{Max} \left\{ E \int_0^T u(c_t) dt + EW(k_T) \right\}.$$

If it is legitimate to divide by T and let $T \to 0$ – surely it is, but justification is difficult – it follows that

$$0 = \text{Max} \left\{ u(c_t) + \left[\frac{d}{ds} E_t W(k_s) \right]_{s=t} \right\}, \qquad (3.5')$$

where E_t is the expectation operator conditional on knowledge of A_t. Since, using (2.2'), we have

$$k_s^* = \frac{A_s}{A_t} \left(k_t^* - \int_t^s \frac{A_t}{A_r} c_r^* \, dr \right),$$

we can evaluate the time derivative in (3.5'). It is equal to

$$\left[\frac{d}{ds} E_t W \left(\left(\frac{A_s}{A_t} e^{-g(s-t)} \right) e^{g(s-t)} \left(k_t^* - \int_t^s \frac{A_t}{A_r} c_r^* dr \right) \right) \right]_{s=t}$$

$$= \left[\frac{d}{ds} E_t W \left(\frac{A_s}{A_t} e^{-g(s-t)} k_t^* \right) + \frac{d}{ds} E_t W(e^{g(s-t)} k_t^*) \right.$$

$$\left. + \frac{d}{ds} E_t W \left(k_t^* - \int_t^s \frac{A_t}{A_r} c_r^* \, dr \right) \right]_{s=t}$$

$$= \left[\frac{d}{ds} E_t W(B_s k_t^*) \right]_{s=t} + g k_t^* W'(k_t^*) - c_t^* W'(k_t^*),$$

where $B_s = \frac{A_s}{A_t} e^{-g(s-t)}$ is a stochastic process with $E_t B_s = 1$ and B_s 'more uncertain' than B_r when $s > r$, in a natural sense. In fact, if $s > r \geq t$,

$$E_t W(B_s k_t^*) = E_t E_r W(B_s k_t^*) > E_t W(B_r k_t^*),$$

since, as is clear from its definition (3.4'), W is a strictly concave function, and $B_r k_t^* = E_r(B_s k_t^*)$. Thus,

$$\omega = \left[\frac{d}{ds} E_t W(B_s k_t^*) \right]_{s=t} < 0.$$

Returning to (3.5'), we see, on differentiating with respect to c_t, that

$$u'(c_t^*) = W'(k_t^*) \qquad (4.1)$$

on the optimum path, and also on that path

$$u(c) + (gk - c)u'(c) = -\omega > 0. \qquad (4.2)$$

Optimum Accumulation Under Uncertainty

In the absence of uncertainty, with $E(A_t)$ the same, $u + (gk - c)u' = 0$. Furthermore, $u + (gk - c)u'$ is a decreasing function of c (provided that $gk - c > 0$, as is implied by (4.2)). Therefore, c_t^* *is less than optimum consumption when there is no uncertainty.* The result has been obtained on the assumption that there is no impatience. The other assumptions, that u is bounded and W well-defined, are very likely almost necessary for the existence of an optimum policy, in the sense that the only other cases in which an optimum policy exists are boundary cases to those here considered, in which the result would hold at least in the weak sense that optimum consumption is not increased when the uncertainty of returns is considered. But this is an unproven conjecture. If it is correct, it would be interesting to have a direct proof of the result, based only on the assumption that an optimum policy exists in the overtaking sense, without the additional assumption that W exists. I suppose it is quite likely that an optimum exists wherever u is bounded above and $g > 0$. It is surprising, if correct, that the assumption of zero impatience should be sufficient to obtain the result.

When there is discounting we obtain, by the same arguments, the equation

$$u(c) + (gk - c)u'(c) = rW - \omega. \tag{4.3}$$

In this case, we can make an interesting remark without further analysis. An increase in uncertainty which has no effect on EA_t leaves g unchanged, but reduces W. This last fact is apparent from (3.4'), since any policy that is feasible for a particular model is also feasible when uncertainty is reduced. Now compare the stochastic model with the deterministic model. The right-hand side of (4.3) is increased, for the stochastic model, by inclusion of the positive term $-\omega$; but diminished by the reduction in W. Thus it seems possible that, when r is great enough, increased uncertainty can be a reason for saving less. (As in the discrete–time model, this is readily verified to hold when u is homogeneous and unbounded above.)

Finally, it is worth noting that, when the stochastic process A_t is the result of independent multiplicative increments, with variance 2β per unit of time, and is normal (i.e. $\log A_t$ is a 'Wiener process'),

$$\omega = \beta k^2 W''(k). \tag{4.4}$$

Using this in (4.3), and combining with (4.1), we have the basic equations for analysis of the optimal policy. But that is another story.

V. CONCLUSIONS

The model used in this paper is a rather special one. It has received more attention than other models of accumulation under uncertainty because it is easier to handle than most of the others that have been thought of. One ought to be able to learn something about the problems from the simplest special case, and one can hope that the techniques developed for it will be capable of extension. The special case does not have all the interesting features of the general. For example, the model we have considered is not a good vehicle for examining the asymptotic behaviour of the optimally developing economy as time tends to infinity; nor does it show up the ways in which uncertainty can cause existence problems for optimum growth. But the model has shown:

(i) That the introduction of uncertainty – i.e. a stochastic specification into the model – may lead to greater or smaller savings requirements, depending upon the utility function and the utility–discount rate. In saying this, it is assumed that comparisons should be made between models with the same mean rate of return to investment. This fact at least shows that simple rules of thumb for dealing with uncertainty, such as the imposition of a finite planning horizon, cannot be justified by an unspecific appeal to uncertainty.

(ii) That the introduction of uncertainty may not, at this aggregative level, have a significantly large influence on optimal policies. This impression can be made precise in those cases where an explicit solution is possible.

(iii) That there may be some justification for supposing that, when a long-run view is taken – i.e. utility is not discounted on account of the mere passage of time – the precautionary reaction to uncertainty is the predominant one: the more uncertainty there is, the more should be saved. Insofar as the analysis of the continuous-time version of the model is as yet incomplete, this conclusion must remain somewhat tentative.

(iv) That competitive realisation of optimal development meets severe difficulties when uncertainty is admitted into the model and no terminal conditions are imposed. For a proper understanding of these problems, it will be necessary to find out more about the possible relationships between central planning and decentralised production and consumption.

APPENDIX

We have to show that $EW(Xk) \to W(0)$ as $k \to 0$. $W(0) = \sum_1^\infty R^{t-1} u(0)$, which may be $-\infty$.

$EW(Xk) \leq \sum_1^\infty R^{t-1} Eu(m^t Xk)$, so that it is sufficient to show that

$$\sum_1^\infty R^{t-1} Eu(m^t Xk) \to \sum_1^\infty R^{t-1} u(0).$$

Take first the case $R = 1$, $u(0) < 0$. Let M be an arbitrarily large number and let T be such that

$$Tu(0) < -M - 2,$$

$$\sum_{T+1}^\infty Eu(m^t X) < 1.$$

Then we can choose $k_0 \leq 1$ such that

$$\sum_1^T Eu(m^t Xk) < Tu(0) + 1 \qquad (k \leq k_0).$$

Adding, we have

$$\sum_1^\infty Eu(m^t Xk) < -M \qquad (k \leq k_0),$$

proving, as desired, that $\sum Eu(m^t Xk) \to -\infty$.

If $R < 1$, we take an arbitrary positive number ϵ, and choose T so that

$$\sum_1^T R^{t-1} u(0) < \frac{1}{1-R} u(0) + \frac{1}{3}\epsilon,$$

$$\sum_{T+1}^\infty R^{t-1} Eu(m^t X) < \frac{1}{3}\epsilon.$$

Then $k_0 \leq 1$ is chosen to give

$$\sum_1^T R^{t-1} Eu(m^t Xk) < \sum_1^T R^{t-1} u(0) + \frac{1}{3}\epsilon \qquad (k \leq k_0).$$

Adding the inequalities, we obtain

$$\sum_1^\infty R^{t-1} Eu(m^t Xk) < \frac{1}{1-R} u(0) + \epsilon \qquad (k \leq k_0),$$

as desired.

REFERENCES

[1] W. Brock and L. Mirman, 'The Stochastic Modified Golden Rule in a One Sector Model of Economic Growth with Uncertain Technology', mimeo, Rochester and Cornell, 1970.
[2] F. H. Hahn, 'Savings and Uncertainty', *Review of Economic Studies*, vol. XXXVII (1970), pp. 21–4.
[3] N. Hakansson, 'Optimal Investment and Consumption Strategies Under Risk for a Class of Utility Functions', *Econometrica*, vol. XXXVIII (1970), pp. 587–607.
[4] D. Levhari and T. N. Srinivasan, 'Optimal Savings under Uncertainty', *Review of Economic Studies*, vol. XXXVI (1969), pp. 153–63.
[5] E. Malinvaud, 'First Order Certainty Equivalence', *Econometrica*, vol. XXXVII (1969), pp. 706–18.
[6] E. Phelps, 'The Accumulation of Risky Capital: A Sequential Utility Analysis', *Econometrica*, vol. XXX (1962), pp. 729–43.
[7] M. Yaari, 'Uncertain Lifetime, Life Insurance, and the Theory of the Consumer', *Review of Economic Studies*, vol. XXXII (1965), pp. 137–50.
[8] M. Yaari, 'A Law of Large Numbers in the Theory of Consumer's Choice Under Uncertainty', Working Paper No. CP-330, Center for Research in Management Science, University of California, Berkeley, March 1971.

Part 2

General Equilibrium

4 Allocation Under Uncertainty: a survey

Roger Guesnerie[1]
CEPREMAP, PARIS

and

Thierry de Montbrial[1]
ECOLE POLYTECHNIQUE AND COMMISSARIAT DU PLAN, PARIS

An extension of the theory of allocation of resources to the case of uncertainty has been realised recently. After the pioneering article of Arrow [2], who with Allais [1] initiated this analysis, the field was explored by Baudier [4], and Debreu [7, 8] whose results have been somewhat generalised by Radner [14]. One can find stimulating discussions about the implications of the theory in Arrow [3], applications in Borch [5] and Hirshleifer [11], or critical comments on various aspects in Drèze [6].

These articles or books are the basic material for the review presented here. The statements of results are generally accompanied by proofs, comments and indications of open problems, and are expected to lead the reader to an understanding of the state of knowledge in this area.

I. THE DESCRIPTION AND FORMALISATION OF UNCERTAINTY

(1)
In the framework of general equilibrium theory, uncertainty may be introduced at several points. On the production side, a typical example is that of agriculture, where the harvest is closely related to meteorological conditions. On the other hand, the arbitrage between investments will be affected by the level of reserves in a mine, not exactly known; this is uncertainty about initial endowments. A factory will become obsolete with the discovery of a new technique; a machine may break down and this would reduce the output. These are examples of technological uncertainties. Uncertainty may concern the tastes of consumers as well. My preference for ice cream

[1] The authors wish to thank Jacques Drèze and Dieter Sondermann for their helpful comments.

over a cup of tea tomorrow may depend on the weather and, perhaps, on other factors that I am more or less able to specify today.

So, different elements in the description of the economy – resources, technology, preferences – are not completely determined at the beginning of the economic process. We will suppose that all these uncertainties can be represented by a list of 'variables', the level of which is partially unknown, and which are independent of the agents' actions. These variables, by definition, cannot be influenced by any economic agent and describe the environment. They must be carefully distinguished from decision variables controlled by economic agents and from the other variables (prices and trades) which are determined by both decisions and environment.

(2)

A specification of possible values for the variables characterising the environment is a state of the environment, or, according to Savage's terminology, a state of nature. The states of nature are mutually exclusive. The set S of all states of nature is supposed to be exhaustive.

An event is a subset of S.[1] An event can be defined from an incomplete description of the characteristics of the states of nature. For instance, the event 'the weather is hot in Paris at a given date' is the set of all states of nature, for which the temperature in Paris, on that day, is – say – greater than 20° C.

A priori, the concept of state of nature or of event applies independently of the temporal specification of the problem. In a many periods economy ($t = 1, ..., T$), a state of nature is a complete specification of the history of the environment from the beginning of time ($t = 1$) to the end ($t = T$). In this case, the temporal structure must be considered explicitly, and leads to define elementary events at every period t: two states of nature belong to the same elementary event at period t if all the variables describing the environment coincide for all periods from 1 to t. Let B_t be the set of all elementary events e_t at date t. This is a partition of S. It is clear that an observation of the characteristics of the environment from period 1 to t allows one to tell in which element e_t of B_t the true state of nature lies, but no more. Moreover, the elementary events at the last period T coincide with the states of nature. Finally, we observe that the sequence of partitions B_t is increasing, or that B_{t+1} is a refinement of B_t for all $t \geqslant 1$. This means that for all E in B_{t+1} there is an F in B_t such that $E \subseteq F$.

The process can then conveniently be represented by a tree – the

[1] If S is infinite, however, there exist subsets of S which cannot be considered as events. This is a familiar difficulty of probability theory. The set of events is a σ algebra or tribe $\mathscr{S}$ of subsets of S. In the sequel, we shall assume, to simplify, that S is finite.

tree structure of events – the vertices of which are the elementary events.

(3)
The definition of the tree of events given here does not refer to the possibility of specific observation of events by any particular agent (although characteristics of the environment which could not be identified by any agent in the economy would, *a priori*, not be relevant for the definition of a state) and is in a sense 'objective'. However, for a given agent i, producer or consumer, two different elementary events might not be discernible, if he could not obtain all the relevant information. His structure of information would then be a sequence $(S_1^i, ..., S_T^i)$ of partitions of S such that he would be able to distinguish two events at period t if, and only if, they belong to two different elements of S_t^i. In particular, S_{t+1}^i is finer than S_t^i (*expanding information*) if, and only if, agent i has a perfect memory between date t and $t+1$, and this is of course not necessarily the case.

In general, two agents i and j will have two different structures of information $(S_1^i, ..., S_T^i)$ and $(S_1^j, ..., S_T^j)$. At period t, if the elementary event e_t obtains, one will observe $E_t^i \supset e_t$ and the other $E_t^j \supset e_t$. The consideration of these differences of knowledge complicates the theory. The extension to this case is possible, as shown by Radner [14]. We prefer to deal first with the case where all the agents can observe the elementary events; that is, they all have the same structure of information $(B_1, ..., B_T)$.

II. REINTERPRETATION OF THE THEORY OF GENERAL EQUILIBRIUM

(1)
The Arrow–Debreu model of equilibrium can be extended to uncertainty, by means of a reinterpretation of the concept of good. The basic idea is due to Arrow and, perhaps, the best way to present the analogy between a 'certain' and an 'uncertain' economy is to come back to the original presentation by Arrow.

Consider m consumers indexed $i = 1, ..., m$ and suppose that the total endowment of the economy depends on $|S|$ mutually exclusive states of nature $s \in S(s = 1, ..., |S|)$. Denote ω_s the vector of scarce resources under state s. ω_s is a vector of the commodity space $\mathbb{R}^l$.

Let x_{is} be a conditional bundle of individual i, restricted to belonging to $\mathbb{R}_+^l$.[1] $x_s = (x_{1s}, ..., x_{ms}) \in \mathbb{R}_+^{lm}$ is an allocation conditional on the realisation of state s if and only if $\sum_{i=1}^{m} x_{is} = \omega_s$.

[1] $\mathbb{R}_+^l$ is the 'conditional' consumption set of individual i.

An allocation of the economy is a vector set of conditional allocations $x = (x_1, ..., x_s, ..., x_{|S|})(x \in \mathbb{R}_+^{l\,m|S|})$. Suppose that the preferences between conditional consumption plans $x_i = (x_{i1}, ..., x_{i|S|}) \in \mathbb{R}_+^{l|S|}$ for consumer i are well-defined,[1] and are representable by a continuous utility function $V_i(x_i)$.[2] It is natural to say that an allocation $x^* = (x_1^*, ..., x_{|S|}^*)$ is Pareto optimal if there exists no other allocation $x = (x_1, ..., x_{|S|})$ such that $V_i(x_i) \geqslant V_i(x_i^*)$ for all i, with at least one strict inequality. This is a concept of 'ex ante' Pareto optimality (see section V).

The problem of characterisation of such a Pareto optimal state is formally the same as in an economy under certainty, and the fundamental theorem of welfare economics applies here and can be stated as follows:

Theorem. If the functions V_i are quasi-concave, then for every Pareto optimal state x^* there exists a price system $p^* \in \mathbb{R}^{l|S|}$ such that $V_i(x_i) \geqslant V_i(x_i^*) \to p^* . x_i \geqslant p^* . x_i^*$.

So, to a Pareto optimal state, is associated a price system, with a price for every good in every state of nature. If x_i^* does not minimise expenditure on $\mathbb{R}_+^{l|S|}$,[3] x_i^* will be for every agent a maximal element in the budget set $\{x_i \in \mathbb{R}_+^{l|S|} | p^* . x_i \leqslant p^* . x_i^*\}$. Moreover, the allocation x^* will be achievable as an equilibrium on the $l|S|$ markets corresponding to all couples, good/state of nature, with $R_i = p^* . x_i^*$ as the wealth of agent i ($i = 1, ..., m$). A Pareto optimal state can be realised 'as a competitive market on contingent claims to commodities'.

We see that the basic concept for the reinterpretation of the theory is that of *contingent good*; a good will be specified not only by its physical nature, its location and its date, but also by the circumstances under which it is available. In a temporal economy, with a tree structure of events as defined above, a good will have a double index, one defining the physical nature of the good, and one defining the relevant vertex of the tree (and therefore, also, the date). Then, we can say that 'the concept of uncertain commodity is derived from the concept of certain commodity by substituting the tree structure of events for the line structure of dates and replacing everywhere

[1] This is acceptable because we consider states of nature. If the likelihood of s could be influenced by the actions of the agents, it would be meaningless to introduce preferences depending only upon the vector x_i.

[2] It is more fundamental to start from a complete preordering $\lesssim_i$ on $\mathbb{R}_+^{l|S|}$ reflecting the choices of agent i. Conditions under which $\lesssim_i$ can be represented by a continuous utility function are well known [7]. This pre-ordering reflects, in particular, the beliefs of i on the chances of realisation of the events, and his attitude towards risk. Note also that $\mathbb{R}_+^{l|S|}$ is the consumption set of consumer i.

[3] It will be so, for example, if $x_i^* \gg 0$.

Allocation Under Uncertainty: a survey

"date" by "event"' ([7], p. 99), and if Q is the number of vertices of the tree, $\mathbb{R}^{lQ}$ is the space of contingent goods.

In a productive economy, the possibilities of production can be described by subsets of the space of contingent goods: a vector y_j of $\mathbb{R}^{lQ}$ belongs to the production set Y_j of producer j if, and only if, the plan of contingent inputs (negative components of y_j) can be transformed into the plan of contingent outputs (positive components of y_j), i.e. if for every possible history of the economy, the associated combination of inputs-outputs is feasible, given that the state obtains.

The concept of contingent goods remains relevant for the extension of the theory.

(2)
Let us give now a detailed interpretation of the general equilibrium in a private ownership economy (with m consumers $i=1, ..., m$ and n producers $j=1, ..., n$) with markets for contingent claims.

The contracts are concluded at the outset, and are relative to contingent goods. An elementary contract specifies an amount of one good, for delivery, conditional on the realisation of an elementary event (as the agents have the same information, they will agree on the realisation of the event). The price has to be paid now. The combination of such elementary contracts allows, for instance, sure delivery at period t. In this case the price to be paid for a unit of good h at time t is: $\sum_{e_t \in B_t} p_{he_t}$.

So, given a price system of contingent goods p, every producer j ($j=1, ..., n$) maximises the value of his production plan, i.e. chooses a plan y_j^* in Y_j such that $p.y_j \leq p.y_j^*$ for all $y_j \in Y_j$.

We remark that, the transactions being made at the outset, the profit is sure, and the profit maximising behaviour does not imply any attitude towards risk. This sure profit $p.y_j^*$ is distributed to the consumers – shareholders of the firm. Let θ_{ij} denote the share of firm j held by consumer i ($\theta_{ij} \geq 0$ and $\sum_{i=1}^{n} \theta_{ij} = 1$ for all j). The wealth of consumer i comes from his shares, $\sum_{j=1}^{n} \theta_{ij} p.y_j^*$, and from the sure value of his contingent initial endowments, $p.\omega_i$. He chooses a consumption plan x_i^* which maximises his utility function V_i on his budget set $B_p = \{x_i \in X_i \mid p.x_i \leq p.\omega_i + \sum_j \theta_{ij} p.y_j^*\}$ (X_i is the consumption set of consumer i).

It is important to note that, although they have a sure wealth, the consumers' choices depend on their attitude towards risk, via their preferences, as in the pure exchange case.

A market equilibrium in this private ownership economy is an $(m+n+1)$-tuple $(\bar{p}, x_i^*, y_j^*)$ of vectors in $\mathbb{R}^{lQ}$, such that:

—x_i^* is a maximal element of the budget set B_p, just defined;
—y_j^* maximises the profit of the firm j for the price system $\bar{p}$;
—$\sum_j y_j^* + \omega = \sum_i x_i^*$ (where ω is the vector of scarce resources of the economy).

Such a private ownership economy is formally analogous to a certain economy and has an equilibrium under the same conditions as those given, for example, in [7]. The other theorems of *Theory of Value* on the relations between optimum and equilibrium also apply.

However, the economic interpretation of the classical conditions of validity of the theorems (convexity of preferences and of production sets) may be specific in the case of uncertainty. We will return to this in section V below.

III. ALLOCATION OF RISK-BEARING BY SECURITIES

If perfectly competitive markets on contingent claims to commodities lead to an optimal allocation of risk-bearing, the number of markets will increase in proportion to the number of states of nature, and will soon become very important. In the same basic article [2], Arrow expressed the idea that the number of markets could be reduced by replacing markets for contingent claims to commodities by markets for securities. Such an assertion is somewhat ambiguous and we will examine its meaning, from the simple model at the beginning of the preceding section (pure exchange economy).

The economy of that section had m agents $i=1, ..., m$, $|S|$ states of nature, and l goods. It is implicitly assumed that there are two periods. Decisions are made in period one (*ex ante*), and executed in period two, when the true state of nature is known (*ex post*). To a Pareto optimal state $x^* = (x_1^*, ..., x_m^*) \in \mathbb{R}^{l|S|m}$, one can associate a price system $p^* \in \mathbb{R}^{l|S|}$ such that the allocation x^* is an equilibrium relative to this price system (theorem 1, p. 56).

Now, let us give the wealth $R_i = p^* . x_i^*$ to every consumer and consider the following markets:

—First, markets for securities. There are $|S|$ securities; one unit of security of type s is a claim to one unit of 'money',[1] conditional on the realisation of state s.
—Simultaneously, conditional markets for goods. The trade contracts indicate delivery and a payment conditional upon a given

[1] Actually the terminology of 'money', used for this asset, is somewhat ambiguous. This will be explained in the following.

state. So, these markets differ from markets for contingent claims, because no payment will take place unless a given state obtains.

Let β_s be the price (at date one) of one unit of security s, and $\Pi_s (\in \mathbb{R}^l)$ the price vector of goods on the conditional market $s (s \in S)$. Consider the procedure defined by the following maximisation problem, for each $i = 1, \ldots, m$:

Max . $V_i(\ldots x_{is}, \ldots)$
subject to
$$\sum_{s \in S} \beta_s y_{is} = R_i$$
$$\Pi_s . x_{is} \leqslant y_{is}, \quad x_{is} \in \mathbb{R}_+^l \text{ for all } s,$$

where y_{is} is the number of securities of type s held by consumer i, and x_{is} is the conditional consumption plan of i.

It is easy to see that if $\beta_s . \Pi_s = p_s$ (with an obvious notation, we write $p = (p_1, \ldots, p_s, \ldots, p_{|S|})$ with $p_s \in \mathbb{R}^l$)) every agent has the same range of alternatives available as he had under the system described in the preceding section. So, every price system $\beta = (\beta_1, \ldots, \beta_s, \ldots, \beta_{|S|}) \in \mathbb{R}^{|S|}$, $\Pi = (\Pi_1, \ldots, \Pi_s, \ldots, \Pi_{|S|}) \in \mathbb{R}^{l|S|}$, such that $\beta_s \Pi_s = p_s$, is a price-equilibrium for the procedure.

We can also use the concept of indirect utility function, defined by: $V_i^*(\ldots y_{is}, \ldots) = \text{Max} . V_i(\ldots x_{is} \ldots)$, subject to $\Pi_s . x_{is} = y_{is}$ and $x_{is} \in \mathbb{R}_+^l$ for all $s \in S$. Then, the $y_{is}^* = \Pi_s . x_{is}^* (s \in S)$ define an optimal portfolio of securities, because for any other such portfolio, with $\sum_{s \in S} \beta_s . y_{is} = R_i$, we have $V_i^*(\ldots y_{is} \ldots) \leqslant V_i^*(\ldots y_{is}^* \ldots)$.

This is analogous to the intertemporal interpretation of general equilibrium (see T. de Montbrial [13]), where time t would replace s and β_t would be the discount coefficient. In either case, we obtain what Arrow calls his second theorem: under classical conditions (those which permit the association of a price system with a Pareto optimal allocation), every optimal allocation of resources under uncertainty can be obtained by perfect competition on the market for contingent claims to money and on conditional markets for goods.

The reader will have noticed that there are many possible choices of the coefficient β_s. This is analogous to the problem of defining a 'normalisation rule' in the intertemporal theory of resource allocation (Malinvaud [12]). In particular, we can choose the β_s such that

$\sum_{i=1}^{m} y_{is}^* = \sum_{i=1}^{m} R_i$ for all s. $\left[\beta_s = \dfrac{p_s \omega_s}{\sum_{i=1}^{m} R_i} \right]$. The interpretation is that the *ex* *post* total 'stock of money' to be distributed is constant, and equal to the *ex ante* stock $\sum_{i=1}^{m} R_i$. We have then $\sum_{s \in S} \beta_s = 1$, which means that it is equivalent to keep one unit of money or to buy claims to one unit of money in every state.

Note also that, all the contracts in Arrow's procedure (transactions on securities and conditional trade on commodities) are concluded at period one, and an equilibrium on these simultaneous markets is an equilibrium of plans, prices, and price expectations in the sense of Radner [15]. Actually, this last framework is adequate in order to extend the above ideas to a general model (see Guesnerie–Jaffray [10]).

Notice finally that the total number of markets is $|S|(l+1)$ ($|S|$ for securities and $l|S|$ for goods), approximately the same as the number of markets for contingent claims.

However, there is a case where another interpretation of the procedure can be given, considering that markets for securities and markets for commodities are not simultaneous but successive. Only $|S|$ markets for securities take place at period one, and when state s obtains at period two, spot markets for commodities take place. This is the case when the y_{is}^*, the price system Π_s and the allocation (... x_{is}^* ...) define an equilibrium of the spot market corresponding to the conditions prevailing under state s.

It is clear that, if the utility function $V_i(\ldots x_{is} \ldots)$ is additively decomposable, i.e. can be written $V_i(\ldots x_{is} \ldots) = \sum_{s \in S} V_{is}(x_{is})$,[1] the problem: Max. $V_i(\ldots x_{is} \ldots)$ subject to $\Pi_s \cdot x_{is} = y_{is}^*$ for all s is equivalent to the $|S|$ problems: Max. $V_{is}(x_{is})$ subject to $\Pi_s \cdot x_{is} = y_{is}^*$.

Then, we can say that a Pareto allocation can be obtained only by $|S|+l$ markets, namely $|S|$ *ex ante* markets for securities and l *ex post* markets for goods, instead of $|S|(l+1)$ markets before.

Nevertheless, this reduction of the number of the markets is only apparent, since a correct allocation of securities can be obtained only if the agents know the future prices on all the spot markets. This knowledge can result only from a simultaneous determination at date one of all the equilibrium prices on all the markets. Rigorously, therefore, the assertion about the reduction of the number of markets is not true. However, it might happen that an approximate determination of equilibrium prices on the spot markets does not require a complete simulation of these markets. In this case the uncertainty about spot prices is not important relatively to other types of

---

[1] Debreu has given conditions under which a preordering $\lesssim_i$ on $I\!R^{l|S|}$ can be represented by such a continuous utility function. His main assumption is equivalent to postulate 2 of Savage.

IV. DIFFERENT STRUCTURES OF THE AGENTS' INFORMATION

Recall that an information structure of an agent is a T-uple of partitions of S, the set of states of nature. We shall use the notation $S^i = (S_1^i, \ldots, S_T^i)$ for consumers ($i = 1, \ldots, m$), $F^j = (F_1^j, \ldots, F_T^j)$ for producers ($j = 1, \ldots, n$), or $U^k = (U_1^k, \ldots, U_T^k)$ for all the agents ($k = 1, \ldots, m+n$).

At any date t, an agent k is able to say to which set H of U_t^k the true state belongs, but no more. Consider, now, the information structure $\alpha = (\alpha_1, \ldots, \alpha_T)$ defined by the intersection of all the information structures U^k of the agents. In other words, an element of α_t is defined by the intersection of elements, one in each of the U_t^k ($k = 1, \ldots, m+n$). This information structure is the least fine among the structures finer than every individual structure. To this maximal structure of information of the economy is associated a tree of events, and the concept of a contingent good associated to the vertices of the tree remains relevant, if we assume memory for all the agents. The commodity space is thus $\mathbb{R}^{l|E|}$ where E is the set of vertices of the tree of events.

To each information structure U^k, we associate the manifold $A(U^k)$ of functions from E to $\mathbb{R}^l$ which are constant on each elementary event of U^k. In other words, for each $H \in U_t^k$ and e_t, e_t' in H where e_t and e_t' are elementary events of α, an element z of $A(U^k)$ should satisfy $z(e_t) = z(e_t')$. In this framework, a *private ownership economy is* defined by the information structures for all the agents and in addition:

— for every consumer $i = 1, \ldots, m$ a consumption set X_i, assumed to be a subset of $A(S^i)$, a complete preordering $\lesssim_i$ on X_i, an initial endowment $\omega_i \in A(S^i)$ and shares θ_{ij} defined as usual:
— for every producer $j = 1, \ldots, n$, a production set Y_j, assumed to be a subset of $A(F^j)$.

The reason why X_i (resp. Y_j) is assumed to belong to $A(S^i)$ (resp. $A(F^j)$) is that an agent is unable to separate any two states of nature in one elementary event of his own information structure, and should not consider plans which would require such a possibility. If we suppose, as we should, that the information structure takes into account all sources of information, we must naturally assume $\omega_i \in A(S^i)$; otherwise, the initial endowment would give the consumer additional information.

There is no problem in formulating and applying the theorems of welfare economics on optima and equilibria and the relations between them.

There are technical difficulties with the problem of the existence of an equilibrium for private ownership economies; the reason is that assumptions such as free disposal become irrelevant. If, for instance, $y_j \in Y_j$, the set of vectors $z_j \leq y_j$ will contain acts that do not belong to $A(F^j)$. Radner gives an existence theorem in [14], which is based on Debreu [9]

To conclude this topic, let us remark that the presentation given here, based on the idea of a maximal information structure of the economy and of contingent goods relative to the events of this maximal information structure, is slightly different from Radner's original approach, which uses the notion of act in the sense of Savage, and of acts compatible with a structure of information. In particular, Radner does not need to assume 'memory'.

V. ON THE MEANING OF THE ASSUMPTIONS

The complete analogy presented here between a certain and an uncertain problem of allocation of resources, does not mean that in both cases the assumptions have the same economic implications. So we will examine first, the significance of the concept of *ex ante* Pareto optimality, and then the significance of the convexity hypothesis for preferences and production sets.

(1) Ex Ante *and* Ex Post *Optimality*

The concept of *ex ante* Pareto optimality as introduced in Arrow's model of sections II and III is the following: an allocation $(x^* = x_1^*, \ldots, x_{|S|}^*)$ (in the notation of section II) was *ex ante Pareto optimal*, if, and only if, there was no other allocation, improving the situation of every agent, with strict improvement for at least one agent.

If the strong independence assumption – Savage's second axiom – is verified by every *ex ante* preordering $\gtrsim_i$ so that the utility function $V_i(\ldots x_{is} \ldots) = \sum_{s \in S} V_{is}(x_{is})$ is additive relative to the vector x_{is}, every conditional allocation x_s^* is also *ex post Pareto optimal*. Precisely for any $s \in S$, there exists no $(x_{is})_{i=1,\ldots,m}$ with $x_{is} \in \mathbb{R}_+^l$ such that $\sum_{i=1}^{m} x_{is} = \omega_s$ and such that $V_{is}(x_{is}) \geq V_{is}(x_{is}^*)$ for all i, strictly for some i'.

If such a conditional allocation x_s were to exist, the allocation $x = (x_1^*, \ldots, x_{s-1}^*, x_s, x_{s+1}^*, \ldots, x_{|S|}^*)$ would be Pareto better than

Allocation Under Uncertainty: a survey

x^*. This is a consequence of the additive form of V_i since $V_{is}(x_{is}) \geq V_{is}(x_{is}^*)$, $\forall i$ would imply $V_i(x_{i1}^*, \ldots, x_{is}, \ldots, x_{i|S|}^*) \geq V_i(x_{i1}^*, \ldots, x_{is}^*, \ldots, x_{i|S|}^*)$ with at least one strict inequality and would contradict the optimality of x^*. The *ex post* Pareto optimality is also a clear consequence of the possibility proved above, of obtaining x_s^* as an equilibrium allocation on the spot market s with initial individual wealth y_{is}^*.

The fact that an *ex ante* optimum is also an *ex post* optimum does not mean, however, that the *ex ante* allocation coincides with that which would result from deferred trading. Suppose the initial resources are owned by the agents with $\sum_{i=1}^{m} \omega_i = \omega$ or $\sum_{i=1}^{m} \omega_{is} = \omega_s$ for all s. Let (x_i^*, p) be a competitive equilibrium of this private ownership economy, if it exists.

We have then

$$\sum_{s \in S} p_s \cdot x_{is} \leq \sum_{s \in S} p_s \cdot \omega_{is} \to V_i(\ldots x_{is} \ldots) \leq V_i(\ldots x_{is}^* \ldots);$$

define

$$\mu_{is} = p_s \cdot x_{is}^* - p_s \cdot \omega_{is} \text{ (so that } \sum_{s \in S} \mu_{is} = 0\text{).}$$

It follows immediately that for all s and i

$$p_s x_{is} \leq p_s \omega_{is} + \mu_{is} \to V_{is}(x_{is}) \leq V_{is}(x_{is}^*) \; \forall i, \; \forall s.$$

Then $(\ldots x_{is}^* \ldots, p)$ is not an equilibrium of the *ex post* economy with distribution of resources defined by the ω_{is}, unless we have $\mu_{is} = 0$ for all i.

The μ_{is}, generally different from zero, are monetary transfers which reflect the *ex ante* choices. A planner who would control the total resources of the economy should obtain different results, from the social welfare point of view, with an *ex ante* or *ex post* distribution of endowments.[1] It seems clear that this planner would achieve his social goals more accurately with the *ex post* distribution. This suggests that, in this case, the concept of *ex ante* optimality is not appropriate. However as pointed out by Drèze [6]: '*No matter what significance one attaches to Arrow optimality in a model of pure exchange, the concept becomes essential in a model of production. In*

---

[1] Suppose that each agent has a differentiable Von Neumann–Morgenstern utility function of the form $V_i(x_i) = \sum_{s \in S} \Pi_{is} U_i(x_{is})$ and that there exists a system of weights α_i for a linear collective utility function such that the *ex ante* collective utility function be $\Sigma \alpha_i V_i$ and the *ex post* one be $\Sigma \alpha_i U_i$. Then we may note that the allocation $(\ldots x_{is}^* \ldots)$ maximising the *ex ante* function would maximise the *ex post* function for every s, if, and 'generally' only if, $\Pi_{is} = \Pi_{js}$ ($\forall i, j, s$) J. Drèze gives a similar argument in his comment ([6] p. 143).

the model of pure exchange, social endowments (... ω_s, ...), s = 1, ..., |S|, are given *quantities of consumption goods. In the model of production, one starts instead with a vector of total resources and a total production set in |S|l-dimensional commodity space. The quantities of all commodities available for consumption depend upon the choice of a point in the production set. Of two such points, one may involve more total consumption of some commodities given state a but less total consumption of some commodities given state s. For the choice among such points, an* ex ante *concept of optimality is needed: redistribution for a given state is constrained by the social endowment available, an endowment that reflects prior choices of economic agents as well as nature's choice. Arrow optimality seems to provide a natural extension of Pareto optimality in such situations, whilst leaving open the problem of redistribution – whether* ex ante *or* ex post.'

(2) *Convexity of Preferences and Risk Aversion*
An important class of utility functions satisfying the axiom of strong independence is the Von Neumann–Morgenstern, or the Savage, utility function:

$$V_i(x_{i1}, ..., x_{i|S|}) = \sum_{s \in S} \Pi_{is} U_i(x_{is}) \tag{5.1}$$

with $\Pi_{is} \geq 0$ and $\sum_{s \in S} \Pi_{is} = 1$.

It can be seen that the representation and interpretation of the Π_{is} as subjective probabilities does not derive strictly from Savage's theorems, since the number of states of nature considered here is finite.

However, as pointed out in another article, one can always enlarge the set S of states of nature by introducing the tossing of a coin. The expected utility theorem requires then, that the axioms be verified on the new set of acts, defined as the applications of the achieved set S' (now infinite) into the set $\mathbb{R}_+^l$ of consequences. What is the meaning then of the quasi-concavity, of utility function of this type? The following theorem gives an answer.

Proposition. Let $g(x_1, ..., x_{|S|}) = \sum_{s \in S} \Pi_s f(x_s)$, be a function of $\mathbb{R}^{l|S|}$ into $\mathbb{R}$. If there exist s and σ such that $\Pi_s = \Pi_\sigma$, $(s \neq \sigma\ \Pi_s, \Pi_\sigma \neq 0)$ the quasi-concavity of g implies the concavity of f.

Proof. Suppose there exists a and b in $\mathbb{R}_+^l$ such that

(1) $$f\left[\frac{a+b}{2}\right] < \frac{f(a)+f(b)}{2}$$

Allocation Under Uncertainty: a survey

(which implies $a \neq b$). Let us choose x^1 and x^2 in $\mathbb{R}^{l|S|}$ differing only by their s and σ components:

$$x_s^1 = a \qquad x_\sigma^1 = b$$
$$x_s^2 = b \qquad x_\sigma^2 = a$$

we have

$$g(x^1) - g(x^2) = \Pi_s[f(x_s^1) - f(x_s^2)] + \Pi_\sigma[f(x_\sigma^1) - f(x_\sigma^2)] = 0.$$

Since g is quasi-concave, this implies

$$g\left[\frac{x^1 + x^2}{2}\right] - g(x^1) \geq 0$$

hence

$$\Pi_s f\left[\frac{x_s^1 + x_s^2}{2}\right] + \Pi_\sigma f\left[\frac{x_\sigma^1 + x_\sigma^2}{2}\right] - \Pi_s f(x_s^1) - \Pi_\sigma f(x_\sigma^1) \geq 0$$

or, since $\Pi_s = \Pi_\sigma > 0$

$$2f\left[\frac{a+b}{2}\right] - f(a) - f(b) \geq 0$$

that is

$$f\left[\frac{a+b}{2}\right] \geq \frac{f(a) + f(b)}{2}$$

which contradicts (1).

It is also clear that the assumption $\exists \ s \neq \sigma$, s.t. $\Pi_s = \Pi_\sigma > 0$ is not necessary in the case of a non-atomic measure space.[1]

In either case, whether we assume $\Pi_s = \Pi_\sigma$, or assume that S is a non-atomic measure space, the quasi-concavity of the V_i-function, in the first case of the contingent bundle (... x_{is} ...), in the second case of the measurable applications $x(.)$ of S into $\mathbb{R}^l$ – implies the concavity of U_i i.e.

$$U_i(\alpha x_1 + (1-\alpha)x_2) \geq \alpha U_i(x_1) + (1-\alpha)U_i(x_2) \ \forall \ \alpha \in [0, 1].$$

Economically, that means that one prefers to have with certainty $\alpha x_1 + (1-\alpha)x_2$, the mathematical expectation of the random lottery, rather than x_1 with probability α and x_2 with probability $(1-\alpha) \ \forall \ \alpha \in [0, 1]$. This property is also a definition of risk aversion.

So *risk aversion*, with the expected utility hypothesis, is equivalent to *concavity of* U_i. Hence, the *quasi-concavity of* V_i is 'nearly' equivalent to *risk aversion*.

---

[1] Precisely the following theorem is true. Let S be a non-atomic measure space, A a σ-algebra of subsets of S, $dP(s)$ a probability measure on S.
Let $x(.)$ be an A-measurable application of S into $\mathbb{R}^l$ and $f(x(.)) = \int g(x(s))dP(s)$. If f is quasi-concave, g is concave.

In the absence of risk aversion, the quasi–concavity of V_i can be reintroduced, by considering opportunities of gambling at fair odds, i.e. opportunities to replace a sure bundle x by any random lottery offering y with probability α, z with probability $(1-\alpha)$ such that $\alpha y + (1-\alpha)z = x$. For instance, if we consider a non-concave utility function of a unidimensional variable (income), it is easy to see that the possibility of gambling at fair odds, 'concavifies' in some way the expected utility (see [6]).

The quasi-concavity assumption, not needed anyway in a many agents economy, would be more innocuous than it appears at first.

(3) *Production*

Apparently, Debreu's treatment of production under uncertainty is fairly general. However, an important qualification on this representation of production activity under uncertainty has been made by Arrow (appendix to Essay 4 in [3]):

> 'The definition of a commodity is seriously affected on the production side by the nature of the theory of uncertainty. For two units to be regarded as part of the same commodity, they must have the same role of production for any possible state of nature. . . . The number of commodities then becomes enormously greater than is ordinarily supposed and indivisibility becomes a much more prevalent phenomenon'.

Arrow gives the following example:

> Suppose we have two machines, each with a fifty-fifty chance of breakdown, and one man. To operate, a machine has to be in action and have a man assigned to it. If neither machine has broken down, then only one machine can be used. Hence, it is clear one machine will be in operation with probability $\frac{3}{4}$ and 0 machine will be in operation with probability $\frac{1}{4}$: so that the expected output is $\frac{3}{4}$ of the potential output of one machine. Now suppose there are four machines and two men and again assume that each machine will break down with probability $\frac{1}{2}$; then 0 machine will be in action with probability $\frac{1}{16}$, one machine with probability $\frac{1}{4}$ and 2 machines with probability $\frac{11}{16}$.
>
> The expected output will therefore be $\frac{13}{8}$ of the potential output of a single machine, which is more than twice as much. In other words, by doubling the number of men and doubling the number of machines we have more than doubled the expected output.

Let us look at this example more closely.

We have two inputs, machines and labour; and one output. Let S be the set of states of the world. The traditional analysis consists of

Allocation Under Uncertainty: a survey

defining a production correspondence from $\Omega = \mathbb{R}_+ \times \mathbb{R}_+$ to $(\mathbb{R}_+)^S$, which specifies, for each input vector (number of machines and men), the quantity of output under each state of the world. There are two difficulties, in defining such a production set. First, the goods are indivisible, and R_+ must be replaced by the set N of non-negative integers. The second and more basic problem is that the states of the world seem to depend on the individual units of production. However, we can overcome this difficulty at the cost of introducing a *continuum* of states of the world, precisely the interval [0, 1] of positive real numbers less than or equal to 1.

Indeed, let us consider n machines. A state of the world must specify those which are in operation and those which have broken down. We can depict all the possibilities as follows: Take [0, 1] and divide it in two segments $[0, \frac{1}{2}]$ and $[\frac{1}{2}, 1]$. If machine 1 does not work, we choose a point in $[0, \frac{1}{2}]$ and if it works, in $[\frac{1}{2}, 1]$. Suppose, for instance, that machine 1 does not work. If machine 2 does not work either we choose a point in $[0, \frac{1}{4}]$ and if it does work, in $[\frac{1}{4}, \frac{1}{2}]$. We repeat this process until we have taken up the n machines. Then, [0, 1] is partitioned into 2^n segments of equal length $\frac{1}{2^n}$, and each one describes one and only one possible situation.

Given a number n of machines and a number p of men, the maximal output one can get is a function $f_{n,p}$ from [0, 1] to N, such that $f_{n,p}(s)$ remains constant on each interval of the partition.

Now we can see in which sense it is true that we have increasing returns. It is clear that the maximal expected output corresponding to n machines and p men is $\int_0^1 f_{n,p}(s)ds$, where ds is the Lebesgue measure on [0, 1]. Arrow's remark can be written as

$$\int_0^1 f_{4,2}(s)ds > 2\int_0^1 f_{2,1}(s)ds.$$

But does this imply increasing returns as they are usually defined on the production set?

We should have, for this

$$f_{4,2}(s) \geq 2f_{2,1}(s) \text{ for all } s \in [0, 1].$$

It is easy to show that this is not true.

The following table shows this. [0, 1] is partitioned into 16 equal intervals, numbered from 1 to 16.

TABLE 4.1

s belongs to segment n°	1 2 3 4	5 6 7 8	9 10 11 12	13 14 15 16
$f_{2,1}[s] =$	0 0 0 0	1 1 1 1	1 1 1 1	1 1 1 1
$f_{4,2}[s] =$	0 1 1 2	1 2 2 2	1 2 2 2	1 2 2 2

Clearly, the returns are not increasing for states which belong to the 5th and the 9th interval.

So, this example does not introduce 'increasing returns' in the sense of the production theory; but it leads certainly to 'non-convexities', and the essence of Arrow's remark, which concerns the difficulties of integrating uncertainties about inputs in the framework of the theory, remains valid.

VI. THE MODEL AND THE 'REAL' WORLD

The model introduced and discussed here is a satisfactory logical extension of microeconomic theory to the case of uncertainty. The conditions stated for Pareto optimality underline the distance between an ideal organisation under uncertainty and the 'real' world. Contrary to the belief of the first theorists of welfare economics, the finer analysis of the economic process recently developed (public goods, uncertainty), has shown that the working of western economies differs from the working of a refined neo-classical world. It is clear that the model of general equilibrium under uncertainty does not provide a good description of our economics where the complete system of insurance postulated by the theory does not exist. Indeed, the shifting of risks is possible by means of some institutions such as the stock market, or insurance for some types of risks. But these opportunities of risk-shifting are limited in number and are far from allowing the complete separation between risk-pooling activity and production activity. The role of entrepreneurs as risk-poolers is essential in a 'real' economy.

Among the obstacles to the application of the conclusions of the theory in its normative aspects, we will quote three, specifically related to uncertainty.

(1) Some implications of the theory have not yet been clearly seen; especially the adaptations of the conclusions to the different types of risks – 'risques globalement éliminables' of M. Allais and other risks[1] – have to be made precise. It is the purpose of some works presented in this volume to do it.

(2) It is clear that the number of events for which it would be necessary to organise conditional contracts would increase exponentially with the number of periods; but more fundamental is the fact that some types of contingent contracts cannot be considered. Take, for example, uncertainties about tastes. A contract implying delivery conditional to a state of nature that would be a state of mind is not conceivable. The terms of the contract must be defined with objectivity. This is an extreme case of the important phenomena pointed

[1] 'Risques globalement inexistants'.

out by Arrow [3] under the name of '*moral hazard*'. In many circumstances, what is observable is not directly the state of nature, but a fact which results both from nature and from human decision, and it is impossible to separate the two causes. For instance, one can observe a fire, but one cannot easily appreciate if it is due to carelessness and determine the human responsibility. So a system of complete insurances, relative to events which originate not only in choices of nature, would suppress the incentives to correct behaviour: there is a constant contradiction between the necessity of risk-shifting and that of maintaining incentives. Real arrangements come from an arbitrage between these two opposite goals.

(3) In an uncertain world, new activities will take place, mainly in relation to what can be called production of information. Resources may be used for improving the observation of events, and refining the 'structure of information of an agent' [14] or more generally for production of 'knowledge' [3]. In both cases, difficulties arise, linked to non-convexities [14] and to 'public good' aspects of information or to more fundamental reasons (read the masterful analysis of Arrow [3] on the production of knowledge). This is a field for further research, but also for reflections on the basic theory.

REFERENCES

[1] M. Allais, 'Généralisation des théories de l'équilibre économique général et du rendement social au cas du risque', in *Econométrie*, Colloque International XL (Paris: CNRS, 1953).
[2] K. J. Arrow, 'Le rôle des valeurs boursières pour la répartition la meilleure des risques', pp. 41–7 in *Econométrie*, Colloque International XL (Paris: CNRS, 1953); translated as 'The Role of Securities in the Optimal Allocation of Risk-Bearing', *Review of Economic Studies*, vol. XXXI (1964), pp. 91–6.
[3] K. J. Arrow, 'Essays in the Theory of Risk-Bearing' (Amsterdam: North-Holland, 1970).
[4] E. Baudier, 'L'introduction du temps dans la théorie de l'équilibre général', *Cahiers Économiques* (December 1959), pp. 9–16.
[5] K. Borch, 'The Safety Loading of Reinsurance Premiums', *Skandinavisk Aktuarietidskrift*, vol. XLIII (1960), pp. 163–84.
[6] J. Drèze, 'Market Allocation under Uncertainty', *European Economic Review*, vol. II (1971), pp. 133–65.
[7] G. Debreu, *Theory of Value* (New York: John Wiley, 1959).
[8] G. Debreu, 'Une économique de l'incertain', *Economie Appliquée*, vol. 13 (1960).
[9] G. Debreu, 'New Concepts and Techniques for Equilibrium Analysis', *International Economic Review*, vol. III (1962), pp. 257–73.
[10] R. Guesnerie and J. Y. Jaffray, 'Optimality of Equilibrium of Plans Prices and Price Expectations', chapter 5 *infra*.
[11] J. Hirshleifer, 'Investment Decision under Uncertainty Applications of the

State Preference Approach', *Quarterly Journal of Economics*, vol. LXXX (1966), pp. 252–77.
[12] E. Malinvaud, 'Decentralized Procedures for Planning', in *Activity Analysis in the Theory of Growth and Planning*, ed. by E. Malinvaud and M. O. L. Bacharach (London: Macmillan, 1967), pp. 170–208.
[13] T. de Montbrial, 'Intertemporal General Equilibrium and Interest Rates Theory', *École Polytechnique* (1970).
[14] R. Radner, 'Competitive Equilibrium under Uncertainty', *Econometrica*, vol. XXXVI (1968), pp. 31–58.
[15] R. Radner, 'Existence of Equilibrium of Plans, Prices and Price Expectations in a Sequence of Markets', *Econometrica*, vol. XL (1972), pp. 289–303.
[16] L. J. Savage, *Foundations of Statistics* (New York: John Wiley, 1954).

5 Optimality of Equilibrium of Plans, Prices and Price Expectations

Roger Guesnerie[1]
CEPREMAP, PARIS

and

Jean-Yves Jaffray[1]
LABORATOIRE D'ÉCONOMETRIE, PARIS

In the classical model of resource allocation, often called the Arrow–Debreu model, all transactions are determined at the outset; the contracts are final and the history of the economy is in accordance with the initial plans; all possibility of reopening the markets can be dispensed with; it would serve no real purpose.

Such a procedure reflects only very imperfectly the 'real' processes of resource allocation, for which 'forward' markets are more often the exception rather than the rule, and most exchanges are 'spot' ones. In these spot markets, the plans of the agents depend on expected future prices, and these subjective expectations generally differ from one agent to another.

Furthermore, these expectations can only be realised by chance, and even in the case where they are common to all the agents, they are not always true. In this sense, the equilibria arising from those markets are 'temporary' according to the definition of Hicks.

Radner's model on equilibrium of plans, prices and price expectations, whose characteristics are presented in the first part of this paper, describes an intermediate world between the 'generalised' forward markets of Debreu, and realistic 'temporary' equilibria. It considers a succession of ideal markets where 'spot' and 'forward' trades coexist. They are ideal because for future markets, all agents have common price expectations and because these expectations will be realised.

The purpose of this paper is to examine this concept of equilibrium of plans, prices and price expectations, and to clarify its

[1] The authors would like to thank Jacques Drèze for his helpful and stimulating comments.
This paper is a revised version of the Core discussion paper 7117 written for the Bergen Conference. It summarises, in that the proofs are only sketched, another paper by the same authors [4], which might be of interest to those readers needing more details.

implications for the question of optimality. On this point, it is clear that although the allocation arising from a sequence of temporary equilibria generally cannot be Pareto optimal – mistakes in forecasting by the agents are a patent source of waste – this cause of inefficiency is eliminated in Radner's model, since the consumer is aware of the true future prices. Actually, it will be proved that in this model, Pareto optimality becomes possible as soon as a sufficient number of markets is organised. This will be the case if appropriate forward contracts are allowed on a good chosen as a numeraire. More generally, in section II we will try to exhibit a series of 'contract structures', which guarantee the optimality of the associated equilibria.

In section III we will substitute a bond market for forward trade on 'real' goods. By introducing a 'fictitious good' we will see that the model is appropriate to the study of the simultaneous equilibrium of real markets and of financial markets (or under uncertainty, of markets for securities). Here again, and it is intuitively reasonable, it will be proved that financial markets take on the functions of a 'generalised' forward market '*à la* Debreu', and as soon as there are enough of them, make the efficient allocations attainable. A similar property of the role of securities in the allocation of risk-bearing will be stated.

Finally, this is a systematic interpretation of the Arrow–Debreu solution as a succession of 'spot' and 'forward' trades which, it is hoped, will clarify the concept of equilibrium of plans, prices and price expectations.

I. EQUILIBRIUM OF PLANS, PRICES AND PRICE EXPECTATIONS: THE MODEL, THEOREMS OF EXISTENCE

The general framework of Radner's model, which is presented here, is similar to Debreu's model in chapter 7 of *Theory of Value* [2], as mentioned in this volume in [3]. It takes into account a temporal economy over a finite number of periods $t=0 \dots T$, with an uncertain environment. Complete specifications of the alternative histories of the environment through dates $0 \dots T$, define a set S of states of nature, supposed to be finite. The elementary events (see [2] and [3]) of the period t, A_t, constitute a partition of S, and define the family $\mathscr{S}_t$.

Here, in contrast to an earlier model of the same author [6], everybody can observe the elementary events A_t, and has complete information. It is supposed that this information increases with time, so that the partition $\mathscr{S}_{t+1}$ is not less fine than $\mathscr{S}_t$.[1] $\mathscr{S}_0 = \{S\}$ and thus the observable events A_t form a tree $\mathscr{A}$.[2]

Now, the consumers are in finite number I, and each of them has a contingent initial endowment (... $\omega_i(A_t)$ ...) where $\omega_i(A_t)$ is conditional on the realisation of the event A_t. $\omega_i(A_t)$ is a vector of $\mathbb{R}^l$, commodity space.

Every consumer has also inter-temporal preferences, represented by a complete preordering on the contingent plans of consumption (... $x_i(A_t)$ ...), a preordering defined on a consumption set X_i. This preordering can satisfy Savage's axioms and so be representable by a cardinal utility function; but this is not necessary.

In this exchange economy E, the Arrow–Debreu model describes a procedure of exchange, consisting of a market for contingent claims: all the trade contracts implying either an immediate delivery, or a future conditional delivery, are allowed for every good. The transactions are determined according to a price system for contingent claims.

Faced with this price system every agent chooses, from all the plans compatible with his budget constraint, that exchange plan which maximises his satisfaction. His constraint is fixed by the prices and his initial endowment. The contingent price systems that make the exchange plans of the agents compatible, by equalising supply and demand for every good, at every period, in every elementary event, are called competitive prices, and the associated allocations are competitive allocations. This describes the classical exchange procedure based on a market for contingent commodities. (See [3].) We will refer to it hereafter as the 'D-procedure'. Formally:[3]

— A D-price P is a sequence of vectors of $\mathbb{R}^l$, (... $p(A_t)$ ...); $p_h(A_t)$, h^{th} coordinate of $p(A_t)$, is the price of good h, the delivery of which is conditional on A_t.

— a conditional consumption plan $x_i = ($... $x_i(A_t)$ ...$)$ is called D-feasible for consumer i, for a D-price P, if and only if

$$x_i = (\ldots x_i(A_t) \ldots) \in X_i$$

$$\sum_{A_t \in \mathscr{A}} p(A_t).x_i(A_t) \leq \sum_{A_t \in \mathscr{A}} p(A_t).\omega_i(A_t)$$

[1] A partition $\mathscr{S}$ is said not to be less fine than $\mathscr{S}'$, if for every A' in $\mathscr{S}'$ and A in $\mathscr{S}$ either $A \subset A'$ or $A \cap A' = \emptyset$.

[2] The single event at date 0 will be called S_0 instead of A_0. The partition $\mathscr{S}_t$ generates the algebra $\mathscr{S}_t^*$ of events at date t, i.e. any union of elementary events at date t is an event at date t.

[3] For the following, we write the D-model, with notations introducing explicitly the elementary events A_t:A_t with brackets, (A_t), means that the preceding objects (vector, number) are contingent to A_t, if they are commodities, or relative to A_t if they are prices. So the meaning of $\omega_i(A_t)$, $x_i(A_t)$, $\Pi(A_t)$ is clear.

—a global consumption plan $x = (\ldots\ x_i\ \ldots)$, $i \in I$, is called D-realisable with the price system P, if and only if
it is D-feasible for every consumer i,
it is physically possible, i.e.

$$\sum_i x_i(A_t) \leqslant \sum_i \omega_i(A_t), \ \forall\ A_t \in \mathscr{A}$$

—a D-equilibrium (P, x) consists of a price system P, and a global consumption plan $x = (\ldots\ x_i\ \ldots)$, D-realisable for the price system P, and such that x_i is 'best' among all the D-feasible plans, for consumer i, $\forall\ i$.

In the context of this D-procedure, all the actions of the agents are fixed at the beginning, and the history takes place according to the original plans, since the characteristics of the environment have already been taken into account at time O. There is no reason to reopen the market in some event A_t, and even if this were done, no modifications of the plans would result.

This possibility of reopening the markets is introduced in Radner's work. He considers that, at time O, not all trade contracts for contingent claims are allowed. More precisely, he defines the *allowed contracts*, for the market A_t, in the following way: with every elementary event A_t, is associated a set $\mathscr{C}(A_t, h)$ of events B_u, for $u \geqslant t$, where B_u belongs to $\mathscr{S}_u^*$, algebra of sets built from $\mathscr{S}_u$. (The B_u's are 'elementary' events A_u or unions of such 'elementary' events.) A trade contract from A_t, for the good h, is allowed if, and only if, it stipulates delivery conditionally to an event $B_u \in \mathscr{C}(A_t, h)$.

It will often be supposed:

—that $A_t \in \mathscr{C}(A_t, h)$, $\forall\ h$, i.e. that trade contracts with immediate delivery are allowed (we have then 'spot' trading);
—and that, $\forall\ B_u \in \mathscr{C}(A_t, h)$, $B_u \subset A_t$, i.e. that B_u is not an impossible event conditionally to A_t (for $u > t$, we have 'forward' trading).

It will be useful to introduce, jointly to $\mathscr{C}(A_t, h)$ the set of events $\mathscr{D}(A_t, h)$, so defined

$$A_u \in \mathscr{D}(A_t, h) \Rightarrow \exists\ B_t \supset A_t\ \text{s.t.}\ B_t \in \mathscr{C}(A_u, h).$$

$(\mathscr{D}A_t, h)$ is the set of all events, from which it is possible to conclude contracts for the good h, conditionally to an event $B_t \supset A_t$, i.e. to trade on good h between A_u and A_t.

It follows from the assumptions made on $\mathscr{C}(A_t, h)$ that

—$A_t \in \mathscr{D}(A_t, h)\ \forall\ A_t,\ \forall\ h$
— $\forall\ A_u \in \mathscr{D}(A_t, h),\ A_u \supset A_t$.

Optimality of Equilibrium of Plans, Prices and Price Expectations

This first characteristic of the model, the possibility of reopening the markets, could lead to the study of something like a 'temporary equilibrium' with coexistence of 'spot' and 'forward' trading. Actually, the price expectations have specific features:

—first, the traders have *common* expectations, i.e. they associate the same (future) prices to the same events; however, this does not imply that they agree as to the joint probability distribution of future prices, since different traders assign generally different subjective probabilities to the same event.
—second, these expectations are equilibrium expectations, i.e. they will actually be verified on A_t, if A_t occurs.[1]

This second assumption is strong; it implies that at the beginning all the plans of the agents are *consistent*; i.e. for each commodity, each date, each event at that date, the planned excess supply of that commodity, at that date in that event, is zero. 'An equilibrium of plans, prices and price expectations is a set of prices on the first market, a set of common price expectations for the future, and a consistent set of individual plans, one for each trader, such that, given the current prices and price expectations, each individual trader's plan is optimal for him, subject to an appropriate sequence of budgetary constraints'.[2] But it is essential that all these plans and prices be simultaneously determined at the beginning. The model cannot be considered a realistic description of a succession of markets; it is an idealisation, a limit case.

In actual fact, complete knowledge of the future prices is conceivable only if all the exchanges are planned from the beginning, i.e. if the contracts are agreed to at the outset, even if the payments are contingent. This procedure, which may be called conditional market equilibrium, is in a certain way as little realistic as the one considered by Arrow–Debreu, unless one assumes that the 'good' expectations are announced by a 'planner' capable of simulating the markets. Nevertheless, the question of realism is not essential here, for the interpretation of the model in terms of spot and forward market equilibria is interesting as a limit case which can provide a reference for less 'ideal' situations, which is the reason for considering it here.

The formal description of the model makes these remarks explicit.

—A price system is a vector with coordinates $\Pi_h(A_t, B_u)$, h running over H, A_t over $\mathscr{A}$ and B_u belonging to $\mathscr{C}(A_t, h)$:

---

[1] The assumptions that all agents have the 'right' price expectations, and that Savage's axiom 2 is verified, are essential for the validity of this assertion (more general assumptions about price expectations go beyond the framework of this model).   [2] See Radner [5].

$\Pi_h(A_t, B_u)$ is the price paid on the market A_t, for delivery at time u, if B_u is realised, of one unit of the good h.

— A plan of exchange and consumption for the consumer i is denoted $[\ldots z_{ih}(A_t, B_u) \ldots x_{ih}(A_t) \ldots]$ where h runs over H, A_t over $\mathscr{A}$, and B_u belongs to $\mathscr{C}(A_t, h)$.

$z_{ih}(A_t, B_u)$ is the quantity of good h exchanged on market A_t, with conditional delivery if B_u obtains and $x_{ih}(A_t)$ is the contingent consumption of good h in A_t.

— A plan of exchange and consumption is said to be feasible for the consumer i and for some price system Π if, and only if:
· the consumption plan $(\ldots x_i(A_t) \ldots)$, $A_t \in \mathscr{A}$, belongs to X_i;
· it is compatible with the trade contracts and the initial endowment

$$\forall A_t \in \mathscr{A}, \forall h, \forall B_t \supset A_t, \sum_{A_u \in \mathscr{D}(A_t, h)} z_{ih}(A_u, B_t) \leqslant \omega_{ih}(A_t) - x_{ih}(A_t)$$

(the summation extends to all exchanges on the preceding markets for $u < t$, and on the market A_t itself);
· it satisfies a sequence of budgetary constraints,

$$\forall A_t \in \mathscr{A}, \sum_h \sum_{B_u \in \mathscr{C}(A_t, h)} \Pi_h(A_t, B_u) \cdot z_{ih}(A_t, B_u) \geqslant 0$$

i.e. on every market A_t, the value of the purchases does not exceed that of the sales.

— A global exchange and consumption plan $(\ldots z_{ih}(A_t, B_u) \ldots x_{ih}(A_t) \ldots) \forall A_t \in \mathscr{A}$, will be called realisable for a given price system if:
· it is feasible for every consumer i,
· all the trade contracts are jointly feasible,

$$\sum_{i \in I} z_{ih}(A_t, B_u) \leqslant 0 \qquad \forall h, \forall A_t \in \mathscr{A}, \forall B_u \in \mathscr{C}(A_t, h).$$

— A price system Π, a global exchange and consumption plan, constitute an equilibrium of plans, prices and price expectations, when:
— The plan is realisable for the price system.
— Every individual plan is a maximal element for the preference preordering of i, from all the feasible plans associated with Π.

References to this procedure of Radner will be made with the letter R. So, we will speak about R-prices, R-feasible plans, R-realisable plans and R-equilibria.

We specify the following assumptions:

(H1) – All spot trades are allowed:
$\forall h \in H, A_t \in \mathscr{C}(A_t, h)$

(H2) – $\forall h$, $\forall t$, $\forall u$, $\{B_u: B_u \in \bigcup_{A_t \in \mathscr{S}_t} \mathscr{C}(A_t, h)\}$ is a partition of S, or is empty.

(H3) – $|z_{ih}(A_t, B_u)| \leq L$ (there is an upper bound for the trades).

(H4) – $\forall i$, X_i is closed and convex, and there is a vector $\bar{x}_i$ s.t. $x \geq \bar{x}_i$ for all x in X_i.

(H5) – The preordering $\lesssim_i$, is represented by a continuous and concave utility function U_i, $\forall i$;

(H6) – For every x in X_i, and every A_t in $\mathscr{A}$, there is an x' in X_i, differing from x only at A_t, s.t. $U_i(x') > U_i(x)$; (i.e. there is no contingent satiation).

(H7) – There is an $\tilde{x}_i$ in X_i such that $\tilde{x}_i \ll \omega_i$.

Under assumptions H1–7, the pure trade economy E has an equilibrium of plans, prices and price expectations (R-equilibrium). Cf. Radner [5]. We make two remarks about this theorem.

Remark 1. It concerns the interpretation of the assumptions under uncertainty. The assumption H6 of non-satiation in each market A_t, implies that the trader has a positive subjective probability for each event, if the consumer behaves in accordance with Savage's axioms. The assumption that U_i is concave implies that the trader does not have a preference for risk. (See [3].)

Remark 2. Considering the price system on the market A_t (which is the restriction to A_t of the global price system), it is easy to see that the multiplication by a positive scalar of all the prices, for 'spot' trades or for 'forward' trades, on A_t, does not modify the set of R-possible plans for the consumers. So, the new price system, obtained after multiplication by $\lambda(A_t) > 0$ of the prices on every market A_t, is still an equilibrium price system; and the comparison of the price of good h on two consecutive markets has no *a priori* meaning.

II. OPTIMALITY OF EQUILIBRIUM OF PLANS, PRICES AND PRICE EXPECTATIONS

So there exists, under classical assumptions, an equilibrium of plans, prices and price expectations. What are the properties of the allocation so obtained in terms of optimality? To this question there is no simple general answer that would hold independently of the allowed trade contract choice. We will show, however, 'structures' of allowed trade contracts, leading to Pareto-optimal allocations. The first of them will be the structure of allowed trade contracts $\mathscr{S}^{h_0}$.

It is defined as follows:
All the trade contracts are forbidden, except
  α) every 'spot' trade contract,

β) for the single good h_0, in every A_t, 'forward' trade contract stipulating delivery in A_{t+1}, $\forall A_{t+1} \subset A_t$.

Formally

$$\forall t = 0 \ldots T-1, \; \forall A_t, \; \mathscr{C}(A_t, h_0) = \{A_t\} \cup \{A_{t+1} \in \mathscr{S}_{t+1}, A_t \supset A_{t+1}\}.$$
$$\mathscr{C}(A_t, h) = \{A_t\}, \; \forall h \neq h_0, \; \forall A_t \in \mathscr{A}.$$

With $\mathscr{S}^{h_0}$, the notations can be more explicit and thus clearer: an R-price is a sequence of vectors $(\ldots \Pi(A_t) \ldots \Pi_{h_0}(A_t, A_{t+1}) \ldots)$ where

· $\Pi(A_t)$ is the price vector relative to 'spot' trade contracts
· $\Pi_{h_0}(A_t, A_{t+1})$ is the price on market A_t of the contingent good h_0 at A_{t+1}.

—A consumption and exchange plan $(\ldots x_i(A_t) \ldots z_{ih_0}(A_t, A_t) \ldots z_{ih_0}(A_t, A_{t+1}))$[1] is R-feasible[2] for consumer i, with the R-price Π if:

· $x_i = (\ldots x_i(A_t) \ldots) \in X_i$;

· $z_{ih_0}(A_{t-1}, A_t) + z_{ih_0}(A_t, A_t) \leq \omega_{ih_0}(A_t) - x_{ih_0}(A_t)$,
   $\forall A_t \in \mathscr{A}$ with $z_{ih_0}(-1, 0) = 0$

· $\Pi(A_t) \cdot x_i(A_t) + \sum_{A_{t+1} \subset A_t} \Pi_{h_0}(A_t, A_{t+1}) \cdot z_{ih_0}(A_t, A_{t+1}) \leq$

$\Pi(A_t) \cdot \omega_1(A_t) + \Pi_{h_0}(A_t) \cdot z_{ih_0}(A_{t-1}, A_t) \; \forall A_t \in \mathscr{A}$,

with $z_{ih_0}(-1, 0) = 0$ and $z_{ih_0}(A_T, A_{T+1}) = 0$.

—A global consumption and exchange plan is R-realisable[2] for the R-price Π, if it is R-feasible for every consumer and if all the markets can be cleared. This is, here, equivalent to the two conditions

$$\sum_i x_i(A_t) = \sum_i \omega_i(A_t), \; \forall A_t \in \mathscr{A}$$
$$\sum_i z_{ih_0}(A_t, A_{t+1}) = 0.$$

The notations being clearly fixed, we are able to compare in the exchange economy E, the allocations corresponding to equilibria of plans, prices and price expectations with the contracts $\mathscr{S}^{h_0}$, and the allocations arising from markets for contingent claims 'à la Arrow–Debreu'; or, in other words, to compare the solutions of the 'D-procedure' and of the 'R-procedure'.

[1] We mention explicitly 'spot' trades only for good h_0.
[2] It will sometimes be said that x_i (resp x) is R-feasible (resp R-realisable), when there exists z_i (resp z) such that (x_i, z_i), (resp (x, z)) is R-feasible (resp. R-realisable).

To this end, we first examine the relations between R-realisable and D-realisable plans.

For this purpose the preliminary work is to define a one-to-one correspondence between D-prices and R-prices, or more exactly between equivalence classes of D-prices and equivalence classes of R-prices.

— Two D-price systems are equivalent if they have proportional components, the factor of proportionality being strictly positive. Formally $P \sim_D \hat{P} \Leftrightarrow P = \lambda \hat{P}$.

— Two R-price systems are equivalent if 'spot' and 'forward' prices are proportional in every market A_t, with a proportionality factor $\lambda(A_t)$ strictly positive. With the structure of allowed contracts

$$\Pi \sim_R \hat{\Pi} \Leftrightarrow \exists \lambda(A_t) > 0 \text{ s.t.} \begin{vmatrix} \Pi(A_t) = \lambda(A_t)\hat{\Pi}(A_t) \\ \Pi_{h_0}(A_t, A_{t+1}) = \lambda(A_t)\hat{\Pi}_{h_0}(A_t, A_{t+1}). \end{vmatrix}$$ [1]

Any property defined with respect to a price system (feasible plans, equilibrium plans) is simultaneously true or false for two price systems belonging to the same equivalence class, for both models. (This is obvious for the D-model and results from remark 2 at the end of preceding section for the R-model.)

Now, considering only the sets of D-prices and R-prices for which all the prices of good h_0 are positive, one can define:

— An application Ψ' of the set of equivalence classes of D-prices into the set of equivalence classes of R-prices, by associating to any D-price P the R-price Π defined by the formulas

$$\forall A_t: \Pi_h(A_t) = p_h(A_t), h \in H; \Pi_{h_0}(A_{t-1}, A_t) = p_{h_0}(A_t).$$

— An application Ψ'' of the set of equivalence classes of R-prices into the set of equivalence classes of D-prices by first choosing in any equivalence class of R-prices a member Π^* verifying

$$\Pi_{h_0}^*(A_t, A_{t+1}) = \Pi_{h_0}^*(A_{t+1}, A_{t+1}), \forall A_{t+1} \subset A_t, \forall A_t.$$

It is not difficult to see that such a member exists, by choosing adequate $\lambda(A_t)$ (see [4]). One can then associate to Π^* the D-prices defined by:

$$p_h(A_t) = \Pi_h^*(A_t), \forall h, \forall A_t.$$

Checking that Ψ' and Ψ'' are indeed equivalence class applications and that $\Psi' \circ \Psi'' = I$, identity application, thus that $\Psi'' = \Psi'^{-1}$, one sees that Ψ' is actually a one-to-one application.

[1] Sometimes, when no risk of confusion is involved, we omit the precision: $\forall A_t, t = 0, \ldots$ etc.

The following key propositions can then be stated:

(1) Every set of consumption plans $(x_i, i \in I)$, D-realisable for a price system P such that all the prices of good h_0 are positive ($\forall A_t : p_{h_0}(A_t) > 0$) is R-realisable for the price system $\Pi = \Psi(P)$.

(2) Every set of consumption plans $(x_i, i \in I)$, R-realisable for a price system Π such that all the prices of good h_0 are positive ($\forall A_t : \Pi_{h_0}(A_{t-1}, A_t) > 0; \Pi_{h_0}(A_t) > 0$) is D-realisable for the price system $P = \Psi'^{-1}(\Pi)$.

Now, suppose that (x, P) is a D-equilibrium; as x is D-realisable for P, x is R-realisable for $\Psi(P)$, by (2). If x and $\Psi(P)$ do not define an R-equilibrium, there is at least one consumer, say i_0, who can increase his satisfaction by choosing x_{i_0}', R-feasible for him, such that $x_{i_0}' \gtrsim_{i_0} x_{i_0}$. But then by (1), and since $\Psi'' = \Psi'^{-1}$, x_{i_0}' is D-feasible for i_0 and this contradicts the assumption. Replacing R by D and vice versa, (1) by (2) and vice versa, P by Π and $\Psi'(P)$ by $\Psi'^{-1}(\Pi)$, the proof can be repeated and we have:

Proposition 1. Let (P, x) be a D-equilibrium (s.t. $\Pi_{h_0}(A_t) > 0$)
$\exists z$ s.t. $(\Psi'(P), x, z)$ is an R-equilibrium.

Proposition 2. Let (Π, x, z) be an R-equilibrium (such that $\Pi_{h_0}(A_t, A_{t+1}), \Pi_{h_0}(A_{t+1}, A_{t+1}) > 0$); $\Psi'^{-1}(\Pi)$, x is a D-equilibrium.

Propositions 1 and 2 imply the following theorem:

Theorem. In an economy where $\forall i \lesssim_i$ has no local maximum in X_i, and where in every A_t, h_0 is desired without satiation[1] by at least one consumer (not necessarily the same), the R-equilibrium allocations with the structure $\mathscr{S}^{h_0}$, are identical to the D-equilibrium allocations and are all Pareto-optimal.

This follows from the fact that in this economy a D-equilibrium is necessarily Pareto-optimal, and that every R-equilibrium is such that $\Pi_{h_0}(A_t) > 0$, $\Pi_{h_0}(A_t, A_{t+1}) > 0$.

This property of Pareto optimality of the R-equilibrium remains true with more general types of structures of allowed trade contracts other than $\mathscr{S}^{h_0}$. As is intuitively reasonable, it suffices, for the property to be true, that spot trades be possible on every market A_t and that some 'transfer of value' be possible, from the initial period to every market A_t.

Several cases, where for this reason the set of markets of the R-model will actually be equivalent to the markets of the D-model, are indicated now:

---

[1] However, even if h_0 is not directly desired, it may be indirectly desired and have a positive price so that proposition 2 applies.

— Forward exchanges are permitted from A_t to A_{t+1}, on a particular good depending on A_t, $h(A_t)$, on the condition that it is desired at A_t, by at least one consumer.

— Forward exchanges are permitted from A_t to A_{t+1}, for two desired goods h_1 and h_2. Their R-equilibrium prices are positive and moreover they fulfil the relations

$$\frac{\Pi_{h_1}(A_{t+1})}{\Pi_{h_1}(A_t, A_{t+1})} = \frac{\Pi_{h_2}(A_{t+1})}{\Pi_{h_2}(A_t, A_{t+1})}.$$

If they did not, any consumer could then arbitrarily loosen his budget constraint at A_t, by buying good h_1 at A_t with delivery at A_{t+1}, by selling an equal value of good h_2 at A_t also with delivery at A_{t+1} and then making at A_{t+1} the inverse purchase and sale.

This relation between the prices of h_1 and h_2 implies that the one-to-one application Ψ still relates the equilibrium prices Π of this variant of the R-model, to the prices P of the D-model; all the properties demonstrated above remain valid.

— Every event A_t is linked to S_0 by a 'chain' of contracts. A chain of contracts between two elementary events A_t and A_θ, is defined as a sequence $A_{u_1} \ldots A_{u_K} (K \geqslant 0, \theta < u_1 < \ldots < u_K < t)$ such that
· $\exists\ B_{u_1} \supset A_{u_\theta}$ and at least one desired good $h(A_\theta)$ with $B_{u_1} \in \mathscr{C}(A_\theta, h(A_\theta))$
· $\exists\ B_t \supset A_t$ and at least one desired good $h(A_{u_K})$ with $B_t \in \mathscr{C}(A_{u_K}, h(A_{u_K}))$.

The proof sketched above can also be transposed (see [4]).

III. AN INTERPRETATION OF THE MODEL: SIMULTANEOUS EQUILIBRIUM OF 'REAL' AND FINANCIAL MARKETS

A financial market is a market for bonds. A bond can be defined as a claim, on the part of its owner, to a payment of some amount of money, at a given due date. If the payment is conditional, we will speak of 'conditional bonds' or of 'securities', and indifferently of markets for conditional bonds, and for securities. The transactions on these markets of bonds, at some given period, enable the agents to modify the sequence of their budgetary constraints, at the given period, and at the due period. Under conditions of certainty, an agent who sells bonds is called a borrower, a buyer is a lender. The payment, at the fixed due date, of the quantity of money indicated on the bond, is the operation of reimbursement.

In the Arrow–Debreu economy there are no bond markets in the sense we have just defined, since money *stricto sensu* does not have any role. In other words, the function of these markets, which is to allow an adequate reallocation of the whole budgetary constraint over all the different periods, or to modify the sequence of budgetary constraints, vanishes in a market with only forward trade concentrated at the beginning of time, since every agent then has one and only one budgetary constraint.

In an economy where both forward trade and spot trade coexist and conform to the ideal procedure described by Radner, bond markets no longer play any role, at least – and this is the conclusion of the preceding paragraph – when appropriate forward-trade contracts are allowed for a particular commodity (the numéraire). But when such forward markets do not exist, bond markets again have a role and generally economists agree that the second can, to some extent, replace the first.

The framework of Radner's model is well suited to make this intuition clear. So we will examine in this paragraph the consequences:

—Without uncertainty, of the opening of bond markets in a temporal economy, where a sequence of spot markets is already organised.
—Under uncertainty, of the introduction of securities markets taking place before all the spot markets corresponding to the vertices of the tree of events.

(1) *Opening of Bond Markets in a 'Temporal' Economy*[1]

The economy $E(X_i, \omega_i, \lesssim_i^E)$ considered here, is a temporal economy without uncertainty, and t suffices for indexing the markets and the goods.

Only 'spot' trades are allowed at every period $t = 0 \ldots T$.

The superposition of financial markets on this sequence of spot markets is obtained by the artefact of introducing a supplementary fictitious good in the economy, This good, denoted h_0', is fictitious in the following sense:

—Its total quantity is zero, and the initial endowment of every consumer is zero.
—It is not desired by anybody, at least directly.

Formally, we have an economy $E'(\omega_i', X_i', \lesssim_i^{E'})$, where

—the initial endowments in real goods, are identical in E and E' i.e. $\omega_{ih}'(t) = \omega_{ih}(t)$, $\forall i$, $\forall t$, $\forall h = 1, \ldots, l$.

[1] For a study of this problem in another context see T. de Montbrial [7].

—the initial endowment in good h_0' is zero for every consumer i.e. $\omega'_{ih'}(t)=0$, $\forall\, i$, $\forall\, t$.
—the consumption set X_i' can be deduced from the set X_i, assuming that every positive amount of good h_0' can be consumed at every period, in addition to some bundle of goods $x_i \in X_i$ i.e. $X_i' = X_i \times (R^+)^q$ (if $q = T+1$).
—an allocation of E', being denoted $x' = (x,\, x_{h_0'})$ where $x = (\ldots x_i(t) \ldots)$ is an allocation of 'real' goods, and $x_{h_0'}$ an allocation of fictitious goods; the preferences $\lesssim_i^{E'}$, in the economy E' are defined by

$$(x_i, 0) \sim_i^{E'} (x_i, x_{ih_0}), \quad \forall\, i, \quad \forall\, x_{ih'_0}$$

$$(x_{i_1}, 0) \lesssim_i^{E'} (x_{i_2}, 0) \Leftrightarrow x_{i_1} \lesssim_i^{E} x_{i_2} \quad \text{(with obvious notations).}$$

If the structure of allowed trade contracts is $\mathscr{S}^{h'0}$, the new economy E' describes exactly the opening of successive financial markets from period t to period $t+1$. Selling 'forward' at t is equivalent to borrowing; buying forward is equivalent to lending, and the delivery of the fictitious good one period later is reimbursement. The R-equilibria of E' can thus be considered as simultaneous equilibria of financial and real markets.

Are these Pareto optimal?

Let us note first that, although the set of allowable contracts is $\mathscr{S}^{h'0}$ (defined above), the theorem of section II on the Pareto optimality of the R-equilibria does not apply, since in this economy E' the good h_0' is never desired 'for itself', thus *a fortiori* is not desired at the equilibrium.

However, it can be noted that, given some D-equilibrium (P, x) for E, (P', x') where $P' = (P, P_{h_0})$ and $x' = (x, 0)$ with $P_{h_0'} = (\ldots p_{h_0'}(t) \ldots) \gg 0$[1] is a D-equilibrium for E'. Using proposition 1 of the last section one can easily verify [4] that any allocation associated with a D-equilibrium of the initial economy can be obtained as associated with an R-equilibrium of the economy with the additional fictitious good.

In this sense, the opening of bond markets in the sequence of spot markets makes it possible to attain every Pareto optimal state, attainable through the forward markets '*à la* Debreu'. Reciprocally, it is true that every R-equilibrium such that $p_{h_0'}(t, t+1) > 0$, $p_{h_0'}(t+1) > 0$, $\forall\, t = 0 \ldots T-1$, i.e. every simultaneous equilibrium of real and financial markets, with a strictly positive spot and forward price of the fictitious good, is Pareto optimal (as follows from proposition 2 of section II).

[1] $\gg 0$ means $p_{h_0'}(t) > 0$, $\forall\, t$.

Nevertheless, if a component of $P_{h_0'}$ is not strictly positive, the property is no longer true. Particularly if (P, x) is an R-equilibrium of E, $\{(P, 0), (x, 0)\}$ is an R-equilibrium of E' and is 'generally' not Pareto optimal. There is here a limit case, when the bond markets are not really active, and it is likely (this should be investigated in more detail) that apart from the case of degenerate financial markets, the simultaneous equilibrium of the markets of goods and bonds leads to efficient allocations.

Finally, let us look at the interest rates arising from the financial markets. Let $(\ldots p(t), p_{h_0'}(t), p_{h_0'}(t, t+1) \ldots)$ be the prices of an R-equilibrium,[1] and let w^* be a reference bundle of goods. A forward purchase of one unit of fictitious good, i.e. a loan of $p_{h_0'}(t, t+1)$, costs $\dfrac{p_{h_0'}(t, t+1)}{p(t) \cdot w^*}$ units of the reference bundle of goods. The yield of the loan at the following period, in units of the reference basket w^*, is $\dfrac{p_{h_0'}(t+1)}{p(t+1) \cdot w^*}$.

The ratio of the yield to the cost of the loan equals one plus the real interest rate of the period t, i_t:

$$1 + i_t = \frac{p_{h_0'}(t+1)}{p_{h_0'}(t, t+1)} \cdot \frac{p(t) \cdot w^*}{p(t+1) \cdot w^*}.$$

Put

$$1 + i_t' = \frac{p_{h_0'}(t+1)}{p_{h_0'}(t, t+1)} \quad \text{and} \quad 1 + \alpha_t = \frac{p(t+1) \cdot w^*}{p(t) \cdot w^*}.$$

We define i_t' as the nominal interest rate, on the market t, and α_t as the inflation rate.

Then $1 + i_t = \dfrac{1 + i_t'}{1 + \alpha_t}$. Approximately, $i_t = i_t' - \alpha_t$: the real interest rate equals the nominal interest rate minus the inflation rate.

(2) *Simultaneous Equilibrium of Markets For Securities at the First Period, and of 'Real' Spot Markets*

Let E be the economy without production, but with uncertainty, introduced at the beginning of this text, where only 'spot' contracts in every market, for every good, are allowed. In the economy E', forward trade contracts on the good h_0', conditional on the realisation of any event A_t, are allowed; and as in E, all the spot contracts

---

[1] Notice that $p_{h_0'}(0)$ has an arbitrary value because, in equilibrium, there are no spot exchanges of the good h_0' at period 0.

on every good (h_0' included), in every date-event, are possible. Formally:

$$A_t \in \mathscr{C}(A_t, h), \; \forall h, \; \forall A_t; \; A_t \in \mathscr{C}(S_0, h_0') \; \forall A_t.$$

The economy E' works as the economy E with a market at the initial period for conditional bonds (securities). The reasonings of subsection (1) of this section may be carried over into this situation and lead to similar conclusions:

. Given a D-equilibrium of E, there exists an R-equilibrium of the economy E', leading to the same allocation of contingent goods.
. An R-equilibrium of the economy E', such that the price at every date-event of the fictitious good is strictly positive, is Pareto optimal. (Nevertheless, as soon as one of these prices at some date-event is zero, this reciprocal property is 'generally' false.)

This is just another way of considering 'the role of securities in the allocation of risk-bearing'. Compared to the Arrow approach [1], this one is different on several points: first, we have here a multi-period and not a one period model; second we reason in an exchange economy and not in a distribution economy, and hence we do not consider, as Arrow does, a numeraire of constant quantity; third, it is proved that the direct theorem which asserts the existence of R-equilibria associated to the D-equilibria has a reciprocal.

Indeed, the concept of equilibrium of plans, prices and price expectations helps to give a systematic meaning to Arrow's remark, underlining the idea of simultaneously determining the equilibria, which is perhaps not always explicit in the original paper [1]. (See on this [3].)

IV. CONCLUSIONS

It is hoped that this text will help to a better understanding of Radner's model. It appears that this model stays very close to the Arrow–Debreu concept, and is concerned more with normative theory, than with a 'realistic' description of economic processes. Two points however, plead in favour of this approach:

(1) It is an adequate way to give precise meaning to intuitive assertions about the introduction of financial markets in a sequence of economies, or on the role of insurance in the allocation of risk-bearing in a trading economy.
(2) In the study of more realistic 'temporary equilibria' with subjective price expectations for the agents, this model seems to

provide a basic frame of reference, as a limit case, where the expectations are common, and are actually verified.

REFERENCES

[1] K. J. Arrow, 'Le rôle des valeurs boursières pour la répartition la meilleure des risques', pp. 41–7 in *Econométrie*, Colloque International XL (Paris, CNRS: 1953); translated as 'The Role of Securities in the Optimal Allocation of Risk-Bearing', *Review of Economic Studies*, vol. XXXI (1964), pp. 91–6.
[2] G. Debreu, *Theory of Value* (New York: Wiley, 1959).
[3] R. Guesnerie and T. de Montbrial, 'Allocation under Uncertainty, a survey', chapter 4 *supra*.
[4] R. Guesnerie and J. Y. Jaffray, 'Optimalité des équilibres de plans, de prix et d'anticipations de prix', mimeographed July 1971.
[5] R. Radner, 'Existence of Equilibrium of Plans, Prices and Price Expectations in a Sequence of Markets'; *Econometrica*, vol. XL (1972), pp. 289–303.
[6] R. Radner, 'Competitive Equilibrium under Uncertainty', *Econometrica*, vol. XXXVI (1968), pp. 31–58.
[7] T. de Montbrial, 'Intertemporal General Equilibrium and Interest Rates Theory'. Ecole Polytechnique (1970).

Part 3

Individual Risks in Large Markets

6 Optimum Allocation of Risk in a Market With Many Traders

Yaffa Caspi[1]
THE HEBREW UNIVERSITY, JERUSALEM

I. INTRODUCTION

In a market with 'many' traders who bear risks, there is the possibility of pooling their independent risks and in this way to eliminate traders' risks. There is a benefit from trade, and the way this benefit is divided between the traders depends on the system of exchange.

There is uncertainty about the initial endowment of the traders, which is a random variable, fixed by the state of nature. In a one-product economy we shall discuss a contingent commodity market as first presented by Arrow [1].

The number of traders will go to infinity in a way similar to that of Debreu and Scarf [3]. We shall take replicas of the economy, but replicating the economy, in the case of uncertainty, raises the problem of dependence between the random endowments of the different cconomies. The model of Debreu and Scarf [3] refers to a case of full correlation between the random endowments of identical economies. We shall, on the other hand, assume full independence.

By going to infinity in this way, we shall see that competitive equilibria will give each trader his expected initial endowment. This result cannot be generalised to the core. The core does not define a unique way to divide the benefit from trade between the traders.

II. THE MODEL

Consider an economy, E, without production and with a finite set of states of nature $\{\omega\} = \Omega$. Traders are denoted by i, $i = 1, ..., m$.

The consumption space is R^Ω, the consumption set of each trader is R_+^Ω, with elements

$$y_i = (y_i(\omega)),$$

---

[1] I am indebted to Professor D. Levhari and Professor M. E. Yaari for many comments and suggestions. I am grateful to the participants at the I.E.A. Workshop for many helpful remarks. In particular, F. Delbaen and J. Drèze supervised a systematic revision of the manuscript. However, I alone am responsible for any mistakes still present in the paper.

where $y_i(\omega)$ is the contingent consumption of the unique good in state ω.

Every trader has a preordering of preferences $\succsim_i$ on R_+^Ω.

Following the assumptions of Savage [5], the preferences can be represented by a utility function

$$U^i(y_i) = \sum_{\omega \in \Omega} \pi_i(\omega) u_i[y_i(\omega)] \qquad i = 1, 2, \ldots, m \qquad (2.1)$$

where $\pi_i(\omega)$

is the subjective probability of the event ω for trader i. $X_i(\omega)$ is the initial random endowment of the i-th trader. The total endowment of the economy is $\sum_{i=1}^{m} X_i(\omega)$ in state $\omega \in \Omega$.

Let us *assume:*
A_1: u_i is strictly concave.
A_1': u_i is differentiable and $u_i' > 0$.
A_2: $\pi_i(\omega) = \pi(\omega) \qquad i = 1, \ldots, m$.

III. OPTIMAL ALLOCATIONS

An allocation $y = (y_1, \ldots y_m)$ is *feasible* if, for every ω,

$$y_i(\omega) \geq 0 \text{ for } i = 1, \ldots, m \qquad (3.1)$$

and

$$\sum_{i=1}^{m} y_i(\omega) = \sum_{i=1}^{m} X_i(\omega). \qquad (3.2)$$

A feasible allocation $y = (y_1, \ldots, y_m)$ is a *Pareto optimum* if for any other feasible allocation $z = (z_1, \ldots, z_m)$

$Eu_i(z_i) \geq Eu_i(y_i)$ for every $i = 1, \ldots, m$ implies that $Eu_i(z_i)$
$$= Eu_i(y_i). \qquad (3.3)$$

Debreu and Scarf [3] defined the *core* in a commodities exchange market. We shall utilise this definition for a market of contingent incomes.

We may say that allocation y is blocked by S if it is possible to find contingent incomes, y_i', for all traders in S such that

$$\sum_{i \in S} X_i(\omega) = \sum_{i \in S} y_i'(\omega) \ \forall \ \omega \in \Omega$$

$$y_i' \succsim_i y_i \text{ for } i \in S$$

with strict preference for at least one member of S. The core of the economy is defined as the collection of all feasible allocations which cannot be blocked by any set S.

Optimum Allocation of Risk

An allocation in the core is Pareto optimal. Now we come to the definition of competitive equilibrium. There is a positive price system $P(\omega)$. $P(\omega)$ is the price paid in advance in order to receive one unit of the good if event ω occurs.

Each trader has a budget constraint

$$\sum_{\omega \in \Omega} P(\omega) X_i(\omega) \geq \sum_{\omega \in \Omega} P(\omega) y_i(\omega) \qquad i=1, \ldots, m \qquad (3.4)$$

and subject to (3.4) each trader wants to maximise

$$E u_i[y_i(\omega)] \qquad i=1, \ldots, m \qquad (3.5)$$

A competitive equilibrium for the economy E, is an $(m+1)$-tuple of vectors in R_+^{Ω}, $(y_1(\omega), \ldots, y_m(\omega), P(\omega))$, such that (3.5) is maximised under (3.4) for each i and (3.1), (3.2) hold. If $(y_1, \ldots, y_m, P)$ is a competitive equilibrium, then the m-tuple $(y_1, \ldots, y_m)$ is called a *competitive allocation* and P is referred to as a competitive price system.

Arrow [1] has shown that in the contingent commodities market, a competitive allocation is a Pareto optimum. Following Debreu and Scarf [3] we may observe that, in our market, a competitive allocation is in the core. Furthermore:

Theorem 1. If $(y_1^*(\omega), \ldots, y_m^*(\omega))$ is a Pareto optimum allocation, and if ω' and ω'' are two states of nature such that

$$\sum_{i=1}^{m} X_i(\omega') = \sum_{i=1}^{m} X_i(\omega'') \qquad (3.6)$$

then, under A_1 and A_2,

$$y_i^*(\omega') = y_i^*(\omega'') \qquad i=1, \ldots, m$$

Proof. Consider $(y_1^*, \ldots, y_m^*)$, a Pareto optimal allocation, and suppose that the theorem is not true; that is, $y_j^*(\omega') \neq y_j^*(\omega'')$ for some j. Consider then the following allocation:

$$\tilde{y}_i(\omega) = y_i^*(\omega) \text{ for every } \omega \text{ other than } \omega' \text{ and } \omega'',$$

$$\tilde{y}_i(\omega') = \tilde{y}_i(\omega'') = \frac{\pi(\omega') y_i^*(\omega') + \pi(\omega'') y_i^*(\omega'')}{\pi(\omega') + \pi(\omega'')}, i=1, \ldots, m.$$

$(\tilde{y}_1, \ldots, \tilde{y}_m)$ is an allocation, i.e. satisfies (3.1) and (3.2); this is obvious for $\omega \neq \omega'$, ω'', and is readily verified for ω' and ω'':

$$\sum_{i=1}^{m} \tilde{y}_i(\omega') = \sum_{i=1}^{m} \tilde{y}_i(\omega'') = \sum_{i=1}^{m} X_i(\omega') = \sum_{i=1}^{m} X_i(\omega'').$$

But according to assumption A_1

$$u_i\left[\frac{\pi(\omega')}{\pi(\omega')+\pi(\omega'')}y_i^*(\omega') + \frac{\pi(\omega'')}{\pi(\omega')+\pi(\omega'')}y_i^*(\omega'')\right] \geq$$

$\frac{\pi(\omega')u_i[y_i^*(\omega')] + \pi(\omega'')u_i[y_i^*(\omega'')]}{\pi(\omega')+\pi(\omega'')}$, $i=1...m$, with strict inequality for $i=j$.

Hence:

$$\tilde{y}_i \succsim_i y_i^* \quad i=1,...,m$$
$$\tilde{y}_j \succ_{jj} y_j^*. \qquad Q.E.D.$$

The idea of the theorem was first presented by Borch [2] while discussing the reinsurance market, but was proved there under stronger assumptions.

IV. INDEPENDENT REPLICAS OF THE ECONOMY E

Let r be a natural number and consider the product space

$$\Omega^r = \Omega \times ... \times \Omega$$

with the probability measure

$$\pi^r(\omega_1 \times \omega_2 ... \times \omega_r) = \pi(\omega_1) \times \pi(\omega_2) ... \times \pi(\omega_r). \quad (A.3.1)$$

Let E^r be an economy with mr traders, indexed (ij), $i=1,...,m$, $j=1,...,r$, whose initial endowments are defined by

$$X_{ij}(\omega^r) = X_{ij}(\omega_1, ... \omega_j ... \omega_r) = X_i(\omega_j) \quad (A.3.2)$$

and whose preferences among consumption vectors $y_{ij} \in R_+^{\Omega^r}$ can be represented by a utility function

$$U_{ij}(y_{ij}) = \sum_{\omega \in \Omega^r} \pi^r(\omega)u^i(y_{ij}(\omega)) = U^i(y_{ij}), \quad j=1,...,r. \quad (A.3.3)$$

We shall refer to conditions (A.3.1)–(A.3.2) and (A.3.3) as assumption A_3. There are m types of traders; two traders of the same type have identical tastes (A.3.3) and independent endowments with identical distributions (A.3.1)–(A.3.2).

In contrast, the replication scheme introduced by Debreu and Scarf [3] would require two traders of the same type to have identical endowments, that is, perfectly correlated endowments.

It was proved by Samuelson [4] that under assumptions A_1, A_1', A_2, A_3 the random income

$\sum_{j=1}^{r} \frac{1}{r} X_{ij}$ is preferred by each trader to any other combination

Optimum Allocation of Risk

$\sum_{j=1}^{r} \lambda_j X_{ij}$ such that $\lambda_j \geq 0$, $\sum_{j=1}^{r} \lambda_j = 1$.

We can conclude that

$$\frac{1}{r}\sum_{j=1}^{r} X_{ij} \gtrsim_i \frac{1}{r-1}\sum_{j=1}^{r-1} X_{ij}, \qquad i=1, \ldots, m. \tag{4.1}$$

Theorem 2. Let ϕ be a permutation $(1 \ldots r) \rightarrow (\phi_1 \ldots \phi_r)$.

$$A \in \Omega^r, A = (\omega_1, \ldots \omega_r),$$
$$B \in \Omega^r, B = (\omega_{\phi_1}, \ldots \omega_{\phi_r})$$

If $P \in R^{\Omega^r}$ is a competitive price system for E^r, then $P(A) = P(B)$, where $P(A)$ and $P(B)$ are the prices of one unit of consumption in states A and B.

Proof.

(1) $\pi^r(A) = \prod_{j=1}^{r} \pi(\omega_j) = \prod_{j=1}^{r} \pi(\omega_{\phi_j}) = \pi^r(B)$.

(2) $\forall i \sum_j X_{ij}(A) = \sum_j X_i(\omega_j) = \sum_j X_i(\omega_{\phi_j}) = \sum_j X_{ij}(B)$.

Hence, $\sum_{ij} X_{ij}(A) = \sum_{ij} X_{ij}(B)$.

(3) In every competitive equilibrium (y, P), the first-order conditions of maximisation under the budget constraint of trader (ij) imply

$$\frac{\pi(A)u_i'(y_{ij}(A))}{\pi(B)u_i'(y_{ij}(B))} = \frac{P(A)}{P(B)} \qquad i=1, \ldots, m \quad j=1, \ldots, r. \tag{4.2}$$

(4) According to Debreu-Scarf and Arrow, every competitive equilibrium of this economy is Pareto optimal. Furthermore, (2) and theorem 1 imply $y_{ij}(A) = y_{ij}(B)$. Thus

$$P(A) = P(B). \qquad \qquad Q.E.D.$$

Theorem 3. Under A_1, A_1', A_2, A_3, every competitive allocation will give two traders of the same type the same contingent income.

Proof. Consider two traders (ik) and (ip) of the same type i. According to theorem 2, their initial endowments have the same value; and they are subject to the same price system. As u_i is strictly concave, they will have the same allocation in every competitive equilibrium.

Theorem 4: There exist economies E^r satisfying A_1, A_1', A_2, A_3 and allocations X in the core of E^r such that two traders of the same type have different contingent incomes.

Illustration: An economy consists of r traders. All of them have the same utility function

$$u_i(X_i) = \sqrt{X_i} \qquad i = 1, \ldots, r$$

X_i is a random variable

Outcome	Probability
1	0.5
$\frac{1}{100}$	0.5

$X_1, \ldots, X_r$ are independent.

For every r there is β, $0 < \beta < \frac{1}{r}$ such that $\beta \sum_{i=1}^{r} X_i \sim_1 X_1$. The allocation $\left(\beta \sum_{i=1}^{r} X_i, \frac{1-\beta}{r-1} \sum_{i=1}^{r} X_i, \ldots, \frac{1-\beta}{r-1} \sum_{i=1}^{r} X_i\right)$ is in the core.

V. A LIMIT THEOREM FOR REPLICA ECONOMIES

We are interested in competitive allocations when r approaches infinity.

Lemma 5.1. $(y_1^r, y_2^r, \ldots, y_m^r)$ is a competitive allocation. Under A_1, A_1', A_2, A_3, for every $\epsilon > 0$ there exists $\bar{R}(\epsilon)$ such that, for all $r > \bar{R}(\epsilon)$, (5.1) holds.

$$|Eu_i(y_i^r) - u_i(EX_i)| < \epsilon, \qquad i = 1, \ldots, m. \tag{5.1}$$

Proof. (1) Let us first prove that

$$Eu_i(y_i^r) \geq u_i(EX_i) - \epsilon \quad \text{for } r > R(\epsilon) \tag{5.2}$$

A competitive allocation is in the core. Therefore,

$$y_i^r \gtrsim_i \frac{1}{r} \sum_{j=1}^{r} X_{ij} \qquad i = 1, \ldots, m; \tag{5.3}$$

otherwise, the allocation will be blocked by r individuals of type i.

We have seen in (4.1) that $Eu_i\left(\frac{1}{r} \sum_{j=1}^{r} X_{ij}\right)$ is an increasing function of r, but bounded by $u_i(EX_i)$.

We first prove that actually

$$\lim_{r \to \infty} Eu_i\left(\frac{1}{r} \sum_{j=1}^{r} X_{ij}\right) = u_i(EX_i).$$

Optimum Allocation of Risk

By the weak law of large numbers, $\frac{1}{r}\sum_{j=1}^{r} X_{ij} \to EX_i$ in probability. Since all the functions X_{ij} are positive, it follows from Scheffé's theorem that

$$\frac{1}{r}\sum_{j=1}^{r} X_{ij} \to EX_i \text{ in } L^1; \text{ i.e. } E|EX_i - \frac{1}{r}\sum_{j=1}^{r} X_{ij}| \to 0 \text{ if } r \to \infty.$$

Since an L^1 converging sequence is uniformly integrable, the sequence $\frac{1}{r}\sum_{j=1}^{r} X_{ij}$ is uniformly integrable. u_1 is a concave function and hence bounded by a linear function; i.e., $a > 0$, $b > 0$ such that for all α: $u(\alpha) \leq a \cdot \alpha + b$. Hence $u_i\left(\frac{1}{r}\sum_{j=1}^{r} X_{ij}\right)$ is uniformly integrable. We now can apply Lebesgue's dominated convergence theorem, which yields:

$$\lim_{r \to \infty} E\left(u_i\left(\frac{1}{r}\sum_{j=1}^{r} X_{ij}\right)\right) = E\left(\lim u_i\left(\frac{1}{r}\sum_{j=1}^{r} X_{ij}\right)\right) = E(u_i(EX_i)) = u_i(EX_i).$$

So, for every $\epsilon > 0$, we can find $R(\epsilon)$ such that:

$$Eu_i\left(\frac{1}{R}\sum_{j=1}^{R} X_{ij}\right) \geq u_i(EX_i) - \epsilon \tag{5.4}$$

and, for $r > R$,

$$Eu_i(y_i^r) \geq u_i(EX_i) - \epsilon.$$

(2) We will now prove that, $\forall\, r > R'(\epsilon)$:

$$Eu_i(y_i^r) - u_i(EX_i) \leq \epsilon. \tag{5.5}$$

Assume the opposite. There is one type, for instance no. 1, such that

$$Eu_1(y_1^r) > u_1(EX_1) + \epsilon \text{ for every } r. \tag{5.6}$$

Now, $u_1(Ey_1^r) \geq Eu_1(y_1^r)$.

So, there is $\delta(\epsilon) > 0$ such that

$$Ey_1^r \geq EX_1 + \delta(\epsilon) \text{ for every } r. \tag{5.7}$$

It is always true that $\sum_{i=1}^{m} Ey_i^r = \sum_{i=1}^{m} EX_i$ for every r, so that:

$$\sum_{i=2}^{m} Ey_i^r \leq \sum_{i=2}^{m} EX_i - \delta(\epsilon),$$

and there exist $(m-1)$ real numbers δ_i such that:

$$\delta(\epsilon) = \sum_{i=2}^{m} \delta_i, \; Ey_i^r \leq EX_i - \delta_i \qquad i = 2, \ldots, m.$$

At least one of the δ_i's is positive. Let us denote a type for which δ_i is positive by i^*.
$$Ey_{i^*}^r \le EX_{i^*} - \delta_{i^*}, \ \delta_{i^*} > 0.$$
As $y_{i^*}^r$ is a random income, while $EX_{i^*} - \delta_{i^*}$ is constant, it is obvious that
$$y_{i^*}^r \prec_{i^*} EX_{i^*} - \delta_{i^*}.$$
There exists $R_{i^*}(\delta_{i^*})$ such that
$$\frac{1}{R_{i^*}(\delta_{i^*})} \sum_{j=1}^{R_i^*} X_{i^*j} \precsim_{i^*} EX_{i^*} - \delta_{i^*},$$
$$\frac{1}{R_{i^*}(\delta_{i^*})} \sum_{j=1}^{R_i^*} X_{i^*j} \succ_{i^*} y_{i^*}^r.$$

The allocation suggested in (5.6) will be blocked by R_{i^*} traders of type i^*, is therefore, not in the core and cannot be a competitive allocation.

(3) $\bar{R}(\epsilon) = \max(R(\epsilon), R'(\epsilon))$ and for $r > \bar{R}(\epsilon)$, inequality (5.1) holds for every i.

Q.E.D.

Corollary 5.2. Under the hypotheses of lemma 5.1,
$$\lim_{r \to \infty} E(y_i^r) = EX_i$$

Proof: It follows from the proof of lemma 5.1 that:

$\forall \ \epsilon > O, \ \exists R$ such that, $\forall \ r > R, \ Eu_i(y_i^r) \ge u_i(EX_i) - \epsilon$.

Hence, applying Jensen's inequality:

$\epsilon > 0, \ \exists R'$ such that, $\forall \ r > R', \ Ey_i^r \ge EX_i - \epsilon$.

On the other hand, it follows from the second part of the proof of lemma 5.1 that:

$\forall \ \epsilon > 0, \ \exists R''$ such that, $\forall \ r > R'', \ Ey_i^r \le EX_i + \epsilon$.

(Indeed, it was verified above that (5.7) leads to a contradiction). So finally $\lim_{r \to \infty} Ey_i^r = EX_i$.

Q.E.D.

Theorem 5.3. Under A_1, A_1', A_2, A_3
$$\forall \ i, \ \forall \ \epsilon > 0: \lim_{r \to \infty} P_r\{\omega \big| |y_i^r(\omega) - EX_i| \ge \epsilon\} = 0$$

Proof: The theorem will follow from lemma 5.1 and the corollary.

Let $\alpha_i^r = u_i'(Ey_i^r)$, $\alpha_i = u_i'(EX_i)$.
From corollary 5.2, it follows that $\alpha_i^r \to \alpha_i$ as $r \to \infty$.

By concavity of u_i, we have: $u_i(x) \leq u_i(EX_i) + \alpha_i(x - EX_i)$.
By strict concavity of u, $\forall\, \epsilon > 0$, $\exists \delta > 0$ such that:

$$u_i(x) > u_i(EX_i) + \alpha_i(x - EX_i) - 2\delta \text{ implies } |x - EX_i| < \epsilon.$$

Hence, $\exists R_0$ such that, $\forall\, r > R_0$:

$$u_i(x) > u_i(Ey_i^r) + \alpha_i^r(x - Ey_i^r) - \delta \text{ implies } |x - EX_i| < \epsilon.$$

Suppose now, contrary to the theorem, that $\lim_{r \to \infty} Pr\{\omega \big| |y_i^r(\omega) - EX_i| \geq \epsilon\} \geq \eta > 0$.

Then, by extracting a subsequence, we may suppose that $\forall\, r$:

$$Pr\{\omega \big| |y_i^r(\omega) - EX_i| \geq \epsilon\} \geq \eta > 0.$$

Let $\Omega_1 = \{\omega | u_i(y_i^r(\omega)) \leq u_i(Ey_i^r) + \alpha_i^r(y_i^r(\omega) - Ey_i^r) - \delta\}$.

By the reasoning above, $P(\Omega_1) \geq \eta$. Denoting by 1_{Ω_1} the function taking the value 1 on Ω_1 and 0 on its complement Ω_1^c, we have:

$$E(u_i(y_i^r(\omega))) = E(u_i(y_i^r(\omega)).1_{\Omega_1}) + E(u_i(y_i^r(\omega)).1_{\Omega_1^c}),$$

and hence by concavity:

$E(u_i(y_i^r(\omega))) \leq E((u_i(Ey_i^r) + \alpha_i^r(y_i^r(\omega) - Ey_i^r) - \delta).1_{\Omega_1}) + E((u_i(Ey_i^r) + \alpha_i^r(y_i^r(\omega) - Ey_i^r)).1_{\Omega_1^c}) \leq E(u_i(Ey_i^r) + \alpha_i^r(y_i^r(\omega) - Ey_i^r)) - \delta \cdot \eta$

$$\leq u_i(Ey_i^r) - \delta \cdot \eta. \tag{5.8}$$

However lemma 5.1 and corollary 5.2 imply $\lim\, (E(u_i(y_i^r)) - u_i(Ey_i^r)) = 0$, a contradiction to (5.8).

Q.E.D.

REFERENCES

[1] K. J. Arrow, 'The Role of Securities in the Optimal Allocation of Risk-Bearing', *Review of Economic Studies*, vol. XXXI (1964), pp. 91–6.
[2] K. Borch, 'The Safety Loading of Reinsurance Premiums', *Skandinavisk Aktuarietidskrift*, vol. XLIII (1960), pp. 163–84.
[3] G. Debreu and H. Scarf, 'A Limit Theorem on the Core of an Economy', *International Economic Review*, vol. IV (1963), pp. 235–46.
[4] P. A. Samuelson, 'General Proof that Diversification Pays', *Journal of Financial and Quantitative Analysis*, vol. II (1967), pp. 1–13.
[5] L. J. Savage, *The Foundations of Statistics*, (New York: Wiley, 1954).

7 Stochastic Preferences and General Equilibrium Theory

Freddy Delbaen[1]

DEPARTMENT OF MATHEMATICS, UNIVERSITY OF BRUSSELS

I. INTRODUCTION

This paper is an attempt to introduce stochastic events in consumer behaviour and the related equilibrium theory. The idea of stochastic behaviour is not very new as may be seen from the literature. Nevertheless, it is not introduced in the current theory of general equilibrium. Indeed, one always supposes that people behave rationally (i.e. their preferences can be represented by a continuous utility function). In psychology such a model is not accepted and one tries to replace the *'homo deterministicus'* by the *'homo stochasticus'* (this is done keeping in mind that they are both *'homo sapiens'*). The introduction of stochastic individuals in general equilibrium theory is an idea of W. Hildenbrand [9]. This paper generalises his results, since we use only asymptotic independence instead of independence. See also [3] for another application to general equilibrium analysis.

Section I is devoted to a brief introduction to probability terminology. Of course, the introduction is far from being complete but it will suffice for the next sections. Section II contains some well-known properties of utility functions; a construction of a space of agents also will be given. Section III introduces the concept of the *'homo stochasticus'*. In section IV we shall introduce stochastic markets and we shall give an asymptotic result. The result says, roughly, that if the number of 'stochastic' agents tends to infinity, and if they are sufficiently independent, then the equilibrium prices of each market tend to a price system which is independent of stochastic influences.

I. PRELIMINARIES

(1)
Many textbooks speak about stochastic values and stochastic functions without saying where they are defined. For a mathema-

[1] I would like to thank J. Drèze and W. Hildenbrand for interesting discussions on this subject.

tician this is unacceptable. Therefore, one introduces the concept of probability space. The set of states of the world will be denoted by Ω. Note that Ω is not assumed to be a finite set. On the contrary we shall always assume that Ω contains sufficiently many points to describe all the events which we consider to be interesting. An event will be a subset of Ω.

Indeed $A \subset \Omega$ represents the event which is realised if, and only if, nature is in a state ω which is a member of A. Not all subsets of Ω will be considered as events, only a subclass of them. Let $\mathscr{A}$ be such a subclass consisting of events. We shall assume that $\mathscr{A}$ is sufficiently rich, namely it is a σ-algebra or tribe, i.e.

(1) $\emptyset \in \mathscr{A}$ (the event which never occurs is an element of $\mathscr{A}$).
(2) If $A \in \mathscr{A}$ then $A^c = \Omega \setminus A \in \mathscr{A}$ (i.e. if A is an event then the event A^c which occurs if, and only if, A does not occur is also in $\mathscr{A}$).
(3) If $A_n, n \geqslant 1$ is a sequence in $\mathscr{A}$ then the union $\bigcup_{n \geqslant 1} A_n \in \mathscr{A}$.

For each $A \in \mathscr{A}$ we define $\mathbb{P}(A)$ as the probability that A occurs. $\mathbb{P}$ is then a function $\mathbb{P}: \mathscr{A} \to [0, 1]$ and we ask that $\mathbb{P}$ satisfies

(1) $\mathbb{R}(\Omega) = 1$
(2) If A_n is a sequence of pairwise disjoint events then

$$\mathbb{P}\left(\bigcup_{n \geqslant 1} A_n\right) = \sum_{n \geqslant 1} \mathbb{P}(A_n).$$

A probability space is a triple $(\Omega, \mathscr{A}, \mathbb{P})$. A measurable space is a couple $(E, \mathscr{E})$ where $\mathscr{E}$ is a tribe on the set E.

Definition 1. A measurable function $f: \Omega \to E$ is a function such that for all $B \in \mathscr{E}: f^{-1}(B) \in \mathscr{A}$. The induced probablity on E is $\mu: \mathscr{E} \to [0, 1]: \mu(B) = \mathbb{P}[f^{-1}(B)]$.

Example. $f: (\Omega, \mathscr{A}, P) \to (\mathbb{R}, \mathscr{R})$ where $\mathbb{R}$ is the set of the reals, is called a random value ($\mathscr{R}$ is the smallest tribe containing all the open intervals). (The induced probability is a mathematical counterpart of the distribution function. Indeed $F(x)$ is the probability that f is smaller than, or equal to, x and hence $F(x) = \mathbb{P}(f^{-1}(-\infty, x])$.

Definition 2. If $f: \Omega \to (E, \mathscr{E})$ is a function then $\mathscr{A}_f$ is the smallest tribe such that f is measurable

$$\mathscr{A}_f = \{A | \exists B \in \mathscr{E}, A = f^{-1}(B)\}.$$

Definition 3. If $(\Omega, \mathscr{A}, \mathbb{P})$ is a probability space then $\mathscr{A}_1$ and $\mathscr{A}_2$, subtribes of $\mathscr{A}$, are called independent if, $\forall A_1 \in \mathscr{A}_1$ and $\forall A_2 \in \mathscr{A}_2$, $\mathbb{P}(A_1 \cap A_2) = \mathbb{P}(A_1) \cdot \mathbb{P}(A_2)$. Two functions $f: \Omega \to E; g: \Omega \to F$ are independent if $\mathscr{A}_f$ and $\mathscr{A}_g$ are independent.

Definition 4. If $(\Omega, \mathscr{A}, \mathbb{P})$ is a probability space and $\mathscr{A}_1$ and $\mathscr{A}_2$ are subtribes of $\mathscr{A}$ then the dependence coefficient between $\mathscr{A}_1$ and $\mathscr{A}_2$ is

$$\rho(\mathscr{A}_1, \mathscr{A}_2) = \sup |P(A \cap B) - P(A).P(B)|$$
$$A \in \mathscr{A}_1$$
$$B \in \mathscr{A}_2$$

Clearly $\rho(\mathscr{A}_1, \mathscr{A}_2) = 0$ if, and only if, $\mathscr{A}_1$ and $\mathscr{A}_2$ are independent.

It is proved by Ibragimov [10] that if X is an $\mathscr{A}_1$ measurable random value and Y is an $\mathscr{A}_2$ measurable random value where $|X| \leq C_1$ and $|Y| \leq C_2$ then

$$|\int X.Y\,d\mathbb{P} - \int X.d\mathbb{P}. \int Y.d\mathbb{P}| \leq 4\rho(\mathscr{A}_1, \mathscr{A}_2).C_1.C_2$$

For a proof we refer to [11].

Definition 5. A sequence $\alpha_n\ n \geq 1$ is called $(C, 2)$ summable with limit 0 if $\lim_{n \to \infty} \frac{1}{n^2} |n\alpha_1 + (n-1)\alpha_2 \ldots + \alpha_n| = 0$.

A sequence α_n tending to zero is $(C, 2)$ summable with limit zero.

Definition 6. A sequence $\mathscr{A}_n$ of subtribes in a probability space $(\Omega, \mathscr{A}, \mathbb{P})$ is called asymptotically independent if $\rho(\mathscr{A}_n, \mathscr{A}_{n+k}) \leq \rho_k$ where ρ_k is $(C, 2)$ summable with limit zero. In particular if $\rho_k \to 0$ then $\mathscr{A}_n$ is asymptotically independent.

Theorem 1. (S. Bernstein [2]). If $\mathscr{A}_n$ is a sequence of tribes which is asymptotically independent, if X_n is $\mathscr{A}_n$ measurable with $\int X_n d\mathbb{P} = 0$ and $|X_n| \leq 1$ then

$$\lim_{n \to \infty} \frac{1}{n} \sum_{k=1}^{n} X_k = 0 \text{ in probability.}$$

Proof. It is sufficient to prove that $Y_n = \frac{1}{n} \sum_{k=1}^{n} X_k$ satisfies

$$\int |Y_n|^2\,d\mathbb{P} \to 0.$$

But : $\int |Y_n|^2\,d\mathbb{P} = \sum_{k=1}^{n} \frac{1}{n^2} \int |X_k|^2\,d\mathbb{P} + \frac{2}{n^2} \sum_{1 \leq i < j \leq n} \int X_i X_j\,d\mathbb{P}$

$$\leq \frac{1}{n} + \frac{2}{n^2} \sum_{1 \leq i < j \leq n} 4\rho(\mathscr{A}_i, \mathscr{A}_j)$$

$$\leq \frac{1}{n} + \frac{2}{n^2} \sum_{1 \leq i < j \leq n} 4\rho(j - i)$$

$$\leq \frac{1}{n} + \frac{2}{n^2} ((n-1)\rho(1) + (n-2)\rho(2) \ldots + \rho(n-1))$$

and this goes to zero since $\rho(k)$ is $(C, 2)$ summable with limit zero.

(2)

A set A and a function $d: A \times A \to \mathbb{R}_+ = \{x | x \geq 0\}$ is called a metric space if d is a distance function on A, i.e.

(1) $d(x, y) = 0$ if, and only if, $x = y$
(2) $d(x, y) = d(y, x)$
(3) $d(x, y) \leq d(x, z) + d(z, y)$.

A distance function measures how far two points in A are from each other.

(1) says that if the distance is zero then the two points are identical
(2) says that the distance from x to y equals that from y to x
(3) is the famous triangle inequality.

Example. $\mathbb{R}$, $d(x, y) = |x - y|$ for all x and y in $\mathbb{R}$. The metric space (A, d) will be called separable if there is a sequence $x_n \in A$ such that for all $\epsilon > 0$, $\forall x \in A$, $\exists n$ $d(x, x_n) \leq \epsilon$ (i.e. every point of A can be approximated by elements of the sequence (x_n)).
It is well known that $\mathbb{R}$ is separable. All the spaces we will need in the sequel are separable.

Definition 7. The open ball of centre x and radius ϵ is $S(x, \epsilon) = \{y | d(x, y) < \epsilon\}$. The smallest tribe on a separable metric space containing all the open balls is called the Borel tribe.

II. THE METRIC SPACE OF 'RATIONAL' AGENTS

(1)

In our model l commodities are available. The commodity vector space will be $\mathbb{R}^l = \{(x_1, ..., x_l) | x_i \in \mathbb{R}\}$ and economic agents are supposed to be interested in

$$\mathbb{R}_+^l = \{(x_1, ..., x_l) | x_i \geq 0\}.$$

Every agent a is supposed to have initial endowment

$$i(a) \in \mathbb{R}_+^l = \{(x_1, ..., x_l) | x_i > 0\}.$$

Prices are supposed to be normalised and strictly positive. The set of prices will be denoted by

$$S = \{(P_1, ..., P_l) | \sum_{i=1}^{l} P_i = 1, P_i > 0\}.$$

Every agent a is supposed to have a preference relation $\leq_a$ on $\mathbb{R}_+$. $\leq_a$ satisfies:

(1) reflexivity: $x \leq_a x$
(2) transitivity: $x \leq_a y$ and $y \leq_a z$ implies $x \leq_a z$

(3) completeness $\forall x, y \in \mathbb{R}_+^l$ one has $x \leqslant_a y$ or $y \leqslant_a x$
(4) monotonicity $x \in \mathbb{R}_+^l$, $t \in \mathbb{R}_+^l$, $t \neq 0$, implies
$$x + t >_a x \ (>_a \text{ means } \geqslant_a \text{ but not } \leqslant_a)$$
(5) continuity $\forall x \in \mathbb{R}_+^l$ $\{y | y \leqslant_a x\}$ and $\{y | y \geqslant_a x\}$ are closed sets
(i.e. if $x_n \leqslant_a y_n$, $x_n \to x$, $y_n \to y$ then $x \leqslant_a y$)
(6) strict convexity: If $x \sim_a y$ then for all $t \in (0, 1)$ $tx + (1-t)y >_a x$.

It will be clear that our assumptions are a little more restrictive than need be; nevertheless we prefer to use these restrictions to avoid some technical difficulties.

Proposition 2. Every preference relation $\leqslant_a$ on $\mathbb{R}_+^l$ satisfying (1) (2) (3) (5) can be represented by a continuous function $u_a: \mathbb{R}_+^l \to \mathbb{R}$ (i.e. $x \leqslant_a y$ if, and only if, $u_a(x) \leqslant u_a(y)$).

Proof. *The Theory of Value* [5], proposition 4.6, p. 56.

The set of all preferences satisfying (1) (2) (3) (4) (5) and (6) will be denoted by $\mathscr{P}$. Proposition 2 can easily be proved for elements of $\mathscr{P}$. The utility we will construct is called the Kannai utility function. All the utility functions we shall use in the sequel will be of this kind.

Proposition 3. Every preference relation $\leqslant_a \in \mathscr{P}$ can be represented by a continuous function $u_a : \mathbb{R}_+^l \to \mathbb{R}$.

Proof. Let $\bar{e} = (e, ..., e)$ for all $e \in \mathbb{R}$.
Let $x \in \mathbb{R}_+^l$ then $0 \leqslant_a x$ and for e large enough $x <_a \bar{e}$. Hence on the

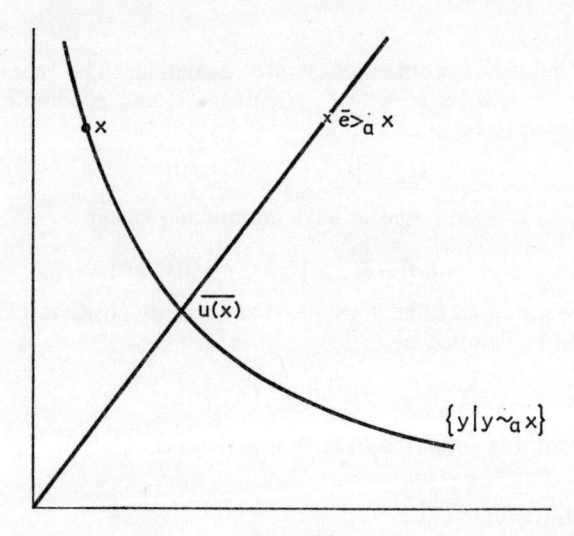

FIG. 7.1

segment $[0, \bar{e}]$ there is one, and only one, point $\overline{u(x)}$ such that $\overline{u(x)} \sim_a x$. The function $x \to u(x)$ is the good representation.

Q.E.D.

As Kannai observed [12] there is a natural metric on $\mathscr{P}$. If $\leqslant_1$ and $\leqslant_2 \in \mathscr{P}$ then let u_1 and u_2 be respective Kannai utilities. Let K_n be the set $\{(x_1, ..., x_l) | 0 \leqslant x_i \leqslant n\}$. Now, let

$$\delta(\leqslant_1, \leqslant_2) = \sum_{n=1}^{\infty} \frac{1}{2^n} \min \{\sup_{x \in K_n} |u_1(x) - u_2(x)|, 1\}.$$

Kannai proved that $\mathscr{P}, \delta$ is a separable metric space. (For more information see [12]; see also [6].)

We can now construct the set of all economic agents,

$$A = \mathscr{P} \times \mathring{\mathbb{R}}_+^l.$$

On A there is a natural metric $d(a_1, a_2) = \delta(\leqslant_{a_1}, \leqslant_{a_2}) + |i(a_1) - i(a_2)|$ (A, d) is still a separable metric space.

Definition 8. A deterministic agent $a = (\leqslant_a, i(a))$ is an element of $A = \mathscr{P} \times \mathring{\mathbb{R}}_+^l$. His preference relation is the first coordinate, his initial endowment, the second.

(2)
We shall now introduce economies with a finite number of participants. A pure exchange economy $\mathscr{E}$ with m participants can best be represented by m agents $(a_1, ..., a_m)$, hence by an element A^m.

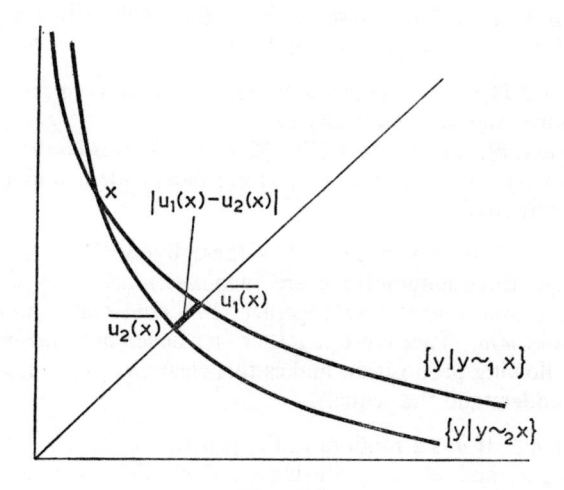

Fig. 7.2

For every price system $p \in S$ and every agent $a_i \in \mathscr{E}$ we can construct his demand $f_{a_i}(p)$. $f_{a_i}(p)$ is the element such that $u_{a_i}(f_{a_i}(p))$ is maximal within $\{u_{a_i}(x) | p.x \leqslant p.i(a_i)\}$ ($f_{a_i}(p)$ is unique since u_{a_i} is strictly quasi-concave).

A price system $p \in S$ is called an equilibrium if $\sum_{i=1}^{m} f_{a_i}(p) = \sum_{i=1}^{m} i(a_i)$. We shall write $f(a_i, p)$ instead of $f_{a_i}(p)$. Hence p is an equilibrium if, and only if,

$$\sum_{i=1}^{m} f(a_i, p) = \sum_{i=1}^{m} i(a_i).$$

Definition 9. The excess demand map $\zeta : A \times S \to \mathbb{R}^l$ is defined as $\zeta(a, p) = f(a, p) - i(a)$. It follows from our assumption that

$$p . \zeta(a, p) = 0.$$

Theorem 3. Every economy $\mathscr{E}$ has at least one equilibrium.

Proof. Theory of Value [5], proposition 5.7, p. 83.

Proposition 4. The set of equilibria is a compact subset of S.

III. THE 'HOMO STOCHASTICUS'

(1)

Thurstone [14] has observed that people behave stochastically and hence he replaced the utility function u by a stochastic equivalent.

Definition 9. $u : \Omega \times \mathbb{R}_+^l \to \mathbb{R}$, $\omega, x \to u(\omega, x)$ is called a random utility function if it satisfies (1) and (2).

(1) $\forall x \in \mathbb{R}_+^l$ $u(-, x) : \Omega \to \mathbb{R}$, $\omega \to u(\omega, x)$ is measurable (it defines the random utility of x).
(2) $\forall \omega \in \mathbb{R}_+^l$ $u(\omega, -) : \mathbb{R}_+^l \to \mathbb{R}$, $x \to u(\omega, x)$ is continuous.
(3) $\forall x \neq y$, $u(-, x)$ and $u(-, y)$ are independent and normally distributed.

Thurstone assumed more or less these hypotheses. As is easily seen, these three assumptions are inconsistent. This is intuitively clear: if x and y are close together then continuity implies that $u(\omega, x)$ and $u(\omega, y)$ are close together and hence not independent.

The following proposition makes this clear (its proof need not be read to understand the sequel).

Proposition 5. If u is a random utility function $u : \Omega \times \mathbb{R}_+^l \to \mathbb{R}$ such that $u(-, x)$ and $u(-, y)$ are independent, then u is constant in $\omega \ \forall x \in \mathbb{R}_+^l$, i.e. u is not subject to stochastic influences.

Proof. If $\mathcal{Q}_+^l$ is the set of elements in $\mathbb{R}_+^l$ having rational coordinates then $\mathcal{Q}_+^l$ is countable. It follows that the tribe generated by $u(-, q)$, $q \in \mathcal{Q}_+^l$ is separable, i.e. generated by a countable number of sets. Suppose that this tribe is $\mathcal{A}$. Since $u(-, x) = \lim_{n \to \infty} u(-, q_n)$ for suitable q_n, it follows that all the $u(-, x)$ are measurable for $\mathcal{A}$. Suppose now that the set L of x such that $u(-, x)$ is non-constant, is not a countable set. Let $\mathcal{A}_x$ be the tribe generated by $u(-, x)$. Since $\mathcal{A}_x$ for $x \in L$ is non-trivial, there exists $\psi_x \in L_2(\Omega, \mathcal{A}_x, \mathbb{P})$ such that ψ_x is non-constant. $\int \psi_x \, d\mathbb{P} = 0$ and $\|\psi_x\|_{L^2} = 1$. Since ψ_x and ψ_y are independent, ψ_x and ψ_y are orthogonal, i.e. $\int \psi_x \cdot \psi_y \, d\mathbb{P} = 0$ (see Dunford-Schwartz [7]). It follows that in $L^2(\Omega, \mathcal{A}, \mathbb{P})$ there is an uncountable set of orthonormal vectors, which contradicts the separability of $L^2(\Omega, \mathcal{A}, \mathbb{P})$. It follows that L is countable. Since a countable set has an everywhere dense complement, it follows from the continuity in x, that $u(-, x)$ is constant for all x. Q.E.D.

Remark. The same proof, except for the last sentence, applies if $u(\omega, x)$ is jointly measurable. The separability of $\mathcal{A}$ is then proved by more sophisticated methods.

In [14] the independence is used to calculate the expressions $\mathbb{P}(x, y) = \mathbb{P}\{\omega | u(\omega, x) \leq u(\omega, y)\}$ which is the probability that the agent prefers y to x. If dependence is allowed, then it is difficult to calculate $\mathbb{P}(x, y)$; on the other hand, independence implies the complete loss of continuity and even of measurability conditions on u.

(2) The Set of Stochastic Agents

It was stated in (1) that a stochastic agent can be described by a stochastic utility function $u : \Omega \times \mathbb{R}_+^l \to \mathbb{R}$. Such a function u induces another function $\psi : \Omega \to \mathcal{P}$. Indeed with every $\omega \in \Omega$ we associate the preference relation on $\mathbb{R}_+^l$ represented by $u(\omega, -) : \mathbb{R}_+^l \to \mathbb{R}$.

If one puts on $\mathcal{P}$ the Borel tribe $\mathcal{B}(\mathcal{P})$ then ψ is measurable (this can be seen using standard measure theoretic concepts). Conversely, if a function $\psi : \Omega \to \mathcal{P}$ is given, i.e. with each $\omega \in \Omega$ we give a preference relation $\psi(\omega)$ on $\mathbb{R}_+^l$ then we can construct a random utility function. Indeed, let $u(\omega, x)$ be $u_{\psi(\omega)}(x)$ where $u_{\psi(\omega)} : \mathbb{R}_+^l \to \mathbb{R}$ is the Kannai utility function representing $\psi(\omega)$.

If Ω denotes the set of influences common to all agents we will consider, then a stochastic agent can be described by a function $\psi : \Omega \to \mathcal{P}$. Let $\mathcal{M}$ be the set

Meas $(\Omega, \mathcal{P}) \times \mathring{\mathbb{R}}_+^l$ where Meas $(\Omega, \mathcal{P})$ denotes the set of all measurable function from Ω into $\mathcal{P}$.

Definition 10. A stochastic agent is an element of $\mathcal{M}$. A stochastic pure exchange economy with m participants is an element of $\mathcal{M}^m$.

Remark. The definition of economies with a measure space of agents can be given in the same way. However, 'small' technical difficulties occur.

(3) Another Approach to Stochastic Agents

If u is a random utility function then one can define

$$\mathbb{P}: \mathbb{R}_+^l \times \mathbb{R}_+^l \to \mathbb{R}$$

$\mathbb{P}(x, y) = \mathbb{P}\{\omega | u(\omega, x) \leq u(\omega, y)\}$. $\mathbb{P}$ has a straightforward interpretation; it gives the probability that y will be preferred to x. Conversely, if given a function $\mathbb{P}: \mathbb{R}_+^l \times \mathbb{R}_+^l \to \mathbb{R}$, when can we define a random utility function $u: \Omega \times \mathbb{R}_+^l \to \mathbb{R}$ such that $\mathbb{P}(x, y)$ describes precisely the probability that $u(\omega, x)$ will be smaller than, or equal to, $u(\omega, y)$? This gives the following problem.

Problem 1. Given $\mathbb{P}: \mathbb{R}_+^l \times \mathbb{R}_+^l \to \mathbb{R}$, when does there exist a measure μ on $\mathcal{P}$ such that $\mu\{\leq | x \leq y\} = \mathbb{P}(x, y)$?

A related problem is

Problem 1'. Given two Polish spaces Z and X, a continuous function $v: Z \times X \to \mathbb{R}$ and a function $\mathbb{P}: X \times X \to \mathbb{R}$, when does there exist a measure μ on Z such that

$$\mu\{z | v(z, x) \leq v(z, y)\} = \mathbb{P}(x, y)?$$

An answer to problem 1 or 1' is unknown to this author. See [13] for some results in this direction.

Since we put some restrictions on elements of $\mathcal{P}$ it is clear that there will be restrictions on $\mathbb{P}: \mathbb{R}_+^l \times \mathbb{R}_+^l \to \mathbb{R}$; e.g. if $y = x + t$ where $t \in \mathbb{R}_+^l$, then y is always preferred to x, hence $\mathbb{P}(x, y)$ should be 1. Another restriction may be $\mathbb{P}(x, y) + \mathbb{P}(y, x) = 1$. This means that the probability that x is indifferent to y is 0, and hence the agent almost always makes a choice between x and y.

IV. STOCHASTIC GENERAL EQUILIBRIUM

(1) The Demand of a Stochastic Agent

As was seen above, an agent is represented by (ψ, i) where

$$\psi: \Omega \to \mathcal{P} \text{ and } i \in \mathring{\mathbb{R}}_+^l.$$

For each price system $p \in S$ and each state of 'influence' ω the agent will maximise his utility in his budget constraint set, i.e. the agent selects the point x such that

Stochastic Preferences and General Equilibrium Theory

(a) $p.x \leq p.i$
(b) if $p.y \leq p.i$ then $u(y, \omega) \leq u(x, \omega)$ or $y \leq_\omega x$.

Such a point clearly depends on ω and p. The function $f: S \times \Omega \to \mathbb{R}_+^l$

$$p, \omega \to x \text{ (as constructed above)}$$

is the random demand function of the agent. It is clearly seen that f is continuous in p and measurable in ω. The function $\zeta(p, \omega) = f(p, \omega) - i$ is the random excess demand of the agent.

(2) Pure Exchange Economies

We consider an economy with m stochastic agents

$$(\psi^1, i^1) \ldots (\psi^m, i^m).$$

For each state of influence ω we obtain a 'deterministic' economy consisting of m agents $(\psi^1(\omega), i^1), \ldots, (\psi^m(\omega), i^m)$. By the famous existence theorem there is a price equilibrium $p \in S$ such that $\sum_{j=1}^m f^j(p, \omega) = \sum_{j=1}^m i^j$. The set of such price systems depends on ω and will be denoted by $W(\omega)$. The mean excess demand $\zeta_m(p, \omega) = \frac{1}{m}\sum_{j=1}^m (f^j(p, \omega) - i^j)$ is continuous in p and measurable in ω. $W(\omega)$ is precisely $W(\omega) = \{p | \zeta_m(p, \omega) = 0\}$. It follows that the graph of $W = \{(\omega, p) | p \in W(\omega)\}$ is measurable in $\Omega \times S$ and has compact sections.

$\bar{\zeta}_m(p) = \int_\Omega \zeta_m(p, \omega) \, d\mathbb{P}$ is the average excess demand per agent. It follows from [1] and [8] that there is $p \in S$ such that $\bar{\zeta}_m(p) = 0$, i.e. there is a price system p such that, in the mean, the excess demand is zero.

(3) A Limit Theorem

Definition 11: A sequence of stochastic agents (ψ^n, i^n) is called asymptotically independent if the sequence of tribes $\mathscr{A}_{\psi^n}$ is asymptotically independent and if i^n is bounded.

Theorem 6. If (ψ^n, i^n) is a sequence of asymptotically independent agents, then $\zeta_n(p, \omega) - \bar{\zeta}_n(p)$ goes to zero uniformly on compact sets.

Proof. We have to prove
$\lim_{n \to \infty} \sup_{p \in K} \mathbb{P}[\omega | \, ||\zeta_n(p, \omega) - \bar{\zeta}_n(p)|| > \epsilon] = 0$ for all $\epsilon > 0$ and all compact sets K in S.

Referring to the proof of Bernstein's theorem we need to prove only that

$$\lim_{n\to\infty} \sup_{p\in K} \int ||\zeta_n(p, \omega) - \bar{\zeta}_n(p)||^2 \, d\mathbb{P} = 0.$$

Since K is compact and lies in S $\exists \delta > 0$ such that $\forall p \in K$ $P_s \geq \delta$ for all $s \leq l$. Since i^n is bounded we obtain from $p.f^j = p.i^j$ that $||f^j(p, \omega)|| \leq \frac{1}{\delta}||i^j|| \leq \frac{1}{\delta}M$ where M is such that $||i^j|| \leq M$ for all j. It follows that $||\zeta_n(p, \omega) - \bar{\zeta}_n(p)||$ is smaller than $\frac{2M}{\delta}$.

The application of Bernstein's theorem now completes the proof.

The interpretation of the above theorem is straightforward. If the sequence of agents is asymptotically independent then the random fluctuations of the mean excess demand tend to zero. See also [9] where more information is given in the case of complete independence.

In a forthcoming paper of Bhattacharya and Majumdar [3] results are given on the set of price systems $W_n(\omega)$.

REFERENCES

[1] R. Aumann, 'Existence of Competitive Equilibria in Markets with a Continuum of Traders', *Econometrica*, vol. 34 (1966), pp. 1–17.

[2] S. Bernstein, 'Sur l'extension du théorème limité du calcul des probabilités aux sommes de quantités dépendantes', *Mathematische Annalen*, vol. XCVII (1927), pp. 1–59.

[3] R. N. Bhattacharya and M. Majumdar, 'On Convergence of Random Price Equilibria', Technical Report, No. 48 (1971), Stanford University: Institute for Mathematical Studies in the Social Sciences.

[4] P. Billingsley, *Convergence of Probability Measures* (New York: Wiley, 1968).

[5] G. Debreu, *Theory of Value* (New York: John Wiley, 1959).

[6] G. Debreu, 'Neighboring Economic Agents', pp. 85–90 in *La Décision* (Paris: CNRS, 1968).

[7] N. Dunford and J. T. Schwartz, *Linear Operators–Part I* (New York: Interscience, 1958).

[8] W. Hildenbrand, 'Existence of Equilibria for Economies with Production and a Measure Space of Consumers', *Econometrica*, vol. 38 (1970), pp. 608–23.

[9] W. Hildenbrand, 'Random Preferences and Equilibrium Analysis', *Journal of Economic Theory*, vol. III (1971), pp. 414–29.

[10] I. A. Ibragimov, 'Some Limit Theorems for Stationary Processes', *Theory of Probability and its Applications*, vol. VII (1962), pp. 349–82.

[11] M. Iosifescu and R. Theodorescu, *Random Processes and Learning* (Berlin: Springer-Verlag, 1969).

[12] Y. Kannai, 'Continuity Properties of the Core of a Market', *Econometrica*, vol. XXXVIII (1970), pp. 791–815.
[13] R. D. Luce, *Individual Choice Behaviour* (New York: John Wiley, 1959).
[14] L. L. Thurstone, 'A Law of Comparative Judgment', *Psychological Review*, vol. XXXIV (1927), pp. 273–86.

8 The Allocation of Individual Risks in Large Markets

Edmond Malinvaud[1]
INSEE, PARIS

I. INTRODUCTION

The modern theory of risk-bearing, as introduced by Arrow [1], Baudier [3] and Debreu [4], although fully general, gives no direct justification for a proposition that common sense suggests: an optimal allocation of resources typically requires that firms ought to maximise the expected value of their profits, and *a contrario* risk aversion at the level of the individual firm is detrimental to efficiency. It is very revealing that this proposition had to be argued by one of the founders of the modern theory against one of its adepts, namely by Arrow and Lind [2] against Hirshleifer [6]. One may also note that the modern approach does not directly exhibit the role of insurance for a proper allocation of resources. Such a role was often emphasised, for instance by F. Knight [7]. To a very large extent a system of insurance can replace the markets for contingent commodities, which were imagined by the theory but hardly exist in fact.

In his argument for maximisation of expected profits, Arrow led us to draw an important distinction that others have also encountered: we should identify on the one hand collective risks that are directly significant for a large proportion of the people or firms and on the other hand individual risks that appear at the level of the individual agents but are socially removed by the operation of the law of large numbers. Expected profit is the appropriate maximand for dealing with the second type of risk.

The natural idea for reaching this proposition is to derive it from the general theory according to which the price system sustaining an optimum specifies a price p_{he} applying for an offer to deliver one unit of good h if state e occurs, this being true for all $h = 1, 2, ..., H$ and $e = 1, 2, ..., E$. Where only individual risks are involved, the state e having probability π_e, it seems that 'contingent' prices p_{he} have the property that they can be given the approximate form

---

[1] The author has benefited from useful comments made by P. Champsaur, B. Grodal, C. Henry and a referee.

$\pi_e p_h$ by an appropriate choice of the H prices p_h for unconditional delivery.[1] Proving that such a particular form almost always holds was the line followed by Arrow, but the argument made a number of simplifying assumptions; integrating it within the general model of resource allocation seems to be difficult.

The recent article by W. Hildenbrand [5] gives us a way to obtain the theoretical result very cheaply by a different approach. Roughly speaking, it consists of introducing the law of large numbers right at the beginning when formal concepts are specified and not at the end for a particularisation of the price system. The clue is to change the definition of feasibility: the balance between supply and demand is required to hold only in expected value across all states and no longer for each single state. The law of large numbers permits this because, *when the economy is large and involves only individual risks*, the excess demand for each commodity almost never deviates significantly from its expected value.

In order to study the theory of resource allocation in the case of individual risks and to see its implications for distribution as well as for production, I should like to put down here the main elements of the new approach limiting myself to a simple model. Economists of the Aumann–Debreu school will soon make this paper obsolete when they will turn their powerful machinery in the direction that I am today exploring.

II. INDIVIDUAL RISKS

Let there be I types of consumers ($i = 1, 2, ..., I$) and J types of producers ($j = 1, 2, ..., J$). The economy is assumed to contain IN consumers and JN producers, precisely N of each type, N being considered as large number. The index of the n-th agent of type i is (i, n) and similarly (j, n) for the n-th producer of type j. What is meant by a 'type' will be made more precise as we proceed; roughly speaking, it means that two agents of the same type have the same set of feasible acts, the same endowments, and the same preferences. Let there also be H commodities ($h = 1, 2, ..., H$). The definition of the latter ought to specify the states with respect to collective risks, as is recommended by the modern theory. We shall not pay special attention to this point in what follows, but we must make explicit here that individual risks are *not* taken into account in the definition of commodities.

---

[1] This special form of contingent prices is also the reason why a Pareto optimum can be sustained by the prices prevailing in a competitive economy in which there is a system of insurance but markets exist only for sure commodities.

For a consumer of type i the individual risk comes from the fact that he will find himself in one of several possible states with respect to his resources, needs and preferences. An index for these states will be (i, s) and $s = 1, 2, ..., S_i$. Each state occurs with an objective probability π_{is}:

$$\sum_s \pi_{is} = 1 \tag{2.1}$$

(to simplify the notation, it will be understood that summations with respect to s run over all the corresponding states). Similarly a producer of type j may find himself in one of S_j possible states (j, s) concerning what he can technically do. These states occur with probabilities π_{js} adding up to one $(s = 1, 2, ..., S_j)$.

If we should like to define a 'state e for the economy' we ought to say that it is a complete specification of the $(I+J)N$ states occurring simultaneously, each one affecting one of the individual agents (assuming there is no collective risk). But we shall not need this concept.

Let now m_{is} and q_{js} designate, respectively, the numbers of individuals who will find themselves in state (i, s) and (j, s). They are random numbers. But the situation is assumed to be such that, if N were to increase indefinitely, the proportions m_{is}/N and q_{js}/N would converge, respectively, to π_{is} and π_{js}. This assumption formalises the idea of individual risks. It could be derived from other hypotheses and from a law of large numbers.

For instance, the various replicas constituting the economy may be taken as stochastically independent from one another: the state obtaining for agent (i, n) or (j, n) is an event independent of the states obtaining for all agents with a different n index. The endowments, needs and preferences of a consumer are stochastically independent of those of other consumers of the same type; similarly for the technical possibilities of a producer. There might, however, be any kind of dependence between agents having the same index n.

The case of independent replicas is, of course, restrictive. But the law of large numbers holds under much more general conditions, which have been studied by probabilists. They concern, in particular, cases in which the dependence may strongly affect 'neighbours', i.e. agents with indices n and n' differing little from one another, but vanishes as $n - n'$ increases (an elementary proof of this is given in the appendix of this essay). They correspond rather well to the notion of individual risks.

In such an economy, a 'program' is a complete specification of the activities of all individual agents *in the various situations that they may face*. For consumer (i, n) the program gives the HS_i numbers x_{insh} defining his consumption of the various commodities in the various states (i, s) that are relevant for him.[1] Similarly the number y_{jnsh} is the net output of good h that producer (j, n) obtains if state (j, s) occurs for him.

Our main concern is the study of the price system sustaining a Pareto optimal program. Since the definition of types is flexible, we may without loss of generality assume that in this program individuals belonging to the same type behave in exactly the same way. We shall therefore be able to drop the index n and to denote by x_{is} and y_{js} the H-vectors defining, respectively, the consumptions of any consumer of type i under state (i, s) and the net outputs of any producer of type j under state (j, s). The Pareto optimal program we are going to study is therefore defined by as many activity vectors as there are types and states.

We shall even take N as being arbitrary, i.e. consider a sequence of economies $\mathscr{E}^N$ differing only by the number N of agents of each type ($N = 1, 2, \ldots$ ad infinitum). The specification of the activity vectors will be assumed to be such that the resulting program is Pareto optimal in each one of the economies $\mathscr{E}^N$.[2]

In such a program the vector of excess demands is

$$\sum_{i=1}^{I} \sum_{s} m_{is}(x_{is} - \omega_{is}) - \sum_{j=1}^{J} \sum_{s} q_{js} y_{js}.$$

(From the definition of types we know that consumers of the same type hold equal quantities of initial resources; we denote by ω_{is} the vector of these endowments for a consumer of type i finding himself in state (i, s).) The vector of 'per capita excess demands' is

$$\frac{1}{I}\left[\sum_{i=1}^{I}\sum_{s}\frac{m_{is}}{N}(x_{is} - \omega_{is}) - \sum_{j=1}^{J}\sum_{s}\frac{q_{js}}{N}y_{js}\right]. \qquad (2.2)$$

On the other hand, the vector of 'per capita *expected* excess demands' is

$$\frac{1}{I}\left[\sum_{i=1}^{I}\sum_{s}\pi_{is}(x_{is} - \omega_{is}) - \sum_{j=1}^{J}\sum_{s}\pi_{js}y_{js}\right]. \qquad (2.3)$$

[1] One may think of programs in which the allocation of good h to consumer (i, n) would depend not only on the events (i, s) concerning him but also on those concerning other agents: this allocation would be a function of the 'state of the economy' and no longer a function of only the individual state (i, s). For small economies, the programs commonly considered would, indeed, not have the special form that we are here assuming from the beginning. The approach of the present article makes it feasible and interesting to limit attention to programs of this form.

[2] This last condition is not restrictive. For instance, with the classical definition of Pareto optimality and with the classical convexity assumptions, a program for $\mathscr{E}^N$ in which agents of the same type have identical activity vectors is optimal if and only if the corresponding program for $\mathscr{E}^1$ is optimal. The proof, which uses the duality between optima and market equilibria, may be transposed so as to apply with the definitions of Pareto optimality that will be considered here.

The assumption on individual risks implies that the random vector (2.2) tends to the sure vector (2.3) as the number N increases indefinitely. Hence we shall be satisfied with an excess demand requirement for feasibility that will be written

$$\sum_{i=1}^{I} \sum_{s} \pi_{is}(x_{is} - \omega_{is}) = \sum_{j=1}^{J} \sum_{s} \pi_{js} y_{js}. \qquad (2.4)$$

It should be emphasised here that this constraint is intended as a representation of the requirement for overall balance between supplies and demands. It does *not* mean that agents are satisfied with a state of affairs in which their demands are fulfilled 'on the average'. It rather means that we neglect the discrepancies that will remain between supplies and demands in the same way as we neglect transaction costs. Such discrepancies may be viewed as being put to or met from inventories. In any case they are negligible when the economy is large.

Using the constraint (2.4) is very convenient because it makes it possible to omit reference to the number N of individuals within each type. In most of the following discussion we shall actually deal with the case $N=1$ and therefore drop the index n. For deriving formal results that are independent of N, this is permissible even though such results would not be adequate to reality if N were not large.

III. AN EXCHANGE ECONOMY WITHOUT RISK LEVELLING

In order to have a first look at the problem and to see the sharp difference between individual and collective risks we shall briefly consider now an exchange economy, for which we shall adopt a simple concept of optimality – one which is too simple as we shall see later. This will, of course, not bring any light on the criterion of maximisation of expected profit but exhibit the special form of the price system and be instructive from the formal viewpoint.

Without loss of essential generality, the definition of states being flexible in practice, let us assume that the number of states is the same for all types of consumers ($S_i = S$) and that all states have the same probability of occurring ($\pi_{is} = 1/S$).

Then condition (2.4) can be written

$$\sum_{i=1}^{I} \sum_{s=1}^{S} (x_{is} - \omega_{is}) = 0. \qquad (3.1)$$

The individual needs and preferences are taken as varying from one state to another, but as being, in a given state (i, s), the same for

The Allocation of Individual Risks in Large Markets

all individuals of the same type. Let us for the moment represent them by a utility function on the H-vector x_{is} defining the consumptions in state (i, s). This utility may be written $u_{is}(x_{is})$.

Let us now consider a program P^0 that allocates the same consumption vectors x_{is}^0 to individuals of the same type facing the same state. P^0 is said to be feasible if it fulfils (3.1). We shall moreover say that it is optimal if it is feasible and if there is no program P^1 consisting of IS vectors x_{is}^1 fulfilling (3.1) and such that

$$u_{is}(x_{is}^1) \geqslant u_{is}(x_{is}^0) \qquad \text{for all } i \text{ and } s, \tag{3.2}$$

with at least one strict inequality.[1] We shall discuss this concept in a moment, but first examine its implications.

They are quite clear because we are now in a situation that is formally identical to the one we get for a riskless exchange economy with IS agents, consumer (i, s) having resources ω_{is} and a utility $u_{is}(x_{is})$. The program P^0 is optimal according to the present definition if it is Pareto optimal in the associated riskless economy.

In such a case, if the u_{is} are defined on convex sets and assumed to be quasi-concave, we know that there exists an H-*dimensional price vector* p such that in each state (i, s) the vector x_{is}^0 maximises $u_{is}(x_{is})$ under the constraint:

$$px_{is} \leqslant px_{is}^0. \tag{3.3}$$

Conversely, if we define an equilibrium as a feasible program P^0 and an H-dimensional price vector p such that the IS vector x_{is}^0 satisfy the preceding condition where in (3.3) the given 'income' R_{is} replaces px_{is}^0, and if there is no satiation, an equilibrium is an optimal program. (If the functions u_{is} are strictly quasi-concave and if the price vector p and the incomes R_{is} are given, then the vectors x_{is}^0 of the equilibrium are uniquely defined so that it is not artificial to impose identical behaviour to individuals of the same type facing the same state.)

The formal association just used is worth noting: to come back to the classical model built for riskless economies we have extended the number of consumers in this case of individual risks whereas one extends the number of commodities in the case of collective risks. We have now *sure prices* p_h that do not depend on the states; but for each agent we have as many budget constraints (3.3) as there are

---

[1] Comparing P^0 to programs P^2 in which the vectors x_{ins}^2 would differ for individuals (i, n) and (i, n') of the same type would not make the condition more stringent to the extent that the u_{is} are quasi-concave and feasibility refers to expected excess demands. Indeed, suppose, for instance, that P^2 allocates $\hat{x}_{is}$ to a proportion α_i of consumers of type i and $\tilde{x}_{is}$ to the remaining consumers of the same type. Define P^1 by $x_{is}^1 = \alpha_i \hat{x}_{is} + (1 - \alpha_i)\tilde{x}_{is}$. If P^2 is feasible, then P^1 also is feasible. If $u_{is}(\hat{x}_{is}) \geqslant u_{is}(x_{is}^0)$, and $u_{is}(\tilde{x}_{is}) \geqslant u_{is}(x_{is}^0)$, then $u_{is}(x_{is}^1) \geqslant u_{is}(x_{is}^0)$.

states concerning him. There is no longer any market for contingent claims. Only markets for sure commodities are considered.[1]

The concept of optimum is not, however, very stringent. With the definition given above no comparison is made between the utility levels $u_{is}(x_{is}^0)$ and $u_{i\sigma}(x_{i\sigma}^0)$ achieved by a consumer in two different states (i, s) and (i, σ). An 'optimal program' may place a particular consumer in a welfare situation that varies very much from one state to another. This may be the case, for instance, with an equilibrium in which each income R_{is} is equal to the value of the corresponding resources $p\omega_{is}$. The budget constraint (3.3) is then written

$$px_{is} \leqslant p\omega_{is}. \tag{3.4}$$

The value of the consumption that consumer i chooses in state s is constrained by the value of the resources that he holds in the same state. Such an equilibrium rules out insurance against individual risks. There is no 'risk-levelling'. That such a situation could be called 'optimal' reveals how inadequate is the present concept. We must therefore look for a formalisation that contains a better representation of individual preferences.

Before leaving the model of this section let us, however, note first that a program that will be called optimal under the more stringent criterion we are going to introduce is also optimal under the criterion of this section if it concerns an exchange economy and if the individual preferences fulfil a rather natural assumption. The result we have reached will therefore still apply. Let us also remark that budget constraints such as (3.4) may turn out to be adequate in some cases, for instance, when ω_{is} does not depend on s and when the state (i, s) concerns only the 'tastes' of the consumers of type i, a case on which is focussed the article by W. Hildenbrand [5].

IV. PARETO OPTIMAL PROGRAMS

Let us now consider the general model in which producers exist as well as consumers. The activity or 'strategy' of an agent will give definite values to his demands and supplies of the various goods in the various states concerning him. For instance, the activity of a consumer of type i will determine his S_iH demands x_{ish}. We shall therefore find it convenient to consider the S_iH-vector x_i having these components x_{ish}. Similarly we shall use the S_jH-vector y_j having the components y_{jsh}, the net outputs of a producer (j, n) in the various states that he may face.

[1] If some collective risks exist, they have been taken into account in the definition of the commodities h; hence p_h are not quite sure prices but prices contingent only on collective risks. Markets for 'collectively contingent' commodities are still required.

The Allocation of Individual Risks in Large Markets

The needs of the consumer (i, n) require that x_i belongs to some set X_i of the $S_i H$-space and this set is the same for all consumers of the same type. In most cases, the needs will concern the S_i separate H-subvectors x_{is}, each one of them defining which consumptions will be made when state (i, s) obtains. The subvector x_{is} will be required to belong to some set X_{is}. The set X_i will then be simply the Cartesian product of the S_i sets X_{is}.

The preferences of the consumer (i, n) define a preordering on the set X_i; and this preordering will be the same for all consumers of the same type. We shall write

$$x_i^1 \gtrsim x_i^2 \tag{4.1}$$

to mean that the consumers of type i consider x_i^1 as at least as good as x_i^2 (the preorderings may, of course, vary from one type to another). Comparing x_i^1 to x_i^2 the consumers evaluate simultaneously how well the vectors x_{is}^1 and x_{is}^2 satisfy them in the various possible states (i, s).

It does not seem that the generality of the theory would be significantly reduced by the assumption that the preordering derives from an additively separable utility function

$$\sum_s u_{is}(x_{is}). \tag{4.2}$$

This form would justify the use made of the u_{is} functions in the preceding section. It would also remind one that consumer choices weigh the advantages derived from the various subvectors x_{is} representing the consumptions in the various states. On the contrary, the stronger von Neumann–Morgenstern assumption that there exists a common function $u_i(x_{is})$ such that

$$u_{is}(x_{is}) = \pi_{is} u_i(x_{is}) \tag{4.3}$$

would be restrictive here. It would rule out the possibility that the needs of the consumers be higher in some states than in others. In any case we may keep here the general formulation (4.1) and shall not even suppose the existence of an additively separable utility function.

So, it appears that the objective probabilities π_{is} of the states (i, s) need not be known or accepted by the consumers. For the theory to be developed it is admissible that the consumers of a given type use their own subjective probabilities when weighing the advantages derived from the various x_{is}.

The net output vector y_j of a producer of type j is subject to some technical constraints, which take into account, in particular, the information that the producer will hold at each stage of his decision.

These constraints limit y_j to a set Y_j, which is the same for all producers of the same type.

The definition of Pareto optimality is now quite clear. A program P^0, in which agents of the same type behave in the same way, is said to be feasible if each x_i belongs to the corresponding X_i, if each y_j belongs to the corresponding Y_j and if equation (2.4) holds. Such a program is optimal if there is no feasible P^1 in which agents of the same type would behave in the same way and for which

$$x_i^1 \succsim x_i^0 \tag{4.4}$$

would hold for all types i, with a strict preference for at least one type.[1]

V. SURE PRICES AND EXPECTED VALUES

In order to study the price system sustaining such a Pareto optimal program we may map the economy $\mathscr{E}$ under discussion into another simpler economy $\bar{\mathscr{E}}$ in which risk disappears, all random variables being replaced by their expected values. As we shall see, this mapping E transforms a program P^0 that is optimal in $\mathscr{E}$ into a program $\bar{P}^0$ that is optimal in $\bar{\mathscr{E}}$. Moreover, the price system sustaining $\bar{P}^0$ is applicable in some sense to P^0.

To the $S_i H$-dimensional vector x_i we associate the H-dimensional vector $\bar{x}_i$ whose components are the expected demands of a consumer of type i for the various goods:

$$\bar{x}_{ih} = \sum_s \pi_{is} x_{ish}. \tag{5.1}$$

Similarly to the vectors y_j and ω_i we associate vectors giving, respectively, expected net supplies and expected endowments

$$\bar{y}_{jh} = \sum_s \pi_{js} y_{jsh}, \qquad \bar{\omega}_{ih} = \sum_s \pi_{is} \omega_{ish}. \tag{5.2}$$

This transformation maps the sets X_i and Y_j, respectively, into the sets $\bar{X}_i$ and $\bar{Y}_j$: a particular H-dimensional vector $\bar{x}_i$ belongs to $\bar{X}_i$ if there is in X_i a vector x_i such that (5.1) holds for all h.

The preordering (4.1) induces on $\bar{X}_i$ a preordering that is easily defined. Given any $\bar{x}_i$ in $\bar{X}_i$, let $E^{-1}(\bar{x}_i)$ be the set of all the vectors x_i that are mapped into $\bar{x}_i$. Let $g(\bar{x}_i)$ be a maximising vector of $E^{-1}(\bar{x}_i)$:

$$g(\bar{x}_i) \succsim x_i \quad \text{for all} \quad x_i \text{ in } E^{-1}(\bar{x}_i). \tag{5.3}$$

[1] Given the classical convexity assumptions, the optimality criterion is not made more stringent if comparison is extended to programs in which agents of the same type do not necessarily behave in the same way.

The Allocation of Individual Risks in Large Markets

(If the π_{is} are positive, if X_i is closed and bounded from below, and if the preordering is continuous, such a maximising vector exists; when there are several maximising vectors, one of them has been selected.) The function g depends on i, but for simplicity this is not made explicit. By definition the relation

$$\bar{x}_i^1 \gtrsim \bar{x}_i^2 \tag{5.4}$$

means

$$g(\bar{x}_i^1) \gtrsim g(\bar{x}_i^2). \tag{5.5}$$

It is obviously a preordering.

The economy $\bar{\mathscr{E}}$ is defined by the sets $\bar{X}_i$, $\bar{Y}_j$, the endowments $\bar{\omega}_i$, and the preference relations introduced above. A program for this economy is given by $I+J$ vectors $\bar{x}_i$ and $\bar{y}_j$. It is feasible if $\bar{x}_i \in \bar{X}_i$ and $\bar{y}_j \in \bar{Y}_j$ for all i and j, and if

$$\sum_{i=1}^{I}(\bar{x}_i - \bar{\omega}_i) = \sum_{j=1}^{J} \bar{y}_j. \tag{5.6}$$

The definition of Pareto optimality is the usual one.

If P^0 is optional in $\mathscr{E}$, then the associated program $\bar{P}^0$ is optimal in $\bar{\mathscr{E}}$. Indeed, suppose to the contrary the existence of a feasible program $\bar{P}^1$ such that

$$\bar{x}_i^1 \gtrsim \bar{x}_i^0 \quad \text{for all } i$$

with a strict preference for at least one i. Define now for $\mathscr{E}$ the program P^1 in which $x_i^1 = g(\bar{x}_i^1)$ and y_j^1 is any vector of Y_j that is mapped into $\bar{y}_j$. Since $\bar{P}^1$ fulfils equation (5.6), the program P^1 fulfils equation (2.4) and is feasible. Moreover,

$$x_i^1 = g(\bar{x}_i^1) \gtrsim g(\bar{x}_i^0) \gtrsim x_i^0 \tag{5.7}$$

for all i, with strict preference for at least one i. This contradicts the assumption that P^0 is Pareto optimal.

One may check that convexity of X_i (or Y_j) implies convexity of $\bar{X}_i$ (or $\bar{Y}_j$) and that convexity of the individual preference relations in $\mathscr{E}$ implies convexity of the corresponding relations in $\bar{\mathscr{E}}$. Hence,[1] associated to the Pareto optimal program $\bar{P}^0$, there is in $\bar{\mathscr{E}}$ a price vector p such that

(i) For all i and all $\bar{x}_i$ in $\bar{X}_i$ such that

$$p\bar{x}_i \leq p\bar{x}_i^0, \tag{5.8}$$

then $\bar{x}_i^0 \gtrsim \bar{x}_i$.

---

[1] Since we are dealing here with large economies we could dispense with convexity assumptions. But the argument would have to be more laborious; the complication does not seem to be advisable here.

(ii) For all j and all $\bar{y}_j$ in $\overline{Y}_j$,

$$p\bar{y}_j \leqslant p\bar{y}_j^0. \tag{5.9}$$

This result has direct implications for the original economy $\mathcal{E}$. In order to exhibit them, we shall use the common expected value operator and write, for instance,

$$Epx_{is} = \sum_s \pi_{is} px_{is}. \tag{5.10}$$

Conditions (i) and (ii) above imply

(i') For all i and all x_i in X_i such that

$$Epx_{is} \leqslant Epx_{is}^0, \tag{5.11}$$

then $x_i^0 \succsim x_i$.

(ii') For all j and all y_j in Y_j,

$$Epy_{js} \leqslant Epy_{js}^0.$$

Indeed, suppose there is some i and some x_i^1 in X_i fulfilling (5.11) such that $x_i^1 \succsim x_i^0$. Then, the corresponding $\bar{x}_i^1$ belongs to $\overline{X}_i$ and fulfils (5.8) so that $\bar{x}_i^0 \succsim \bar{x}_i^1$. The following chain of preferences

$$g(\bar{x}_i^0) \succsim g(\bar{x}_i^1) \succsim x_i^1 \succsim x_i^0. \tag{5.12}$$

implies that $g(\bar{x}_i^0)$, which belongs to X_i and has the same expected value as x_i^0, is preferred to x_i^0. But this contradicts the optimality of P^0, because replacing x_i^0 by $g(\bar{x}_i^0)$ is feasible (in particular (2.4) is maintained). Similarly, (ii) implies (ii'): suppose there is some y_j^1 in Y_j such that $Epy_{js}^1 > Epy_{js}^0$, then the vector $\bar{y}_j^1$ belongs to $\overline{Y}_j$ and contradicts (ii).

Rules (i') and (ii') show that, in the economy $\mathcal{E}$, the price system has the special form announced earlier in this article. In order to compute 'the value' of consumption by i we must multiply each component x_{ish} of x_i by 'the contingent price' $\pi_{is} p_h$.

Rule (ii') is precisely maximisation of expected profit. In rule (i') the budget constraint may look queer because it concerns the expected value of consumption: if markets for contingent commodities do not exist how could a consumer, who is not even supposed to know the objective probabilities, meet such a constraint? We are now going to see that, if a costless system of insurance exists, then (i') and (ii') follow from rather natural behavioural rules.

VI. THE INSURANCE SYSTEM

We now assume that *there exists a full system of insurance operating as a risk-neutral redistribution scheme*; insurance is costless in the sense that the premium is equal to the expected value of the damage

The Allocation of Individual Risks in Large Markets

covered. The assumption is a strong one, but not so much because of the latter feature. Since we are dealing with large economies, individual risks may be pooled and the insurance institutions may operate with a very small margin above expected value (this point will be taken up again later).

But assuming that one may insure against all individual risks is assuming that objective contracts can be concluded about any of them.[1] The insurance institution must be able to identify which state (i, s) occurs for consumer i as well as this consumer does it himself. Such a condition rules out in practice any distinction between states based on purely subjective changes about wants; I cannot insure myself against the risk of being greedy tomorrow because the occurrence of this risk cannot be observed by anyone but me.

The assumed existence of such a 'perfect' insurance system does not claim to be realistic. It is introduced here so that we can clearly exhibit conditions for an efficient allocation of individual risks. As is often the case with general theories, some hypotheses relate to an ideal situation that is in fact not even approximated, but towards which it might be interesting to move.

A system of insurance, as is assumed here, implies that each individual consumer i can subscribe contracts giving him any set of net transfers v_{is} (for $s = 1, 2, ..., S_i$) that he may wish, under just one constraint,

$$\sum_s \pi_{is} v_{is} = 0, \qquad (6.1)$$

the expected value of the transfer must be zero. Similarly each individual producer can obtain any set of net transfers w_{js} that he may wish under the condition

$$\sum_s \pi_{js} w_{js} = 0. \qquad (6.2)$$

The rates prevailing for insurance premiums are here assumed to be determined from objective probabilities. The market conditions then reveal these probabilities to the individual agents, but agents do not need to be aware of it.

Let us now consider what the behaviour of consumer i will be if he is to receive an exogenous 'income' R_{is} in each state (i, s). (This income may be the value $p\omega_{is}$ of his endowment, to which may possibly be added a share of the profits of some firms.) He will have to choose simultaneously a consumption vector x_i and a vector v_i of net transfers (with the S_i components v_{is}). He will then remember that, in each state (i, s), the value of his consumption x_{is} must not

---
[1] This point was made previously by R. Radner.

exceed his resources $R_{is}+v_{is}$, i.e. he will consider the S_i budget requirements

$$px_{is} \leq R_{is}+v_{is}. \qquad (6.3)$$

But, the vector v_i being subject to no other constraint than (6.1), he may adopt the following two-stage procedure: choose first the best vector x_i under the single condition

$$p\bar{x}_i \leq \bar{R}_i; \qquad (6.4)$$

determine thereafter

$$v_{is}=p(x_{is}-\bar{x}_i)-(R_{is}-\bar{R}_i). \qquad (6.5)$$

The transfers computed in this way fulfil condition (6.1). Moreover, (6.4) and (6.5) imply (6.3). Conversely, if (6.1) and (6.3) are satisfied, the inequality (6.4) holds. In other words the constraints imposed on x_i by (6.3) and (6.1) are identical to (6.4).

The existence of the insurance system makes it possible to reduce the budget requirements to just one constraint on expected values, even though markets for contingent commodities do not exist. Rule (i') of the preceding section is indeed equivalent to

(i'') For any i, any vectors v_i^0 and v_i both satisfying (6.1) and any x_i in X_i such that

$$px_{is}+v_{is} \leq px_{is}^0+v_{is}^0, \qquad s=1, 2, ..., S_i; \qquad (6.6)$$

then $x_i^0 \gtrsim x_i$.

Similarly maximisation of expected profits is now a natural rule for producers. Indeed, the profits py_{js} earned in the various states (j, s) may be supplemented by transfers w_{js}, subject only to condition (6.2). The net gains are then

$$z_{js}=py_{js}+w_{js}. \qquad (6.7)$$

No matter what the behaviour of producer j towards risk may be, as long as higher gains are preferred to lower ones, his decision will result in a vector y_j maximising Epy_{js}. Conversely, if there are several such vectors, they make possible precisely the same gains. In order to understand these facts, suppose the producer selects vectors y_j^* and w_j^* that do not result in maximisation of Epy_{js}. Let y_j^1 be such that

$$p\bar{y}_j^1 > p\bar{y}_j^*. \qquad (6.8)$$

Then determine

$$w_{js}^1=w_{js}^*+p(y_{js}^*-\bar{y}_j^*)-p(y_{js}^1-\bar{y}_j^1). \qquad (6.9)$$

These transfers satisfy condition (6.2). Moreover,

$$z_{js}^1=py_{js}^1+w_{js}^1=z_{js}^*+p\bar{y}_j^1-p\bar{y}_j^*$$

The Allocation of Individual Risks in Large Markets

and (6.8) implies $z_{js}^1 > z_{js}^*$ for all s, which is a contradiction to the assumption that the producer prefers higher gains to lower ones. Now, if y_j^* and y_j^1 are both maximising $p\bar{y}_j$, then the second vector leads to precisely the same gains as the first one when it is associated with transfers defined by (6.9). Any vector y_j^0 maximising Epy_{js} is therefore consistent, under the assumed market and insurance system, with any kind of attitude towards risk.

Finally, in the absence of transaction costs, the budget of the insurance system will be approximately balanced if the economy is large. This is again a result of the law of large numbers. We shall not look here for a general proof, but limit ourselves to check that the result holds for a program P^0 in which agents of the same type take precisely the same insurance contracts: a given vector v_i^0 of net insurance transfers applies to each one of the N consumers of type i. If m_{is} of them find themselves in state (i, s) the aggregate net transfer to consumers of type i will be

$$\sum_s m_{is} v_{is}^0,$$

and the average per capita will be

$$\sum_s \frac{m_{is}}{N} v_{is}^0. \tag{6.10}$$

By assumption, m_{is}/N tends to π_{is} when N increases indefinitely. In view of equality (6.1), the average (6.10) tends to zero. We may then say that in a finite but large economy the aggregate net insurance transfer per capita will be negligibly small.

The results we have just reached support claims that have long been made on the useful role of insurance against individual risks. They show that, for an efficient allocation, such insurance should be introduced quite systematically – at least if their administrative costs can be neglected. They also seem to provide the appropriate framework for a justification of the statement according to which maximisation of expected net value is the correct criterion for decentralised economic calculations.

APPENDIX
LARGE NUMBERS WITH DEPENDENT NEIGHBOURS

Each one of N individuals ($n = 1, 2, ..., N$) will find himself in one of S possible states ($s = 1, 2, ..., S$) (for simplicity reference to the type of agents concerned is omitted in this appendix). The probability of state s is π_s, but the occurrence of states for the various individuals does not define independent events. The two states that obtain, respectively, for individuals n and n' are stochastically dependent although the dependence vanishes as $n - n'$ increases in absolute value.

In order to state precisely the last property let us consider the random variable e_{ns} that takes value 1 when s obtains for n and value zero otherwise:

$$Ee_{ns} = E(e_{ns})^2 = \pi_s. \tag{A.1}$$

(There are NS such random variables.) The 'mixing condition' we are going to assume states the existence of some positive function Ψ, defined on the set of positive and negative integers, decreasing to zero when its argument tends to infinity, and such that

$$| E(e_{ns}e_{n's}) - \pi_s^2 | \leq \Psi(n' - n). \tag{A.2}$$

The discrepancy between $E(e_{ns}e_{n's})$ and the value that it would have under independence tends to zero as $|n' - n|$ increases indefinitely.

Under this condition we may prove that m_s/N tends in the mean square to π_s, the random variable m_s being the number of individuals who find themselves in state s. Indeed, we may write

$$m_s = \sum_{n=1}^{N} e_{ns}. \tag{A.3}$$

From (A.1) it follows that m_s/N has expected value π_s. Its variance is

$$V_s = \frac{1}{N^2} \sum_{n,n'=1}^{N} [E(e_{ns}e_{n's}) - \pi_s^2]. \tag{A.4}$$

Condition (A.2) implies

$$V_s \leq \frac{1}{N^2} \sum_{n,n'=1}^{N} \Psi(n' - n). \tag{A.5}$$

This inequality proves that V_s tends to zero and m_s/N to π_s as N increases indefinitely. Indeed,

$$\frac{1}{N^2} \sum_{n,n'=1}^{N} \Psi(n' - n) < \frac{1}{N} \sum_{r=-N}^{N} \Psi(r) \tag{A.6}$$

(as is easily seen by changing the variable n' to $n + r$) and, given any $\epsilon > 0$, the right-hand member of (A.6) is made smaller than ϵ by choosing R and N such that

$$\Psi(r) \leq \frac{\epsilon}{4} \quad \text{for} \quad |r| \geq R \geq 1,$$

and
$$N \geqslant \frac{4R\Psi^*}{\epsilon},$$

Ψ^* being the maximum of $\Psi(r)$:

$$\sum_{r=-N}^{N} \Psi(r) \leqslant \sum_{r=-R+1}^{R-1} \Psi(r) + 2(N-R+1)\frac{\epsilon}{4}$$

$$\leqslant (2R-1)\Psi^* + (N-R+1)\frac{\epsilon}{2}$$

$$< \frac{\epsilon N}{2} + \frac{\epsilon N}{2} - (R-1)\frac{\epsilon}{2} \leqslant \epsilon N.$$

REFERENCES

[1] K. J. Arrow, 'Le rôle des valeurs boursières pour la répartition la meilleure des risques', in *Econométrie*, Colloques Internationaux du Centre National de la Recherche Scientifique (Paris, 1953). English translation in *Review of Economic Studies*, vol. XXXI (1964), pp. 91–6.
[2] K. J. Arrow and R. C. Lind, 'Uncertainty and the Evaluation of Public Investment Decision', *American Economic Review*, vol. LX (1970), pp. 364–78.
[3] E. Baudier, 'L'introduction du temps dans la théorie de l'équilibre général', *Cahiers Economiques*, (1954), pp. 9–16.
[4] G. Debreu, *Theory of Value* (New York: John Wiley, 1959).
[5] W. Hildenbrand, 'Random Preferences and General Economic Equilibrium', *Journal of Economic Theory*, vol. III (1971), pp. 414–29.
[6] J. Hirshleifer, 'Investment Decision under Uncertainty: Applications of the State-Preference Approach', *Quarterly Journal of Economics*, vol. LXXX (1966), pp. 252–77.
[7] F. Knight, *Risk, Uncertainty and Profit* (Boston: Houghton Mifflin), 1921.

Part 4

Optimum Investment with Asset Markets

9 Investment Under Private Ownership: Optimality, Equilibrium and Stability

Jacques H. Drèze[1]
CORE, LOUVAIN

I. INTRODUCTION

(1) *General Equilibrium Under Uncertainty*
The theory of equilibrium and efficiency of resource allocation, initially developed for a world of certainty, has been reinterpreted for a world of uncertainty, thanks to a suggestion made by Arrow [1] and pursued further by Debreu [7].[2]

An economy is defined by (i) a set of commodities, with the total resources (quantities of these commodities) initially available; (ii) a set of consumers, with their consumption sets and preferences; (iii) a set of producers, with their production sets. The resources, consumption sets and production sets define the physical environment. In a world of certainty, the environment is given. In a world of uncertainty, the environment depends upon uncertain events. Let these be determined by 'the choice that nature makes among a finite number of alternatives' ([7], p. 98).

The reinterpretation consists in defining a commodity not only by its physical properties (including the time and place at which it is available) but also by an event *conditional* upon which it is available. An allocation then specifies the consumption of every consumer and the production of every producer, *conditional* on every event. Uncertainty means that these consumptions and productions may vary with the event that obtains.

Consumer preferences are defined over commodity vectors, that is, over plans specifying fully the consumption associated with every event. These preferences are introduced as a primitive concept. Underlying these preferences among consumption plans, there may exist subjective judgements about the likelihood of the various

---

[1] I am grateful to Mordecai Avriel, Freddy Delbaen, Louis Gevers, Roger Guesnerie and Dieter Sondermann for helpful comments and discussions. Earlier work on this subject with Dominique de la Vallée Poussin led to [11]. Support of the Fonds de la Recherche Fondamentale Collective, Brussels, under contract No. 611 is gratefully acknowledged.

[2] See also Baudier [5] and Borch [6].

events and subjective attitudes towards risk, as well as conditional preferences among alternative consumptions given some event.

Production sets reflect the 'games against nature' to which the economy has access.

The interpretation of a price system is facilitated if one normalises prices by choosing as a unit the price of a numeraire commodity, available at time 0 (i.e. unconditionally). The price of a given commodity, defined conditionally on an event A, may then be interpreted as an insurance premium: the premium giving title to one unit of that commodity if, and only if, event A obtains. Thus a price system defines a full set of insurance premiums, one for each physical commodity conditionally on each event. In a market context, a price system is predicated upon the organisation of a full set of insurance markets.

With commodities and preferences so defined, the theory developed for a world of certainty is formally applicable to a world of uncertainty, without modification. In particular, the concepts of price equilibrium (or 'equilibrium relative to a price system') and Pareto optimum, the existence and equivalence theorems, carry over.

(2) *Private Ownership*

A private ownership economy is completely described if, in addition to the consumption sets, preferences and production sets, one specifies, for each consumer, his resources and his shares of all firms (producers). Given a price system, the net value of a firm's production plan defines its profits; for each consumer the value of his initial resources plus his shares in the profits of all firms defines his budget constraint. Markets for shares can be substituted, to some extent, for insurance markets. Since the value of a firm is automatically equal to the market value of its production plan, one could replace the market for one of the firm's outputs by a market for shares of the firm. The price of that output would then be inferred from the price of the firm, instead of proceeding in the other direction. This operation could be repeated as many times as there are firms with linearly independent production plans. Similar remarks apply to the substitution of futures markets (and asset markets) for insurance markets.

When there exists a mixture of insurance markets, of futures markets, and of markets for shares and other assets, the question naturally arises whether together the prices on these markets provide the same information as the prices on a full set of insurance markets. This question is relevant for existing economies, which do indeed operate through such a mixture of markets.[1]

[1] It is noteworthy that new financial assets are regularly created (e.g. shares in investment trusts; real estate certificates . . .).

(3) Unrealistic Implications of Competitive Equilibria

A competitive equilibrium for a private ownership economy is defined by a price system and an allocation such that (i) the profits of each firm are maximised over its production set; (ii) the consumption of each consumer is best, from the viewpoint of his preferences, over his budget set.

Such an equilibrium has two important properties. (i) The firms operate exactly in the same way as in a world of certainty. The price system provides all the information needed to guide their production and investment decisions. Profit maximisation amounts to choosing the conditional production plan with the highest insurance value, and collecting that insurance value at once. The firms need not make any probability judgements or adopt any attitude towards risk. Because the firms automatically maximise the wealth of their stockholders, no problem of control arises. (ii) Since the insurance markets on all events are cleared simultaneously at the outset, the occurrence of any event simply calls for realisation of the conditional plans, and no *new* adjustments are required.

These two properties may be contrasted with observed features of existing economies. (i) Firms do engage continuously in activities designed to improve their assessments of the probabilities of future events. Sometimes, important debates take place, regarding the choice of investment policies, when these investments are surrounded by considerable uncertainty.[1] The control problems are obvious in small firms, especially family owned firms. In the case of large firms, such problems sometimes come out in the open, through proxy fights or takeover bids that point unmistakably to interactions between ownership and control. (ii) The need to reconsider investment decisions in the light of new information is particularly obvious in times of change.[2] Revisions in international parities and monetary arrangements, new trade agreements, new public programs or forms of concern about the environment, temporary investment credits, are some key elements to which investment policies (and asset

---

[1] A particularly obvious example was provided in the late 1950s by the Belgian Steel Industry, which was then planning plant modernisation and capacity expansion. Whereas several major firms pooled their resources to build a large modern plant on the seashore, another firm planned instead to extend the capacity of its inland facilities. That plan was extensively debated between stockholders, management and financial institutions. A major argument in favour of the plan was the much shorter delay required for its realisation, as opposed to the new seashore complex. The plan was clearly perceived as a gamble on the rate of capacity utilisation in the 1960s, and opposing views were expressed about both the probabilities and the attitude towards risk that should guide the firm's policy. The plan was approved, and the firm faced severe financial difficulties in the late 1960s. . . .

[2] The second half of 1971 provides a good example.

prices) must adjust. Clearly, the process does not reduce to realisation of predetermined conditional plans.

(4) *Outline of the Paper*

Considering these shortcomings of the price information and insurance opportunities available in existing private ownership economies, it seems worthwhile to develop models which aim at capturing the essential operating features of these economies. Models of private ownership economies, with asset markets (in particular, with a stock market) but with restricted (in the limit, with no) insurance markets are natural candidates. The simplest models one can build involve a single commodity and two dates, with information about the true state of nature accruing at the later of these dates.

Among previous investigations of such models, the most relevant for my purposes here are those by Diamond [9] and Stiglitz [23]. Diamond's paper concentrates on the special case where the firms choose only a scale of operation, and produce (conditional) outputs in exogenously given proportions. Some sections of Stiglitz's paper recognise output substitution, but describe them in terms of two parameters only (mean and variance of output). The results presented below are fully consistent with those of Diamond and Stiglitz but they are more general and explicitly linked to the underlying general equilibrium model.

The stability analysis presented in the second part of this paper and dealing with the issue raised under (ii) in (3) seems new. Because adjustment processes take place simultaneously at the level of markets for *assets* held by consumers, and at the level of investment decisions within firms, the standard literature on the dynamic stability of adjustment processes for commodity markets is not directly relevant, and a new theory is needed.

The plan of the paper is as follows. An economy with a stock market and no insurance markets is described in section II, where the notation and assumptions are also introduced. Section III is devoted to static analysis. An equilibrium concept, reflecting the special features of the economy, is introduced; equilibria are characterised and related to Pareto optima. Section IV gives three examples of equilibria that are not Pareto optimal, and an example of a Pareto optimum that is technologically inefficient. Section V is devoted to stability analysis, and contains a quite general convergence theorem. Applications of this theorem are discussed in section VI. An application of the theory presented here to semi-public goods and some possible extensions are collected in a concluding section. Reference should also be made to a companion paper [10], where some of these issues are approached with the tools of calculus, under differentiability assumptions. The results in the present paper are more general, but the two presentations are complementary.

II. THE MODEL

(1) Consumers

The economy considered in this paper consists of I consumers, indexed $i = 1 \ldots I$, and J firms, indexed $j = 1 \ldots J$. There is a single physical commodity, but there are two periods of time, labelled 0 and 1 respectively. The true state of the world is unknown in period 0, but will be known in period 1. There are S mutually exclusive states, indexed $s = 1 \ldots S$.

A *consumption plan* for consumer i is a non-negative vector in R^{S+1}: $x^i = (x_0^i, x_1^i \ldots x_S^i)$; x_0^i denotes the consumption of i in period 0, x_s^i his consumption in period 1 if state s obtains. The consumption set of i is the non-negative orthant of the commodity space, R_+^{S+1}.

As a minimal survival requirement, it is assumed that future consumption is useless unless there is some current consumption (a stronger requirement could easily be introduced). Otherwise, R_+^{S+1} is assumed to be completely ordered by a preordering $\succsim_i$, which is continuous, strictly convex and monotone. Monotonicity is a natural assumption, when there is a single physical commodity (but several periods and/or states). Convexity is needed for most results below, but strict convexity is used only once.[1]

Let $x_s^i = x_1^i$, $s = 1 \ldots S$; strict convexity of preferences in the (x_0^i, x_1^i) plane is then equivalent to a 'diminishing marginal rate of time preference'. Let x_0^i be fixed; strict convexity of preferences in the $(x_1^i \ldots x_S^i)$ space is then basically equivalent to risk aversion (for a detailed discussion of this point, see [16], section 5.2).

Assumption 1. $\succsim_i$ is representable by the continuous, non-decreasing function $U^i(x^i)$; $\bar{x}_0^i = 0$ implies $U^i(x^i) \geq U^i(\bar{x}^i)$ for all $x^i \epsilon R_+^{S+1}$; $\bar{x}_0^i > 0$ implies that U^i is strictly quasi-concave at $\bar{x}^i$.

For some of the results in section III and applications in section VI, the stronger assumption of differentiability is needed.

Assumption 1 bis. $\succsim_i$ is representable by the non-decreasing, twice continuously differentiable function $U^i(x^i)$; $\dfrac{\partial U^i}{\partial x_0^i} > 0$; when $\bar{x}_0^i = 0$, $\dfrac{\partial U^i}{\partial x_s^i} = 0 \ \forall \ s$ at $\bar{x}$; when $x_0^i > 0$, U^i is strictly quasi-concave at $\bar{x}^i$.

---

[1] In step 2 of the proof of the convergence theorem 5.3. The role of strict convexity assumptions is not as clearly known in stability analysis as in the static theory, and it may well be that the strict assumption is not necessary.

Remarks (1).
(i) An example of utility function satisfying assumptions 1 and 1 *bis* is:
$$U(x) = x_0^{\alpha_0} \prod_{s=1}^{S} (x_s + c_s)^{\alpha_s}, \alpha_s > 0, s = 0, 1 \ldots S, \alpha_0 < 1, c_s > 0, s = 1 \ldots S.$$
(ii) When U^i is strictly quasi-concave, it is also strictly increasing.

(2) *Producers*
A production plan for firm j is a non-negative vector in R^{S+1}: $b^j = (a^j, b_1^j \ldots b_S^j)$, belonging to a production set Y^j; a^j denotes the input of firm j in period 0, b_s^j its output in period 1 if state s obtains; notice that inputs are treated as non-negative quantities. The following is assumed about Y^j:

Assumption 2. Y^j is closed and convex; $0 \in Y^j$; $\forall b^j \in Y^j$, $b_s^j > 0$ for some s implies $a^j > 0$. $\forall c \in R$, the set $\{b^j | b^j \in Y^j, a^j \le c\}$ is compact.

For some applications in section VI, a stronger assumption is needed, namely:

Assumption 2 bis. Y^j is defined by $f^j(b^j) \le 0$, $b^j \ge 0$, where f^j is a twice continuously differentiable convex function, with $\frac{\partial f_j}{\partial a_j} < 0$, $\frac{\partial f_j}{\partial b_s^j} > 0$, and $f(0) = 0$.

A few comments are in order about the interpretation of Y^j. Let there be two states, s and t, and consider a firm which has access to two basic activities, and to free disposal. With one unit of input, the first activity yields $1\frac{1}{2}$ units of output in state s and $\frac{1}{2}$ in state t, whereas the second yields 1 unit of output in both states. Let these two activities be subject to constant returns to scale. The production possibilities in the (b_s^j, b_t^j) plane, when $a^j = 1$, are then described by figure 1, where point a corresponds to the first activity and point b corresponds to the second.[1]

As a further illustration, let the first activity yield 1 unit of b_s^j and 0 unit of b_t^j, the second activity yield 0 unit of b_s^j and 1 unit of b_t^j, when $a^j = 1$. Let, further, the input requirement be equal to the square of the output in the relevant state, for both activities. The production possibilities corresponding to $a^j = 1$ are then depicted in Fig. 9.2. The production set of Fig. 9.2 satisfies assumption 2 *bis*, and serves to illustrate how a continuous marginal rate of substitution among outputs may result from diminishing returns to a finite set of basic activities with fixed output proportions.

[1] The assumption of 'multiplicative uncertainty', on which the analysis of Diamond [9] rests, would require the firm to have access to a single activity. In principle, 'multiplicative uncertainty' allows for the ratio b_s^j/b_t^j to vary with a^j; but these variations are constrained by the requirement that Y^j is convex. Under constant returns to scale, any variation is ruled out by convexity.

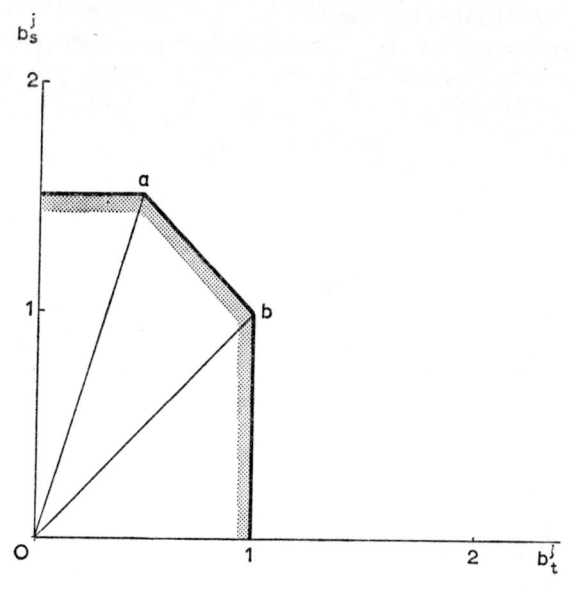

FIG. 9.1

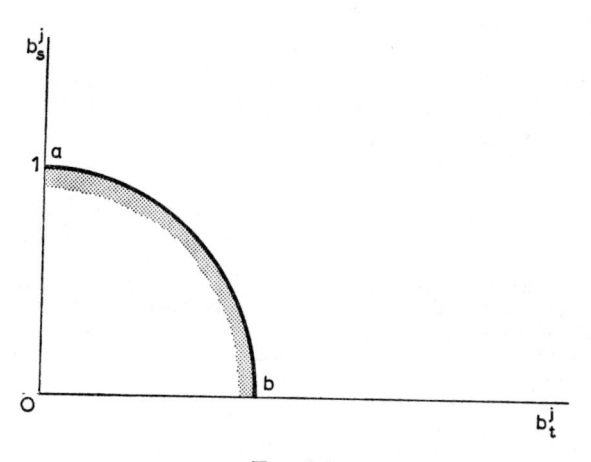

FIG. 9.2

(3) *Stock Ownership Programs*

Let the *endowment* of the economy consist of an amount W_0 of initial resources.[1] A *feasible program* for the economy is then an $(I+J)$-tuple of vectors in R_+^{S+1}, $(x, b) = (x^1 \ldots x^I, b^1 \ldots b^J)$ with:

$$\sum_i x_0^i + \sum_j a^j \leq W_0 \tag{2.1}$$

$$\sum_i x_s^i - \sum_j b_s^j \leq 0 \qquad s = 1 \ldots S \tag{2.2}$$

$$b^j \in Y^j \qquad j = 1 \ldots J. \tag{2.3}$$

A feasible program is attainable through joint stock ownership of the firms – in short, it is a *stock ownership program*[2] – if, and only if, there exists a matrix $\Theta = [\theta_{ij}]$, $\theta_{ij} \geq 0$,[3] $\sum_i \theta_{ij} \leq 1$, such that

$$x_s^i - \sum_j \theta_{ij} b_s^j \leq 0 \qquad i = 1 \ldots I, \quad s = 1 \ldots S. \tag{2.4}$$

Condition (2.4) states that the consumption vector x^i can be attained through ownership of the shares θ_{ij}, $j = 1 \ldots J$, of all firms, where such ownership gives right to the same fraction θ_{ij} of firm j's output in every state, $j = 1 \ldots J$.

A stock ownership program will be denoted (x, b, Θ). As announced in the introduction, this paper deals exclusively with stock ownership programs.

By definition, every stock ownership program is feasible – but not all feasible programs can be attained through stock ownership. Thus, when $J = 1$ (there is a single firm), conditions (2.4) impose that consumer i should receive the same fraction of society's output in every state – whereas (2.2) allows for these fractions to vary with the states, so long as their sum over all consumers does not exceed unity. In order for an arbitrary (feasible) program to be attainable through stock ownership, it is necessary that the I vectors of future consumption $(x_1^i \ldots x_S^i)$, $i = 1 \ldots I$, be contained in the (sub)space spanned by the J output vectors $(b_1^j \ldots b_S^j)$, $j = 1 \ldots J$.[4]

---

[1] Because no exchanges of future resources will be allowed, the endowment for period 1 may remain implicit in the consumer preferences and production sets of the firms.

[2] In [10] I have used instead the term 'private ownership program'; it was aptly pointed out to me that confusion with the standard concept of 'private ownership economy' should be avoided.

[3] $\theta_{ij} \geq 0$ rules out short-holdings of securities; that assumption seems more realistic, except in the very short run; dropping the assumption would not affect the results in this paper, so long as short-holdings are bounded.

[4] Taking the non-negativity constraints $\Theta \geq 0$ into account, the set of feasible stock ownership programs is a convex polyhedron in the space spanned by the b^j's.

Investment Under Private Ownership

An important implication of conditions (2.4) is the following:

Lemma 2.3. Under assumption 2, the set of feasible programs is convex, but the set of stock ownership programs is not always convex.

Proof: The first proposition is well known and its proof is immediate. To prove the second proposition, let $\bar{b}_s{}^j > b_s{}^j > 0$ and $\bar{b}_s{}^k = b_s{}^k = 0$, $k \neq j$; let furthermore $\bar{\theta}_{ij} > \theta_{ij} > 0$ and $\bar{x}_s{}^i - \bar{\theta}_{ij}\bar{b}_s{}^j = 0$, $x_s{}^i - \theta_{ij}b_s{}^j = 0$. Then, $\forall\, \lambda \epsilon (0, 1)$:

$$\lambda \bar{x}_s{}^i + (1-\lambda) x_s{}^i - (\lambda \bar{\theta}_{ij} + (1-\lambda)\theta_{ij})(\lambda \bar{b}_s{}^j + (1-\lambda)b_s{}^j) =$$

$$\lambda \bar{\theta}_{ij}\bar{b}_s{}^j + (1-\lambda)\theta_{ij}b_s{}^j - (\lambda \bar{\theta}_{ij} + (1-\lambda)\theta_{ij})(\lambda \bar{b}_s{}^j + (1-\lambda)b_s{}^j) =$$

$$\lambda(1-\lambda)(\bar{\theta}_{ij}\bar{b}_s{}^j + \theta_{ij}b_s{}^j - \bar{\theta}_{ij}b_s{}^j - \theta_{ij}\bar{b}_s{}^j) = \lambda(1-\lambda)(\bar{\theta}_{ij} - \theta_{ij})(\bar{b}_s{}^j - b_s{}^j) > 0$$
$$Q.E.D.$$

The non-convexities introduced by conditions (2.4) may be illustrated graphically, with the help of Figs. 9.3 and 9.4. For the case considered in the proof of the lemma, (2.4) reduces to $x_s{}^i - \theta_{ij}b_s{}^j \leq 0$, and we may drop all subscripts.

Let x be fixed; the feasible region in (b, θ) space is convex, being defined by a rectangular hyperbola (see Fig. 9.3). Now, let x vary, and look at the intersection of the feasible region in (x, b, θ) space with the plane $\theta = b$ (the plane containing the x axis and the dotted line in Fig. 9.3). That intersection is the complement of the convex set defined by $x \geq \theta^2 = b^2$ (see Fig. 9.4). Putting Figs. 9.3 and 9.4

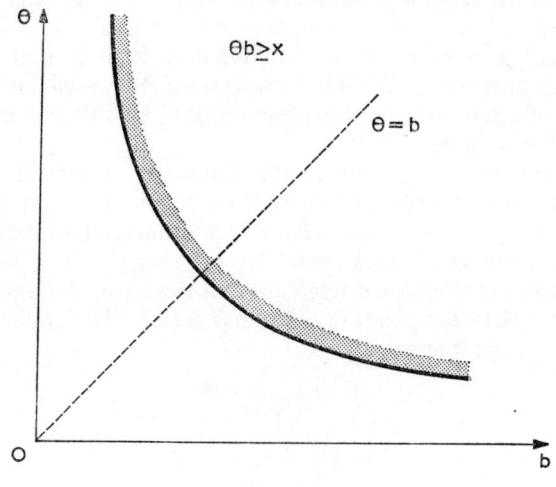

Fig. 9.3

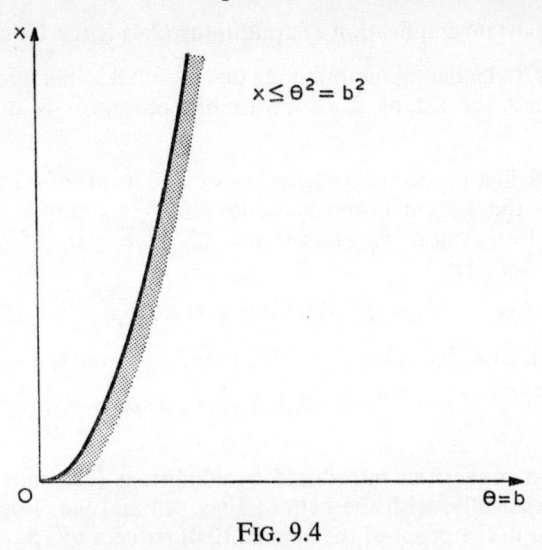

[Figure 9.4: graph showing $x \leq \theta^2 = b^2$, with axes x and $\theta = b$.]

FIG. 9.4

together, one may visualise the feasible region in (x, b, θ) space as delineated by a sort of 'plough' with hyperbolic (convex) sections for fixed x and quadratic (concave) sections for fixed ratio of θ to b.

(4) *Constrained Pareto Optima*

A feasible program (x, b) is a *Pareto optimum* if, and only if, there exists no other feasible program $(\bar{x}, \bar{b})$ with $\bar{x}^i \gtrsim_i x^i \; \forall \; i$ and $\bar{x}^h \succ_h x^h$ for some h.

We shall now state as an additional definition[1] that a stock ownership program (x, b, Θ) is a *constrained Pareto optimum* if there exists no other stock ownership program $(\bar{x}, \bar{b}, \bar{\Theta})$ with $\bar{x}^i \gtrsim_i x^i \; \forall \; i$ and $\bar{x}^h \succ_h x^h$ for some h.

An equivalent definition is the following: define the *Pareto preordering* over I-tuples of consumption plans x by: $x \gtrsim \bar{x}$ whenever $x^i \gtrsim_i \bar{x}^i \; \forall \; i$. Then, a constrained Pareto optimum is a maximal element for $\gtrsim$ over the set of stock ownership programs.

We recall for convenient reference that the set of stock ownership programs is the set of points (x, b, Θ) in $(I+J)(S+1) + IJ$ dimensional Euclidian space that satisfy:

$$\sum_i x_0^i + \sum_j a^j \leq W_0 \qquad (2.1)$$

$$b^j \epsilon Y^j \qquad j = 1 \ldots J \qquad (2.3)$$

[1] A similar definition is used by Diamond [9].

$$x_s^i - \sum_j \theta_{ij} b_s^j \le 0 \qquad i=1 \ldots I,\ s=1 \ldots S \qquad (2.4)$$

$$\sum_i \theta_{ij} \le 1 \qquad j=1 \ldots J \qquad (2.5)$$

$$x, b, \Theta \ge 0. \qquad (2.6)$$

For economy of notation, let $z=(x, b, \Theta)$ denote a stock ownership program and $Z \subset R_+^{(I+J)(S+1)+IJ}$ denote the set of such programs, i.e. the set of z's satisfying (2.1) and (2.3)–(2.6).

III. STOCKHOLDERS EQUILIBRIA AND CONSTRAINED PARETO OPTIMA

(1) Outline of the Section

The fact that the set Z of stock ownership programs is, in general, not convex, places severe restrictions on the decentralisation properties of the economy. Actually, it is not immediately clear how a suitable concept of equilibrium should be defined.

In [10] I have used the necessary optimality theorem for non-linear programming with differentiability (see, e.g., theorem 7.3.7 in [20]) to deduce from assumptions 1 *bis* and 2 *bis* necessary conditions for a constrained Pareto optimum. As an alternative, one which does not use differentiability, I will consider here successively the set of reallocations that can be attained through the decisions of a single firm (III.2), then through exchanges of shares among individuals (III.3). In each case, a natural equilibrium concept will be borrowed from accepted theory. These concepts will then be combined to define a 'stockholders equilibrium'. Properties of such equilibria, and their relationship to constrained Pareto optima, will be studied (III.4).

The approach followed in this section also serves as a natural introduction to the stability analysis of sections V and VI.

(2) Pseudo Equilibria for the Firms

Given a stock ownership program $\bar{z}=(\bar{x}, \bar{b}, \bar{\Theta})$, firm j can generate alternative programs by choosing in Y^j some alternative production plan $b^j \ne \bar{b}^j$. Whenever $a^j \ne \bar{a}^j$, the adjustment of the input level must somehow be accompanied by adjustments in the current consumptions of the consumers, if the production plans of the other firms remain fixed.

Denoting by $F^j(\bar{z})$ the set of stock ownership programs attainable from a given starting point $\bar{z}$, through decisions of firm j and adjustments in current consumptions (the production plans of the other firms and the ownership matrix being given), we have:

$$F^j(\bar{z}) = \{z | z \epsilon Z, b^k = \bar{b}^k \not\forall k \neq j, \Theta = \bar{\Theta}\} \quad (3.1)$$
$$= \{z | \sum_i x_0^i + a^j \leq W_0 - \sum_{k \neq j} \bar{a}^k$$
$$x_s^i - \bar{\theta}_{ij} b_s^j \leq \sum_{k \neq j} \bar{\theta}_{ik} \bar{b}_s^k, \quad i = 1 \ldots I,$$
$$s = 1 \ldots S, \quad b^j \epsilon Y^j, x \geq 0\}.$$

The preferences of the consumers among such programs are representable by the continuous, quasi-concave,[1] monotonic functions

$$V^i(x_0^i, b_1^j \ldots b_S^j | \bar{z}) =_{def} U^i(x_0^i, \sum_{k \neq j} \bar{\theta}_{ik} \bar{b}_1^k + \bar{\theta}_{ij} b_1^j \ldots \sum_{k \neq j} \bar{\theta}_{ik} \bar{b}_S^k$$
$$+ \bar{\theta}_{ij} b_S^j), \quad i = 1 \ldots I. \quad (3.2)$$

$F^j(\bar{z})$ is also the set of feasible allocations for an economy, say $\mathscr{E}^j(\bar{z})$, with S public goods $(b_1^j \ldots b_S^j)$ and a single private good (x_0), where the preferences of the I consumers are defined by $(V^1 \ldots V^I)$ and the constraints on production and distribution reduce to:

$$\sum_i x_0^i + a^j \leq W_0 - \sum_{k \neq j} \bar{a}^k \quad (3.3)$$
$$b^j \epsilon Y^j \quad (3.4)$$
$$x_0^i \geq 0, \quad i = 1 \ldots I. \quad (3.5)$$

All the results obtained for such an economy (see e.g. [11], [13], [18], [21]) are thus valid in our context as well. In particular, a *pseudo equilibrium* for such an economy is defined by an allocation $\hat{z} \epsilon F^j(\bar{z})$, and a set of I vectors $\phi^i \epsilon R_+^{S+1}$, $\phi_0^i = 1$, such that:

(1) $V^i(x_0^i, b_1^j \ldots b_S^j) > V^i(\hat{x}_0^i, \hat{b}_s^j \ldots \hat{b}_S^j)$ implies
$$x_0^i + \sum_s \phi_s^i b_s^j > \hat{x}_0^i + \sum_s \phi_s^i \hat{b}_s^j, \quad i = 1 \ldots I.$$
(2) $\hat{b}^j$ maximises $\sum_s b_s^j (\sum_i \phi_s^i) - a^j$ on Y^j.

The set of Pareto optima for $\mathscr{E}^j(\bar{z})$, to be denoted $F_{P^j}(\bar{z})$, is defined as usual by:

$$F_{P^j}(\bar{z}) = \{z | z \epsilon F^j(\bar{z}), \not\exists \hat{z} \epsilon F^j(\bar{z}), \hat{x}^i \gtrsim_i x^i \not\forall i, \hat{x}^h \gtrsim_h x^h \text{ for some } h\}. \quad (3.6)$$

The following properties are well known.[2]

Proposition 3.2. Under assumptions 1 and 2, for all $\bar{z} \epsilon Z$ with $\sum_i \bar{x}_0^i > 0$, $\mathscr{E}^j(\bar{z})$ is such that:

[1] When $\bar{\theta}_{ij} = 0$, V^i is still well-defined and quasi-concave, but not strictly so.
[2] See the excellent survey paper by Milleron [21]. Milleron does not use the term 'pseudo equilibrium', introduced by Malinvaud, and refers instead to a 'Lindahl equilibrium'.

Investment Under Private Ownership

(i) there exists a pseudo equilibrium;
(ii) every pseudo equilibrium is a Pareto optimum;
(iii) with every Pareto optimum $z \epsilon F_P{}^j(\bar{z})$, one can associate a set of I vectors $\phi^i \epsilon R_+{}^{S+1}$, $\phi_0{}^i = 1$, such that $\{z, \phi^i\}$ is a pseudo equilibrium.

The transposition of these results to our context is immediate. Using the monotonicity of $\succsim_i$, we may impose the equality conditions

$$x_s{}^i - \bar{\theta}_{ij} b_s{}^j = \sum_{k \neq j} \bar{\theta}_{ik} \bar{b}_s{}^k, \quad i = 1 \ldots I, s = 1 \ldots S. \tag{3.7}$$

Define then the vectors $\Pi^i \epsilon R_+{}^{S+1}$ by: $\Pi_0{}^i = 1$, $\phi_s{}^i = \Pi_s{}^i \bar{\theta}_{ij}$. It follows that

$$x_0{}^i + \sum_s \phi_s{}^i b_s{}^j > \hat{x}_0{}^i + \sum_s \phi_s{}^i \hat{b}_s{}^j \Leftrightarrow x_0{}^i + \sum_s \Pi_s{}^i \bar{\theta}_{ij} b_s{}^j > \hat{x}_0{}^i + \sum_s \Pi_s{}^i \bar{\theta}_{ij} \hat{b}_s{}^j$$

$$\Leftrightarrow \Pi^i x^i > \Pi^i \hat{x}^i. \tag{3.8}$$

We may then define a *pseudo equilibrium for firm j* (relative to $\bar{z}$) by an allocation $\hat{z} \epsilon F^j(\bar{z})$, and a set of I vectors $\Pi^i \epsilon R_+{}^{S+1}$, $\Pi_0{}^i = 1$, such that:

(1) $x^i \succ_i \hat{x}^i$ implies $\Pi^i x^i > \Pi^i \hat{x}^i$, $i = 1 \ldots I$;
(2) $\hat{b}^j$ maximises $\sum_s b_s{}^j \left(\sum_i \bar{\theta}_{ij} \Pi_s{}^i \right) - a^j$ on Y^j.

As a corollary of proposition 3.2, we then have:

Theorem 3.2. Under assumptions 1 and 2, and given any stock ownership program $\bar{z}$ such that $\sum_i \bar{x}_0{}^i > 0$:

(i) there exists a pseudo equilibrium for firm j, $j = 1 \ldots J$;
(ii) every pseudo equilibrium for firm j belongs to $F_P{}^j(\bar{z})$;
(iii) with every $z \epsilon F_P{}^j(\bar{z})$, one can associate I vectors $\Pi^i \epsilon R_+{}^{S+1}$, $\Pi_0{}^i = 1$, such that $\{z, \Pi^i\}$ is a pseudo equilibrium for firm j.

The definition of a pseudo equilibrium for the firm states that the firm maximises the present value of its production plan, using shadow prices $\left(\sum_i \bar{\theta}_{ij} \Pi^i \right)$ obtained as weighted averages of individual shadow prices Π^i reflecting the consumption preferences of the shareholders, with the weights given by their respective ownership fractions.[1] Theorem 3.2 says that efficient production (investment) decisions by the firms imply the existence of such shadow prices.

The definition does not place any restrictions on the allocation

---

[1] See the paper by Gevers [14] on the (remote) possibility of obtaining these shadow prices, through majority voting, as weighted medians of the Π^i's.

among consumers of the adjustments in current consumption required to offset the adjustment in input level $a^j - \bar{a}^j$. Alternatively stated, the definition is consistent with arbitrary transfers of initial resources among consumers.[1]

(3) *Price Equilibria for the Stock Market*

Given a stock ownership program $\bar{z} = (\bar{x}, \bar{b}, \overline{\Theta})$, exchanges of shares among individuals can generate alternative programs through the choice of an alternative ownership matrix $\Theta \neq \overline{\Theta}$ accompanied by adjustments in the current consumptions x_0^i, $i = 1 \ldots I$.

Let $E(\bar{z})$ denote the set of stock ownership programs attainable, from a given starting point $\bar{z}$, through such exchanges (the production plans of all firms being given); we have:

$$E(\bar{z}) = \{z \mid z \in Z, b = \bar{b}\} \tag{3.9}$$

$$= \{z \mid \sum_i x_0^i \leq W_0 - \sum_j \bar{a}^j$$

$$x_s^i - \sum_j \theta_{ij} \bar{b}_s^j \leq 0, i = 1 \ldots I, s = 1 \ldots S$$

$$\sum_i \theta_{ij} \leq 1, j = 1 \ldots J, x, \Theta \geq 0\}.$$

The preferences of the consumers among such programs are representable by the continuous, quasi-concave,[2] monotonic functions:

$$W^i(x_0^i, \theta_{i1} \ldots \theta_{iJ} \mid \bar{z}) =_{\text{def}} U^i\left(x_0^i, \sum_i \theta_{ij} \bar{b}_1^j, \ldots \sum_i \theta_{ij} \bar{b}_S^j\right), i = 1 \ldots I.$$

$$\tag{3.10}$$

$E(\bar{z})$ is also the set of feasible allocations for an exchange economy, say $\mathcal{E}(\bar{z})$, with $J + 1$ private goods, namely the shares of the J firms and current consumption, where the preferences of the I consumers are defined by $(W^1 \ldots W^I)$ and the market clearing conditions reduce to:

$$\sum_i x_0^i \leq W_0 - \sum_j \bar{a}^j = \sum_i \bar{x}_0^i \tag{3.11}$$

$$\sum_i \theta_{ij} \leq 1 = \sum_i \bar{\theta}_{ij}, \quad j = 1 \ldots J \tag{3.12}$$

$$x_0^i \geq 0, \quad i = 1 \ldots I, \overline{\Theta} \geq 0. \tag{3.13}$$

---

[1] In the literature on public goods, some attention has been paid to the problem of existence of a pseudo equilibrium when the transfers of private goods are restricted; Foley [13] has proved a theorem to that effect. A particular transfer mechanism, and its specific merits, are discussed in [11]. Realism would call for individual contributions to $a^j - \bar{a}^j$ in proportion to the $\bar{\theta}_{ij}$'s.

[2] Strict quasi-concavity is not preserved by this transformation, when the vectors $\bar{b}^j$ are not linearly independent.

Investment Under Private Ownership

All the results obtained for such an economy are thus valid in our context as well. In particular, a *price equilibrium* for such an economy is defined by an allocation $\hat{z} \in E(\bar{z})$ and a (price) vector $\bar{p} \in R_+^{S+1}$, $\bar{p}_0 = 1$, such that

(1) $W^i(x_0^i, \theta_{i1} \ldots \theta_{iJ}) > W^i(\hat{x}_0^i, \hat{\theta}_{i1} \ldots \hat{\theta}_{iJ})$ implies $x_0^i + \sum_j \theta_{ij} \bar{p}_j > \hat{x}_0^i + \sum_j \hat{\theta}_{ij} \bar{p}_j$.

The set of Pareto optima for $\mathscr{E}(\bar{z})$, to be denoted $Ep(\bar{z})$, is defined as usual by:

$$E_p(\bar{z}) = \{z \mid z \in E(\bar{z}), \nexists \hat{z} \in E(\bar{z}), \hat{x}^i \gtrsim_i x^i \,\forall\, i, \hat{x}^h \gtrsim_h x^h \text{ for some } h\}. \quad (3.14)$$

The following properties are well known:

Proposition 3.3. Under assumption 1, for all $\bar{z} \in Z$ with $\sum_i \bar{x}_0^i > 0$, $\mathscr{E}(\bar{z})$ is such that:

 (i) there exists a price equilibrium;
 (ii) every price equilibrium is a Pareto optimum;
 (iii) with every Pareto optimum $z \in E_p(\bar{z})$ such that $x_0^i > 0 \,\forall\, i$, one can associate a price system $\bar{p}$, such that $(z, \bar{p})$ is a price equilibrium.

The transposition of these results to our context is obvious.

Because the correspondence between the ownership fractions $(\theta_{i1} \ldots \theta_{iJ})$ and the consumption vector $(x_1^i \ldots x_S^i)$ is not one-to-one, the relation of the price vector for shares $\bar{p}$ to the shadow prices reflecting consumption preferences ($\bar{\Pi}^i$ of section III.2) is not entirely straightforward. For reasons that will become clear in III.4, I will consider only the case where U^i is differentiable (assumption 1 *bis*). In that case, W^i is also differentiable, and

$$\frac{\partial W^i}{\partial \theta_{ij}} = \sum_s \bar{b}_s^j \frac{\partial U^i}{\partial x_s^i}, \quad \frac{\partial W^i}{\partial \theta_{ij}} \bigg/ \frac{\partial W^i}{\partial x_0^i} = \sum_s \bar{b}_s^j \frac{\partial U^i}{\partial x_s^i} \bigg/ \frac{\partial U^i}{\partial x_0^i} = \sum_s \bar{b}_s^j \bar{\Pi}_s^i. \quad (3.15)$$

With differentiability of W^i, a price equilibrium $(z, \bar{p})$ has the property:

(2) $\dfrac{\partial W^i}{\partial \theta_{ij}} \bigg/ \dfrac{\partial W^i}{\partial x_0^i} \leq \bar{p}_j, \quad \theta_{ij}\left(\bar{p}_j - \dfrac{\partial W^i}{\partial \theta_{ij}} \bigg/ \dfrac{\partial W^i}{\partial x_0^i}\right) = 0.$

Consequently:

Theorem 3.3. Under assumption 1 *bis*, with every $\hat{z} \in E_p(\bar{z})$ such that $\hat{x}_0^i > 0 \,\forall\, i$, one can associate I vectors $\bar{\Pi}^i \in R_+^{S+1}$, $\bar{\Pi}_0^i = 1$, and a vector $\bar{p} \in R_+^{S+1}$, $\bar{p}_0 = 1$, such that:

 (i) $x^i \succ_i \hat{x}_i$ implies $\bar{\Pi}^i x^i > \bar{\Pi}^i \hat{x}^i$, $i = 1 \ldots I$;
 (ii) $\sum_s \bar{b}_s^j \bar{\Pi}_s^i \leq \bar{p}_j$, $\theta_{ij}\left(\sum_s \bar{b}_s^j \bar{\Pi}_s^i - \bar{p}_j\right) = 0$, $i = 1 \ldots I$, $j = 1 \ldots J$.

Conditions (i) and (ii) define portfolios of shares that are optimal from the viewpoint of the individual consumers, given the production plans of the firms and the (stock) market prices $\bar{p}$.

(4) *Stockholders Equilibria*

We can now combine the concepts and results of sections III(2) and III(3). The definitions of pseudo equilibria for the individual firms and of price equilibria for the stock market can be combined in the following:

Definition 3.4. A stock ownership program z is a *stockholders equilibrium* if, and only if:

(i) for every firm j, there exist I vectors $\Pi^i(j)$ such that $\{z, \Pi^i(j)\}$ is a *pseudo equilibrium* for firm j (relative to z);
(ii) there exists a (price) vector p such that (z, p) is a *price equilibrium* for $\mathscr{E}(z)$.

That is, a stockholders equilibrium combines production plans in the individual firms which have the properties of pseudo equilibria for the corresponding public-goods economies $\mathscr{E}^j$, with an allocation of shares which has the properties of a price equilibrium for the corresponding exchange economy $\mathscr{E}$. In particular, the production plan of each firm is Pareto optimal, given the production plans of the other firms and the ownership matrix Θ; and the allocation of shares is Pareto optimal, given the production plans of the firms. This definition provides, in my opinion, a natural concept of equilibrium for stock ownership programs. Indeed, the firms have no incentive to change their production plans, and the consumers have no incentive to exchange shares, given the actions of the other agents. One could, of course, look for a stronger equilibrium concept, ruling out incentives for *simultaneous* adjustments in production plans and portfolios. But no natural definition of this stronger concept seems to present itself.

Two important properties of stockholders equilibria may be stated at once.

Theorem 3.4.1. Under assumptions 1 and 2, and provided $W_0 > 0$, there exists a stockholders equilibrium.

Proof. This follows as an immediate corollary of theorem 5.3 below.

Theorem 3.4.2. Under assumptions 1 and 2, every constrained Pareto optimum z with $x_0^i > 0 \; \forall \; i$ is a stockholders equilibrium.

Proof. Follows as an immediate corollary of theorem 3.2 (iii), and of proposition 3.3 (iii).

Investment Under Private Ownership

The converse of theorem 3.4.2 is not true: there exist stockholders equilibria which are *not* constrained Pareto optima. Examples are given in section IV below. This shortcoming of decentralised decision procedures reflects the non-convexity of the feasible set Z. Thus a price mechanism on the stock exchange and efficient decision procedures within individual firms will always *sustain* a Pareto optimum, but could equally well sustain an allocation that is *not* Pareto optimal.

Under differentiability, the price implications of a stockholders equilibrium are sharper: the shadow price vectors $\Pi^i(j)$ in (i) of definition 3.4 do not depend upon j. That is, $\Pi^i(j) = \Pi^i(k)$, $i = 1 \ldots I$, $j, k = 1 \ldots J$. This has an important implication for productive efficiency. Formally:

Theorem 3.4.3. Under assumptions 1 *bis* and 2, one can associate with every stockholders equilibrium $\hat{z}$ such that $\hat{x}_0^i > 0 \; \forall \; i$ a set of I vectors $\hat{\Pi}^i \in R_+^{S+1}$, $\hat{\Pi}_0^i = 1$, and a vector $\hat{p} \in R_+^{S+1}$, $\hat{p}_0 = 1$ such that:

(i) $x^i \succ_i \hat{x}^i$ implies $\hat{\Pi}^i x^i > \hat{\Pi}^i \hat{x}^i$, $i = 1 \ldots I$;

(ii) $\hat{b}^j$ maximises $\sum_s b_s^j \left(\sum_i \hat{\theta}_{ij} \hat{\Pi}_s^i \right) - a^j$ on Y^j, $j = 1 \ldots J$;

(iii) $\sum_s \hat{b}_s^j \hat{\Pi}_s^i \leq \hat{p}_j$, $\hat{\theta}_{ij} \left(\sum_s \hat{b}_s^j \hat{\Pi}_s^i - \hat{p}_j \right) = 0$, $i = 1 \ldots I, j = 1 \ldots J$.

Proof. By definition 3.4, there exist J sets of I vectors $\Pi^i(j)$ satisfying (i) and (ii); by theorem 3.3, there exist I vectors Π^i and a vector p satisfying (i) and (iii). Let $\hat{p} = p$.

Under differentiability, with $\hat{x}_0^i > 0$ and $\hat{\Pi}_0^i = 1$, the inequality $\hat{x}_s^i > 0$ implies uniqueness of $\hat{\Pi}_s^i$ in (i). Accordingly, for all i, s such that
$$\hat{x}_s^i > 0, \; \Pi_s^i(j) = \Pi_s^i = \hat{\Pi}_s^i, \quad j = 1 \ldots J.$$

When $\hat{x}_s^i = 0$, we know that $\sum_j \hat{\theta}_{ij} \hat{b}_s^j = 0$ (at a stockholders equilibrium). Consequently, conditions (iii), which are satisfied by (Π^i, p), will be satisfied by $(\hat{\Pi}^i, p)$ provided $\hat{\Pi}_s^i \leq \Pi_s^i$. Similarly, conditions (ii), which are satisfied by $\Pi^i(j)$, will be satisfied by $\hat{\Pi}^i$ provided $\hat{\Pi}_s^i \leq \Pi_s^i(j)$: indeed, if $\hat{\theta}_{ij} = 0$, then $\hat{\Pi}_s^i$ is irrelevant to conditions (ii), for that j; if $\hat{b}_s^j = 0$, then $\sum_s \hat{b}_s^j \sum_i \hat{\theta}_{ij} \hat{\Pi}_s^i - a^j \leq \sum_s \hat{b}_s^j \sum_i \hat{\theta}_{ij} \Pi_s^i(j) - a^j \leq \sum_s \hat{b}_s^j \sum_i \hat{\theta}_{ij} \Pi_s^i(j) - \hat{a}^j = \sum_s \hat{b}_s^j \sum_i \hat{\theta}_{ij} \hat{\Pi}_s^i - \hat{a}^j$. We may thus define: $\hat{\Pi}_s^i =$ Min $\{\Pi_s^i, \Pi_s^i(j), j = 1 \ldots J\}$. The vectors $\{\hat{p}, \hat{\Pi}^i\}$ so defined satisfy (i)–(iii).   Q.E.D.

Using theorem 3.4.3, it is easy to prove the following corollary, which states that a stockholders equilibrium entails productive efficiency, not only for each firm considered in isolation, but for all firms considered simultaneously.

Corollary 3.4.3. Under assumptions 1 *bis* and 2, every stockholders equilibrium $\hat{z}$ such that $\hat{x}_0{}^i > 0 \;\forall\; i$ is a Pareto optimal element of the set $F(\hat{z}) = \{z | z \epsilon Z,\; \Theta = \hat{\Theta}\}$.

In the absence of differentiability, $\Pi^i(j) \neq \Pi^i(k)$ in definition 3.4 may entail additional inefficiencies which are illustrated in example 4.4 below.

Conditions (i)–(iii) in theorem 3.4.3 are analogous to the necessary conditions derived from assumptions 1 *bis* and 2 *bis* in [10], where assumption 2 *bis* is further used to state (ii) in the usual terms of marginal costs.

We may thus conclude that no additional necessary optimality conditions of a local nature can be deduced from assumptions 1 and 2.

IV. EXAMPLES OF INEFFICIENT EQUILIBRIA

(1) *Equilibrium at a Local Optimum*

Four examples will now be presented, illustrating successively:

(i) a stockholders equilibrium that is not efficient, being a local optimum but not a constrained Pareto optimum;
(ii) a stockholders equilibrium that is not efficient, being a saddle point;
(iii) a constrained Pareto optimum with technologically inefficient production;
(iv) a stockholders equilibrium that is not technologically efficient, because the utility functions are not differentiable.

All four examples are constructed after the same pattern: there are 2 states, 2 consumers and 2 firms. These simplifications make it possible to present the examples graphically, by displaying the production possibilities of the firms when the input level is equal to one (this construction, underlying Figs. 9.1 and 9.2, was explained in section II(2)). The preferences of both consumers, for fixed current consumption $x_0{}^i$, are similarly represented by indifference curves in the space of future consumption under both states.

Example 4.1. In Fig. 9.5 the production possibilities of firm j, when $a^j = 1$, are given by the triangle ost.[1] With $\theta_{ij} = 1$, that firm is fully owned by individual i, whose preferences about future outputs

[1] In terms of the discussion in section II(2), the firm has access to two basic activities, defined respectively by points s and t.

Investment Under Private Ownership

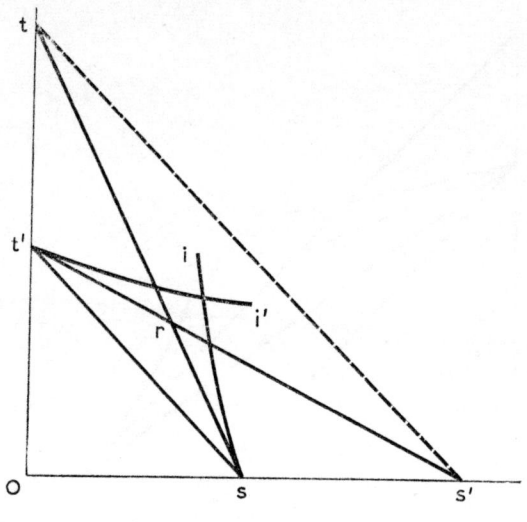

147

Fig. 9.5

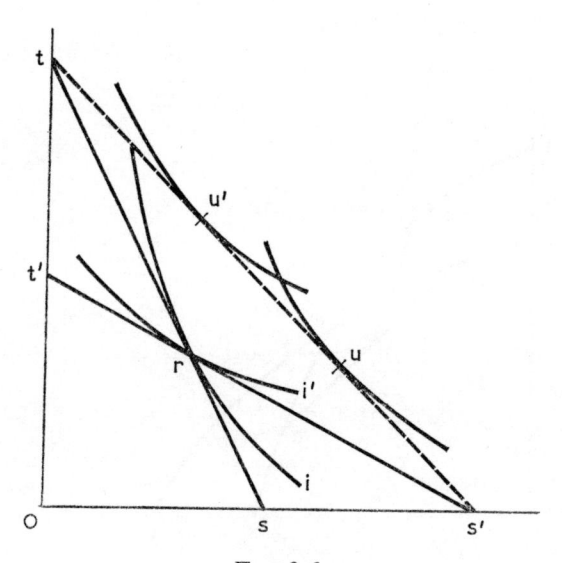

Fig. 9.6

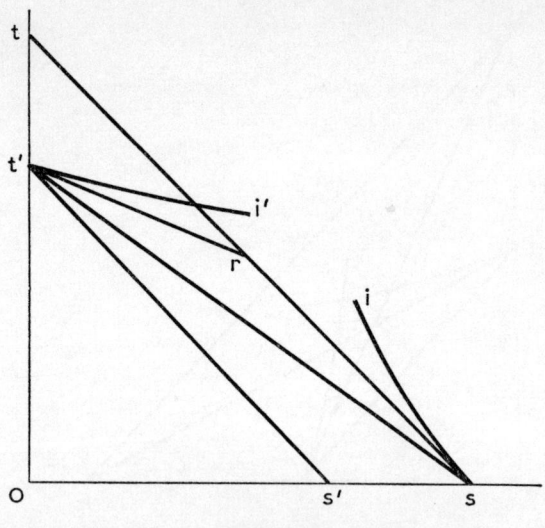

FIG. 9.7

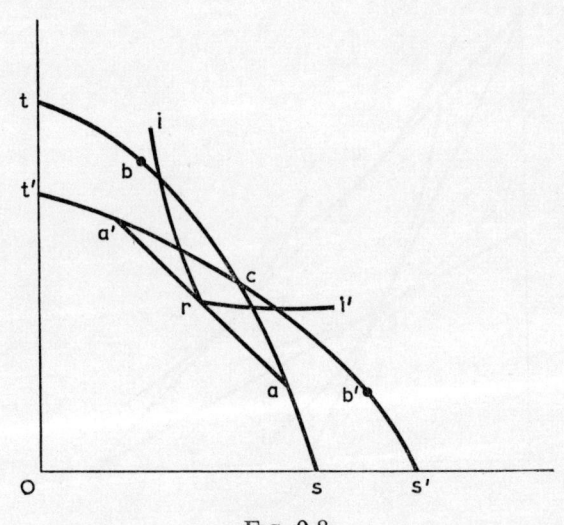

FIG. 9.8

are represented by the curve si. With the ratio $\Pi_s{}^i/\Pi_t{}^i$ corresponding to the slope of that indifference curve at point s, firm j maximises $\Pi_s{}^i b_s{}^j + \Pi_t{}^i b_t{}^j$ at point s, given $a^j = 1$. Thus, let $\bar{b}_s{}^j = \overline{os}$, $\bar{b}_t{}^j = 0$.

Similarly, firm j' has the production set $os't'$ when $a^{j'} = 1$, and is fully owned by individual i', whose preferences are represented by the curve $t'i'$. Again, firm j' maximises $\Pi_s{}^{i'} b_s{}^{j'} + \Pi_t{}^{i'} b_t{}^{j'}$ at point t', given $a^{j'} = 1$. Thus, let $\bar{b}_s{}^{j'} = 0$, $\bar{b}_t{}^{j'} = \overline{ot'}$.

Finally, let $\Pi_s{}^i = \Pi_t{}^{i'}$ and set $\bar{p}_j = \Pi_s{}^i \bar{b}_s{}^j = \bar{p}_{j'} = \Pi_t{}^{i'} \bar{b}_t{}^{j'}$. It follows that $\bar{p}_{j'} - \Pi_s{}^i \bar{b}_s{}^{j'} - \Pi_t{}^i \bar{b}_t{}^{j'} = \bar{p}_{j'} - \Pi_t{}^i \bar{b}_t{}^{j'} > 0$, calling for $\theta_{ij'} = 0$; similarly, $\bar{p}_j - \Pi_s{}^{i'} \bar{b}_s{}^j - \Pi_t{}^{i'} \bar{b}_t{}^j = \bar{p}_j - \Pi_s{}^{i'} \bar{b}_s{}^j > 0$, calling for $\theta_{i'j} = 0$. The allocation defined by $\theta_{ij} = \theta_{i'j'} = 1$, $\theta_{ij'} = \theta_{i'j} = 0$, with firm j producing at s and firm j' producing at t', is thus a stockholders equilibrium.

The inefficiency of this allocation is obvious. Output in period 2 will be $\overline{os} = \overline{ot'}$ irrespective of which state obtains. With the same input level in each firm, but with firm j producing at point t and firm j' producing at s', output in period 2 would rise to $\overline{os'} = \overline{ot}$ in either state – that is, it would double at no cost!

The economics of this situation are straightforward. Each firm produces optimally, *given the preferences of its owner*. With these production plans taken as given, and with the shares in both firms selling at the same price, the set of consumption plans available at a given cost is the line segment st'. Over this set, the optimal portfolio for i is at point s, for i' at point t'. Thus, each consumer carries an optimal portfolio, *given the production plans of the firms*. The inefficiency results from 'mismatching' between the production possibilities of the firms and the preferences of their owners.

There are two possible remedies to this situation. The first consists in changing the production plans of the firms, in the expectation that portfolio readjustments will follow. It may be argued that the 'opportunity-line' st' provides information about the direction of desirable changes in production plans. Examples 4.2 and 4.3 will show that such information may be missing (4.2) or misleading (4.3). It should also be noted that in order for this remedy to be effective, major changes in production plans are required: firm j must move above and to the left of point r, firm j' must move below and to the right of point r, in order for the adjustments to be beneficial.

The other remedy consists in changing the ownership fractions in the firms, in the expectation that modified ownership will lead to the desired adjustments in production plans. The initiative now lies with the consumers. But this requires additional information on their part: each consumer must know the production *set* of the other firm, not only its production *plan*. Furthermore, major changes in ownership fractions are again required: in order to exert enough influence on the decision within firm j' to move its production plan to the right of r, consumer i may have to acquire a majority interest.

The unprofitability of small moves confirms that the situation under consideration is a local optimum. Traditional market mechanisms, which are effective under convexity, are ineffective here. The first remedy might be implemented by managers disregarding the immediate interests of stockholders. The second remedy might be implemented (in a world with many small stockholders) through a proxy fight or a takeover bid.

Note, finally, that a merger would not help: with a single asset left, both consumers should consume a fixed proportion of output in both states, in spite of their diverging preferences.

Example 4.2. (2) *Equilibrium at a Saddle-Point.* This example is a variation of the previous one. The production possibilities of the two firms are unchanged, but the preferences of the two consumers are now represented by the indifference curves ri and ri' respectively. The analysis can be repeated, with $\bar{\theta}_{ij} = \bar{\theta}_{i'j'} = 1$ once more. Both firms are now in equilibrium at the same point r. But this equilibrium is unstable, in the sense that the slightest modification in ownership fractions will tilt the 'shadow prices' ($\prod_s{}^i \theta_{ij} + \prod_s{}^{i'} \theta_{i'j}, \prod_t{}^i \theta_{ij} + \prod_t{}^{i'} \theta_{i'j}$) and move firm j towards point t or firm j' towards point s'. This example depicts a 'saddle-point' situation.

The global optimum calls for $\theta_{ij} = \theta_{i'j'} = \frac{1}{3}$, $\theta_{ij'} = \theta_{i'j} = \frac{2}{3}$, leading to the consumption plans u and u'. Thanks to the saddle-point property, this optimum could easily be achieved through portfolio adjustments. Changes in production plans offer a less natural remedy, because at the point r the market opportunities for portfolio choices provide no information whatever about desirable production adjustments.

Example 4.3. (3) *Optimum with Technological Inefficiency.* This example is another variation of example 4.1. The preferences of the two consumers are kept unchanged, but the production possibilities are modified. When $a^j = 1$, firm j can choose a production plan in the triangle ost; when $a^{j'} = 1$, firm j' can choose a production plan in the triangle $os't'$. Thus, firm j' is technologically less efficient than firm j. When $\theta_{ij} = \theta_{i'j'} = 1$, firm j produces at point s, firm j' at point t'. The import of this example is that *this situation may well define a genuine constrained Pareto optimum*. Whereas firm j' would not produce at all in the presence of markets for contingent claims, the absence of such markets may justify its activity: the added opportunities for portfolio diversification compensate for its productive inefficiency. In order for consumer i' to be attracted by shares of firm j, the production plan of that firm should be moved above and to the left of point

r – but this would be detrimental to consumer i, which explains why the initial situation may well define a constrained Pareto optimum.[1]

This example shows that the opportunity line st' provides misleading, or at best irrelevant, information. If the management of firm j went by the shadow prices implicit in the opportunity line, it would move to point t, and there might result a local optimum with $\theta_{i'j} = \theta_{ij'} = 1$, firm j' producing at point s', and consumer i worse off than in the starting situation.

Example 4.4. (4) *Equilibrium with Technological Inefficiency.* The last example illustrates the possible consequences of lack of differentiability. The production sets of the two firms are defined by ost and $os't'$ respectively, when $a^j = a^{j'} = 1$. Both consumers have identical preferences represented by the indifference curve iri'. When firm j produces at point a, firm j' at point a', and $\bar{p}_j = \bar{p}_{j'}$, the set of consumption plans available at a given cost is the line segment aa'. Both consumers choose the point r, at which $\bar{\theta}_{ij} = \bar{\theta}_{i'j} = \bar{\theta}_{ij'} = \bar{\theta}_{i'j'} = \frac{1}{2}$. There exist vectors $\Pi^i(j) = \Pi^{i'}(j) \neq \Pi^i(j') = \Pi^{i'}(j')$ for which this allocation is a stockholders equilibrium. Clearly, if firm j were producing at b and firm j' at b', a better allocation could be reached.[2]

V. LOCAL OPTIMA AND STABILITY

(1) *Mixed Tâtonnement/Non-Tâtonnement Processes*

As explained in the introduction, one of the consequences of the absence of markets for contingent claims is the need for new adjustments in production plans and consumer portfolios, whenever new information accrues. The question of interest here is the following. Consider a stock ownership program z_0; in the light of recent information (e.g. a currency devaluation, a new trade agreement, a new tax structure, a technological discovery, etc.), that program? is not (any more) a stockholders equilibrium. Suppose that a specific process of adjustments in production plans and consumer portfolios takes place; will the process converge to a new stock ownership program and, if so, what will be the properties of the new program (Will it be a stockholders equilibrium? Will it be more efficient, in the Pareto sense, than the initial program?)

This topic is totally unexplored and the analysis here is very limited. It consists in establishing the convergence of a decentralised adjustment process, operating in discrete time through a sequence of realised exchanges of shares alternating with tentative revisions of the production plans of the firms. That is, the adjustments in

[1] Furthermore, with firm j producing to the left of r, consumer i might prefer to operate firm j' at point s'.

[2] Note also the existence of a saddle-point with both firms producing at point c.

consumer portfolios will proceed on a non-tâtonnement basis, whereas the adjustments in production plans will proceed on a tâtonnement basis.[1] The tâtonnement process seems natural for production (i.e. investment) decisions, which involve real resources and are irreversible. But stock exchange adjustments are more realistically reflected in non-tâtonnement processes: portfolios are modified through trading, and existing institutions make no provisions for tâtonnements (except on special occasions, like takeover bids whereby a purchase price is announced conditionally on the supply of a given quantity).

The process defined below is thus a 'mixed tâtonnement/non-tâtonnement process'. It may be described informally as follows. Each 'morning' the stock exchange meets, and shares are exchanged until some equilibrium is reached, at which no further trading is forthcoming. Each 'afternoon' the firms revise their production plans, according to the preferences of their shareholders, taking into account the ownership fractions generated by the transactions that have actually taken place on the stock exchange in the morning; these plans are announced but not physically carried out until a final equilibrium is reached. The next 'morning', new stock exchange transactions take place, on the basis of information about the production plans chosen the previous afternoon. When, on some morning, no transactions take place on the stock exchange, the production plans of the firms are regarded as definitive and are carried out.

(2) *Individually Rational and Pareto Optimal Processes*

In order to complete the description of the process, one should specify the properties of the stock exchange equilibrium reached in the morning and of the production decisions reached in the afternoon. I will assume that these decisions are always individually rational and Pareto optimal (over the set of reallocations attainable through exchange of shares, or through the decisions of individual firms, respectively).

There are two reasons why individual rationality is a natural requirement to impose upon such a process. The first is that one cannot expect the process to converge towards a constrained Pareto optimum, when the feasible set Z is not convex.[2] Considering that only a local optimum, or a saddle-point, may be reached, one should guard against the possibility of ending up at an allocation which is

---

[1] These features may be contrasted with those of the simultaneous tâtonnement process in continuous time defined and studied in [10].

[2] Indeed, no mathematical programming algorithm with such a strong property is currently available.

worse than the starting point.[1] The only natural safeguard that I can think of is individual rationality of each move.

The second reason is that individually rational processes have a natural Lyapunov function, namely individual utilities. To see why this is important, consider exchanges of shares leading each morning to a competitive equilibrium on the stock exchange. Because preferences among portfolios are not strictly convex,[2] no reasonable assumptions will guarantee even local uniqueness of the competitive equilibrium. There is accordingly no natural way to base stability analysis on a Lyapunov function defined in the space of prices and/or quantities.

The other requirement – Pareto optimality over the set of reallocations attainable at each step – could certainly be relaxed, but seems easier to justify (as will be done in the applications of section VI) because the attainable set at each step is convex, so that procedures for reaching optima are available.

A major drawback of both requirements is the implicit assumption that the problem arising at each step will be solved as if that step were to be the last one; that is, no consideration of advantages to be realised at *later* steps is recognised. More specifically, acquisition of shares for the purpose of gaining control over a firm and changing its production plan, or choice of a disliked production plan susceptible of raising the price at which stockholders will sell out, are implicitly ruled out by the requirements of individual rationality and Pareto optimality. The process is thus better viewed as an illustration of the possibilities offered by decentralised, rational, but 'myopic', decisions, rather than as a description of the functioning of the stock exchange.[3]

Two definitions are needed to formalise the requirement of individual rationality. Given a stock ownership program $\bar{z}$, I have defined in equation (3.1) the set $F^j(\bar{z})$ of reallocations attainable through decisions of firm j and adjustments in current consumption; and I have defined in equation (3.6) the subset $F_P{}^j(\bar{z})$ of $F^j(\bar{z})$ consisting of Pareto optimal programs. Building upon these definitions, I will now define, and denote by $F_{IP}{}^j(\bar{z})$, the subset of $F^j(\bar{z})$ consisting of individually rational *and* Pareto optimal programs:

$$F_{IP}{}^j(\bar{z}) = \{z \mid z \in F_P{}^j(\bar{z}),\ x^i \succsim_i \bar{x}^i \ \forall\ i\}. \tag{5.1}$$

Similarly, I have defined in equation (3.9) the set $E(\bar{z})$ of reallocations attainable through exchanges of shares among consumers, and

---

[1] Examples of seemingly sensible adjustment processes under which that perverse result may obtain can be constructed.

[2] See equation (3.10) and the remark surrounding that formula.

[3] The same remark applies to most dynamic models in mathematical economics.

in (3.14) its Pareto optimal subset, $E_P(\bar{z})$. I will now define, and denote by $E_{IP}(\bar{z})$, the subset of $E(\bar{z})$ consisting of individually rational *and* Pareto optimal programs:

$$E_{IP}(\bar{z}) = \{z | z \epsilon E_P(\bar{z}), x^i \gtrsim_i \bar{x}^i \not\forall i\}. \tag{5.2}$$

(3) A Convergence Theorem

We are now ready to define a 'Mixed Tâtonnement/Non-Tâtonnement Process' for our economy. The process (P) is defined by a sequence of steps $q = 0, 1, 2, \ldots$

At each step q, a stock ownership program z_q is generated. $z_0 \epsilon Z$ is given, with positive current consumption $\not\forall i$, but otherwise arbitrary. If q is odd, $z_q \epsilon E_{IP}(z_{q-1})$. If q is even, z_q is the J-th element of a sequence $\{z_{q,\,j}\}, j = 1 \ldots J$, where $z_{q,\,1} \epsilon F_{IP}{}^1(z_{q-1})$

$$z_{q,\,j} \epsilon F_{IP}{}^j(z_{q,\,j-1}), j = 2 \ldots J;$$

that is, z_q belongs to the composition of correspondences $F_{IP}{}^J \circ F_{IP}{}^{J-1} \circ \ldots F_{IP}{}^1(z_{q-1})$.

Thus:

Definition 5.3. The process (P) is defined by:

—an initial step: z_0, with $x_{00}{}^i > 0 \not\forall i$.
—a general step:
if q is odd, $z_q \epsilon E_{IP}(z_{q-1})$
if q is even, $z_q \epsilon F_{IP}{}^J \circ F_{IP}{}^{j} \circ^{-1} \ldots F_{IP}{}^1(z_{q-1})$.[1]
—a termination rule:
if $z_q = z_{q-2}$, the process terminates.

Theorem 5.3. Under assumptions 1 and 2, the process (P) is well defined, its solution is bounded, and:

—either the process terminates at some q, and z_q is a stockholders equilibrium,
—or the limit of any convergent subsequence of solutions, $\{z_{qv}\}$, $v \to \infty$, is a stockholders equilibrium.

The proof of the theorem rests upon two lemmata.

Lemma 5.3.1. The correspondences $F^j(z)$ and $F_{IP}{}^j(z)$ are upper hemicontinuous, $j = 1 \ldots J$.

[1] The results below would remain valid if one specified instead: 'if q is even, $z_q \epsilon F_{IP}{}^{\phi_q J} \circ F_{IP}{}^{\phi_q J - 1} \circ \ldots F_{IP}{}^{\phi_q 1}(z_{q-1})$, where ϕ_q is an arbitrary permutation of the integers $1 \ldots J$'. Although z_q may be affected by the order in which the production plans of the J firms are revised, convergence of the process is unaffected by that order (which may vary at each step, or be random, a.s.o.).

Investment Under Private Ownership

Proof. Let $\hat{z}^q \to \hat{z}^0$, $z^q \to z^0$, $q \to \infty$.

To prove that $z^q \epsilon F^j(\hat{z}^q) \not\vdash q$ implies $z^0 \epsilon F^j(\hat{z}^0)$, it is enough to note that z^0 satisfies all the linear inequalities in the definition (3.1) and that Y^j is closed (assumption 2).

To prove that $z^q \epsilon F_{IP}{}^j(\hat{z}^q) \not\vdash q$ implies $z_0 \epsilon F_{IP}{}^j(\hat{z}^0)$, one first notes that continuity of $\succsim_i$ implies $x^{i0} \succsim_i \hat{x}^{i0}$, so that z^0 is individually rational (relative to $\hat{z}^0$). There remains to prove that $F_{IP}{}^j(\hat{z}^0)$ does not own $\tilde{z}$ such that $\tilde{x}^i \succsim_i x^{i0} \not\vdash i$, $\tilde{x}^h \succsim_h x^{h0}$ for some h.

Suppose that such a $\tilde{z}$ exists. Then $\tilde{x}_0^h > 0$ by assumption 1. Without loss of generality, we may assume that $\tilde{z}$ satisfies (2.1) and (2.4) in equality form, and that $\tilde{x}^i \sim_i x^{i0}$, $i \neq h$. Because $\tilde{z} \epsilon F^j(\hat{z}^0)$, $\tilde{\Theta} = \hat{\Theta}^0$ and $\tilde{b}^k = \hat{b}^{k0} \not\vdash k \neq j$, by (3.1). Define then a sequence $\{\tilde{z}^q\}$ as follows:

$$\tilde{\Theta}^q = \hat{\Theta}^q, \ \tilde{b}^{kq} = \hat{b}^{kq}, \ k \neq j; \ \tilde{b}^{jq} = \tilde{b}^j;$$

$$\tilde{x}_s{}^{iq} = \sum_{k=1}^J \tilde{\theta}_{ik}{}^q \tilde{b}_s{}^{kq} \not\vdash i, s; \ \tilde{x}_0{}^{iq} \ni \tilde{x}^{iq} \sim_i x^{iq}, \ i \neq h;$$

$$\tilde{x}_0{}^{hq} = \max \ \{0, \ W_0 - \sum_{k=1}^J \tilde{a}_k{}^q - \sum_{i \neq h} \tilde{x}_0{}^{iq}\}. \text{ Whenever } \tilde{x}_0{}^{hq} > 0, \text{ then } \tilde{z}^q \epsilon F^j(\hat{z}^q).$$

Let $B_\epsilon(.)$ denote the ball with radius ϵ centered at $(.)$. There exist ϵ, $\delta = (I + J)\epsilon$ and Q such that:

(i) $\tilde{x} \succ_h x$ for all $\tilde{x} \epsilon B_\delta(\tilde{x}^h)$, $x \epsilon B_\epsilon(x^{h0})$;
(ii) $\tilde{x}_0{}^h > \delta$;
(iii) $\not\vdash q \geq Q$, $\tilde{x}^{iq} \epsilon B_\epsilon(\tilde{x}^i) \not\vdash i \neq h$, $\tilde{b}^{kq} \epsilon B_\epsilon(\tilde{b}^k) \not\vdash k \neq j$, so that $\tilde{x}^{hq} \epsilon B_\delta(\tilde{x}^h)$;
(iv) $\not\vdash q \geq Q$, $x^{hq} \epsilon B_\epsilon(x^{h0})$.

Properties (ii) and (iii) imply $\tilde{x}_0{}^{hq} > 0$, $\tilde{z}^q \epsilon F^j(\hat{z}^q)$, $\not\vdash q \geq Q$.
Properties (i), (iii) and (iv) imply $\tilde{x}^{hq} \succ_h x^{hq}$, $q \geq Q$. But $\tilde{x}^{iq} \sim_i x^{iq}$, $i \neq h$, by construction. This contradicts $z^q \epsilon F_{IP}{}^j(\hat{z}^q)$ and the proof is complete. Q.E.D.

Lemma 5.3.2. The correspondences $E(z)$ and $E_{IP}(z)$ are upper hemicontinuous.

Proof. Let $\hat{z}^q \to \hat{z}^0$, $z^q \to z^0$, $q \to \infty$.

To prove that $z^q \epsilon E(\hat{z}^q) \not\vdash q$ implies $z^0 \epsilon E(\hat{z}^0)$, it is enough to note that z^0 satisfies all the linear inequalities in (3.9). That z^0 is individually rational (relative to $\hat{z}^0$) follows from continuity of $\succsim_i$, as noted in the proof of lemma 5.3.1. To complete the proof that $z^q \epsilon E_{IP}(\hat{z}^q) \not\vdash q$ implies $z^0 \epsilon E_{IP}(\hat{z}_0)$, suppose, on the contrary, that $E_{IP}(\hat{z}^0)$ owns $\tilde{z}$ such that $\tilde{x}^i \succsim_i x^{i0} \not\vdash i$, $\tilde{x}^h \succ_h x^{h0}$ for some h.

Reasoning as in the proof of lemma 5.3.1, we define $\{\tilde{z}^q\}$ by:

$\tilde{b}^q = \hat{b}^q$; $\tilde{\Theta}^q = \tilde{\Theta}$; $\tilde{x}_s^{iq} = \sum_j \tilde{\theta}_{ij} \tilde{b}_s^j \ \forall\ i, s$;

$\tilde{x}_0^{iq} \ni \tilde{x}^{iq} \sim_i x^{iq}$, $i \neq h$; $\tilde{x}_0^{hq} = \max\{0, W_0 - \sum_j \tilde{a}_j^q - \sum_{i \neq h} \tilde{x}_0^{iq}\}$.

There exist ϵ, $\delta = (I+J)\epsilon$ and Q with properties (i)–(iv) in the proof of lemma 5.3.1, leading to the same contradiction of $z^q \epsilon E_{IP}(\hat{z}^q)$, $q \geq Q$. Q.E.D.

Proof of theorem 5.3.
(1) $\forall\ z \epsilon Z$, $E_{IP}(z)$ and $F_{IP}{}^j(z)$ are non-empty and contained in the compact set Z. Hence, $\forall\ q$, a solution z_q exists and is bounded. Because $x_{00}^i > 0$, it follows from assumption 1 and individual rationality that $x_{0q}{}^i > 0 \ \forall\ q$, $i = 1 \ldots I$.

(2) Let $\hat{z} \epsilon Z$ with $\hat{x}_0{}^i > 0 \ \forall\ i$. $\forall\ z \epsilon F_{IP}{}^j(\hat{z})$, either $z = \hat{z}$, or $\sum_i U^i(x^i) > \sum_i U^i(\hat{x}^i)$. Indeed, $x^i \gtrsim_i \hat{x}^i$ by individual rationality, so that $\sum_i U^i(x^i) \geq \sum_i U^i(\hat{x}^i)$, with strict inequality if $x^i \succ_i \hat{x}^i$ for some i. Suppose that $x^i \sim \hat{x}^i \ \forall\ i$ but $x^h \neq \hat{x}^h$ for some h. Then $F^j(z)$, a convex set, owns $\frac{z + \hat{z}}{2} = \tilde{z}$, and $\tilde{x}^i \gtrsim_i x^i \ \forall\ i$, $\tilde{x}^h \succ_h x^h$, contradicting the Pareto optimality of $z \epsilon F_{IP}{}^j(\hat{z})$. Hence, $\sum_i U^i(x^i) = \sum_i U^i(\hat{x}^i)$ implies $x^i = \hat{x}^i \ \forall\ i$. By (3.1) $x = \hat{x}$ implies $b^j = \hat{b}^j$ and $z = \hat{z}$.

(3) Similarly, $\forall\ z \epsilon E_{IP}(\hat{z})$, either $x = \hat{x}$, or $\sum_i U^i(x^i) > \sum_i U^i(\hat{x}^i)$. This follows from the convexity of $E(\hat{z})$ and the reasoning under 2. Note further that $\forall\ z \epsilon E_{IP}(\hat{z})$, $b = \hat{b}$ by (3.9).

(4) $\forall\ z \epsilon F_{IP}{}^J \circ F_{IP}{}^{J-1} \circ \ldots F_{IP}{}^1 \circ E_{IP}(\hat{z}) =_{def} G(\hat{z})$ and $\forall\ z \epsilon E_{IP} \circ F_{IP}{}^J \circ F_{IP}{}^{J-1} \circ \ldots F_{IP}{}^1(\hat{z}) =_{def} H(\hat{z})$,
either $x = \hat{x}$, $b = \hat{b}$ and $z \epsilon E_{IP}(\hat{z})$, or $\sum_i U^i(x^i) > \sum_i U^i(\hat{x}^i)$.

This follows directly from 2 and 3.

(5) Suppose that $z_q = z_{q-2}$. Because $z_q \epsilon F_{IP}{}^j(z_q)$ with $x_{0q}{}^i > 0 \ \forall\ i$, there exist vectors $\Pi_q{}^i$ such that $\{z_q, \Pi_q{}^i\}$ is a pseudo-equilibrium for firm j (theorem 3.2), $j = 1 \ldots J$. Because $z_q \epsilon E_{IP}(z_q)$ with $x_{0q}{}^i > 0 \ \forall\ i$, there exists a vector p_q such that (z_q, p_q) is a price equilibrium (proposition 3.3); therefore, z_q is a stockholders equilibrium.

(6) Suppose next that an infinite sequence $\{z_q\}$ is generated. Because Z is compact, $\{z_q\}$ contains a convergent subsequence, say $\{z_{q_\nu}\}$; $\{z_{q_\nu}\}$ contains a subsequence $\{z_{q_\mu}\}$ such that $q_{\mu+1} - q_\mu$ is even $\forall\ \mu$; let $\rho = 1$ if q_μ is odd, $\rho = -1$ if q_μ is even; in either case, $\{z_{q_\mu + 2\nu}\}$

contains a convergent subsequence, say $\{z_{q_\lambda+2\rho}\}$. Consider then the two converging subsequences:

$\{z_{q_\lambda}\} \underset{\lambda\to\infty}{\longrightarrow} \bar{z} = \lim_{\nu\to\infty} \{z_{q_\nu}\};$

$\{z_{q_\lambda+2\rho}\} \underset{\lambda\to\infty}{\longrightarrow} \bar{\bar{z}}.$

(7) $U^i(x_{q+1}{}^i) \geq U^i(x_q{}^i)$ by individual rationality. Because U^i is continuous and Z compact, U^i converges, so that $U^i(\bar{x}^i) = U^i(\bar{\bar{x}}^i) \ \forall \ i$.

(8) When q_λ is odd, $z_{q_\lambda+2\rho} = z_{q_\lambda+2} \epsilon H(z_{q_\lambda})$ (as defined under 4 above). $H(z)$ is upper hemicontinuous, as a composition of upper hemicontinuous correspondences defined on compact sets (see, e.g. lemma 4.2 in [24]). Consequently, $\bar{\bar{z}} \epsilon H(\bar{z})$. By 7 and 4, $\bar{x} = \bar{\bar{x}}$, $\bar{b} = \bar{\bar{b}}$ and $\bar{\bar{z}} \epsilon E_{IP}(\bar{z})$. It follows that $\bar{z} \epsilon F_{IP}{}^j(\bar{z})$, $j = 1 \ldots J$, $\bar{z} \epsilon E_{IP}(\bar{z})$, with $\bar{x}_0{}^i > 0 \ \forall \ i$. The reasoning under 5 shows that $\bar{z}$ is a stockholders equilibrium.

(9) When q_λ is even, $z_{q_\lambda+2\rho} = z_{q_\lambda-2}$ and $z_{q_\lambda} \epsilon G(z_{q_\lambda-2})$ (as defined under 4 above). $G(z)$ is upper hemicontinuous, so that $\bar{z} \epsilon G(\bar{\bar{z}})$. By 7 and 4, $\bar{x} = \bar{\bar{x}}$, $\bar{b} = \bar{\bar{b}}$ and $\bar{z} \epsilon E_{IP}(\bar{\bar{z}})$. It follows that $\bar{z} \epsilon E_{IP}(\bar{z})$, $\bar{z} \epsilon F_{IP}{}^j(\bar{z})$, $j = 1 \ldots J$, with $\bar{x}_0{}^i > 0$. $\bar{z}$ is a stockholders equilibrium, and the proof is complete.   Q.E.D.

(4) Two Remarks

(i) In the proof of theorem 5.3, strict convexity of preferences is used only to rule out situations where $z \epsilon F_{IP}{}^j(\hat{z})$ with $\sum_i U^i(x^i) = \sum_i U^i(\hat{x}^i)$ but $z \neq \hat{z}$. Unless one specifies more narrowly how $z_{q,j} \epsilon F_{IP}{}^j(z_q,\ _{j-1})$ is selected, strict convexity is required to rule out cycling among indifferent programs.

The same difficulty has led me to define the process so that all firms in succession revise their production plans between two meetings of the stock exchange. I would have found it more general to allow for exchanges of shares between any pair of revisions of the production plans. But cycling among indifferent portfolios might then prevent convergence to a stockholders equilibrium. Indeed, a subset of the consumers might hold a majority interest in firm j whenever that firm revises its production plan (calls a stockholders meeting), and also hold a majority interest in firm j' whenever that firm revises its production plan, and switch indefinitely back and forth between these two portfolios through exchanges that are indifferent from the viewpoint of the remaining consumers. Such cycling cannot be excluded by strict convexity, as explained in connection with (3.10). But it would be ruled out by any kind of transaction costs.

(ii) Theorem 5.3 does not assert that process (*P*) converges. Non-convexity of the feasible set entails the possibility of multiple limit points among which all consumers would be indifferent. The convergence properties of the process are similar to those of mathematical programming algorithms for non-linear problems. Actually, the proof of theorem 5.3 was inspired by convergence theorems for mathematical programming algorithms (see, e.g., Zangwill [24], or Avriel and Williams [4]). Furthermore, the theorem implies the convergence of a simple algorithm for non-linear programming problems with bilinear constraints.

Consider indeed the following three problems ($\lambda^i \geq 0 \; \forall \; i$):

(P1) $\underset{(x, b, \Theta)}{\text{Max}}$ $\sum_i \lambda^i U^i(x^i)$ subject to (2.1) and (2.3)–(2.6);

(P2) $\underset{(x, b)}{\text{Max}}$ $\sum_i \lambda^i U^i(x^i)$ subject to (2.1), (2.3), (2.4) and (2.6), given $\Theta = \overline{\Theta}$;

(P3) $\underset{(x, \Theta)}{\text{Max}}$ $\sum_i \lambda^i U^i(x^i)$ subject to (2.1), (2.3), (2.5) and (2.6), given $b = \overline{b}$.

Problems (P2) and (P3) are convex, problem (P1) is not.
Consider the following algorithm for solving (P1):

initial step z_0
general step:
if q is odd, solve problem (P3), given $b = b_q$
if q is even, solve problem (P2), given $\Theta = \Theta_q$.
termination: if $z_q = z_{q-2}$, the algorithm terminates.

The convergence properties of this algorithm are covered by theorem 5.3. The algorithm consists in solving a sequence of *convex* programming problems, obtained upon linearising the bilinear constraints (2.3) – by keeping fixed b and Θ alternatively. This linearisation would be particularly helpful if Y^j were a polyhedron – in which case all the constraints in problems (P2) and (P3) would be linear.[1,2]

[1] This algorithm seems more appealing than the alternative contained in a previous, unpublished, version of this paper where it was suggested to solve at step $q+1$ the following problem:

(P_q): $\underset{(x,b,\Theta)}{\text{Max}} \sum_i \lambda^i U^i(x^i)$ subject to (2.1), (2.4)–(2.6) and

$$x_s^i - \sum_j \theta_{ij}^q \, b_s^{jq}\left(1 + \log \frac{\theta_{ij} \, b_s^j}{\theta_{ij}^q \, b_s^{jq}}\right) \leq 0.$$

That algorithm would have similar properties. It is a special case of a more general theory developed by Avriel [3].

[2] Reference should also be made to recent work on bilinear programming, Konno [17], which might open new possibilities for defining processes yielding constrained Pareto optima rather than mere stockholders equilibria.

VI. APPLICATIONS

(1) *Competition on the Stock Exchange*
Any application of theorem 5.3 must rest upon an institutional specification of the ways in which decisions within the firms are arrived at and exchanges of shares are carried out; that is, it must rest upon specific assumptions about the general step of process (P). I will discuss first the institutional specification of exchanges of shares (general step with q odd), then turn to decision making within the firms (general step with q even), and finally compare my results with the simpler rule of market value maximisation by firms.

At step q, q odd, the set $E(z_{q-1})$ of reallocations attainable through exchanges of shares is the set of feasible allocations for an exchange economy $\mathscr{E}(z_{q-1})$ with $J+1$ private goods – the shares of the J firms and current consumption (see section III(3)). Every *competitive equilibrium* for $\mathscr{E}(z_{q-1})$ is individually rational (relative to z_{q-1}) and Pareto optimal (over $E(z_{q-1})$), and thus belongs to $E_{IP}(z_{q-1})$. Should a competitive equilibrium for $\mathscr{E}(z_{q-1})$ always exist, an institutional organisation of the stock exchange generating competitive equilibria would satisfy the requirements of the general step of (P) for odd q.

With monotonicity of preferences and $x_{0q}{}^i > 0$ for all i and all q, existence of a competitive equilibrium for $\mathscr{E}(z_{q-1})$ is readily ascertained (e.g. by means of the proposition in section 4 of [8]).

Does the stock exchange generate competitive equilibria? That assumption would be somewhat too strong, in my opinion. During a meeting of the stock exchange, some trading typically takes place out of equilibrium, at prices which are successively adjusted until no further trading is forthcoming. The resulting allocation is a *price equilibrium*, not necessarily a competitive equilibrium. Of course, every price equilibrium for $\mathscr{E}(z_{q-1})$ is Pareto optimal, over $E(z_{q-1})$, (see proposition 3.3); but not every price equilibrium is individually rational.

In a non-tâtonnement exchange process guided by price adjustments, individually irrational allocations can only result from (ill-advised) speculative behaviour.[1] As intimated in section V(2), theorem 5.3 may be viewed as a result on stability in the absence of speculation.

---

[1] Looking at such a process as a game, with strategies defined by the net demands announced at each stage as functions of past and current prices, one could also state that the α-core must be contained in the set $E_{IP}(.)$ of individually rational and Pareto optimal allocations (on the α-core concept, see [2], section 10). Game theoretic analysis of economic adjustment processes is an intriguing but uncharted territory. . . .

(2) Decision-making Within the Firms

Let us now consider decision-making within the firms. At step q, q even, each firm in succession is called upon to choose a reallocation in $F_{IP}{}^j(.)$. As explained in section III(2) above, that problem amounts to finding an individually rational and Pareto optimal allocation for an economy $\mathscr{E}^j(.)$ with S public goods and a single private good. Tâtonnement processes solving that problem, under assumptions 1 *bis* and 2 *bis*, have been defined by Malinvaud [19] and Drèze–de la Vallée Poussin [11].

Using the differentiability assumptions, one may define $\Pi_s{}^i = \dfrac{\partial U^i}{\partial x_s{}^i} \Big/ \dfrac{\partial U^i}{\partial x_0{}^i}$, i's marginal rate of substitution between $x_s{}^i$ and $x_0{}^i$, $\gamma_s{}^j = -\dfrac{\partial f^j}{\partial b_s{}^j} \Big/ \dfrac{\partial f^j}{\partial a^j}$, the marginal cost of $b_s{}^j$ (in terms of a^j). The tâtonnement process – say (T^j) – studied in [11] is defined as follows (in continuous time, for all $t \geq 0$, with $\Theta \equiv \bar{\Theta}$):

$$\frac{db_2^i}{dt} = \begin{cases} \sum_i \bar{\theta}_{ij} \Pi_s{}^i(t) - \gamma_s{}^j(t), & b_s{}^j(t) > 0 \\ \max[0, \sum_i \bar{\theta}_{ij} \Pi_s{}^i(t) - \gamma_s{}^j(t)], & b_s{}^j(t) = 0 \end{cases} \quad s = 1 \ldots S; \quad (6.1)$$

$$\frac{da^j}{dt} = \sum_s \gamma_s{}^j(t) \frac{db_s{}^j}{dt}; \quad (6.2)$$

$$\frac{dx_0{}^i}{dt} = \bar{\theta}_{ij} \left[-\sum_s \Pi_s{}^i(t) \frac{db_s{}^j}{dt} + \sum_s \left(\frac{db_s{}^j}{dt} \right)^2 \right], \quad i = 1 \ldots I. \quad (6.3)$$

This process (T^j) may be viewed as a procedure for collective choice during stockholders meetings. Equation (6.1) indicates that production plans are adjusted according to the preferences $\Pi_s{}^i$ of the stockholders, weighted by their respective ownership fractions $\bar{\theta}_{ij}$. (6.3) indicates that these adjustments are accompanied by transfers among stockholders, of which the first component is in the nature of an exact compensation for these adjustments, whereas the second component is in the nature of a dividend (per share). Under assumptions 1 *bis* and 2 *bis*, the process (T^j) converges to an individually rational Pareto optimum.[1]

The process requires that the stockholders reveal to the firm their consumption preferences. It is shown in [11] that the process entails incentives for correct revelation of these preferences. Looking at the process as a game, where individual strategies consist in the choice of revealed (as opposed to true) vectors $\Pi_s{}^i(t)$, one finds that correct revelation of preferences is the only minimax strategy, for every player or coalition; and that an equilibrium of the process is a Nash

---
[1] See [11], theorem 1.

Investment Under Private Ownership

equilibrium of the game if, and only if, all consumers reveal their preferences correctly.[1]

The transfers (6.3) are indispensable to generate these incentives. Consider indeed the natural alternative

$$\frac{dx_0^i}{dt} = -\hat{\theta}_{ij}\frac{da_j}{dt}, \qquad i=1\ldots I. \tag{6.4}$$

It is readily verified that, at an equilibrium of the process [(6.1), (6.2), (6.4)], the game is *not* in Nash equilibrium. That is, market exchange of shares and production decisions based upon revealed preferences of stockholders imply incentives for *incorrect* revelation of preferences, in the absence of compensating transfers.

To sum up, theorem 5.3 proves the stability of decentralised mixed tâtonnement/non-tâtonnement processes based upon a stock exchange that generates individually rational price equilibria and decision procedures within the firms that generate efficient production plans, rendered individually rational through differentiated dividends (transfers). Reference to competitive equilibria and to the Malinvaud-Drèze-de la Vallée Poussin procedure for public goods, shows that the class of such processes is not empty. But the realism of these processes is severely limited, in particular because they ignore speculative transactions on the stock exchange and rely upon compensating transfers among stockholders of the firms.

(3) *Market Value Maximisation*

The complexity of the tâtonnement process (T^j) may be contrasted with the simplicity of the recommendation typically found in the finance literature, namely that a firm should always adopt a revision of its production plan (an investment) that will increase its market value on the stock exchange.[2] The recommendation is based upon the explicit assumption that an increase in the market value of firm j may be viewed as an increase in the wealth of all stockholders of firm j, with prices of consumption goods unchanged. Such an increase should give the stockholders access to a preferred consumption plan. Consequently, any revision increasing market value is individually rational.

Within the present model, the assumption of unchanged prices for consumption goods is not acceptable. Indeed consumption goods reduce here to consumptions in the various states; in so far as they

---

[1] See [11], theorems 3 and 4. The last statement must be qualified somewhat for goods s such that $b_s^j = 0$ – but the qualification is a minor one. It is also shown in [11] that the α-core of this game *coincides* with the set of individually rational and Pareto optimal allocations.

[2] See, e.g., [12] pp. 176 ff. and 299 ff.

exist, the prices of those goods are implicit in the prices of shares on the stock exchange. It seems hardly meaningful to assume that consumption prices *implicit in stock prices* do not change when the market value of a given firm increases (even though the increase is due to a change in production plan).

The reasoning underlying the market value rule may still be pursued, within the present model, without assuming unchanged prices for consumption goods. Indeed the basic idea is that an adjustment in production plan is beneficial for all the stockholders of a firm, whenever it brings about a new situation where everyone has access to the consumption vector which he had *chosen* in the initial situation. This is the familiar 'revealed preference' criterion. A weaker criterion can be devised only through reference to the consumption preferences of the stockholders, the very reference which one would like to avoid. But the revealed preference criterion can, in principle, be applied even under price changes.

In order to make that criterion unambiguous, let us assume that the stock exchange generates competitive equilibria, and let us investigate under what conditions an adjustment in production plan is 'revealed individually rational'.

To that effect, consider a stock ownership program $\bar{z}$, and a price vector for shares $\bar{p}$ such that $(\bar{z}, \bar{p})$ is a price equilibrium. Let firm 1 announce a change of its production plan from $\bar{b}^1$ to $\hat{b}^1$, and assume for simplicity that $\hat{a}^1 = \bar{a}^1$. Let this announcement be followed by a meeting of the stock exchange generating a new competitive price vector for shares, $\hat{p}$.

Let $\bar{\theta}_{i1} > 0$.[1] The consumption plan of consumer i in the old situation $\bar{z}$ was $\bar{x}^i$, with $\bar{x}_s^i = \sum_j \bar{\theta}_{ij} \bar{b}_s^j$, $s = 1 \ldots S$. In order for $\bar{x}^i$ to be available in the new situation, there must exist a vector of ownership fractions $(\hat{\theta}_{i1} \ldots \hat{\theta}_{iJ})$ such that:

(i) $\hat{\theta}_{i1} \hat{b}_s^1 + \sum_{j=2}^{J} \hat{\theta}_{ij} \bar{b}_s^j \geq \sum_{j=1}^{J} \bar{\theta}_{ij} \bar{b}_s^j$, $s = 1 \ldots S$.

(ii) $\sum_{j=1}^{J} (\hat{\theta}_{ij} - \bar{\theta}_{ij}) \hat{p}_j \leq 0$.

These conditions may also be expressed as follows. There must exist a vector $\beta \epsilon R^J$, $\beta_j = \dfrac{\hat{\theta}_{ij} - \bar{\theta}_{ij}}{\bar{\theta}_{i1}}$, such that:

---

[1] If $\bar{\theta}_{i1} = 0$, consumer i cannot lose, since his portfolio entails unchanged consumption.

(i') $\hat{b}_s^1 - \bar{b}_s^1 \geq \beta_1 \hat{b}_s + \sum_{j=2}^{J} \beta_j \bar{b}_s^j$, $s = 1 \ldots S$.

(ii') $\sum_{j=1}^{J} \beta_j \hat{p}_j \geq 0$.

Conditions (i') and (ii') state that the adjustment ($\hat{b}^1 - \bar{b}^1$) must be greater than, or equal to, some linear combination of the new production plans, defining a portfolio (short sales permitted) with non-negative value at the new prices $\hat{p}$. In other words, *the adjustment in the production plan must have non-negative value at the consumption prices implied by the new stock prices.*

This condition is quite different from the market value rule: $\hat{p}_1 > \bar{p}_1$ is neither sufficient nor necessary for (i')–(ii'). Conceivably, this new condition could be used as a starting point to define an individually rational adjustment process. But the condition does not possess the operational simplicity of the market value rule.[1]

VII. CONCLUDING REMARKS

Remark (1)

The analysis of the present paper could fruitfully be extended to a model involving several commodities, in period 0 and in period 1 under state *s*. Several commodities in period 0, with exchange opportunities for allocating these commodities, seems to call for an immediate and uninteresting extension. Several commodities in period 1, with limited (no) exchange opportunities for these commodities beyond those made possible by the markets for assets, raises more interesting issues. The analysis of temporary equilibrium under uncertainty ([15], [22]) offers a natural and promising tool with which to approach these issues. Extensions of that analysis, in the direction of optimality and of equilibrium decisions for firms not endowed with preferences of their own, would be welcome.

Perhaps the most interesting and most accessible extension to several commodities will consist in distinguishing between labour and physical goods in an input vector a^j for firm *j*. A major interest of this distinction rests in the symmetrical treatment of human capital and physical capital that it permits. When physical capital is embodied in the inputs of a firm, the supplier of that capital surrenders control over its use to the firm. In the present model, such surrender is accompanied by a proportional right to the yield of the firm's capital, and should ideally be accompanied by a proportional

---

[1] I have derived great benefit from discussion of this topic with my colleagues Jean Jaskold Gabszewicz and Jean-Philippe Vial, who had studied independently a related problem.

weight in determining shadow prices guiding the use of the firm's capital.

When human labour is embodied in the inputs of a firm, there frequently results a creation of 'embodied human capital'. The productivity of a person who has worked for some time in a given firm is typically higher if he continues to work there, than if he shifts to some other occupation. But that extra productivity typically depends upon the state that obtains. The production (investment) decisions of a firm in a world of uncertainty are not only gambles with the physical capital of stockholders, they are also gambles with the embodied human capital of the firm's employees. Naïve extensions of the model used in this paper point clearly towards the desirability of production decisions that aggregate not only the consumption preferences of the stockholders (in proportion to their shares), but also those of the employees (in proportion to the quantities of embodied human capital at stake). One may thus expect from this extension new insights into the intriguing problems of control for firms using both physical and human capital.

Remark (2)

The analysis of the present paper could fruitfully be extended to a model with more than two time periods. Serious consideration of such a model would raise a very difficult problem, which is ignored in sections V and VI above; namely the problem of *timing investment decisions*. Existing private ownership economies probably simulate, to some extent, the kind of adjustment process discussed in section V, where consumer portfolios are revised (through stock exchange transactions and other transfers of assets) in the light of new information about the environment and about the production plans of the firms, and investment decisions are revised in the light of new information about the environment and about asset prices. But these adjustments take place in real time and with limited information. At some stage, irreversible investment decisions are realised; that 'stage' must correspond to some step of an underlying adjustment process. Limit points are hardly ever observed, in real time, under sequential information about the environment. For this reason, and because carrying out an investment tomorrow is a typical alternative to carrying out the same investment today, the optimal timing of investment decisions raises a problem of enormous difficulty. What model could capture some essential aspects of that problem, in a framework amenable to analysis, is an open question.

Remark (3)

The set of private ownership programs defined by (2.1), (2.3)–(2.6) is analogous to the set of feasible programs for an economy with semi-public goods and 'consumer mobility'. As a particular case that admits of a straightforward interpretation in terms of (2.1) and (2.3)–(2.6), consider an economy with J regions (or 'clubs'). In each region, a vector of S 'semi-public' goods is produced; by 'semi-public' good is meant a good of which the total production in the region is at any time consumed in full by all the consumers present in that region, but *only* by these.[1] Let these semi-public goods be produced by means of a single input, that can be freely moved across regions. Denote by a^j the input used in region j, by b_s^j the amount of good s produced there, $s = 1 \ldots S, j = 1 \ldots J$, and let Y^j be the production set of region j. The I consumers of the economy consume (or supply) the input (in quantities x_0^i) and consume the semi-public goods of the region where they reside. Let each consumer be free to move at no cost[2] across the regions, and denote by θ_{ij} the fraction of his time that consumer i spends in region j; thus,

$$\sum_j \theta_{ij} \leq 1, \qquad i = 1 \ldots I.\text{[3]} \tag{7.1}$$

The total amount of semi-public good s consumed by i will then be $x_s^i = \sum_j \theta_{ij} b_s^j$. If the preferences of consumer i are completely represented by a preordering among vectors $x^i = (x_0^i, x_1^i \ldots x_S^i)$ in R_+^{S+1}, then the problem of efficient production of the S semi-public goods in the J regions is formally equivalent to the problem of Pareto optimality for stock ownership programs, with the *single* modification that (7.1) replaces (2.5). Most of the analysis in the present paper is directly applicable to the study of efficient production of semi-public goods.[4]

REFERENCES

[1] K. J. Arrow, 'Le rôle des valeurs boursières pour la répartition la meilleure des risques', pp. 41–7 in *Econométrie*, Colloque International XL (Paris: CNRS, 1953); translated as 'The Role of Securities in the Optimal Allocation of Risk-Bearing', *Review of Economic Studies*, vol. XXXI (1964), pp. 91–6.
[2] R. J. Aumann, 'A Survey of Cooperative Games without Side Payments',

---

[1] Local police protection, public lighting, control of air pollution, street cleaning, ... provide natural examples.
[2] Transportation costs in this model would play a role analogous to transaction costs on the stock exchange in private ownership economies.
[3] The alternative constraints: $\theta_{ij} = \theta_{ij}^2$, $i = 1 \ldots I$, $j = 1 \ldots J$, imposing that each consumer resides in a single region, would of course create additional non-convexities.
[4] In particular, the examples of section IV admit of a natural interpretation in terms of relocating consumers i and i' between regions j and j' (town and suburbs?), and simultaneously modifying the supply of public goods in both regions.

pp. 3–27 in *Essays in Mathematical Economics*, edited by M. Shubik (Princeton: Princeton University Press, 1967).
[3] M. Avriel, 'Solution of Certain Non-Linear Programs Involving r-convex Functions', *Journal of Optimization Theory and Applications*, vol. XI (1973), pp. 159–74.
[4] M. Avriel and A. C. Williams, 'Complementary Convex Programming', Mobil R. & D. Corporation, Progress Memorandum (May 1968).
[5] E. Baudier, 'L'introduction du temps dans la théorie de l'équilibre général', *Cahiers Economiques* (1959), pp. 9–16.
[6] K. Borch, 'The Safety Loading of Reinsurance Premiums', *Skandinavisk Aktuarietidskrift*, vol. XLIII (1960), pp. 163–84.
[7] G. Debreu, *Theory of Value*, (New York: Wiley, 1959).
[8] G. Debreu, 'New Concepts and Techniques for Equilibrium Analysis', *International Economic Review*, vol. III (1962), pp. 257–73.
[9] P. A. Diamond, 'The Role of a Stock Market in a General Equilibrium Model with Technological Uncertainty', *American Economic Review*, vol. LVII (1967), pp. 759–76.
[10] J. H. Drèze, 'A Tâtonnement Process for Investment under Uncertainty in Private Ownership Economies', pp. 3–23 in *Mathematical Methods in Investment and Finance*, ed. by G. P. Szegö & K. Shell (Amsterdam: North-Holland, 1972).
[11] J. H. Drèze and D. de la Vallée Poussin, 'A Tâtonnement Process for Public Goods', *Review of Economic Studies*, vol. XXXVIII (1971), pp. 133–50.
[12] E. Fama and M. H. Miller, *The Theory of Finance* (New York: Holt, Rinehart and Winston, 1972).
[13] D. K. Foley, 'Resource Allocation and the Public Sector', *Yale Economic Essays*, vol. VII (1967), pp. 45–98.
[14] L. Gevers, 'Competitive Equilibrium of the Stock Exchange and Pareto Efficiency', chapter 10 *infra*.
[15] J. M. Grandmont, 'On the Short-Run Equilibrium in a Monetary Economy', chapter 12 *infra*.
[16] R. Guesnerie and T. de Montbrial, 'Allocation under Uncertainty: a survey', chapter 4 *supra*.
[17] H. Konno, 'Bilinear Programming: Part I: Algorithm for Solving Bilinear Programs; Part II: Application of Bilinear Programming', (Stanford University, California, Technical Reports 9 and 10, 1971).
[18] E. Malinvaud, *Leçons de théorie microéconomique* (Paris: Dunod, 1969).
[19] E. Malinvaud, 'Procédures pour la détermination d'un programme de consommations collectives', mimeographed (Paris, 1969) (paper presented at the European Meeting of the Econometric Society, Brussels, 1969).
[20] O. Mangasarian, *Non-Linear Programming* (New York: McGraw-Hill, 1969).
[21] C. Milleron, 'Theory of Value with Public Goods: A Survey Article', *Journal of Economic Theory*, vol. V (1972), pp. 419–77.
[22] D. Sondermann, 'Temporary Competitive Equilibrium under Uncertainty', chapter 13 *infra*.
[23] J. Stiglitz, 'On the Optimality of the Stock Market Allocation of Investment', *The Quarterly Journal of Economics*, vol. LXXXVI (1972), pp. 25–60.
[24] W. I. Zangwill, *Non-Linear Programming, A Unified Approach* (Englewood Cliffs: Prentice Hall, 1969).

10 Competitive Equilibrium of the Stock Exchange and Pareto Efficiency

Louis Gevers[1]
CORE, LOUVAIN

INTRODUCTION

The simplest model of a productive economy is based on the following assumptions: agents live only for one period, they take input and output prices as given, and production involves no risks.

In this economy, it does not matter whether production is financed through output sales or through share flotation. In the first case, all agents who own a share in the profit of a firm want the firm to maximise profit. In case of share flotation, all stockholders spontaneously agree that the market value of a share should be maximised. The latter must be equal to the market value of the dividends. Hence both criteria have the same implications. In particular, a competitive equilibrium is known to be Pareto efficient in a wide variety of circumstances.

Introducing time and technological uncertainty changes nothing essential, provided one specifies, for each good, its date and the state of the world upon which its delivery is contingent, and provided there is a market for every such good.

Common observation suggests that markets are not universal in the world we know. Transaction costs explain why most futures markets and most markets for contingent goods are lacking.

Shares in firms must be viewed as composite goods when there is more than one output. The stock exchange is an allocating device which economises on transaction costs when there are fewer firms than there are produced commodities.

The present paper attempts to answer the following question: under what conditions is the allocation of resources through a

[1] I am much indebted to J. H. Drèze for suggesting many improvements. I wish to thank K. J. Arrow, R. Guesnerie, A. Kirman, M. Marchand and J. E. Stiglitz for helpful discussions. I alone am responsible for any remaining errors. A preliminary version of part of this paper was presented at the European Research Conference on Economy Theory sponsored by the IEA, Bergen, summer 1971. Part of this research was carried out while the author was associated with the Center for Operations Research and Econometrics, Louvain, Financial support of the Fonds de la Recherche Fondamentale Collective (under contract 611) is gratefully acknowledged.

competitive stock exchange Pareto-efficient in a suitably restricted sense?

The relevant concept of Pareto efficiency is developed in section I. Competitive equilibria of the stock exchange are defined in sections II and III.

The descriptive literature is notoriously fuzzy about the firm's objectives under uncertainty. Perhaps the only virtue of this paper is to clarify the issue in a simplified world, where natural objectives are dictated to firms by the decision-makers' preferences regarding consumption.

The paper is not concerned with the question of existence. It is easy to show, by means of examples, that the set of competitive allocations that can be sustained by a stock exchange is nonempty. However, no general proof of existence is offered in the sequel. Some counter-examples based on the Condorcet paradox can be found in the appendix.

Two papers by Drèze [6], [7] stimulated this work. Papers by Diamond [5], Plott [9] and Stiglitz [11] have also been important sources of inspiration.

I proceed with a summary of the paper.

A simple two-period general equilibrium framework is used repeatedly. There is a finite number of goods, only one of which is used as input in production. Society's initial endowment is made up of that good. All other commodities are produced goods. Agents derive satisfaction from consuming all goods.

In section I, Pareto-efficient allocations are defined and characterised. A general form of the constraint governing the distribution of outputs is presented. It can be specialised to accommodate both public and private goods among the outputs. An intermediate form of the constraint is needed for our study. It goes as follows: if an agent consumes a fraction of a firm's output, he must also consume the same fraction of all other outputs of that particular firm. Shares in one firm must be non-negative and add up to one.

We need the constraint in this form because no exchange is allowed to take place in our economy outside the stock market.

An allocation (a list of levels of all relevant variables in the model) achieves (constrained) Pareto efficiency when it is feasible, and when there exists no other feasible allocation which makes every agent better off.

Differentiability is assumed, and first-order conditions which characterise Pareto-efficient allocations are provided. These conditions are necessary but not sufficient. Indeed, the set of feasible allocations corresponding to the intermediate form of the constraint is not convex. This was pointed out by Drèze in [6] and [7].

Competitive Equilibrium of the Stock Exchange

We need a descriptive theory of the firm to define a stock exchange equilibrium. This theory is developed in several directions. The aim is to find out whether equilibria are Pareto-efficient.

A quick presentation of the classical version of the competitive model concludes section I. Section II is concerned with technological uncertainty when separate markets for contingent goods are lacking. Section III deals with uncertainty about future spot prices when separate forward markets are lacking.

In all versions of the model, firms issue shares to finance production. The stock exchange is assumed free of transaction costs.

In section II, the various outputs of the firms are interpreted as physically identical goods, which are associated with several *a priori* possible states of the world. Technological choices made at period one, and the state of the world that obtains at period two, determine together the amount of output which is actually delivered.

The model rests on two main assumptions. The first one generalises the customary assumption of free competition; when agents choose their portfolio, they take the price of every share as a datum; moreover, they do not perceive any influence of their portfolio choice on production plans of firms.

The other assumption pertains to the market valuation of a share as it is perceived by the firm's decision-makers. The latter choose a production plan and the number of shares that must be floated in order to finance it. When there is a market for every contingent good, the price of a share must be equal to the value of the dividends and thus must depend on the production plan. When no such markets exist, decision-makers may be assumed to believe that the observed price of a share would change in a definite fashion if they selected another production plan.

This change in market valuation is in the nature of a conjecture; it is less so when short sales of shares are permitted, and there are at least as many firms with linearly independent output vectors as there are states of the world, or when output ratios are fixed. In the latter case, meaningful aggregates can be defined; in the former case, each unit of contingent good may be priced separately, albeit indirectly.

Except for some unlikely cases such as the ones I have just mentioned, stockholders generally disagree about the optimal production plan, although they may be in agreement about the way the price of a share depends on the production plan. There are three further sources of disagreement: risk aversion, probability judgements, and initial endowment. They are thus faced with a problem in group decision.

The literature suggests two ways of dealing with this problem. Following one trend (see, e.g. [12]), one may consider the firm manager as a 'dictator' who selects that production plan which suits him best. The model may then be closed by exogenously assigning a manager to every firm.

In a more traditional perspective, one may assume that the manager executes what stockholders decide through majority voting.

Further assumptions, under which these decisions result in an allocation that satisfies the first-order conditions for a constrained Pareto optimum, are described in detail. They are all highly unlikely to be satisfied exactly in reality. This suggests that there may be better ways of organising production than through the market structure I have stylised. Other forms of organisation, such as the Drèze process [7], surely imply various costs too. Some kind of empirical comparison is needed before a final judgement can be attempted.

In section III, the various outputs of the firms are interpreted as physically distinct goods. There is no uncertainty about the results of technical processes. However, there are no futures markets and agents face uncertain future spot prices. It is shown that the formalism and the results of section II apply also to this case. Of course, reinterpretation is in order, particularly as far as the relevant concept of Pareto efficiency is concerned.

Some comments about possible extensions of the model conclude the paper.

I. SOME BASIC CONCEPTS

In order for a market to exist, it must be possible to exclude non-buyers from the use of the goods which are exchanged. Information about price, and the nature of the goods, must be produced, transmitted and received. Bargaining time and uncertainty about the outcome must also be taken into account, especially when there are few sellers or buyers.

As Arrow lucidly shows in [1], these various costs may be so high that exchange fails to take place. Externalities and public goods provide good instances of market failures.

These principles are illustrated in the following threefold example,[1] two cases of which will be used as reference throughout the rest of the paper.

Consider an economy with I consumers, indexed $i=1, ..., I$. Moreover, assume there are J firms, indexed $j=1, 2, ..., J$, and $S+1$ goods. One good, called good zero, is singled out because it is the only component of the agents' physical endowment and also the only input used in production. The other goods are referred to by the index $s=1, 2, ..., S$.

[1] The basic model and the notation are directly taken from Drèze [6].

Competitive Equilibrium of the Stock Exchange

A consumption plan for consumer i is a non-negative vector in R^{S+1}: $x^i = (x_0^i, x_1^i, \ldots, x_s^i, \ldots, x_S^i)$. His preferences among consumption plans are described by the utility function

$$U^i = U^i(x^i). \tag{1.1}$$

U^i is assumed differentiable. Marginal utilities are denoted: U_0^i, U_s^i ($s = 1, \ldots, S$). By assumption $U_0^i > 0$, $U_s^i \geq 0$ with strict positivity for at least one s. We define also $\Pi_s^i = \dfrac{U_s^i}{U_0^i}$, the marginal rate of substitution of good s for good zero.

A production plan for firm j consists of an input level a^j together with a non-negative output vector in R^S. The latter is denoted by $(b_1^j, \ldots, b_s^j, \ldots, b_S^j)$.

A cost function

$$a^j = \gamma^j(b_1^j, \ldots, b_S^j) \tag{1.2}$$

associates to each output vector, the minimal quantity of input needed to produce it. Thus, the set of feasible plans is given by $a^j \geq \gamma^j(b_1^j, \ldots, b_S^j)$, $a^j \geq 0$, $b_s^j \geq 0$ $\forall s$.

The function $\gamma^j(\ )$ is assumed differentiable and its partials with respect to outputs, denoted by γ_s^j, ($s = 1, \ldots, S$), are all positive.

The economy as a whole cannot use more good zero than is available; denoting the economy's endowment of good zero by $\sum_i \omega^i + \sum_j \omega^j$,

$$\sum_i \omega^i + \sum_j \omega^j \geq \sum_i x_0^i + \sum_j a^j. \tag{1.3}$$

Material balances for output may take several forms. For instance, the outputs may be public goods; they may also be private goods. The following formulation fits either case.

For each i, each j and each $s \geq 1$, define a number θ_{ij}^s such that $0 \leq \theta_{ij}^s \leq 1$. Material balances may be partly expressed in the form

$$x_s^i - \sum_j \theta_{ij}^s b_s^j \leq 0 \qquad \forall\, i, s. \tag{1.4}$$

This means that agent i's consumption of good s is at most equal to a sum of fractions of each firm's output.

By adding more restrictions to the θ_{ij}^s's, one can define (1) an economy with public goods, (2) an economy with private goods and (3) an intermediate case. In subsections (1) to (3), I adhere to the same plan: assumptions, interpretation and conditions for Pareto efficiency. Subsection (4) introduces private ownership and stock market organisation; it concludes with a quick review of the Arrow–Debreu economy.

(1) An Economy with Public Goods

Suppose first that the $\theta_{ij}{}^s$'s are fixed exogenously, or that they are prohibitively expensive to change. Then, all the outputs are public goods. If this is due to the high cost of exclusion, one may assume that all $\theta_{ij}{}^s$'s are equal to one, but this is not mandatory. Take for instance a flood protection scheme. The fraction of land protected may be a multiple of the height of the dam, which varies from one acre to the next.

In this context, a planner has to allocate society's endowment of good zero to consumption and to the production of other goods by firms. This he must do without violating constraint (1.3). Within each firm, he must choose a production plan consistent with (1.2).

Our planner does not only want a feasible allocation; he also wants a Pareto-efficient allocation. A reduction of the output $b_s{}^j$ of firm j, while leaving the other output levels unchanged, releases a quantity of good zero which is approximately equal to $\gamma_s{}^j d\, b_s{}^j$. Suppose this can be shared among agents in a way that more than compensates each of them for the loss they suffer through the reduction of $b_s{}^j$. Then the allocation is not Pareto-efficient.

The amount of good zero which just compensates agent i is approximately $\theta_{ij}{}^s \Pi_s{}^i db_s{}^j$. Unless the solution lies at a corner, Pareto efficiency then requires:

$$\gamma_s{}^j = \sum_i \theta_{ij}{}^s \Pi_s{}^i \qquad \forall j, s. \tag{1.5}$$

In other words, this means that the marginal cost of good s in terms of good zero must be equalised for each firm with a weighted sum of marginal rates of substitution between the same goods. The weights are the $\theta_{ij}{}^s$'s, i.e. the scale factors linking firm j's output of good s and its maximum contribution to individual i's consumption of the same good.

(2) An Economy with Private Goods

Referring again to inequalities (1.4), one may take the extreme view that every $\theta_{ij}{}^s$ can be changed without cost. There is a global constraint however; total consumption of each good must not exceed total output.

$$\sum_i x_s{}^i - \sum_j b_s{}^j \leq 0 \qquad \forall s. \tag{1.6}$$

In view of (1.4), this certainly holds if, for all j and all s,

$$\sum_i \theta_{ij}{}^s = 1. \tag{1.7}$$

Our planner has a lot more freedom than under section I(1): now he must also select a distribution rule for each output. He can do this by choosing non-negative $\theta_{ij}{}^s$'s which satisfy (1.7).

Pareto efficiency now requires that all agents' marginal rate of substitution between good s and good zero be the same. Put together with (1.5) and (1.7), this further implies equality with the marginal cost of good s in terms of good zero in each firm.

This presentation of the problem could be simplified: constraint (1.6) is all that matters under the present circumstances. Constraints (1.4) and (1.7) are used to clarify the relationship between private and public goods. When there are at least two suppliers and two customers of a commodity, infinitely many $\theta_{ij}{}^s$ values are compatible with fixed consumption and production levels.

(3) *An Intermediate Case*

It may happen that the planner has more freedom with respect to the $\theta_{ij}{}^s$'s than under section I(1), although he is less free than under section I(2). This is the case if he must satisfy (1.7) and also:

$$\theta_{ij}{}^1 = \theta_{ij}{}^2 = \ldots = \theta_{ij}{}^S = \theta_{ij} \qquad \forall\, i, j. \tag{1.8}$$

In other words, the share of a firm's outputs received by any particular agent must be the same for every output of that firm. However, one agent may hold different shares in different firms, and two different agents may hold two different shares in the same firm.

In view of (1.8), the allocative rule (1.5) becomes

$$\gamma_s{}^j = \sum_i \theta_{ij} \Pi_s{}^i \qquad \forall\, s, j. \tag{1.9}$$

This is of interest if the various goods which make up the output of a firm are difficult to sort out and to distribute separately.

In contrast with the private goods case, consumers are generally not indifferent with respect to the origin of the goods; receiving a larger share of firm j's output of good s generally involves a change in the consumption of all other goods.

A share in firm j's output must be considered as a composite good. Unless there is a corner solution, Pareto efficiency requires that the marginal rate of substitution between this composite good and good zero be equalised for all consumers. Taking agent α as a reference

$$\left[\frac{\partial U^i(x_0{}^i, \sum_k \theta_{ik} b_1{}^k, \ldots, \sum_k \theta_{ik} b_S{}^k)}{\partial \theta_{ij}}\right] \Bigg/ \left(\frac{\partial U^i}{\partial x_0{}^i}\right)$$

$$= \sum_s \Pi_s{}^i b_s{}^j = \sum_s \Pi_s{}^\alpha b_s{}^j \qquad \forall\, i, j. \tag{1.10}$$

Searching for a Pareto-efficient allocation is, of course, a programming problem. Conditions (1.9) and (1.10), which are here presented heuristically, are shown by Drèze [6] to be necessary for an interior solution. He also points out that these conditions are not sufficient, even if preferences and production sets are convex. Indeed, the constraints in (1.4) are not quasi-convex if $\theta_{ij}{}^s$ and $b_s{}^j$ are allowed to vary.[1] His article contains some striking examples of allocations which are inefficient although they satisfy our necessary conditions.[2]

The reader will have noticed that equation (1.4) is also constraining in the pure private goods case, with $\theta_{ij}{}^s$ used as a control variable. As it was pointed out, however, this is not the only possible presentation of the problem. Agent i's utility depends on his share in the total of each good.

Every good may be allocated independently. This is why the $\theta_{ij}{}^s$'s can be dropped in the classical presentation, where the constraints (1.6) are quasi-convex.

In the intermediate case, the $\theta_{ij}{}^s$'s are no longer allowed to vary with s. They cannot be disposed of unless very special conditions are met. For instance, if output ratios are fixed, utilities can be re-expressed, without ambiguity, in terms of as many goods as there are firms. Every such good may be allocated independently. The θ_{ij}'s are allowed to vary with j, and this makes it possible to use quasi-convex constraints, as in the private goods case.

Under special circumstances, allocations which are fully Pareto efficient are compatible with constraint (1.8). This may hold in particular when $J > S$. For fixed production plans, it may also be true for special utility functions. Borch has pursued the latter question in a related model [4].

(4) Universal Markets and the Stock Exchange

For future comparison, it is convenient to describe here a private ownership economy with perfect forward markets, which can be associated with the private goods model of section I(2). By assumption, production is financed exclusively through the stock exchange. Notation introduced at this stage will be used throughout the rest of the paper.

Each agent i is assumed to own at the outset a quantity ω^i of good zero, as well as v_{ij} shares in firm j.

Let p^j be the price of a share of firm j in terms of good zero; let

---

[1] To see this easily, suppose there is only one good and one firm and consider one individual. Dropping the indices let $x = \theta b$ and $x^* = \theta^* b^*$, with $\theta^* > \theta$, $b^* > b$. Choose λ positive and smaller than one; then
$$(1 - \lambda)x + \lambda x^* > [(1 - \lambda)\theta + \lambda \theta^*][(1 - \lambda)b + \lambda b^*].$$
As a result, the set of feasible allocations is not convex.

[2] For the sake of completeness, one of Drèze's examples is shown in the appendix to be consistent with the definition of competitive equilibrium that is used in this paper.

y_{ij} denote the number of shares of the same firm owned by agent i when the market closes. The following restriction is in order:

$$x_0^i + \sum_j p^j y_{ij} \leqslant \omega^i + \sum_j p^j v_{ij} \quad \forall\, i \quad (1.11)$$

where by assumption $\omega^i > 0$ and $v_{ij} > 0$; it is also assumed that short sales are not allowed: $y_{ij} > 0$, $\forall\, i, j$.

When the market opens, firm j owns a quantity ω^j of good zero and its ownership is represented by m_j shares, so that

$$\sum_i v_{ij} = m_j \quad \forall\, j. \quad (1.12)$$

Firm j may change its holding of good zero by floating or buying shares at the ruling price p^j. Denoting by n_j the final number of shares outstanding we write down two accounting constraints:

$$\sum_i y_{ij} = n_j \quad \forall\, j \quad (1.13)$$

$$\omega^j + p^j(n_j - m_j) \geqslant a^j \quad \forall\, j \quad (1.14)$$

where a^j denotes firm j's total physical capital.

Firm j is liquidated at period two, and each stockholder receives his share of the output $(b_1^j, ..., b_S^j)$. If each output may be sold at a price p_s, agent i's budgetary constraint (1.11) must be completed as follows:

$$\sum_i p_s x_s^i \leqslant \sum_s p_s \sum_j \frac{y_{ij}}{n_j} b_s^j \quad \forall\, i. \quad (1.15)$$

If perfect forward markets exist, the prices p_s may be observed. Riskless arbitrage must be profitless. This is true only if

$$p^j n_j = \sum_s p_s b_s^j \quad \forall\, j. \quad (1.16)$$

Agents may check that this equation is verified in equilibrium. The firm's decision-makers must also believe that formula (1.16) is valid for every production plan. Otherwise they would always select a plan that makes arbitrage profitable, in order to take advantage of it.

The model of a private ownership economy with perfect forward markets may be closed by assigning one, or several, decision-makers to each firm. Like every other agent, these decision-makers choose a consumption plan and a portfolio that maximise their utility; moreover, they select a production plan and a financial plan for the firms they manage, which best serve their interest as consumers.

The reader will easily verify that agents who take the prices p_s as given and the share prices p^j as determined by (1.16) are indifferent about the composition of their portfolio and they always agree about what firms ought to do: in the case of an interior solution, the marginal cost of each output must be equated with its price. Thus the assignment of decision-making responsibilities has no bearing on the outcome.

Moreover, the same equilibrium emerges if there is no stock exchange, and firms buy their input outright, and this equilibrium is fully Pareto-efficient.[1]

We have seen that the private goods model of section I(2) is relevant in the case of perfect forward markets. It turns out that we need the model of section I(3) when forward markets (or markets for contingent goods) are lacking. This is the subject matter of the next two sections.

II. TECHNOLOGICAL RISKS

(1) *Stochastic Interpretation of the Model*

The general assumptions laid down at the beginning of section I allow for a stochastic interpretation. Consider firm j. Its input level a^j may be interpreted as investment. By assumption, output (say corn) is reaped at the next period. Given the investment level, and given the production technique, the amount of output is assumed to depend on which of S possible states of the world has obtained by that time. Output is best considered a different good under each state of the world. *Ex post*, only one kind of good will be delivered. However, the firm can choose *ex ante* what bundle of goods it pleases in its production set. For instance, the corn harvest depends on past rainfalls and also on how investment expenditures were allocated between seeds and irrigation.

The assumption that the number of techniques available is infinite and that $\gamma^j(\ )$ is differentiable, is generally retained throughout the paper. This is clearly an idealisation. Indeed S must be considered a large number. Some elementary events (say u and t) are likely to be distinguishable for a firm j only by observing facts that are physically independent of its production process, although other firms are affected. Then, the level of all other variables being given, the set of (b_u^j, b_t^j) bundles that the firm has to choose from is a square. The differentiability assumption is thus violated.

Another extreme idealisation would be to assume that all output ratios are fixed within each firm. A few implications of this assumption are sketched in section II(2).

If the supply of output to consumers is contingent on the state of the world, one has to distinguish *ex ante* as many goods in consump-

[1] However, when $\sum_s p_s b_s^j - a^j = \omega^j = 0$, financing through sales is possible, while stock financing is not.

Competitive Equilibrium of the Stock Exchange

tion as there are possible states of the world; x_s^i stands for the second period consumption level of agent i under state s, $(s = 1, ..., S)$.

When every contingent good can be exchanged separately before the true state of the world is known, we may denote the price of good s by p_s and apply the model with universal markets that was described in section I. The resulting allocation of risks is fully Pareto-efficient. Let us now turn to an economy without independent markets for contingent goods.

(2) *Risk Allocation Through Joint Ownership*

Suppose that contingent goods are exchanged only in bundles, by means of shares. The outputs of firm j are distributed among its shareholders proportionately to their shares, as in the model with universal markets. However, what shareholders receive as dividends, they also consume; they can no longer dissociate the package of contingent goods, which every share represents, in order to sell them on separate markets. Equations (1.11) to (1.14) remain valid. Equation (1.15) must be replaced by the following:

$$x_s^i \leqslant \sum_j \frac{y_{ij}}{n_j} b_s^j \qquad \forall\, i, s. \tag{2.1}$$

In view of (1.4), (1.7) and (1.8) the relevant first-order conditions for Pareto efficiency are those of the intermediate case in section I, viz. (1.9) and (1.10).

Explicit assumptions are needed to specify the behaviour of consumers and producers. First, I shall consider the selection of portfolios and consumption plans.

Assumption 1. When selecting his portfolio and his consumption plan, agent i considers p^j and b_s^j/n_j as given $\forall\, j, s$.

This assumption was also implicit in the model with universal markets. In the present context its implications may appear very restrictive; indeed, stockholders generally disagree about optimal production plans, and a stockholder's bearing on production decisions may be influenced by the share he owns.

For instance, the case of a producer–owner who refuses to set up a corporation, for fear of losing control of his firm, is ruled out by assumption 1. The latter is a natural generalisation of the assumption of perfect competition; it is defensible only if each agent holds a tiny fraction of total resources.

The implications of assumption 1 are easy to unravel; since utility is increasing, constraints (1.11) and (2.1) are binding. Combining these equations with (1.1);

$$U^i = U^i(\omega^i + \sum_j p^j(v_{ij} - y_{ij}), \sum_j \frac{y_{ij}}{n_j} b_1^j, ..., \sum_j \frac{y_{ij}}{n_j} b_s^j, ...). \tag{2.2}$$

As a necessary condition for an unconstrained maximum,

$$\frac{\partial U^i}{\partial y_{ij}} = -U_0^i p^j + \sum_s \frac{b_s^j}{n_j} U_s^i = 0. \tag{2.3}$$

Dividing through by $\dfrac{U_0^i}{n_j}$ and rearranging

$$\sum_s \Pi_s^i b_s^j = p^j n_j \qquad \forall\, i, j. \tag{2.4}$$

The right-hand side of (2.4) is independent of i. Hence condition (1.10) for Pareto efficiency is satisfied. It is not at all surprising that a competitive market for composite goods equates the relevant marginal rates of substitution.

We can now turn to the choice of production plans; we want to find out when condition (1.9), which is also necessary for Pareto efficiency, is satisfied.

Two special cases must be disposed of beforehand. First, suppose there are fewer states than firms. If proposed output vectors are linearly independent, and if short sales of shares are allowed (that is, if the sign restrictions concerning the y_{ij}'s are dropped), then any consumption plan can be obtained by a suitable portfolio and every contingent good has an implicit price. Thus, in order to test whether these proposed production plans are equilibrium plans, one must turn to the model involving perfect markets for contingent goods (section I(4)).

Secondly, if output ratios are fixed within each firm (contrary to equation (1.2)), meaningful aggregates can be defined. The market value of a share determines the price of the aggregate for the production plan which is in fact chosen. In a competitive setting, this price is deemed constant. The value of a share associated with any production plan is thus unambiguous and the universal market apparatus may be used again.[1] Price-taking agents spontaneously agree that the quantity of output per outstanding share should be maximised; and constrained Pareto efficiency obtains if such production plans are adopted. This case is treated extensively by Diamond in [5].

Except for such special cases, no market evidence allows stockholders to predict how the price of a share is affected by a change of output ratios. Equation (1.16) is of no help.

---

[1] Let b be the aggregate output of a firm. By assumption, there exist constant numbers $\alpha_1, \ldots \alpha_S$ such that $b = \alpha_1 b_1 = \ldots = \alpha_S b_S$.

Let b^0 be the output that is in fact produced; the price of aggregate output is defined by $\phi b^0 = p^0 n^0$ where $p^0 n^0$ denotes the observed market value of the firm. The value of the firm for any other production plan is $pn = \phi b$.

In principle, the answer can be discovered by solving the system of $(I+4)$ J equations of the form (1.2), (1.12), (1.13), (1.14) and (2.4). Under favourable circumstances, the solution is unique, and it is possible to construct a mapping $\mathscr{M}$ from a set of arrays of output vectors into the set of firms' valuations. This mapping $\mathscr{M}$ reflects the demand side of the market.

However, I shall not assume that agents are perfectly informed. For each agent, expectation formulae will be specified only in broad terms, which can disagree with $\mathscr{M}$ unless there is equilibrium. In other words, by our definition of equilibrium, expectations must coincide with the market valuations associated by $\mathscr{M}$ with the array of output vectors which is in fact chosen. This feature reminds one of the analysis of imperfect competition.

To conclude these remarks, I introduce formally

Assumption 2. Agent i perceives the market valuation $p^j n_j$ of every firm j as an increasing differentiable function of its outputs.

These market valuations functions will be written

$$p^j n_j = \phi^{ij}(b_1^j, \ldots, b_S^j) \qquad \forall\, i, j \qquad (2.5)$$

and their partial derivatives will be denoted by ϕ_s^{ij}.

According to assumption 2, firm j's market value is not affected by the plans of other firms. This kind of myopia is fully consistent with the competitive spirit.[1]

The implications of assumption 2 are particularly clear, if it is supplemented by

Assumption 3. For some arrays of output vectors, portfolios and 1st-period consumption levels, either $\phi_s^{ij} = \Pi_s^i$ or $\phi_s^{ij} = \gamma_s^j$ $\forall\, i, j, s$.

The economic meaning of this assumption is as follows: agent i wants to predict how much the market is ready to pay in terms of good zero to get one extra unit of b_s^j; either he extrapolates his own feelings and assumes that the market is willing to pay exactly as much as he does, or he believes that value is somehow determined by marginal cost; in either case he pays no attention to the circularity of that kind of argument.

We are now ready to explore the implications of assumptions 2 and 3. First, what are the stockholders' preferences regarding production plans? Secondly, who is to make a decision? Thirdly, when are first-order conditions for Pareto efficiency satisfied? These are the questions to be dealt with in turn.

---

[1] One might get one step closer to equation (1.16) and assume that $\phi^{ij}(\ )$ is homogeneous of order one. This is consistent with the last footnote, but it has no bearing on what follows.

Suppose first that production plans and consumption plans have been established. What would be the effect of a small increase of $b_s{}^j$? By assumption, all other outputs remain unchanged and the increased input level must be financed by floating new shares.

In view of (2.2), we want to find an expression for dU^i when $db_s{}^j > 0$.

Adjustment of a^j, p^j, m^j and y_{ij} must be taken into account by differentiating totally not only (2.2), but also (2.5), and (1.2) combined with (1.14) (where inequality signs may be ruled out). Simple, but tedious, algebraic manipulations to be found in the appendix yield the following result. Three versions are listed to facilitate interpretation. As a matter of notation, final and initial share in firms are respectively denoted by

$$\theta_{ij} = \frac{y_{ij}}{n_j} \quad \text{and} \quad \sigma_{ij} = \frac{v_{ij}}{m_j} \tag{2.6}$$

$$\frac{1}{U_0{}^i} \frac{\partial U^i}{\partial b_s{}^j} = \theta_{ij}(\Pi_s{}^i - \phi_s{}^{ij}) + \sigma_{ij}(\phi_s{}^{ij} - \gamma_s{}^j) \tag{2.7}$$

$$= \theta_{ij}(\Pi_s{}^i - \gamma_s{}^j) + (\sigma_{ij} - \theta_{ij})(\phi_s{}^{ij} - \gamma_s{}^j)$$

$$= \sigma_{ij}\left[\frac{\theta_{ij}}{\sigma_{ij}}\Pi_s{}^i + \left(1 - \frac{\theta_{ij}}{\sigma_{ij}}\right)\phi_s{}^{ij} - \gamma_s{}^j\right].$$

Stiglitz's remarks about his own model [11] become perhaps even clearer in the present context. A stockholder who had no initial share ($\sigma_{ij} = 0$), despite our assumption to the contrary, would be affected only by his increased expenditure on y_{ij} and his increased consumption of good s. A stockholder who sells the whole of his initial share ($\theta_{ij} = 0$) would like to maximise the price of a share, or equivalently the value of his initial wealth.[1] If the stockholder maintains his share constant ($\sigma_{ij} = \theta_{ij}$), he wants to equalise the marginal cost of $b_s{}^j$ in terms of good zero with his marginal rate of substitution.

In the general case, the stockholder would like to obtain a compromise between the two principles: the marginal cost of $b_s{}^j$ should be equated with a linear combination of his marginal rate of substitution and the marginal income from $b_s{}^j$, with weights adding up to one.

If two stockholders have the same $\phi_s{}^{ij}$'s, i.e. the same beliefs regarding marginal income, they still have plenty of ground for clashing about what the firm ought to do; the ratio of their final share to their initial share may be different, and/or their marginal rates of substitution may diverge.

[1] From (1.14), (1.2) and (2.5), we can write $p^j m_j = p^j n_j - \gamma^j(b_1{}^j, \ldots b_S{}^j) + \omega^j = \phi^{ij}(b_1{}^j, \ldots b_S{}^j) - \gamma^j(b_1{}^j, \ldots b_S{}^j) + \omega^j$.

In the Arrow–Debreu economy with universal markets, both marginal revenue and marginal rate of substitution equal p_s for every agent; hence stockholders are spontaneously unanimous.

By assumption, our economy fails to have enough markets for contingent goods. No invisible hand is available to take care of production plans. In private ownership economies, this group decision problem is solved, at least in principle, by majority-voting among stockholders. Following one trend in the literature, however, the voting process is paralysed by its working costs and the manager who happens to be picked up may, in Williamson's words [12], exercise discretionary powers. I shall deal with the latter case first, as it is the easier one.

Suppose agents satisfy assumption 1 when choosing their portfolio.

Assume that each firm is managed by a particular agent who is selected exogenously. Then every manager chooses for his firm the production plan and the financial plan which suit him best. If assumption 2 is satisfied, and if, for these plans, the decision-makers' perceived valuation of their firm is consistent with demand as expressed by (1.2), (1.12), (1.13), (1.14) and (2.4), then the resulting allocation may be called, for short, a managerial equilibrium of the stock exchange.

Excluding corner solutions, such an equilibrium is characterised by equations (2.4) and (2.7), where the right-hand side is set equal to zero. They must be compared respectively with equations (1.10) and (1.9), in order to test for Pareto efficiency. Before explaining how it is reached, I shall summarise the results of the comparison in the following

Proposition I. Excluding corner solutions, a managerial equilibrium of the stock exchange fulfils the first-order necessary conditions for constrained Pareto efficiency, if and only if

$$(\sigma_{\beta j} - \theta_{\beta j})\phi_s^{\beta j} = \sigma_{\beta j}\sum_i \theta_{ij}\Pi_s^i - \theta_{\beta j}\Pi_s^\beta \qquad \forall j, s \qquad (2.8)$$

where β is the index associated with firm j's manager. Equation (2.8) is arrived at by inserting γ_s^j from (1.9) into (2.7), where the right-hand side is equated to zero, and by rearranging.

The economic meaning of (2.8) must be sought in the interpretation of (2.7). If the manager's relative share has not changed ($\sigma_{\beta j} = \theta_{\beta j}$), his $M R S$ should be equal to the average $M R S$; in this precise sense, he should be a representative individual.

The same conclusion is valid when assumption 3 holds locally in equilibrium. Generally, the manager's perceived market valuation of an extra unit of good s in terms of good zero should be equal to a linear combination of his own MRS and the average MRS. The weights depend on his initial and final share ($\sigma_{\beta j}$ and $\theta_{\beta j}$); they are of opposite sign and they add up to unity.

Now, if there are fewer firms than goods, there is no reason for the MRS to be equated. I cannot think of any natural specification of the market valuation functions $\phi^{ij}(\ )$ whereby (2.8) would be generally upheld. Assumption 3 fails in this respect.

My general conclusion is the following: production plans in a managerial equilibrium of the stock exchange are Pareto-efficient only by accident.

We turn next to what might be a less arbitrary decision-making process. From dictatorship, we turn to plutocracy. By assumption, each stockholder has voting rights proportional to his share, and production plans are selected through majority-voting. It is supposed that every agent selects that consumption plan and that portfolio which suit him best in conformity with assumption 1.

It is only natural to complete the latter by adding that stockholders do not perceive their influence on the outcome of the vote.

When ranking production plans, every stockholder predicts their financial implications with the help of market valuation functions which satisfy assumption 2. Voting is assumed to be a costless activity. Every stockholder may require a vote about any pair of production plans which are technically feasible in a stochastic sense.

Moreover, cooperative behaviour among stockholders is prohibitively costly. It was pointed out earlier that separate markets for contingent goods were too costly to run, and we do not want to reintroduce them under the guise of log-rolling.

A feasible allocation which is based on plans that are not outvoted by a majority in each firm, will be called, for brevity's sake, a voting equilibrium of the stock exchange, if it satisfies the above list of assumptions and if the shareholders' market valuations agree with (1.2), (1.12), (1.13), (1.14) and (2.4) for these plans. Production plans which are part of a voting equilibrium will be called equilibrium plans.

Prior to testing whether voting equilibria are Pareto-efficient, we have to characterise them.

Under assumption 1, portfolio choices satisfy equation (2.4); previous analysis has indicated that share allocation is Pareto-efficient under these circumstances. What about the choice of production plans? The following analysis is based on the works of Black [3] and Plott [9].

Under our assumptions, it never hurts a stockholder to let his voting strategy simply reflect his preferences preordering among production plans.

Competitive Equilibrium of the Stock Exchange

Consider an equilibrium plan of firm j such that non-negativity constraints are not binding. Suppose there is a small increase of $b_s{}^j$. Then $\frac{\partial U^i}{\partial b_s{}^j}$ as determined by (2.7), must not be positive for shareholders controlling together over one-half of the shares. Otherwise the plan would be out-voted. A small decrease of $b_s{}^j$ may also be proposed. No majority must approve this proposal.

Therefore marginal cost must be, in equilibrium, a median value of the distribution among stockholders of the quantity

$$\frac{\theta_{ij}}{\sigma_{ij}}\Pi_s{}^i + \left(1 - \frac{\theta_{ij}}{\sigma_{ij}}\right)\phi_s{}^{ij},$$

each stockholder being weighted by his share θ_{ij}. If this production plan is to be Pareto-efficient it must also satisfy equation (1.9); in other words, the marginal cost of good s must be equal to $\sum_i \theta_{ij}\Pi_s{}^i$, the average $M R S$.

I can now summarise the conclusion of the above analysis:

Proposition 2. Excluding corner solutions, a voting equilibrium of the stock exchange is not Pareto-efficient, if for some firm, the average $M R S$ of some output s in terms of good zero $\sum_i \theta_{ij}\Pi_s{}^i$ is not a median value of the distribution among stockholders of the quantity

$$\frac{\theta_{ij}}{\sigma_{ij}}\Pi_s{}^i + \left(1 - \frac{\theta_{ij}}{\sigma_{ij}}\right)\phi_s{}^{ij}$$

weighted by the θ_{ij}'s.

The meaning of this condition must again be sought in the interpretation of equation (2.7).

If the first condition of assumption 3 is satisfied locally by each stockholder in equilibrium, and if each set of median values contains only one element, the first-order necessary conditions for constrained Pareto efficiency are satisfied when the median $M R S$ coincides with the average $M R S$ for each firm and each good.

This happy coincidence can only be accidental when there are fewer firms than states of the world. Again I cannot think of any natural specification of the market valuation functions $\phi^{ij}(\ )$ that would allow a more optimistic conclusion.

Moreover, the first-order necessary conditions for Pareto efficiency are not sufficient. For an example taken from Drèze [7], see the appendix.

There is another theoretical problem which is associated with majority voting, namely the question of existence. Occurrence of the Condorcet paradox cannot be ruled out, as an example in the appendix shows. A paper by Hamada [8] contains an interesting contribution to this topic.

III. PRICE UNCERTAINTY

The formalism of section II may also be used in the analysis of temporary equilibrium, to test whether some kind of Pareto efficiency is achieved by a competitive stock exchange.

By assumption, there exists one commodity which agents may use for present consumption or for investment in a number of firms. Firms finance their needs by floating shares; they produce many commodities which appear at period two and are distributed to stockholders; the latter are allowed to sell them on spot markets. By assumption, separate forward markets are lacking.

There is no uncertainty about the productive processes. The only source of uncertainty is the following: agents have no sure method of forecasting future spot prices. I assume that many distinct vectors of future spot prices are considered as possible.[1]

The analysis is centred on two problems: portfolio selection and production decisions.

When production plans are known, selecting a portfolio mainly amounts to choosing a favourable endowment in anticipation of the future exchange opportunities. Every vector of future spot prices which is deemed possible must receive its proper weight.

The same consideration may guide the choice of production plans. However, there is an added complication; indeed, the price of a share depends on the output vector which it represents. An agent's judgement concerning production is influenced by his portfolio policy; *ceteris paribus*, an agent who decreases his share in a firm clashes with an agent whose share has increased.

With a minimal amount of reinterpretation, the apparatus of the previous sections proves relevant in the present context.

Equations (1.2) and (1.11) to (1.14), which are valid in the model with universal markets, must be retained here as building blocks.

Equation (1.15) might still be used if agents were to know future spot prices with full certainty. As was just mentioned, I am interested in a more general situation: I assume that there are $T < \infty$ possible future price vectors. Each one may be interpreted *ex ante* as a

---

[1] The model presented here has much in common with the model of Sondermann [10]. However, it is less ambitious at least in two respects; the world ends after period two and there are no monetary assets. Also the problem of existence is not tackled. This model throws some light on two questions which are not studied by Sondermann: (i) what are the natural objectives of the firms; and (ii) is a competitive equilibrium Pareto-efficient?

different state of the world; it is natural to enlarge the commodity space to accommodate these contingencies.

Let p_{st} and $x_{st}{}^i$ denote respectively the future spot price of good s in state t ($t=1, \ldots T$) and agent i's associated consumption of the same good.

We now give $x_s{}^i$ ($s=1, \ldots, S$) a new interpretation: $x_s{}^i$ stands for the quantity of good s which is delivered to agent i by the production sector at the beginning of period two, whatever the state of the world may be. The quantity $x_s{}^i$ must satisfy inequality (2.1) for every pair i, s.

If state t obtains, agent i's spot budgetary constraint is given by

$$\sum_{s=1}^{S} p_{st} x_{st}{}^i \leqslant \sum_{s=1}^{S} p_{st} x_s{}^i \quad \forall\, t. \tag{3.1}$$

It is assumed that the set of feasible consumption plans of agent i is the non-negative orthant $R_+{}^{ST+1}$. By assumption, this set is completely preordered by a preference relation which is peculiar to agent i. Given $x_s{}^i$ ($s=0, 1, \ldots, S$) and given p_{st} ($\forall\, t, s \geqslant 1$), agent i is assumed to choose a maximal element among the consumption plans which satisfy (3.1). By this procedure, an indirect ordering of the vectors $x^i = (x_0{}^i, x_1{}^i, \ldots x_s{}^i, \ldots, x_S{}^i) \in R_+{}^{S+1}$ may be derived. I assume that the latter ranking can be represented by a differentiable function $U^i(x^i)$ which satisfies the restrictions applying to (1.1).

From this point on, all the other assumptions of section II may be used again in the present context. The concept of constrained Pareto efficiency requires an obvious reinterpretation. Indeed, the analysis proceeds from the functions $U^i(x^i)$ which are taken as exogenous. In other words, the final allocation of goods at period two is to be a market allocation, and the structure of the agents' information with respect to future spot prices is taken as a datum.

Then a feasible allocation which satisfies constraints (1.4), (1.7) and (1.8) is Pareto-efficient in a restricted sense if the choice of first-period consumptions, portfolios and production plans is such that nobody can be made better off without making someone else worse off.[1]

The conclusions are the same as in section II. Neither managerial dictatorship nor majority voting is likely to bring about a constrained Pareto optimum.

---

[1] In a more sophisticated model, there would be as many physical goods in period one as in period two and the price expectations would depend on period one spot prices. Then, the derived utility functions would also depend on period one spot prices, and the relevant concept of Pareto efficiency would be even more restrictive than the one which is used in this section. Arrow and Hahn use an analogous concept of Pareto efficiency in [2].

IV. CONCLUSION

If separate markets for contingent goods or future goods are lacking at period one and if there are fewer firms than commodities, then there is no obvious way of guessing how a production change affects the value of a share.

Unless the decision-makers' share in the firm is the same when the stock exchange opens as when it closes down, the choice of market valuation functions is critical for the selection of production plans, and thus for Pareto efficiency.

I have defined these functions very broadly (assumption 2) and offered a specific hypothesis (assumption 3).

I have tried to put the odds in favour of the stock exchange by assuming competitive behaviour wherever it seemed tenable (assumption 1).

Decision-making responsibilities have been put in such hands that Pareto-efficient allocations would emerge if there were enough markets.

Then, managerial equilibria and voting equilibria, as defined in this paper, may be aptly considered to be particular instances of competitive equilibria, and the title of the paper can be justified.

If there are fewer firms than goods, such equilibria achieve constrained Pareto efficiency only by accident under my specific assumption 3. And I fail to see any plausible specification of the market valuation functions which would be generally consistent with Pareto efficiency.

To set up a more realistic model, one should allow for the indirect control of a firm through the portfolio of other firms. One should also relax assumption 1 pertaining to the competitive behaviour of some consumers.

I am told that firms check their market valuation function through controlled leaks in the financial press. All these features point to the need for a more general model which would blend the analysis of imperfect competition with bargaining theory. I conjecture that the outcome is highly unlikely to be Pareto-efficient, so that there may be some scope for devising a more satisfactory organisation of production.

APPENDIX

(1) *Derivation of Equation* (2.7) *in the Text*

Differentiate totally (2.2), (2.5) and (1.2) combined with (1.14), ruling out the inequality sign in the latter:

Competitive Equilibrium of the Stock Exchange

$$dU^i = \frac{\partial U^i}{\partial y_{ij}} dy_{ij} + U_0^i(v_{ij} - y_{ij})dp^j + U_s^i \frac{y_{ij}}{n_j} db_s^j$$

$$- \sum_{t=1}^{S} U_t^i \frac{y_{ij}}{n_j} \frac{b_t^j}{n_j} dn_j \quad \text{(A.1)}$$

$$n_j dp^j + p^j dn_j = \phi_s^{ij} db_s^j \quad \text{(A.2)}$$

$$(n_j - m_j)dp^j + p^j dn_j = \gamma_s^j db_s^j. \quad \text{(A.3)}$$

Subtracting (A.3) from (A.2), and substituting successively in (A.2) and (A.1)

$$m_j dp^j = (\phi_s^{ij} - \gamma_s^j) db_s^j \quad \text{(A.4)}$$

$$p^j dn_j = \phi_s^{ij} db_s^j - \frac{n_j}{m_j}(\phi_s^{ij} - \gamma_s^j) db_s^j \quad \text{(A.5)}$$

$$dU^i = U_0^i(v_{ij} - y_{ij}) \frac{1}{m_j}(\phi_s^{ij} - \gamma_s^j) db_s^j + U_s^i \frac{y_{ij}}{n_j} db_s^j$$

$$- \sum_{t=1}^{S} U_t^i \frac{b_t^j}{n_j} \frac{y_{ij}}{n_j} \frac{1}{p_j}\left(\phi_s^{ij} - \frac{n_j}{m_j}\phi_s^{ij} + \frac{n_j}{m_j}\gamma_s^j\right) db_s^j \quad \text{(A.6)}$$

where use made of (2.3). Substituting from (2.3)

$$\frac{\partial U^i}{\partial b_s^j} = U_0^i(v_{ij} - y_{ij})\frac{1}{m_j}(\phi_s^{ij} - \gamma_s^j) + U_s^i \frac{y_{ij}}{n_j}$$

$$- U_0^i \frac{y_{ij}}{n_j}\left(\phi_s^{ij} - \frac{n_j}{m_j}\phi_s^{ij} + \frac{n_j}{m_j}\gamma_s^j\right)$$

$$= U_0^i\left(\frac{v_{ij}}{m_j} - \frac{y_{ij}}{n_j}\right)\phi_s^{ij} - U_0^i \frac{v_{ij}}{m_j}\gamma_s^j + U_s^i \frac{y_{ij}}{n_j}. \quad \text{(A.7)}$$

Equation (2.7) in the text is obtained by substituting from (2.6) and rearranging.

(2) *Example of a Competitive Equilibrium which is Inefficient Although the First-Order Conditions for an Optimum are Satisfied*
The following example is due to Drèze [7]. Suppose there are two states of the world, and two firms wholly owned by their respective founder when the stock market opens.

The first firm has its transformation loci described by a set of straight lines running parallel, with slope different from -1. In isolation, its owner is supposed to select a point on the 45° ray through the origin.

Now, suppose the transformation curves of firm two and the indifference curves of its owner are the mirror-image of those which were just described. Hence, in isolation, the same point on the 45° ray is selected.

If we let these agents meet at a stock exchange, we recognise at once that the initial situation is fully compatible with a competitive equilibrium. The stock exchange remains idle. However, it would be possible to increase each agent's utility level by letting each firm specialise, and by reallocating the outputs through an exchange of shares.

(3) *The Voting Paradox Under Technological Uncertainty*
Suppose there are three agents, three states of the world, and one firm. The production function is of the form

$$b_1 + b_2 + b_3 = \sqrt{a} \tag{A.8}$$

which is a special case of (1.2).

Each agent i ($i = 1, 2, 3$) has the same physical endowment ω and the same initial share in the firm $\frac{v}{m} = \frac{1}{3}$. His preferences are described by

$$U^i = \log x_0^i + q_1^i \log x_1^i + q_2^i \log x_2^i + q_3^i \log x_3^i \tag{A.9}$$

where the q_s^i's are positive constants such that $\sum_s q_s^i = q$.

This is a special case of (1.1).

Substituting in (A.9) from (1.11) and (2.1) where inequality signs may be dropped,

$$U^i = \log\left[\omega + p(v - y_i)\right] + \sum_s q_s^i \log\left(\frac{y_i}{n} b_s\right), \tag{A.10}$$

where p denotes the price of a share in terms of good zero. It is assumed that $b_s > 0$, $\forall s$.

Letting $\partial U^i / \partial y_i$ vanish, we have successively:

$$\frac{p}{\omega + p(v - y_i)} = \frac{q}{y_i} = \frac{1}{\frac{\omega + v - y}{p}} \tag{A.11}$$

$$y_i = \frac{q}{1+q}\left(\frac{\omega}{p} + v\right). \tag{A.12}$$

For all i, this implies

$$\frac{y_i}{n} = \tfrac{1}{3} \text{ if } b_s > 0, \text{ all } s. \tag{A.13}$$

Competitive Equilibrium of the Stock Exchange

Suppose that stockholders agree on some level of investment a, and they are discussing the output mix. The transformation locus may be represented by an equilateral triangle. Motions in six directions are considered: $db_s = -db_t$; $s, t = 1, 2, 3$.

By (A.10) and (A.13),

$$dU^i = \left(\frac{q_t^i}{b_t} - \frac{q_s^i}{b_s}\right) db_t, \qquad (A.14)$$

if agents believe that the value of the firm is unaffected.

Thus for every pair of goods (s, t) there is an optimal ratio:

$$\frac{b_s}{b_t} = \frac{q_s^i}{q_t^i}. \qquad (A.15)$$

The amount of the third good being constant, individual i always votes in favour of a motion which brings him closer to the optimal ratio:

$$\frac{q_s^i}{q_t^i}.$$

Consider the side of the triangle joining vertices s and t and select the point that divides it into two segments proportional respectively to q_s^i and q_t^i. From that point draw a line to the opposite vertex.

One such line may be associated with each pair (s, t). Their intersection marks the optimal plan from agent i's viewpoint.

Suppose now the q_s^i's are such that these figures are identical for the three agents concerned, except for the fact that the triangle rotates from one agent to the next.

Superimpose the triangles on each other and observe that three lines are drawn from vertex s to the opposite side: all points which do not belong to the median line are outvoted by a majority. If the median lines drawn from each vertex do not have a common intersection, i.e. if no two states of the world are equally probable, there is no equilibrium production plan.

(4) *The Voting Paradox Under Price Uncertainty*

Suppose there are three agents, one firm, one input, and three distinct categories of output. Each good has a utility value. Preferences are described by (A.9) with $q_s^i = 1$, $\forall i, s$.

Endowments are the same as in the previous example.

There are no forward markets for outputs.

Each agent has point expectations concerning future spot prices $(p_s^i, s = 1, 2, 3)$.

Letting p stand for the price of a share, and using (1.11) and (1.15), we can write the Lagrangian expression:

$$\mathscr{L}^i = \log\,[\omega + p(v - y_i)] + \log x_1^i + \log x_2^i + \log x_3^i$$

$$-\lambda \sum_s p_s^i \left(x_s^i - y^i \frac{b_s}{n}\right) \qquad (A.16)$$

Setting the partial derivatives equal to zero,

$$\frac{p}{\omega + p(v - y_i)} = \lambda \sum_s p_s^i \frac{b_s}{n} \qquad (A.17)$$

$$\frac{1}{x_s^i} = \lambda p_s^i. \qquad (A.18)$$

Substituting from (1.15) and (A.18) in (A.17);

$$\frac{1}{\omega/p + v - y_i} = \frac{\lambda}{y_i} \sum_s p_s^i x_s^i = \frac{1}{y_i} \sum_s \left(\frac{x_s^i}{x_s^i}\right) = \frac{3}{y_i}. \qquad (A.19)$$

Rearranging, we get

$$y_i = \tfrac{3}{4}\left(\frac{\omega}{p} + v\right). \qquad (A.20)$$

This expression is the same as (A.12). By assumption, each agent has the same initial endowment. Therefore $\frac{y_i}{n} = \tfrac{1}{3}\ \forall\ i$.

Suppose agents are in agreement about the investment level and they have to select an output mix through majority voting. By assumption, every agent believes that p does not depend on the output mix.

The transformation surface is again an equilateral triangle.

To achieve a voting paradox, it is necessary that each output be considered by one agent as getting the highest future spot price.

Given a particular assignment of the most preferred output among agents that satisfies our necessary condition, there are two different ways of completing each man's ordering. Thus there are altogether $2^3 = 8$ ways of completing the picture of the voters' preferences. A voting paradox occurs only in two cases.[1]

[1] An agent's preferences may be represented by arrows pointing towards his preferred output mixtures, as in the following table.

A given state of preferences among agents is obtained by associating a num-

REFERENCES

[1] K. J. Arrow, 'Political and Economic Evaluation of Social Effects and Externalities', pp. 1–23 in J. Margolis (ed.), *The Analysis of Public Output* (NBER, New York: Columbia University Press, 1970).
[2] K. J. Arrow and F. H. Hahn, *General Competitive Analysis* (San Francisco: Holden-Day, 1971).
[3] D. Black, *The Theory of Committees and Elections* (Cambridge: Cambridge University Press, 1958).
[4] K. Borch, 'General Equilibrium in the Economics of Uncertainty', pp. 247–58 in K. Borch and J. Mossin (eds.), *Risk and Uncertainty* (London: Macmillan, 1968).
[5] P. A. Diamond, 'The Role of a Stock Market in a General Equilibrium Model with Technological Uncertainty', *American Economic Review*, vol. LVII (1967), pp. 759–76.
[6] J. H. Drèze, 'A Tâtonnement Process for Investment under Uncertainty in Private Ownership Economies', pp. 3–23 in *Mathematical Methods in Investment and Finance*, ed. by G. P. Szegö and K. Shell (Amsterdam: North-Holland, 1972).
[7] J. H. Drèze, 'Investment Under Private Ownership: Optimality, Equilibrium and Stability', chapter 9 *supra*.
[8] K. Hamada, 'A Simple Majority Rule on the Distribution of Income', *Journal of Economic Theory*, vol. VI (1973), pp. 273–64.
[9] C. R. Plott, 'A Notion of Equilibrium and its Possibility under Majority Rule', *American Economic Review*, vol. LVII (1967), pp. 787–806.
[10] D. Sondermann, 'Temporary Competitive Equilibrium Under Uncertainty', chapter 13 *infra*.
[11] J. E. Stiglitz, 'On the Optimality of the Stock Market Allocation of Investment', *The Quarterly Journal of Economics*, vol. LXXXVI (1972), pp. 25–60.
[12] O. Williamson, *The Economics of Discretionary Behavior: Managerial Objectives in a Theory of the Firm* (Englewood Cliffs: Prentice Hall, 1964).

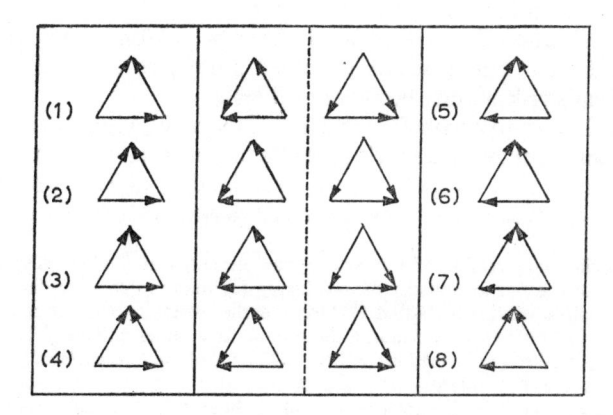

bered triangle with the two triangles on the same line in the two middle columns. Only case 1 and case 7 imply intransitivity of the voting process.

11 Discount Rates for Public Investment Under Uncertainty

Agnar Sandmo[1]
NORWEGIAN SCHOOL OF ECONOMICS, BERGEN

I. INTRODUCTION

The problem of efficient allocation of capital in a world of uncertainty has played a major role in the debate on the social rate of discount. One view, which has been advanced by Hirshleifer [7, 8] and supported by Diamond [6], is that differences in rates of return on capital in the private sector of the economy reflect differences in riskiness among alternative lines of investment, and that these differences are of normative significance for the allocation of capital in the public sector. Thus, when discounting costs and benefits of a particular type of public investment, the government should take as its discount rate the rate of return on capital in a private industry of similar riskiness. Another view, which counts Samuelson [17] and Vickrey [22] among its supporters, is that because of the extremely large and diversified investment portfolio held by the public sector, the marginal return from public investment as a whole is practically risk free and should be equated to the market rate on riskless bonds. In an important recent contribution Arrow and Lind [2] come to the same conclusion for a somewhat different reason; the total risk carried by the public sector is shared among so many that each individual's risk burden becomes negligible.

How is one to reconcile the Hirshleifer view with the result of Arrow and Lind, whose article provides the most rigorous foundation for the alternative view? A close examination of the two sets of arguments reveals that they are really based on entirely different

---

[1] A preliminary version of this article was presented at the Workshop. I am indebted to the participants in the workshop for many interesting discussions. Special thanks are due to Jaques H. Drèze, earlier work with whom resulted in [20], and to Louis Gevers, Maurice Marchand and James Mirrlees. The paper has previously been published in the June 1972 issue of the *International Economic Review*, where two referees provided constructive and interesting criticisms. The present version is identical to the one published in the IER except for a minor reformulation of the model in section III; this is described in note 1, p. 198 below.

assumptions concerning the relationship between private and public investment with respect to risk.[1] Arrow and Lind assume that the returns on private and public investment are uncorrelated; indeed, this assumption is crucial for their main result. The Hirshleifer view, however, is clearly based on the assumption that for each type of public investment it is possible to find a private industry such that the returns are highly correlated. To represent this situation theoretically it is tempting to substitute 'perfectly' for 'highly' and invoke the Modigliani–Miller [12] concept of risk classes, so that we can compare the yield on any type of public investment with that of private investment in the same risk class.

Which set of assumptions is the more realistic one is not easily decided. However, a good case can be made for the position that in a mixed economy of, e.g., the western European variety, the latter provides some crucial elements for the description of real-world conditions. In such an economy private and public production frequently coexist in industries like mining, iron and steel manufacturing, transportation etc.; it is for this type of economy that the Hirshleifer view would seem to be most relevant. In the following we shall formulate a stylised model of such an economy, derive conditions for optimal allocation of capital and present rules for public investment decisions under alternative assumptions about the structure of private capital markets.

General equilibrium models of capital markets have been explored in recent years by Sharpe [21], Lintner [10] and Mossin [13], [14]; an important forerunner of these contributions is the classic article of Modigliani and Miller [12]. This development has not had much influence on the debate over public investment criteria. To some extent this may be due to lack of contact between the two specialised fields of business finance on the one hand and public finance on the other; another explanation may be sought in the fact that these models are pure exchange models in which the real investment decisions of firms are taken as given. The first paper to give an explicit treatment of production and investment decisions within the framework of a general equilibrium model with portfolio decisions and asset markets is that of Diamond [6]; analytically, the models to be presented in the present paper may be seen as extensions of his. The new features introduced are first, explicit treatment of public investment and government transactions in the bond market and second, consideration of the case where there is no stock market in the private sector and only unincorporated business firms. Both of these extensions would seem to be crucial for a better understanding of the allocation problems involved.

[1] This observation has also been made by Hirshleifer and Shapiro [9], p. 298.

II. TECHNOLOGY AND PREFERENCES

In the economy there are m private industries or 'risk classes'. There may be several firms in each industry; we shall, however, take the industry as our basic unit of production and analyse microeconomic decision problems on that level.[1] The output of industry j will be denoted by x_j ($j=1, ..., m$), and total output in the private sector is defined as

$$x = \sum_j x_j. \tag{2.1}$$

This formulation implies that we are in a one-good economy, where the distinctions between industries are made solely on the basis of differences in production functions. The basic defence of this assumption is that relative prices of consumer goods are of little interest for the analysis, so that we can simplify the model by leaving them out.

The uncertainty in the model is technological; given the level of investment in industry or risk class j, y_j, output is known only in a probabilistic sense. Let θ be a stochastic parameter which describes the state of the world.[2] Then we can write the production function for industry j as

$$x_j = F_j(y_j, \theta) \qquad j = 1, ..., m. \tag{2.2}$$

Now we assume that there are also m public industries with production functions

$$x_j^* = G_j(z_j, \theta) \qquad j = 1, ..., m \tag{2.3}$$

such that z_j is public investment in industry j.[3] The interpretation is then that in each industry production takes place partly in private, partly in public firms, and that total output in industry j is simply $x_j^* + x_j$. It follows that total public output is

$$x^* = \sum_j x_j^*. \tag{2.4}$$

---

[1] No explicit attention is paid to the problem of aggregation from the firm to the industry. The step requires an assumption of constant returns to scale, and this cannot be accommodated in a model with only one input. Formally, the introduction of a second factor of production (labour) would have made it possible to assume constant returns to scale as well as decreasing marginal productivity of capital; aggregation would then be justified. However, this would complicate the model without adding much of economic interest. As it is, the identification of a production function with an industry rather than with a firm should be seen as an intuitive interpretation of the model and not as a result of rigorous analysis.

[2] The assumption that states of the world can be parametrised in this way is not important for subsequent results.

[3] It is not essential to assume that public investment takes place in all industries; this assumption is made for convenience only.

Discount Rates for Public Investment

The way in which production functions (2) and (3) have been written is a little too general to be useful in the present context. In industry j we wish public and private production to be of the same risk class; following Modigliani and Miller [12] this means that the *ratio* of the outputs must be independent of the state of the world. This condition will be satisfied if we write the production functions as

$$x_j = f_j(y_j)\phi_j(\theta) \qquad j=1, ..., m, \qquad (2.5)$$

$$x_j^* = g_j(z_j)\phi_j(\theta) \qquad j=1, ..., m. \qquad (2.6)$$

Thus, the production functions are multiplicatively separable in a deterministic and a random factor. With this formulation it is clearly seen that the ratios x_j/x_j^* – or, alternatively, the output shares $x_j/(x_j+x_j^*)$ and $x_j^*/(x_j+x_j^*)$ – are independent of θ. Outputs in the private and public parts of each industry are perfectly correlated.

For any given state of the world we assume that all production functions are everywhere increasing and – at least locally – with diminishing marginal productivities. This assumption may seem particularly restrictive for public production, and it could indeed be dispensed with, but it is preferable to make matters simple in this respect and to concentrate attention on the main issues.

There are n consumers in the economy. Each has a preference ordering over present (c_{1i}) and future (c_{2i}) consumption which can be represented by a continuous and differentiable cardinal utility function. Thus, the utility of consumer i is

$$U^i = U^i(c_{1i}, c_{2i}) \qquad i=1, ..., n. \qquad (2.7)$$

Consumers are assumed to be expected utility maximisers and to be risk averters in the sense that the marginal utility of future consumption is decreasing. The expected utility of consumer i becomes

$$E[U^i(c_{1i}, c_{2i})] = \int U^i(c_{1i}, c_{2i})h(\theta)d\theta. \qquad (2.8)$$

Here E is the expectations operator and $h(\theta)$ is the probability density function for states of the world. The formulation implies that all consumers use the same probabilities in evaluating states of the world. This restrictive assumption is defensible first as an approximation, second as a consequence of our desire to explore the specific role of private risk aversion as a possible source of distortion in the allocation of resources in the economy; to concentrate on this aspect it is convenient to eliminate differences in the probabilities.

With identical probability beliefs we can assume without loss of generality that production functions can be normalised in such a way that

$$E[\phi_j(\theta)] = 1 \qquad j=1, ..., m. \qquad (2.9)$$

This implies that $f_j'(y_j)$ and $g_j'(z_j)$ are the expected marginal productivities of private and public capital, respectively.

III. EFFICIENCY AND OPTIMALITY

It cannot be taken as axiomatic that public investment criteria should be derived solely from considerations of efficiency. The investment policies of the public sector will surely have redistributive effects, and a case may be made for letting the choice of discount rate reflect social welfare evaluations of these effects; this has been discussed extensively by Marglin [11]. It is clear, however, that the need for taking account of redistributive effects arises from a lack of policy tools; with compensatory income payments this need disappears. That such compensatory payments do in fact take place must be the assumption underlying most of the literature, which concentrates on the efficiency aspects of the problem. We shall follow in the same tradition and assume explicitly that compensatory payments are made. Without this assumption few operational results can be derived.

The relationship between competitive equilibrium and Pareto optimality under uncertainty was first explored by Arrow [1] and Debreu [5]. However, their model of state contingent commodities is not well suited for a descriptive analysis of the economic system. We shall therefore prefer to work with a definition of Pareto optimality which is due to Diamond [6]; a somewhat related analysis of a pure exchange model can be found in Sandmo [18]. Relative to the Arrow–Debreu concept of an optimum this is a second-best or constrained optimum, the constraint being that the share of output from any given industry going to any one consumer must be independent of the state of the world.

In industry or risk class j total output is the sum of private and public output, which is simply

$$\{f_j(y_j) + g_j(z_j)\}\phi_j(\theta).$$

In this initial period an optimum is determined by means of three sets of variables relating to the distribution of output in the second period. First, each consumer is allotted a fraction α_{ij} of the output of private industry j. Second, he receives a fraction τ_i of the total output of the public sector. Third, interpersonal transfers are made, so that each consumer receives a net amount a_i from other consumers – this amount may be negative or zero. It should be stressed that although these distributional parameters take effect in the second period, they must be determined in the first period before the state of the world becomes known.

Discount Rates for Public Investment

The future consumption of consumer i is then

$$c_{2i} = \sum_j \alpha_{ij} f_j(y_j)\phi_j(\theta) + \tau_i \sum_j g_j(z_j)\phi_j(\theta) + a_i,$$

and his expected utility becomes

$$E\left[U^i\left(c_{i1}, \sum_j \alpha_{ij} f_j(y_j)\phi_j(\theta) + \tau_i \sum g_j(z_j)\phi_j(\theta) + a_i\right)\right]. \quad (3.1)$$

To find the characteristics of a Pareto optimum we maximise a weighted sum of expected utilities, using arbitrary positive weights; any specific Pareto optimum is then found by assigning numerical values to the weights. In the maximisation problem we have the following constraints:

$$\sum_i c_{1i} + \sum_j y_j + \sum_j z_j = w \quad (3.2)$$

$$\sum_i a_i = 0 \quad (3.3)$$

$$\sum_i \alpha_{ij} = 1 \quad j = 1, \ldots, m. \quad (3.4)$$

$$\sum_i \tau_i = 1 \quad (3.4')$$

(3.2) is of course the constraint on initial resources, the total of which is given and equal to w; (3.3) says that interpersonal transfers must sum to zero; (3.4) expresses the fact that in each private industry the shares of output received by consumers must add up to unity; and (3.4') gives the same condition for the total of public sector output. Our problem can then be formulated as the maximisation of a Lagrange function

$$\sum_i \lambda_i E[U^i] - \alpha \left\{\sum_i c_{1i} + \sum_j y_j + \sum_j z_j - w\right\}$$

$$- \beta \sum_i a_i - \sum_j \gamma_j \left(\sum_i \alpha_{ij} - 1\right) - \delta \left(\sum_i \tau_i - 1\right).$$

Here λ_i is the weight given to consumer i's expected utility, and α, β, γ_j ($j=1, \ldots, m$) and δ are Lagrangian multipliers. The variables to be determined are c_{1i}, a_i, α_{ij}, τ_i, y_j and z_j. Differentiating in that order we obtain the following first-order conditions:

$$\lambda_i E[U_1^i] - \alpha = 0 \quad i = 1, \ldots, n. \quad (3.5)$$

$$\lambda_i E[U_2^i] - \beta = 0 \quad i = 1, \ldots, n. \quad (3.6)$$

$$\lambda_i E[U_2^i f_j(y_j)\phi_j(\theta)] - \gamma_j = 0 \quad i = 1, \ldots, n, j = 1, \ldots, m. \quad (3.7)$$

$$\lambda_i E\left[U_2^i \sum_j g_j(z_j)\phi_j(\theta)\right] - \delta = 0 \qquad i=1, ..., n. \qquad (3.7')$$

$$\sum_i \lambda_i E[U_2^i \alpha_{ij} f_j'(y_j)\phi_j(\theta)] - \alpha = 0 \qquad j=1, ..., m. \qquad (3.8)$$

$$\sum_i \lambda_i E[U_2^i \tau_i g_j'(z_j)\phi_j(\theta)] - \alpha = 0 \qquad j=1, ..., m. \qquad (3.9)$$

From (3.5) and (3.6) we obtain

$$\frac{E[U_1^i]}{E[U_2^i]} = \frac{E[U_1^k]}{E[U_2^k]} \qquad i, k = 1, ..., n. \qquad (3.10)$$

This condition is easy to interpret; the marginal rate of time preference should be the same for all consumers.

Substituting from (3.6) into (3.7) we get[1]

$$\frac{E[U_2^i]}{E[U_2^i \phi_j(\theta)]} = \frac{E[U_2^k]}{E[U_2^k \phi_j(\theta)]} \qquad \begin{aligned} i, k &= 1, ..., n. \\ j &= 1, ..., m. \end{aligned} \qquad (3.11)$$

This condition should be interpreted with care, since it will be a crucial one in our subsequent discussion. Observe first that in the case of risk neutrality, where U_2^i is constant, (3.11) is reduced to an identity. In the general case the fractions in (3.11) are the marginal rates of substitution between a unit of uncertain and a unit of sure claims to future consumption; these fractions can therefore be interpreted as *risk margins*. Each of them gives consumer i's risk margin for output of risk class j; at the optimum this should be the same for all consumers. This interpretation can be elucidated by substituting (3.5) into (3.8) and then using (3.10) and (3.11) to obtain

$$f_j'(y_j) = \frac{E[U_1^i]}{E[U_2^i]} \cdot \frac{E[U_2^i]}{E[U_2^i \phi_j(\theta)]} \qquad j=1, ..., m. \qquad (3.12)$$

The expected marginal productivity of private capital should be equal to the marginal rate of time preference multiplied by the risk margin; in other words, the risk margin is the ratio between the expected marginal productivity of capital and the marginal rate of time preference. Since conditions (3.10) and (3.11) imply that the right-hand side is the same for all consumers (3.12) contains as many conditions as there are risk classes.

It can be proved that all risk margins are greater than unity in the

[1] The formulation in this section is slightly different from the one published in the *International Economic Review*. There I assumed that the fractions α_{ij} applied to total output in sector j, both private and public. The present formulation leads to exactly the same results, but is somewhat closer to the models in later sections. That the two formulations are equivalent can be seen by the fact that equations (3.11) can be derived either from (3.6) and (3.7) or from (3.6) and (3.7').

case where the returns on all investments are non-negatively correlated.[1] If some returns are negatively correlated, however, this is not necessarily true.

Using the same procedure of substitution with equation (3.9) instead of (3.8) we get a similar condition for public investment:

$$g_j'(z_j) = \frac{E[U_1^i]}{E[U_2^i]} \cdot \frac{E[U_2^i]}{E[U_2^i \phi_j(\theta)]} \qquad j = 1, \ldots, m. \qquad (3.13)$$

The right-hand side is identical to that of (3.12), so that an immediate implication is that the expected marginal productivity of public capital should be equal to the expected marginal productivity of private capital in the same risk class, the risk margins on private and public capital should be the same. This conclusion has also been reached by Hirshleifer [8] and Diamond [6]. It is important to realise that it does not necessarily follow that this result describes the correct evaluation procedure in a given market environment; it does follow, however, that any argument for deviation from this rule must be based on second-best considerations.

IV. A STOCK MARKET ECONOMY

We first study an economy in which firms are organised as corporations. Consumers own shares in the firms as part of their initial endowment, and there are markets for exchange of these shares. Firms finance their investment by issuing bonds bearing a perfectly certain rate of return r (we abstract from default risk); the shares give the right to a part of the firms' profits as realised in the second period.

The profit of industry j in the second period – the amount earned by the stockholders – is then:

$$\pi_j = f_j(y_j)\phi_j(\theta) - (1+r)y_j. \qquad (4.1)$$

Since profit is stochastic there is nothing in the formulation which prevents it from becoming negative. The stockholders thus share in the losses of the firms on the same basis as they share in its gains.

The first-period budget constraint of consumer i is

$$c_{1i} + b_i + k_i + \sum_j s_{ij} = w_i. \qquad (4.2)$$

b_i is the amount lent to the government in the form of bond purchases, while k_i is the amount of private bonds bought. s_{ij} is the value of the consumer's purchase of shares in industry j, and w_i is initial wealth, which is composed of initial share holdings plus initial commodity stocks held, if any. Since we take the industry as

[1] A proof is given in the appendix.

the basic microeconomic unit on the production side, consumers' share holdings are only specified with respect to industries, not with respect to individual firms. This is immaterial, however, since all firms in the industry must be assumed to be identical, so that their shares are perfect substitutes for each other.

Let M_j be the market value of the stock of industry j, so that

$$\sum_i s_{ij} = M_j. \qquad j=1, ..., m. \tag{4.3}$$

In the second period the consumer receives a part of the profit of industry j corresponding to his share of its stock, $s_{ij}M_j^{-1}$. He also receives interest on his total bond holdings, $b_i + k_i$. Since both types of bonds bear a sure rate of return, this return must be the same and equal to r. Finally, the consumer also receives a share, τ_i, of the total profits earned by public firms, ξ. Consumption in the second period thus becomes

$$c_{2i} = (b_i + k_i)(1+r) + \sum_j s_{ij} M_j^{-1} \pi_j + \tau_i \xi. \tag{4.4}$$

Substituting from (4.2) we obtain

$$c_{2i} = \left(w_i - c_{1i} - \sum_j s_{ij}\right)(1+r) + \sum_j s_{ij} M_j^{-1} \pi_j + \tau_i \xi. \tag{4.5}$$

Expected utility becomes

$$E\left[U^i\left(c_{1i}, \left(w_i - c_{1i} - \sum_j s_{ij}\right)(1+r)\right.\right. \tag{4.6}$$
$$\left.\left. + \sum_j s_{ij} M_j^{-1} \pi_j + \tau_i \xi\right)\right],$$

and the consumer maximises expected utility with respect to c_{1i} and s_{ij} ($j=1, ..., m$). The first-order conditions are

$$E[U_1^i - (1+r)U_2^i] = 0 \qquad i=1, ..., n. \tag{4.7}$$

$$E[U_2^i\{-(1+r) + M_j^{-1}\pi_j\}] = 0 \qquad i=1, ..., n, j=1, ..., m. \tag{4.8}$$

They can be rewritten as follows:

$$\frac{E[U_1^i]}{E[U_2^i]} = 1 + r \qquad i=1, ..., n. \tag{4.7'}$$

$$M_j = (1+r)^{-1} \frac{E[U_2^i \pi_j]}{E[U_2^i]} \qquad i=1, ..., n, j=1, ..., m. \tag{4.8'}$$

The first of these conditions says that all consumers equate the marginal rate of time preference to the rate of interest. The second one may be interpreted as saying that the market value of firm j is equal to the present value of the certainty equivalent of profits.

Substituting into (4.8′) from the definition of profits (4.1) we obtain

$$M_j = (1+r)^{-1} \left\{ \frac{E[U_2^i \phi_j(\theta)]}{E[U_2^i]} f_j(y_j) - (1+r)y_j \right\}. \qquad (4.9)$$

This can be rewritten as

$$M_j + y_j = \left\{ (1+r) \frac{E[U_2^i]}{E[U_2^i \phi_j(\theta)]} \right\}^{-1} f_j(y_j). \qquad (4.9')$$

The value of stocks plus the value of bonds is equal to the expected value of output discounted by the risk-adjusted rate of interest. This is another restatement of the Modigliani–Miller theorem [12].

From (4.9′) it is clear that one effect of stock market trading is to equalise consumers' risk margins. Let us introduce the symbol R_j^i to denote consumer i's risk margin for investment in risk class j. Since we have that $R_j^i = R_j$, the risk margin in (4.9′) represents the *market* evaluation of the riskiness of investment in industry j.

The objective of the firm is assumed to be maximisation of stock market value, which is the natural counterpart to the usual assumption of maximisation of profit or present value.[1] We further assume that firms take the market's risk premium for their particular risk class as given; with many firms in each industry or risk class this is simply an assumption of price-taking behaviour. Using (4.9) the level of investment which maximises the market value of the stock in the industry is then given by

$$f_j'(y_j) = (1+r)\frac{E[U_2^i]}{E[U_2^i \phi_j(\theta)]} = (1+r)R_j. \qquad (4.10)$$

Thus, the expected marginal productivity of capital is set equal to one plus the rate of interest (the sure rate of discount) multiplied by the market risk margin. This is the risk-adjusted cut-off rate for private investment in risk class j.

Summing up our analysis of the stock market model, what are its implications in terms of efficiency? To see this we check one by one the efficiency conditions of the previous section. It is then easily seen that our equilibrium conditions (4.7′), (4.9′) and (4.10) guarantee the satisfaction of the optimum conditions (3.10), (3.11) and (3.12), respectively. Both marginal rates of time preference and risk margins are equalised among consumers, and the marginal productivity of

[1] The assumption of multiplicative uncertainty is important for the following argument; the reader is referred to Diamond's article [6] for a discussion of the complexities that arise in the general case.

investment in industry j bears the correct relationship to consumers' time and risk preferences. We are left, therefore, with one set of efficiency conditions, viz. those giving the rules for optimal public investment (3.13). The government should then obviously choose its own investment program so as to satisfy these conditions, which in the stock market economy take the form

$$g_j'(z_j) = (1+r)\frac{E[U_2{}^i]}{E[U_2{}^i\phi_j(\theta)]} = (1+r)R_j. \qquad (4.11)$$

Thus, in this economy the rule governing public investment should be: imitate private investment! There are perfect opportunities for pooling of risks in the private sector, and the market risk margins represent a social evaluation of the risk associated with each type of investment. They are thus far from being distortions, as is implied by Baumol [3].[1] On the contrary, they should serve the government as a guide to efficient investment,[2] and there is nothing to the argument that the government should use a riskless discount rate because it is a more efficient pooler of risk.

Evidently, in economies with stock markets there usually exist imperfections which have not been taken account of in this analysis and which may prevent the complete equalisation of risk margins. There may be indivisibilities which make it possible only for the wealthy to diversify efficiently and there may be transaction costs with similar effects. Although the importance of these considerations may easily be exaggerated, it is probably wise to see this analysis as an illustration of what an ideal stock market can do and only as an approximate description of what the real-world stock market actually does. How close the approximation may be is of course an empirical question of the same nature as the general problem of the closeness of a free enterprise economy to the competitive idealisation.

V. IMPERFECT MARKETS: AN ECONOMY WITH UNINCORPORATED BUSINESS

In the stock market economy each consumer has unlimited possibilities for portfolio diversification, so that the government has no

---

[1] A similar criticism of Baumol's view has been advanced by Pauly [15].

[2] How can the risk margin R_j be observed in the market? From (4.9′) we find that

$$R_j = \frac{f_j(y_j)}{(M_j + y_j)(1+r)}$$

The right-hand side is directly observable as the expected average yield on total capital, discounted to the present.

advantage over the individual consumer in this respect. The argument that the government is a more efficient pooler of risk must therefore be based on different assumptions concerning the nature of private capital markets. To analyse the effect of such assumptions we shall now construct a model in which consumers have no possibilities for diversifying investment portfolios in the private sector. We assume now that every consumer is also a producer and that he has access to a bond market but not to a stock market; thus he is completely unable to shift the risk burden. As a further simplification we assume that consumers are identical within each risk class, so that decisions on the industry level can be treated as if they were made by a representative individual. In other words, industry i is run by consumers of type i. Artificial as they may seem, these assumptions are not serious; a subdivision of industries on firms and consumers is perfectly possible, but it would entail a significant increase in notational complexity.[1]

The production function in industry i is

$$f_i(y_i)\phi_i(\theta), \qquad i=1, \ldots, n \tag{5.1}$$

and the budget restriction for type i consumers in the initial period is

$$c_{1i} + b_i + k_i + y_i = w_i, \tag{5.2}$$

where the symbols have the same meaning as before. Consumption in period 2 becomes

$$c_{2i} = (b_i + k_i)(1+r) + f_i(y_i)\phi_i(\theta) + \tau_i \xi. \tag{5.3}$$

Substituting from (5.2) into (5.3) we can write expected utility as

$$E[U^i(c_{1i}, (w_i - c_{1i} - y_i)(1+r) + f_i(y_i)\phi_i(\theta) + \tau_i \xi)]. \tag{5.4}$$

The first-order conditions for a maximum with respect to c_{1i} and y_i are

$$\frac{E[U_1^i]}{E[U_2^i]} = 1 + r. \qquad i=1, \ldots, n. \tag{5.5}$$

$$f_i'(y_i) = (1+r)\frac{E[U_2^i]}{E[U_2^i \phi_i(\theta)]} = (1+r)R_i^i \qquad i=1, \ldots, n. \tag{5.6}$$

---

[1] One extension which is not trivial is to assume that each industry is run by a partnership or syndicate, i.e. by a group of non-identical consumers. This raises all the familiar problems of aggregation of individual preference orderings, and there is as yet no well established theory in this field; see however [23]. For further aspects of the theory of the utility-maximising firm under uncertainty see [19].

The first of these conditions says that the marginal rate of time preference is the same for all consumers, so that our first set of optimality conditions (3.10) is satisfied. The second condition says that the expected marginal productivity of private capital is equal to the sure rate of discount multiplied by the risk margin. At first glance this may suggest the satisfaction of yet another set of optimality conditions (3.12), but this is not so. The reason is that there is no market equalisation of risk margins in this model. The risk margin in (5.6) is the personal risk margin of type i consumers; it does not represent any social evaluation of the riskiness of investment in this industry. This is the fundamental difference between the market solution in this model and in the stock market economy.

What is the implication of this for public investment criteria? There is no ready answer to this question. Because some of the optimality conditions are not satisfied in the private sector, the criterion for optimal public investment (3.13) has no longer any clear normative implication; we are in the world of the second best. Moreover, since the market risk margins no longer exist, conditions (3.13) are hardly meaningful any longer. We must accordingly seek investment criteria for the public sector in the solution to an explicitly formulated second-best optimisation problem. In this formulation the government is seen as choosing that investment program which is the best one in the Pareto efficiency sense, relative to the imperfections in the private sector of the economy. We must begin, therefore, with a clarification of the interrelationship between investment, borrowing and transfer policies of the public sector.

As in the previous models we assume that public investment takes place in all industries. In the initial period public investment is financed by borrowing from consumers, so that we have[1]

$$\sum_k z_k = \sum_i b_i. \tag{5.7}$$

The surplus (or deficit) of the public sector in the second period is

$$\xi = \sum_k g_k(z_k)\phi_k(\theta) - (1+r)\sum_i b_i, \tag{5.8}$$

or, after substitution from (5.7),

$$\xi = \sum_k g_k(z_k)\phi_k(\theta) - (1+r)\sum_k z_k. \tag{5.9}$$

---

[1] To avoid confusion we now use k as an index for the various industries in which public investment takes place while continuing to use the index i for the private components of the same industries.

Discount Rates for Public Investment

This surplus must be disposed of in some way. We shall assume that it is distributed among consumers in such a way that consumer i's share is τ_i. We must evidently require that

$$\sum_i \tau_i = 1. \qquad (5.10)$$

We also assume that the public sector is able to carry out an ideal non-distortive redistribution policy. This means that it can determine $w_i (i = 1, \ldots, n)$ in accordance with the weights attached to the utility functions of the consumers, subject only to the overall constraint on initial resources, viz.

$$\sum_i w_i = w. \qquad (5.11)$$

Substituting from (5.9) into (5.4), our problem is to maximise

$$\sum_i \lambda_i E\left[U^i(c_{1i}, \left(w_i - c_{1i} - y_i\right)(1+r) + f_i(y_i)\phi_i(\theta) + \right. \\ \left. \tau_i \left\{ \sum_k g_k(z_k)\phi_k(\theta) - (1+r)\sum_k z_k \right\} \right) \right] - \beta(\sum_i w_i - w). \qquad (5.72)$$

Here β is a Lagrangian multiplier.

The formulation may require a comment, since it is significantly different from the usual definition of the maximand in Paretian welfare analysis, as e.g. in section III of the present paper. First, preferences are represented by means of the derived or indirect utility functions of consumers, so that utility becomes a function of the arguments of the consumer's demand functions. The indirect utility function of consumer i is then defined by

$$V_i(r, w_i; \tau_i \xi) = E[U^i(c_{1i}, (w_i - c_{1i} - y_i)(1+r) \\ + f_i(y_i)\phi_i(\theta) + \tau_i \xi)]. \qquad (5.13)$$

Here c_{1i} and y_i must be seen as the demand functions which depend on the equilibrium values of the market variables r and w_i. The public sector chooses its investment and redistribution policies so as to obtain a Pareto optimum subject to the demand functions of the private sector and to the constraints (5.10) and (5.11).[1]

Differentiating (5.12) with respect to r, w_i, and z_k we obtain

$$\sum_i \lambda_i E\left[U_1^i \frac{\partial c_{1i}}{\partial r} + U_2^i \left\{ \left(-\frac{\partial c_{1i}}{\partial r} - \frac{\partial y_i}{\partial r} \right)(1+r) + (w_i - c_{1i} - y_i) \right. \right. \\ \left. \left. + f_i'(y_i)\phi_i(\theta)\frac{\partial y_i}{\partial r} - \tau_i \sum_k z_k \right\} \right] = 0. \qquad (5.14)$$

---

[1] For further examples of this approach in a related but deterministic framework see [20].

$$\lambda_i E\left[U_1^i \frac{\partial c_{1i}}{\partial w_i} + U_2^i \left\{\left(1 - \frac{\partial c_{1i}}{\partial w_i} - \frac{\partial y_i}{\partial w_i}\right)(1+r)\right.\right.$$

$$\left.\left. + f_i'(y_i)\phi_i(\theta)\frac{\partial y_i}{\partial w_i}\right\}\right] - \beta = 0. \qquad i=1,\ldots,n. \qquad (5.15)$$

$$\sum_i \lambda_i E[U_2^i \tau_i \{g_k'(z_k)\phi_k(\theta) - (1+r)\}] = 0. \qquad k=1,\ldots,n. \qquad (5.16)$$

Substituting in these equations from the first-order conditions for the consumers, (5.5) and (5.6), they reduce to

$$\sum_i \lambda_i E\left[U_2^i \left(w_i - c_{1i} - y_i - \tau_i \sum_k z_k\right)\right] = 0 \qquad (5.14')$$

$$\lambda_i E[U_2^i](1+r) - \beta = 0 \qquad i=1,\ldots,n \qquad (5.15')$$

$$\sum_i \lambda_i E[U_2^i \tau_i \{g_k'(z_k)\phi_k(\theta) - (1+r)\}] = 0 \qquad k=1,\ldots,n. \qquad (5.16')$$

Substituting from (5.15') into (5.14') we have that

$$\frac{\beta}{1+r} \sum_i (w_i - c_{1i} - y_i - \tau_i \sum_k z_k) = 0. \qquad (5.17)$$

Using (3.2), (5.10) and (5.11) we see immediately that the summation factor is equal to zero. By (5.15'), β must be positive. Substituting from (5.15') into (5.16') one obtains

$$\frac{\beta}{1+r}\sum_i \tau_i \left\{\frac{E[U_2^i \phi_k(\theta)]}{E[U_2^i]}g_k'(z_k) - (1+r)\right\} = 0 \qquad k=1,\ldots,n. \qquad (5.18)$$

Let R_k^i denote, as before, consumer i's risk margin for investment in risk class k. (5.18) then becomes, after utilising the constraint (5.10),

$$g_k'(z_k) = (1+r)\left\{\sum_i \tau_i (R_k^i)^{-1}\right\}^{-1} \qquad k=1,\ldots,n. \qquad (5.19)$$

Thus, the expected marginal productivity of public capital in risk class k should be equal to the sure rate of discount multiplied by a risk margin. This risk margin is a weighted harmonic mean of all consumers' risk margins for investment of risk class k, the weights being consumers' shares of the surplus in the public sector.[1]

The similarity of the solution to the one derived for the stock market economy is obvious. The difference is that instead of observing a market-determined risk margin the government must now

---

[1] The harmonic mean formula arises in a related context in the article by Bradford [4], which is concerned with the case where individual rates of time preference are not identical.

Discount Rates for Public Investment

compute it on the basis of knowledge about individual risk margins. In the stock market the individual risk margins become equalised so that $R_k{}^i = R_k$ for all i; substituting this into (5.9) yields (4.11) and provides us with a check on that result.

The solution (5.19) implies that the higher is the share of the government's surplus received by consumer i, the larger is the weight accorded to his risk margin; the risk margins of those whose shares are zero do not count at all. If the benefits of a given type of public investment accrue to a limited group of individuals, it is only risk margins within this group which are taken into account.

The computation of the harmonic mean of risk margins is by no means an easy task. Of the n risk margins entering the averaging only one – the kth – is directly observable; the remaining $n-1$ must be arrived at by direct questioning in some way. Theoretically, the situation is somewhat reminiscent of the problem of optimal allocation with public goods, where one also needs knowledge of private marginal rates of substitution which are not revealed in the market. As a practical matter a simplified procedure, which would still capture the essentials of the optimality rule, would be to take as one's point of departure the only risk margin which is directly observable, viz. that of the individual or group actually undertaking the corresponding investment in the private sector. This risk margin could then be adjusted upwards or downwards according to one's beliefs about this investor's risk margin and share of the government's surplus as compared to the average for the economy.

One sometimes sees statements to the effect that with imperfect pooling of risk in private capital markets the risk aversion of individual investors will lead to a distortive allocation of capital in the private sector, and the rates of return on private capital will have no normative implications for the allocation of capital in the public sector. We see now that this view cannot be correct in any literal sense. The expected marginal productivities of private and public capital in risk class k should be different only to the extent that the private risk margin of type k investors differs from the 'social risk margin', which is the weighted harmonic mean in (5.19). It is this kind of distortion which provides the rationale for using discount rates for public projects which are different from those for private projects in comparable risk classes.

VI. EVALUATION OF THE RESULTS

Formally, the argument of this paper is now complete. We have presented a definition of Pareto optimality under uncertainty and used this as a basis for deriving rules for correct discounting in public investment evaluation. The most prominent feature of these rules is that the public sector's discount rates should always contain a risk margin, and that this margin should correspond to the one used in the private sector for investment in the same risk class. In the stock market economy this margin can be inferred directly from market data; in the unincorporated economy an averaging of individual risk margins is required.

It deserves to be stressed once more that this is not *the* solution to the problem of the treatment of risk in public investment evaluation. The Arrow–Lind solution is another one, proceeding from different assumptions regarding the nature of public investment. Finally, much public investment is for purposes of production of public goods in the Samuelson sense [16]; this case raises additional problems concerning the criteria for allocation of resources which fall outside the framework of the present discussion.

Another important point to note is that in this model all risks are true risks to society as well as to individuals. Since the sources of risk are to be found in the nature of technology, these sources cannot be removed by changes in society's economic organisation. Default risk is one type of risk which can be so removed, and so are the game-theoretic risks associated with oligopolistic markets. Unfortunately, neither type of risk seems easy to incorporate in a general equilibrium framework.

The assumption of identical probability beliefs is another limitation of the model. It is well known that differences in probabilities raise problems for the definition of Pareto optimality: should expected utilities be calculated by using consumers' personal probabilities, or should the probabilities used reflect any superior information that the government might have? This question is of particular importance for the solution arrived at for the unincorporated economy, which requires assessment of individual's risk margins for investments that they do not themselves undertake. The only reasonable answer seems to be that in such a case the government should use its own best estimates of the probabilities involved, which may well be identical to those of the actual private investor.

It is natural to stress once more that the assumption of ideal lump-sum transfers eliminates the problem of the distributional effects of public investment, so that the criteria developed here are pure efficiency criteria. This is the framework within which the recent discussions of the subject has moved. It would clearly be desirable to extend this framework so that one can incorporate more realistic assumptions about the possibilities of income redistribution. It would take us too far afield, however, to explore these problems in more detail here.

APPENDIX

We shall prove here that in the case where the returns on all investments are non-negatively correlated, all risk margins are greater than unity. Actually, we have three models for which a proof of this is needed; viz. the model from which we derive the optimality criteria, the stock market model, and the model of the unincorporated economy. The proofs for the three cases differ only in inessential details, however, so we give the proof only for the first of the three models, as set out in section III above.

Let utility be written as in (3.1) above. Let $\bar{U}_2^i$ be the marginal utility of future consumption for $\theta = \bar{\theta}$ such

$$\phi_k(\bar{\theta}) - 1 = 0 \qquad (A.1)$$

for some k. Since the marginal utility of future consumption is decreasing and since all returns are non-negatively correlated we must have that

$$U_2^i \leq \bar{U}_2^i \quad \text{for } \theta \text{ such that } \phi_k(\theta) - 1 \geq 0. \qquad (A.2)$$

Multiplying both sides of this inequality by $\phi_k(\theta) - 1$ we obtain

$$U_2^i(\phi_k(\theta) - 1) \leq \bar{U}_2^i(\phi_k(\theta) - 1). \qquad (A.3)$$

This inequality must hold for all θ. For if $\phi_k(\theta) - 1 \leq 0$ inequality (A.2) must be reversed and multiplication will then leave the inequality sign in (A.3) unaffected. Taking expectations we get

$$E[U_2^i(\phi_k(\theta) - 1)] \leq \bar{U}_2^i E[\phi_k(\theta) - 1] = 0, \qquad (A.4)$$

where the last equality follows from (2.9). It then follows immediately that[1]

$$\frac{E[U_2^i]}{E[U_2^i \phi_k(\theta)]} \geq 1, \qquad (A.5)$$

which was to be proved.

REFERENCES

[1] K. J. Arrow, 'Le rôle des valeurs boursières pour la répartition la meilleure des risques', in *Econométrie* (Paris, CNRS: 1953). Reprinted as 'The Role of Securities in the Optimal Allocation of Risk-Bearing', *Review of Economic Studies*, vol. XXXI (April 1964), pp. 91–6.
[2] K. J. Arrow, and R. C. Lind, 'Uncertainty and the Evaluation of Public Investment Decisions', *American Economic Review*, vol. LX (June 1970), pp. 364–78.

[1] Since output cannot become negative we must have that $\phi_k(\theta) \geq 0$ for all θ. With positive marginal utility it then follows that $E[U_2^i \phi_k(\theta)] > 0$.

[3] W. J. Baumol, 'On the Social Rate of Discount', *American Economic Review*, vol. LVIII (September 1968), pp. 788–802.

[4] D. F. Bradford, 'Constraints on Public Action and Rules for Social Decisions', *American Economic Review*, vol. LX (September 1970), pp. 642–654.

[5] G. Debreu, *Theory of Value* (New York: Wiley, 1959).

[6] P. A. Diamond, 'The Role of a Stock Market in a General Equilibrium Model with Technological Uncertainty', *American Economic Review*, vol. LVII (September 1967), pp. 759–76.

[7] J. Hirshleifer, 'Efficient Allocation of Capital in an Uncertain World', *American Economic Review*, vol. LIV (May 1964), pp. 77–85.

[8] J. Hirshleifer, 'Investment Decision under Uncertainty: Applications of the State-Preference Approach', *Quarterly Journal of Economics*, vol. LXXX (May 1966), pp. 252–77.

[9] J. Hirshleifer and D. L. Shapiro, 'The Treatment of Risk and Uncertainty', in R. H. Haveman and J. Margolis (eds.), *Public Expenditure and Policy Analysis* (Chicago: Markham, 1970).

[10] J. Lintner, 'The Valuation of Risk Assets and the Selection of Risky Investments in Stock Portfolios and Capital Budgets', *Review of Economics and Statistics*, vol. XLVII (February 1965), pp. 13–37.

[11] S. A. Marglin, *Public Investment Criteria* (London: Allen and Unwin, 1967).

[12] F. Modigliani and M. H. Miller, 'The Cost of Capital, Corporation Finance and the Theory of Investment', *American Economic Review*, vol. XLVIII (June 1958), pp. 261–97.

[13] J. Mossin, 'Equilibrium in a Capital Asset Market', *Econometrica*, vol. XXXIV (October 1966), pp. 768–83.

[14] J. Mossin, 'Security Pricing and Investment Criteria in Competitive Markets', *American Economic Review*, vol. LIX (December 1969), pp. 749–56.

[15] M. V. Pauly, 'Risk and the Social Rate of Discount,' *American Economic Review*, vol. LX (March 1970), pp. 195–98.

[16] P. A. Samuelson, 'The Pure Theory of Public Expenditures', *Review of Economics and Statistics*, vol. XXXVI (November 1954), pp. 387–89.

[17] P. A. Samuelson, 'Discussion', *American Economic Review*, vol. LIV (May 1964), pp. 93–6.

[18] A. Sandmo, 'Equilibrium and Efficiency in Loan Markets', *Economica*, vol. XXXVII (February 1970), pp. 23–38.

[19] A. Sandmo, 'On the Theory of the Competitive Firm under Price Uncertainty', *American Economic Review*, vol. LXI (March 1971), pp. 65–73.

[20] A. Sandmo, and J. H. Drèze, 'Discount Rates for Public Investment in Closed and Open Economies', *Economica*, vol. XXXVIII (November 1971), pp. 395–412.

[21] W. F. Sharpe, 'Capital Asset Prices: A Theory of Market Equilibrium under Conditions of Risk', *Journal of Finance*, vol. XIX (September 1964), pp. 425–42.

[22] W. Vickrey, 'Discussion', *American Economic Review*, vol. LIV (May 1964), pp. 88–92.

[23] R. Wilson, 'The Theory of Syndicates', *Econometrica*, vol. XXXVI (January 1968), pp. 119–32.

Part 5

Short-Run Equilibrium with Money

12 On the Short-Run Equilibrium in a Monetary Economy

Jean-Michel Grandmont[1]
CEPREMAP, PARIS

A model of an exchange economy is presented where money is the only asset. It is shown that, under some assumptions, a short-run equilibrium exists if the traders' price expectations do not depend 'too much' on current prices.

I. INTRODUCTION

In order to take into account financial phenomena in a formal model of the economy, it seems worthwhile to consider an abstract world where several successive markets are held, to study the conditions which determine the equilibrium of each market and to find how these equilibria are linked together. This is a very old idea indeed, which underlies almost all economic thinking; it was in particular advanced by J. Hicks in his book *Value and Capital* under the name of 'temporary' equilibrium within a 'week' (see also J. Hicks [17], chapter 6). The same idea is present in the Keynesian theory and Don Patinkin [22] explicitly used this framework in his attempt to integrate money and credit in a general equilibrium theory. In a similar context, the recent work of E. Drandakis [8], R. Radner [23], [24] and B. P. Stigum [26] is in the same spirit.

However, the present state of economic theory in this area is not satisfactory, and there are still many difficulties to be solved before we have a consistent, formal theory of the temporary, or *short-run Walrasian equilibrium* (for a good survey of some of these difficulties, the reader may consult F. H. Hahn [14]). The research which is reported here was intended to make some progress in that direction. The simplified economy which is used to this effect is very similar to the economy which is studied by Don Patinkin in ([22], chapters 2 and 3) or M. Friedman in ([10], chapter 1). As the formal treatment of the model is somewhat technical, it is perhaps useful to give here

[1] I would like to express my deep gratitude to Gérard Debreu for his encouragement throughout this research. I also wish to thank Truman Bewley, Richard Cornwall, Emmanuel Drandakis, Werner Hildenbrand, Henry Lavaill, Thierry de Montbrial and Roy Radner for many helpful suggestions. I am also indebted to Jacques Drèze, Roger Guesnerie, Frank Hahn, Serge-Christophe Kolm and Yves Younes for their comments on an earlier draft. They of course bear no responsibility for any remaining error.

a brief account of the basic structure of the model and of the main results.

We consider an exchange economy where money is the only store of value. Time is divided into an infinite sequence of 'Hicksian' weeks; each week is indicated by an integer t. Markets are held on each 'Monday'; they are of the Walrasian type. All commodities which can be traded on any Monday are either consumption goods or (fiat) money. Consumption goods are perishable and cannot be stored from one week to the next; their number is N. Accordingly, a trader's consumption in the t-th week is noted by q_t, a point of R^N. Further, the consumption goods' *monetary* prices at time t are represented by a price system p_t; all prices considered in this study must be positive (formally, p_t must belong to $P_t = \{p \in R^N | p \gg 0\}$).[1] On the other hand, money has no 'direct' utility but is the only means to store wealth (at no cost) from one market to the next one. Finally, the total stock of money is invariant through time.

As in Patinkin's world, each trader receives on the t-th Monday a real income in kind, which is represented by a consumption bundle ω_t. His stock of money m_{t-1} was carried over from the previous week. The object of the t-th market is to allow for a reallocation of these endowments among traders. One of the objectives of our study is, precisely, to find sufficient conditions ensuring the existence of a short-run market equilibrium at time t.

A preliminary task is obviously to define the traders' behaviour on the t-th Monday. In order to do so, we consider a particular trader and assume that p_t is quoted on the floor of exchange. The consumer must choose his current consumption q_t and the money balances m_t he wishes to carry over until the next market. For the sake of simplicity, we assume that the trader makes plans only for the current week and for the next one. It follows that our trader must forecast next week's prices in order to make his choice. In this expository introduction, we shall take the trader's price expectations as certain (in the text, they will take the form of a probability distribution). They are based upon the consumer's information, which in our model consists only of past price systems and of p_t. Since past price systems are fixed, we shall not mention them and we shall note these price expectations $\psi(p_t)$, an element of P_{t+1}. Now let the consumer's intertemporal preferences at time t be represented by the 'direct' utility function $u(q_t, q_{t+1})$. If we assume that he knows with certainty next week's endowment ω_{t+1}, the trader's problem is to maximise $u(q_t, q_{t+1})$ subject to[2] $p_t . q_t + m_t \leq p_t . \omega_t + m_{t-1}$ and

---

[1] The following notation is used. If p, q belong to R^N, $p \geq q$ means $p_n \geq q_n$ for all n in N, $p > q$ means $p \geq q$ and $p \neq q$, and $p \gg q$ means $p_n > q_n$ for all n.

[2] For all p, q in R^N, $p.q$ denotes the inner product $\Sigma p_n q_n$.

Short-Run Equilibrium in a Monetary Economy

$\psi(p_t).q_{t+1} \leq \psi(p_t).\omega_{t+1} + m_t$, where q_t, q_{t+1}, m_t are unknown. The optimal solution (s) gives us the trader's demand for consumption goods q_t, and money balances m_t, in response to p_t.

This demand can equivalently be obtained by a two-step procedure,[1] which allows us to introduce the concept of the 'indirect' or expected utility of money (a similar two-step procedure will actually be used in the text for the case of stochastic expectations). First, given p_t and for every $(\bar{q}_t, \bar{m}_t)$, choose $\bar{q}_{t+1}$ so as to maximise $u(\bar{q}_t, q_{t+1})$ subject to $\psi(p_t).(q_{t+1} - \omega_{t+1}) \leq \bar{m}_t$ with q_{t+1} as unknown. Then define $v(\bar{q}_t, \bar{m}_t, p_t) \equiv u(\bar{q}_t, \bar{q}_{t+1})$. This procedure gives us the expected utility v of the action $(\bar{q}_t, \bar{m}_t)$; this expected utility depends, through price expectations on current prices p_t (and implicitly on past prices). It is clear that the trader's demand in the t-th week is obtained by maximising $v(q_t, m_t, p_t)$ subject to $p_t.q_t + m_t \leq p_t.\omega_t + m_{t-1}$ with q_t, m_t as unknowns.

This procedure 'introduces money in the utility function' as well as prices, and allows us to discuss an important question: is the expected utility v homogeneous of degree zero with respect to m_t and p_t? In general the answer is no; for instance price expectations may depend only on past prices and not at all on p_t, in which case v does not depend on p_t. On the other hand, this homogeneity property holds if the elasticity of price expectations with respect to current prices is unity, i.e. if $\psi(\lambda p_t) = \lambda \psi(p_t)$ for all positive λ (this condition is in particular satisfied by Patinkin's assumption of static expectations: $\psi(p_t) = p_t$ for all p_t). This is obvious if price expectations are certain; it will be shown in the text that the result is still valid when they are stochastic.

As was stated earlier, the main objective of the study is to find sufficient conditions which ensure the existence of a price system p_t^* which equilibrates demand and supply of all commodities (consumption goods and money) on the t-th Monday. We shall prove an existence theorem when, among other conditions, the traders' price expectations do not depend 'too much' on current prices. It must be noted that this condition is incompatible with the hypothesis of a unitary elasticity of price expectations which was discussed earlier. As a matter of fact, it is easy to construct counter-examples which show that an equilibrium may not exist when $\psi(\lambda p_t) = \lambda \psi(p_t)$ for all λ and p_t. Such a counter-example will be given in the text for the case of static expectations ($\psi(p_t) = p_t$ for all p_t). In that case if $\omega_t = \omega_{t+1}$ for all traders, and if the traders display a preference for present consumption, then the money market *cannot* be in equilibrium (if some other technical conditions are satisfied).

[1] The reader will recognise a standard dynamic programming technique. It was used by B. P. Stigum in a similar context [26].

The remainder of the study is devoted to a precise proof of these heuristic statements in the case of stochastic expectations. The paper is organised as follows. In section II we formally state the main definitions and assumptions. In section III we study the properties of an expected utility index. The traders' demand for consumption goods and money balances is analysed in section IV. The existence of a short-run market equilibrium is established in section V. Finally, conclusions are briefly given in section VI.

In what follows, it is taken for granted that the reader is well acquainted with the techniques which are used in G. Debreu's book *Theory of Value*. In addition, the reader should be familiar with the basic concepts of probability theory. References for additional material will be given in the text. Finally, a mathematical appendix gathers a few results for which no reference could be found.

II. DEFINITIONS AND ASSUMPTIONS

We fix t and focus the attention on the t-th week. There are by assumption K consumers (or traders) each of whom is indicated by an index k which varies from 1 to K. The symbol K will also denote the set $\{1, \dots K\}$.

The set of all consumption bundles available in the j-th week ($j = t, t+1$) which are admissible for the k-th consumer (his consumption set for the j-th week) is noted Q_{kj}. By assumption, Q_{kj} is equal to R_+^N, for all j (this assumption is inessential). The k-th trader's endowment of real goods at the beginning of the j-th week is noted ω_{kj}, a point of R_+^N. We shall always assume that ω_{kt} and $\omega_{k,\,t+1}$ are known with certainty by the k-th consumer on the t-th Monday. The k-th consumer's endowment of money at time t is $m_{k,\,t-1}$, a non-negative real number. The whole endowment is noted $e_{kt} = (\omega_{kt}, m_{k,\,t-1})$, a point of R_+^{N+1}. We shall make the following assumption. For all k in K,

(a) $\omega_{kj} > 0, \quad j = t, t+1.$

An *action* x_{kt} of the k-th trader on the t-th market is a complete description of his consumption q_{kt} (a point of Q_{kt}) in the t-th week and of the money balance m_{kt} (a non-negative real number) he wants to carry over from the current week to the next one. Formally, $x_{kt} = (q_{kt}, m_{kt})$ is an element of the action space $X_{kt} = Q_{kt} \times R_+$. The purpose of this section is to describe the k-th consumer's preferences among actions on the t-th Monday.

We assume for the simplicity of the exposition that the trader makes plans only for the t-th week and the next one. Then, the trader's *intertemporal preferences* at time t are defined on the space

Short-Run Equilibrium in a Monetary Economy

of consumption streams $Y_{kt} = Q_{kt} \times Q_{k,\,t+1}$. A generic element $y_{kt} = (q_{kt},\, q_{k,\,t+1})$ of Y_{kt} describes the trader's consumption at time t and $t+1$. It will be assumed that the trader's intertemporal preferences can be represented by a complete preordering $\succsim_{kt}$ defined on Y_{kt}. Then $y \succsim_{kt} y'$ is to be read: y is preferred or indifferent to y'. Note that this preference relation can depend upon past consumption. We shall assume for all k:

(b.1) For all y_0 in Y_{kt}, the sets $\{y \in Y_{kt} | y \succsim_{kt} y_0\}$ and $\{y \in Y_{kt} | y_0 \succsim_{kt} y\}$ are closed in Y_{kt}.

(b.2) For all y, y' in Y_{kt} such that $y \succ y'$, one has $y \succ_{kt} y'$.

When making his choice on the t-th market, the trader must forecast what his consumption will be in the following week, according to the price system p_{t+1} which will prevail on the next Monday, if he now takes the action $\bar{x}_t = (\bar{q}_t, \bar{m}_t)$ in X_{kt}. Given any $\bar{x}_t$ in X_{kt} and any p_{t+1} in P_{t+1}, let the set of feasible consumption streams $\gamma_{kt}(\bar{x}_t, p_{t+1})$ be defined as the set of elements $y_{kt} = (q_t, q_{t+1})$ of Y_{kt} such that $q_t = \bar{q}_t$ and $p_{t+1} \cdot (q_{t+1} - \omega_{k,\,t+1}) \leq \bar{m}_t$. Next week's consumption will then be determined by the maximisation of the consumer's preferences $\succsim_{kt}$ over $\gamma_{kt}(\bar{x}_t, p_{t+1})$. This procedure gives a set $\phi_{kt}(\bar{x}_t, p_{t+1})$, a subset of Y_{kt}, which is interpreted as the set of *conditional consumption programs* associated with the action $\bar{x}_t$ and the price system p_{t+1}. When $\bar{x}_t$ and p_{t+1} vary, this defines a correspondence ϕ_{kt} from $X_{kt} \times P_{t+1}$ into Y_{kt}. One shows by a standard argument:[1]

Proposition 2.1. The correspondence ϕ_{kt} is nonempty-, compact-valued and u.h.c.[2] on $X_{kt} \times P_{t+1}$.

In order to make a choice at time t, the trader must also forecast next week's equilibrium price system. This forecast will depend upon the consumer's information, which in our model consists only of the sequence of past equilibrium prices and of the price system p_t which is currently quoted. Past prices are fixed in our analysis: we shall omit them. For each p_t in P_t, the trader's forecast will take the form of a probability measure defined on P_{t+1}. Loosely speaking, a forecast is a random variable on R^N which assigns probability one to P_{t+1}. Formally, let $B(P_{t+1})$ be the Borel σ-algebra of P_{t+1}, i.e. the σ-algebra generated by its open subsets. Let $M(P_{t+1})$ be the set of probability measures defined on the measurable space $(P_{t+1},$

---

[1] See G. Debreu ([6], chapter 4) which can be easily adapted.

[2] Let X (resp. Y) be a subspace of R^N (resp. R^M). A correspondence ϕ from X to Y is P-valued if $\phi(x)$ has the property P for all x in X. Further, ϕ is upper hemi-continuous (u.h.c.) on X if for all open sets G of Y, the set $\{x \in X | \phi(x) \subset G\}$ is open in X.

$B(P_{t+1})$) (see K. R. Parthasarathy ([21], p. 1) for a definition). By assumption, the k-th trader's pattern of expectations at time t is given by a mapping ψ_{kt} which takes P_t into $M(P_{t+1})$. Then, for every E in $B(P_{t+1})$, $\psi_{kt}(p_t, E)$ is the probability assigned by the k-th consumer to the Borel set E if p_t is quoted on the t-th market.

We shall use, later on, the 'continuity' of a consumer's expectations. We must therefore introduce a topology on the set $M(P_{t+1})$. We shall choose the usual topology of weak convergence of probability measures (K. R. Parthasarathy ([21], chapter 2, section 6) and make the following assumption. For all k:

(c.1) *The mapping $\psi_{kt}: P_t \to M(P_{t+1})$ is continuous.*

We are now able to describe the k-th consumer's *preferences among actions* on the t-th market. These preferences will reflect his tastes, his expectations and his attitude towards risk. Since the trader's expectations may vary according to the price system p_t, his preferences among actions may themselves depend upon it. They will be described by a *family of complete preorderings* $\{\pi_{kt}(p_t) : p_t \in P_t\}$ defined on X_{kt}. Then $x[\pi_{kt}(p_t)] x'$ is to be read: 'the action x is preferred or indifferent to the action x' if p_t is quoted on the t-th market'.

The consumer's preferences will obey the so-called expected utility hypothesis,[1] which is now formally stated:

(d) *There exists a real-valued function u_{kt} defined on Y_{kt} such that:*
  (i) *u_{kt} is continuous, bounded, concave[2] and order preserving with respect to $\succsim_{kt}$;*
  (ii) *if for all (x_t, p_{t+1}) in $X_{kt} \times P_{t+1}$, $u_{kt}(\phi_{kt}(x_t, p_{t+1}))$ is defined as $u_{kt}(y)$ for some y in $\phi_{kt}(x_t, p_{t+1})$, the real-valued function v_{kt} defined on $X_{kt} \times P_t$ by $v_{kt}(x_t, p_t) = \int_{P_{t+1}} u_{kt}(\phi_{kt}(x_t, .)) d\psi_{kt}(p_t, .)$ is for each p_t order preserving with respect to $\pi_{kt}(p_t)$.*

We remark that this assumption makes sense. First, $u_{kt}(\phi_{kt}(., .))$ is a well-defined continuous function according to proposition 2.1. Since it is bounded, the function v_{kt} is well defined. The function u_{kt} is called a *von Neumann–Morgenstern utility* (for short, a von N.–M. utility) and $u_{kt}(y)$ is interpreted as the utility for the k-th consumer on the t-th week of the consumption stream y. Then $u_{kt}(\phi_{kt}(x_t, p_{t+1}))$ is the utility of the conditional consumption program associated with x_t and p_{t+1}, and $v_{kt}(x_t, p_t)$ is the expected utility

---

[1] I greatly benefited from the work of J. Tobin [27] and K. J. Arrow [2].
[2] That is, for all λ in [0, 1], and any y, y' in Y_{kt}, one has $u_{kt}(\lambda y + (1-\lambda) y') \geqq \lambda u_{kt}(y) + (1-\lambda) u_{kt}(y')$.

of the action x_t if p_t is quoted on the t-th market. In what follows, such a function v_{kt} will be called an *expected utility index*. Although we wrote the expected utility index as a function of current prices alone, it must be emphasised that this index depends also on the past equilibrium price systems. Finally, the concavity of u_{kt} on Y_{kt} means that the trader is *risk-averse*.

It must be noted that if we start from an *arbitrary* representation u of the preferences $\succsim_{kt}$ and we apply the formula given in (d), we shall not get, in general, a representation of the preordering $\pi_{kt}(p_t)$. What (d) says is that there exists *at least* one representation u of $\succsim_{kt}$ such that this is true (it can then be shown that the representations of $\succsim_{kt}$ which satisfy (d) are determined up to a linear transformation). In short,

Definition 2.2. A trader who satisfies (a), (b.1), (b.2), (c.1) *and* (d) *is called a regular trader.*

III. PROPERTIES OF AN EXPECTED UTILITY INDEX

We consider the k-th (regular) trader at time t. We choose a particular von N.–M. utility u_{kt} and focus the attention on the properties of the expected utility index v_{kt} which is derived from it as in (d). We shall drop the index k when no confusion is possible. We first establish a few technical properties of v_{kt}.

Proposition 3.1. Consider an expected utility index v_t.
 (1) *v_t is continuous on $X_t \times P_t$;*
 (2) *given p_t in P_t, the function $v_t(., p_t)$ is concave on X_t;*
 (3) *given p_t in P_t, for any x and x' such that $x > x'$ one has $v_t(x, p_t) > v_t(x', p_t)$.*

Proof. Assertions (2) and (3) are straightforward. We shall only prove (1). Fix (x^0, p^0) in $X_t \times P_t$ and consider a sequence (x^j, p^j) in $X_t \times P_t$ converging to (x^0, p^0). We wish $\lim v_t(x^j, p^j) = v_t(x^0, p^0)$. Now the sequence of functions $u_t(\phi_t(x^j,.))$ from P_{t+1} to R is uniformly bounded and converges continuously[1] to $u_t(\phi_t(x^0,.))$ on P_{t+1}. In addition, for each j, $u_t(\phi_t(x^j,.))$ is continuous on P_{t+1}. Finally, by (c.1), the sequence $\psi_t(p^j)$ converges weakly to $\psi_t(p^0)$. Therefore, according to [12, section 5, theorem A.3], $\lim v_t(x^j, p^j) = v_t(x^0, p^0)$.
Q.E.D.

We now turn our attention to the *homogeneity properties* of v_{kt}. Monetary theorists often assume that only 'real' balances enter a

---
[1] A sequence of functions f^j from a subspace Z of R^N to R converges continuously to f^0 on Z if for every z^0 in Z and all sequences z^j converging to z^0, one has $\lim f^j(z^j) = f^0(z^0)$.

typical trader's utility function (or in our terminology his expected utility index). In its most general form (see for instance P. A. Samuelson ([25], pp. 117–24)), this theory asserts that a trader's expected utility index must be homogeneous of degree zero in nominal money holdings and *current* prices. This property is often called 'absence of money illusion'. It should be clear that in our framework, a regular trader will not in general satisfy this requirement. In particular, if there is a lag in the adjustment of a trader's expectations, these expectations – hence the expected utility index – will depend upon past equilibrium price systems, but not on the current one. In this case, the trader suffers from 'money illusion'. But one cannot say that he is inconsistent.

It is interesting to find a condition which implies the above homogeneity property of the expected utility index. We first give some definitions. Fix any positive real number λ. For any subset E of P_{t+1}, the meaning of λE is clear. For any element μ of $M(P_{t+1})$, define the probability measure $\lambda\mu$ of $M(P_{t+1})$ which assigns to any Borel set E of P_{t+1} the probability $\mu((1/\lambda)E)$. Finally for any x: (q, m) in X_t, define $\lambda^* x$ as $(q, \lambda m)$. With these notations, the property we are looking for is $v_t(\lambda^* x, \lambda p) = v_t(x, p)$ for all positive real numbers λ, any action x in X_t and any price system p in P_t. It is intuitive that such a property will depend upon some kind of 'collinearity' between the trader's expectations and current prices. More precisely, let us consider:

(c.2) *For any $\lambda > 0$ and any p_t in P_t, $\psi_{kt}(\lambda p_t) = \lambda \psi_{kt}(p_t)$.*

This condition corresponds to the classical assumption of a 'unit elasticity of expectations with respect to current prices'; it is a very strong condition. We get as a particular case the assumption which is made by Don Patinkin in [22]: each trader is sure that p_{t+1} will be equal to p_t (from now on, this case will be called the case of *static expectations*).

Proposition 3.2. Under (c.2), *for any positive real number λ, any action x in X_t, and any p_t in P_t, one has $v_t(\lambda^* x, \lambda p_t) = v_t(x, p_t)$ (i.e. the expected utility index is homogeneous of degree zero with respect to nominal money holdings and current prices).*

Proof. Fix $\lambda > 0$, x in X_t and p in P_t. In order to simplify the notation, let $h(p_{t+1}) = u_t(\phi_t(x, p_{t+1}))$ and $\bar{h}(p_{t+1}) = u_t(\phi_t(\lambda^* x, p_{t+1}))$ for every p_{t+1} in P_{t+1}. It is easy to show that $\phi_t(x, p_{t+1}) = \phi_t(\lambda^* x, \lambda p_{t+1})$ in which case $h(p_{t+1}) = \bar{h}(\lambda p_{t+1})$. Then, the proposition follows immediately from proposition 1, section A.2 of the appendix.

Q.E.D.

Is it true that the homogeneity of the expected utility index implies (c.2)? I have no definite answer to that question. If, however, we consider the case $N=1$ and if the consumer's expectations are required to be certain (i.e. for each p_t in P_t, the probability measure $\psi_{kt}(p_t)$ is concentrated on a single element of P_{t+1}), it is easy to show that the homogeneity of v_{kt} implies (c.2).

The foregoing analysis suggests that the assumptions of 'static expectations' and of 'absence of money illusion' which Patinkin made in ([22], chapters 2 and 3) are consistent but too specific. On the other hand, our model, which allows for 'money illusion', seems to be in agreement with an idea which was put forward by, for instance, M. Allais [1], P. Cagan [4], or M. Friedman [9], [10]. These authors assume that at any given point in time, the aggregate demand for real money balances depends, among other things, on the expected rate of inflation, which in turn is a function – a weighted average – of current and past actual rates. It is easy to see that such an assumption about the formation of expectations leads to 'money illusion' in the above sense.

Remarks. (1) The 'classical' homogeneity postulate can be interpreted as a proposition dealing with money balances and *expected* prices. One can show that this type of homogeneity holds in our model. We only sketch the argument. Consider a trader at time t and let $\psi \in M(P_{t+1})$ be any probability distribution defined on P_{t+1}. Choose a von N.–M. utility as in (d) and define

$$\bar{v}_t(x_t, \psi) = \int_{P_{t+1}} u_t(\phi_t(x_t, .)) d\psi.$$

Then $\bar{v}_t$ can be interpreted as representing the trader's preferences among actions when his price expectations are ψ. By the reasoning of proposition 3.2, one has $\bar{v}_t(x_t, \psi) = \bar{v}_t(\lambda^* x_t, \lambda \psi)$ for all λ.[1]

(2) Another interpretation is that the homogeneity postulate deals with stationary states. This type of homogeneity also holds in our model. We first recall that a trader's expected utility index depends, through his expectations, on past prices: it can be written $v_{kt}(x_t, p_t, p_{t-1}, \ldots)$. Now assume that past and current prices are stationary and equal to $p \gg 0$. Assume that the trader expects with certainty in that case p_{t+1} to be equal to p. Looking back at the formula giving v_{kt}, we find that $v_{kt}(x_t, p, p, \ldots) = u_{kt}(\phi_{kt}(x_t, p))$. Therefore, trivially, $v_{kt}(\lambda^* x_t, \lambda p, \lambda p, \ldots) = v_{kt}(x_t, p, p, \ldots)$ holds: v_{kt} is homogeneous of degree zero with respect to m_t and the *stationary sequence* of current and past price systems. Note that this result holds even if price expectations are independent of current prices (for instance if the trader expects with certainty p_{t+1} to be equal to p_{t-1}).

[1] This remark is due to F. Hahn.

IV. DEMAND CORRESPONDENCES

Given p_t in P_t, the k-th (regular) trader must choose an action in his budget set $\beta_{kt}(p_t) = \{x \in X_{kt} | s_t \cdot x \leq s_t \cdot e_{kt}\}$ (with $s_t = (p_t, 1)$). His gross demand is then as usual given by the satisfaction of the (conditional) preferences $\pi_{kt}(p_t)$ over $\beta_{kt}(p_t)$:

$$\xi_{kt}(p_t) = \{x^* \in \beta_{kt}(p_t) | x^*[\pi_{kt}(p_t)] \, x \text{ for all } x \text{ in } \beta_{kt}(p_t)\}.$$

Here again, it must be emphasised that the consumer's demand depends also on past equilibrium price systems. When p_t varies in P_t, this relation defines a correspondence ξ_{kt} from P_t into X_{kt}. One shows by a standard reasoning:

Proposition 4.1. For any regular trader, the correspondence ξ_{kt} is nonempty-, compact-, convex-valued and u.h.c.. For all p_t in P_t and all x in ξ_{kt}, one has $s_t \cdot (x - e_{kt}) = 0$.

We next study the behaviour of the correspondence ξ_{kt} when the price of the n-th good tends to zero, or when the price level tends to infinity on the t-th market. In the first case, in view of the monotonicity assumption (b.2), it would seem reasonable to expect that the consumer's demand for the n-th good increases indefinitely; in the second case, one would expect that the consumer's demand for money will tend to infinity. Unfortunately, it is easy to show that this may not be the case if no additional restriction is put on the agent's pattern of expectations (see below). In this case, an equilibrium on the t-th market may not exist. We need a new assumption.

(c.3) *The set $\{\psi_{kt}(p_t) | p_t \in P_t\}$ is relatively (weakly) compact.*

Formally, this means that the closure of the above set is a compact subset of $M(P_{t+1})$. This assumption is automatically fulfilled if the k-th trader's expectations are independent of p_t, or if there exists a compact C such that $\psi_{kt}(p_t, C) = 1$ for all p_t in P_t (K. R. Parthasarathy [21], chapter 2, theorem 6.4). These remarks show the economic meaning of the above assumption: although the trader's expectations can depend upon the price system which is currently quoted, the range of variation of these anticipations must not be 'too large' when p_t varies in P_t. Finally, it should be noted that the above condition and (c.2) are incompatible.

Proposition 4.2. Assume that the k-th (regular) trader satisfies (c.3) and $e_{kt} \gg 0$. Consider any sequence p^j in P_t and any sequence $x^j \in \xi_{kt}(p^j)$. If p^j tends to $p^0 \in R_+^N \setminus P_t$, or if $\|p^j\|$ tends to $+\infty$, then $\|x^j\|$ tends to $+\infty$.[1]

[1] For any x in R^N, $\|x\|$ denotes the usual norm of x.

Short-Run Equilibrium in a Monetary Economy

Proof. We omit the index k. Assume that the proposition is false. This means that there exists a subsequence (which can be taken to be equal to the original sequence) such that x^j converges to $x^0 = (q^0, m^0) \in X_t$. One can assume that there exists an element ψ^0 of $M(P_{t+1})$ such that $\psi_t(p^j)$ converges weakly to ψ^0. Choose a von N.-M. utility u_t and let v_t be the corresponding expected utility index. Define a function h on X_t by $h(x) = \int_{P_{t+1}} u_t(\phi_t(x,.)) d\psi^0(.)$. As in proposition 3.1, one shows that for any x in X_t, one has $\lim v_t(x, p^j) = h(x)$ and $\lim v_t(x^j, p^j) = h(x^0)$. In addition, by the Dominated Convergence Theorem [3, A. 28 of the appendix], h is continuous. Finally, as in proposition 3.1, $h(x) > h(x')$ whenever $x > x'$. Let us distinguish the two cases.

$$\text{(i) } \lim p^j = p^0 \in R_+^N \setminus P_t$$

We have $p^0 . q^0 + m^0 \leq p^0 . \omega_t + m_{t-1}$ and $p^0 . \omega_t + m_{t-1} > 0$. It is not difficult to show, as in proposition 4.1, that $h(x^0) \geq h(x)$ for all $x = (q, m)$ in X_t such that $p^0 . q + m \leq p^0 . \omega_t + m_{t-1}$. But this leads to a contradiction, since there exists an index n such that $p_n^0 = 0$.

$$\text{(ii) } \lim \|p^j\| = +\infty$$

We claim that $h(x^0) \geq h(x)$ for all x in X_t such that $x = (q^0, m)$ where m is arbitrary. Fix such an x. Let for all j, $\mu^j = p^j / \|p^j\|$. Since $\|\mu^j\| = 1$, we can assume that μ^j converges to $\mu^0 > 0$. Clearly, $\mu^0 . q^0 \leq \mu^0 . \omega_t$. Now $\mu^0 . \omega_t > 0$ implies that there exists $\bar{q}$ in Q_t such that $\mu^0 . \bar{q} < \mu^0 . \omega_t$. Choose λ in $[0, 1]$ and define $q^\lambda = \lambda \bar{q} + (1 - \lambda) q^0$. Then $x^\lambda = (q^\lambda, m)$ belongs to X_t. We have $\mu^0 . q^\lambda < \mu^0 . \omega_t$, hence for j large enough, $p^j . q^\lambda + m < p^j . \omega_t + m_{t-1}$, which implies $v_t(x^j, p^j) \geq v_t(x^\lambda, p^j)$. In the limit, $h(x^0) \geq h(x^\lambda)$ and when λ tends to zero, $h(x^0) \geq h(x)$. But this leads to a contradiction: if $x = (q^0, m)$ is such that $m > m^0$, then $h(x) > h(x^0)$. This proves the proposition. Q.E.D.

We now give an example which shows why an assumption such as (c.3) cannot be avoided. We shall assume, as Patinkin does in [22], that the consumer's expectations are static. In addition, we shall focus the attention on the case $\omega_{kt} = \omega_{k, t+1}$. Finally, we shall assume that the preferences $\gtrsim_{kt}$ are separable and that the preorderings induced on Q_{kt} and $Q_{k, t+1}$ are identical. Then, the following result says that if the consumer displays a preference for present consumption, he will not keep more than one-half of his stock of money $m_{k, t-1}$. If all traders are of this type, and if the total stock of money is positive, the money market cannot be in equilibrium.

Proposition 4.3. Consider the k-th (regular) trader and assume:
(1) $\psi_{kt}(p_t, \{p_t\}) = 1$ for all p_t in P_t;
(2) $\omega_{kt} = \omega_{k, t+1} = \omega_k$;

(3) Given q_{t+1} (resp. q_t) in $Q_{k,t+1}$ (resp. Q_{kt}), the preordering $\gtrsim_{kt}$ induces a preordering on Q_{kt} (resp. $Q_{k,t+1}$) which is independent of q_{t+1} (resp. q_t). The two induced preorderings are identical and are noted $\gtrsim_{kt}^*$;

(4) for all q_t and q_{t+1} in R_+^N with $q_{t+1} >_{kt}^* q_t$, one has $(q_{t+1}, q_t) >_{kt} (q_t, q_{t+1})$;

Then, for every p_t in P_t and every $x_t = (q_t, m_t)$ in $\xi_{kt}(p_t)$, one has $m_t \leq (\frac{1}{2}) m_{k,t-1}$.

Proof. We drop the index k. Assume the contrary. Then, for some p_t in P_t, there is an $x_t = (q_t, m_t)$ in $\xi_t(p_t)$ with $m_t > (\frac{1}{2}) m_{t-1}$. Let $y = (q_t, q_{t+1})$ in $\phi_t(x_t, p_t)$. Let u_t be a von N.–M. utility, and let $v_t(x, p_t) = u_t(\phi_t(x, p_t))$ for all x in X_t. Clearly, $v_t(x_t, p_t) = u_t(y)$. Since $p_t \cdot q_t = p_t \cdot \omega + m_{t-1} - m_t$ and $p_t \cdot q_{t+1} = p_t \cdot \omega + m_t$, one has $p_t \cdot q_t < p_t \cdot q_{t+1}$, hence $q_{t+1} >_t^* q_t$. Now, let $\bar{q} = (\frac{1}{2})(q_t + q_{t+1})$, $\bar{y} = (\bar{q}, \bar{q})$ and $\bar{m} = (\frac{1}{2}) m_{t-1}$. Consider $\bar{x} = (\bar{q}, \bar{m})$. From $p_t \cdot \bar{q} + \bar{m} = p_t \cdot \omega + m_{t-1}$, it follows that $\bar{x}$ belongs to $\beta_t(p_t)$, hence $v_t(x_t, p_t) \geq v_t(\bar{x}, p_t)$. But $\bar{y}$ belongs to $\gamma_t(\bar{x}, p_t)$ which implies $v_t(\bar{x}, p_t) \geq u_t(\bar{y})$. Now, by (4) and the concavity of u_t, $u_t(\bar{y}) > u_t(y)$. Therefore, $v_t(\bar{x}, p_t) > v_t(x_t, p_t)$. This contradiction completes the proof. Q.E.D.

V. MARKET EQUILIBRIUM

We study the problem of the existence of an equilibrium on the t-th Monday. This study will allow us to test the logical consistency of the model which was presented in the preceding section. We first introduce some definitions.

A *regular economy* E_K is an economy composed of K regular traders. An *allocation* in the t-th week of the regular economy E_K is a K-tuple $x_t = (x_{1t}, \ldots, x_{Kt})$ where x_{kt} belongs to X_{kt} for all k, such that $\sum_k (x_{kt} - e_{kt}) = 0$. An *equilibrium price system* of the t-th market is a price system p_t^* of P_t such that there exists an allocation $x_t^* = (x_{1t}^*, \ldots, x_{Kt}^*)$ with $x_{kt}^* \in \xi_{kt}(p_t^*)$ for all k.

Theorem 5.1. Consider a regular economy at the moment of the t-th market. Assume that for some trader k, (c.3) and $e_{kt} \gg 0$ both hold. Then, there exists an equilibrium price system p_t^*.

Proof. Define $\bar{S} = \{s = (p, 1) \in R^{N+1} | p \in R_+^N\}$ and $S = \{s \in \bar{S} | s \gg 0\}$. For every $s = (p, 1)$ in S, define the aggregate excess demand correspondence ζ by $\zeta(s) = \sum_k \xi_{kt}(p) - \left\{\sum_k e_{kt}\right\}$.

It is easily seen that the correspondence ζ satisfies all the conditions of theorem 1 of section A.1 of the appendix. The result then follows by a standard argument. Q.E.D.

This result says that relative prices and the price level are *jointly* determined, provided the total stock of money is positive. Thus, we reach the same conclusion as Patinkin: the 'classical dichotomy' is invalid in the short run.

The foregoing existence theorem still holds for a regular economy when we assume $\sum_k e_{kt} \gg 0$ provided that *every* trader satisfies (c.3). The details are left to the reader.[1]

VI. CONCLUSIONS

We have presented a model of an exchange economy where money is the only store of value. We showed that a short-run market equilibrium exists if the traders' price expectations do not depend too much on current prices. This type of result and the methods we used to reach it should be useful for most sophisticated and more realistic models.

We assumed for the simplicity of the exposition that a trader made plans only for the current week and the next one. As a matter of fact it is not difficult to extend the analysis to the case of an arbitrary finite or infinite planning horizon when the traders' expectations are certain.[2] Our results are then still valid. The case of stochastic expectations is more complicated. Its study will probably require the use of stochastic dynamic programming techniques. However, it is likely that the main conclusions of this paper will continue to hold.

This research has been voluntarily restricted to a short-run analysis. The framework which was developed in this paper should, however, be useful for the study of the long-run properties of a monetary economy. The same type of approach should also be useful for the study of an economy with credit. It will then be possible to examine the effect of various monetary policies.

APPENDIX

Section A.1

The following theorem is an extension of a well-known result (see D. Gale [11], H. Nikaido [20], G. Debreu [5] or [6, (1) of 5.6]). A version of it is implicitly contained in L. McKenzie [19] (see also G. Debreu [7, Proposition]). The set $\{1, ..., N\}$ is noted N.

---

[1] It should be noted that the assumption of strong monotonicity of preferences (b.2) is essential to our result. An example due to E. Drandakis shows that it might be difficult to weaken this assumption.

[2] For the case of an infinite planning horizon, see [13].

Theorem 1. Let I be a nonempty subset of N and define $\bar{S} = \left\{ p \in R_+^N \mid \sum_{n \in I} p_n = 1 \right\}$. Let S be any subset of $\bar{S}$ containing $S^0 = \{p \in \bar{S} \mid p \gg 0\}$. If $\xi : S \to R^N$ is a nonempty-valued correspondence whose graph is closed in $S \times R^N$ and which satisfies:

(a) ξ is bounded below, i.e., there is an element b of R^N such that for each p in S and all x in $\xi(p)$, one has $x \geq b$;
(b) for any p in S, $\xi(p)$ is convex and $p \cdot x \leq 0$ for all x in $\xi(p)$;
(c) for any sequence $p^j \in S$ such that $\lim p^j = p^0 \in \bar{S} \setminus S$ or $\lim \|p^j\| = +\infty$ and for any sequence $x^j \in \xi(p^j)$, there is an index n in N such that $\overline{\lim}\, x_n^j > 0$;

then there exists p^* in S and x^* in $\xi(p^*)$ such that $x^* \leq 0$.

Proof. Let S^j be a non-decreasing sequence of nonempty, compact, convex subsets of S^0 such that $S^0 \subset \bigcup_1^\infty S^j$. Then for each j, there is a compact X^j such that $\xi(p) \subset X^j$ for all p in S^j. One shows by a standard argument ([5], for instance) that there exists a p^j in S^j and an x^j in $\xi(p^j)$ such that $p \cdot x^j \leq 0$ holds for all p in S^j.

The sequence x^j is bounded. Thus there is a subsequence (retain the same notation) such that $\lim x^j = x^* \in R^N$. For each p in $\bar{S}$, there is a sequence $\pi^j \in S^j$ such that $p = \lim \pi^j$. Since $\pi^j \cdot x^j \leq 0$, in the limit $p \cdot x^* \leq 0$. This holds for all p in $\bar{S}$, hence $x^* \leq 0$. This shows that the sequence p^j is bounded, for otherwise one could contradict (c). One can therefore assume that the sequence p^j converges to $p^* \in \bar{S}$. But $x^* \leq 0$ and (c) together imply that p^* cannot belong to $\bar{S} \setminus S$. Therefore $p^* \in S$. Finally $x^* \in \xi(p^*)$ since ξ has a closed graph.
Q.E.D.

Section A.2
Let X be a subspace of R^N which is assumed to be a cone with vertex zero, i.e. if $x \in X$, then $\lambda x \in X$ for all positive real numbers λ. Let $B(X)$ be the Borel σ-algebra of X and $M(X)$ the set of all probability measures defined on the measurable space $(X, B(X))$. For any μ in $M(X)$ and any $\lambda > 0$, define the new element $\lambda\mu$ of $M(X)$ which assigns the probability $\mu((1/\lambda)E)$ to any Borel set E of $B(X)$.

Proposition 1. Let $\lambda > 0$ and consider two real-valued functions h and $\bar{h}$ defined on X such that $h(x) = \bar{h}(\lambda x)$ for all x in X. Choose μ in $M(X)$ and assume that h is μ-integrable. Then:

$$\int_X h\,d\mu = \int_X \bar{h}\,d(\lambda\mu)$$

Proof. We only sketch the proof which is elementary. First, it is clearly sufficient to consider only non-negative functions. Second, it is not difficult to show the proposition when h (hence $\bar{h}$) is a simple function. Finally, when h is arbitrary but non-negative, there exists a non-decreasing sequence of non-negative simple functions h^j which converges pointwise to h ([18, (C') of 5.3]). The sequence $\bar{h}^j$ of simple functions defined by $\bar{h}(x) = h^j((1/\lambda)x)$ is non-decreasing and converges pointwise to $\bar{h}^j$. The result then follows from the Monotone Convergence Theorem ([3], A.26 of the appendix). $Q.E.D.$

REFERENCES

[1] M. Allais, 'A Restatement of the Quantity Theory of Money', *American Economic Review*, vol. LVI (1966), pp. 1123–57.
[2] K. J. Arrow, *Aspects of the Theory of Risk-Bearing* (Helsinki: Academic Bookstore, 1965).
[3] L. Breiman, *Probability* (Addison-Wesley: Reading (Mass.), 1968).
[4] P. D. Cagan, 'The Monetary Dynamics of Hyperinflation', pp. 25–117 in [9].
[5] G. Debreu, 'Market Equilibrium', *Proceedings of the National Academy of Sciences of the U.S.A.*, vol. XLII (1956), pp. 876–8.
[6] G. Debreu, *Theory of Value* (New York: Wiley, 1959).
[7] G. Debreu, 'Economies with a Finite Set of Equilibria', *Econometrica*, vol. XXXVIII (1970), pp. 387–92; *ibid.*, p. 790.
[8] E. M. Drandakis, 'On the Competitive Equilibrium in a Monetary Economy', *International Economic Review*, vol. VII (1966), pp. 304–28.
[9] M. Friedman (ed.), *Studies in the Quantity Theory of Money* (Chicago: University of Chicago Press, 1956).
[10] M. Friedman, *The Optimum Quantity of Money* (Chicago: Aldine, 1969).
[11] D. Gale, 'The Law of Supply and Demand', *Mathematica Scandinavica*, vol. III (1955), pp. 155–69.
[12] J.-M. Grandmont, 'Continuity Properties of a von Neumann–Morgenstern Utility', *Journal of Economic Theory*, vol. IV (1972), pp. 45–57.
[13] J.-M. Grandmont and Y. Younès, 'On the Role of Money and the Existence of a Monetary Equilibrium', *Review of Economic Studies*, vol. XXXIX, (1972), pp. 799–803.
[14] F. H. Hahn, 'On Some Problems of Proving the Existence of an Equilibrium in a Monetary Economy', pp. 126–35 in [15].
[15] F. H. Hahn and F. P. R. Brechling (eds.), *The Theory of Interest Rates* (London: Macmillan, 1965).
[16] J. R. Hicks, *Value and Capital* (2nd edition) (Oxford: Clarendon Press, 1946).
[17] J. R. Hicks, *Capital and Growth* (New York: Oxford University Press, 1965).
[18] M. Loève, *Probability Theory* (3rd edition) (Princeton: van Nostrand, 1963).
[19] L. S. McKenzie, 'On Equilibrium in Graham's Model of World Trade and Other Competitive Systems', *Econometrica*, vol. XXII (1954), pp. 147–61.
[20] H. Nikaido, 'On the Classical Multilateral Exchange Problem', *Metroeconomica*, vol. VIII (1956), pp. 135–45.
[21] K. R. Parthasarathy, *Probability Measures on Metric Spaces* (New York: Academic Press, 1967).
[22] D. Patinkin, *Money, Interest and Prices* (2nd edition) (New York: Harper and Row, 1965).
[23] R. Radner, 'Equilibre des marchés à terme et au comptant en cas d'incertitude', *Cahiers du Séminaire d'Econométrie*, vol. IX (1966), pp. 35–52.

[24] R. Radner, 'Existence of Equilibrium of Plans, Prices and Price Expectations in a Sequence of Markets', *Econometrica*, vol. XL (1972), pp. 289–303.
[25] P. A. Samuelson, *Foundations of Economic Analysis* (Cambridge: Harvard University Press, 1966).
[26] B. P. Stigum, 'Competitive Equilibria under Uncertainty', *Quarterly Journal of Economics*, vol. LXXXIII (1969), pp. 533–61.
[27] J. Tobin, 'Liquidity Preference as Behaviour Towards Risk', *Review of Economic Studies*, vol. XXV (1958), pp. 65–86.

13 Temporary Competitive Equilibrium Under Uncertainty

Dieter Sondermann[1]

C.O.R.E., LOUVAIN, AND UNIVERSITY OF THE SAARLAND
SAARBRUECKEN

INTRODUCTION

Short-run equilibrium analysis is concerned 'with an economy where several successive markets are held, to study the conditions which determine the equilibrium of each market and to find how these equilibria are linked together' (Grandmont [11]). This analysis has been advanced, in particular, by Hicks in his book *Value and Capital* [13] under the name, *temporary equilibrium* within a 'week'. In this paper both terms are used synonymously.

At first sight, short-run equilibrium analysis, being concerned only with the analysis of spot markets, seems to be simpler than general Walrasian equilibrium analysis, which studies the conditions for the existence of an equilibrium on a complete system of spot and future markets, covering the whole period from now till the economic planning horizon. This seems, in particular, to be true under the case of uncertainty, where the general Walrasian equilibrium analysis also includes contingent claim markets (see Arrow [2], Debreu [7, chapter 7]), whereas in the short-run equilibrium analysis the existence of such markets is excluded. However, the 'temporary' equilibrium analysis raises problems which do not occur in an Arrow–Debreu economy. In the latter all trading occurs at one time, and people have fixed expectations on the development of the 'world' which are not altered through trading. But in an economy where only a sequence of spot markets exists trading is carried out successively and does influence expectations of the economic agents, since it conveys information about the future development of the economy. Loosely speaking, whereas the Arrow–Debreu analysis is essentially *static*, the short-run equilibrium analysis studies the *dynamic* features of the economy within a short time interval. A survey of some of the formal difficulties arising from this question can be found in Hahn [12]. An important recent contribution, which solves some of these

[1] I am grateful to F. Delbaen, J. Drèze, L. Gevers, J.-M. Grandmont, J. Green and W. Hildenbrand for stimulating discussions and helpful comments.

problems for the case of a pure exchange monetary economy, is that of Grandmont [11].

In the first part of this paper a general decision model is presented, which provides the formal framework for a broad class of short-run equilibrium models. In the second part, the decision model is applied to a private ownership economy with production and capital markets, to study the conditions which guarantee the existence of a temporary equilibrium for such an economy.

PART I: THE GENERAL STRUCTURE OF TEMPORARY EQUILIBRIUM ANALYSIS

I. A DECISION MODEL FOR TEMPORARY EQUILIBRIUM ANALYSIS

Following the line of von Neumann–Morgenstern [17], Savage [20] and Arrow [1], the problem of individual decision-making under uncertainty can be formalised as follows:

(1) Let $(\tilde{\Omega}, \mathscr{F})$ and $(C, \mathscr{C})$ be two measurable spaces[1] and $\mathscr{A}$ be a set of measurable functions from $\tilde{\Omega}$ to C. The elements of $\tilde{\Omega}$ are called *states of the world*, the elements of the σ-algebra $\mathscr{F}$ are called *events*, and the elements of C, *consequences*. The decision-maker has to choose from the elements of the set $\mathscr{A}$, called *actions*. If the decision-maker chooses the action $a \in \mathscr{A}$ and the (unknown) state of the world turns out to be $\tilde{\omega}$, then he receives the consequence $a(\tilde{\omega}) \in C$. It is assumed that the decision-maker has a complete preference ordering $\precsim$ over the set $\mathscr{A}$ of all actions available to him; an action $a_0 \in \mathscr{A}$ is called an optimal decision if a_0 is maximal in $\mathscr{A}$ with respect to $\precsim$. The fundamental theorem of decision theory then states: if the preference ordering $\precsim$ on $\mathscr{A}$ satisfies a certain set of axioms (see e.g. Savage [20], Arrow [1]), then there exist a (subjective) probability measure P on $(\tilde{\Omega}, \mathscr{F})$ and a (cardinal) real-valued measurable utility function u on $(C, \mathscr{C})$ such that

$$a_1 \precsim a_2 \text{ if and only if } \int_{\tilde{\Omega}} u(a_1(\tilde{\omega})) P(d\tilde{\omega}) \leq \int_{\tilde{\Omega}} u(a_2(\tilde{\omega})) P(d\tilde{\omega}). \tag{1.1}$$

This is the well known *expected utility theorem*.

[1] $(M, \mathscr{M})$ is called a *measurable space*, if M is a nonempty set and $\mathscr{M}$ a σ-algebra of subsets of M; i.e. $\mathscr{M}$ has the properties:
    (i) $M \in \mathscr{M}$,
    (ii) $E \in \mathscr{M}$ implies $E^c = M \setminus E \in \mathscr{M}$,
    (iii) $(E_v)_{v=1}\ldots \in \mathscr{M}$ implies $\bigcup_{v=1}^{\infty} E_v \in \mathscr{M}$.

Temporary Competitive Equilibrium Under Uncertainty

On the other hand, to say that the decision-maker behaves according to the *expected utility hypothesis*, is to assume that his preference ordering $\precsim$ on $\mathscr{A}$ can be represented in the form (1.1) and that he behaves as if he were maximising 'expected utility'.

(2) The decision model of (1) will now be combined with a second decision model, which is also well known and which can be found in Debreu [7, 1.9].

Consider a second set Ω of states of the world, and a correspondence ϕ from Ω to the set $\mathscr{A}$ of actions defined in (1). Contrary to the set $\tilde{\Omega}$, which represents the future and unknown states of the world, the elements of Ω are present, observable states of the world, and according to Debreu [7, 1.9] will be called the *environment* of an economic agent. For instance, an element of Ω may be the price system prevailing on the present markets, and the elements of $\tilde{\Omega}$, all possible price paths over all points of the time axis when future spot markets will be held.

Note. From now on we make the assumption that all sets Ω, $\tilde{\Omega}$, $\mathscr{A}$, $\mathscr{C}$ are metric topological spaces. Furthermore, we assume that the σ-algebras $\mathscr{F}$ and $\mathscr{C}$ are the Borel fields; i.e. the σ-algebras generated by the closed (or open) subsets of $\tilde{\Omega}$ and C.

The environment Ω influences the decisions of an economic agent in two ways:

(i) It restricts his set of *a priori* available actions $\mathscr{A}$ to a certain subset, denoted by $\phi(\omega)$, if the environment is characterised by $\omega \in \Omega$.
(ii) The economic agent will base his expectations as to the future states of the world on his observations of his environment (i.e. present states of the world).

The first implication of Ω is completely described by the correspondence ϕ from Ω to $\mathscr{A}$. For instance, if Ω is the set of present market prices, and the set $\mathscr{A}$ consists of different consumption plans, $\phi(\omega)$ will be the budget set at price ω.

(3) The second role of Ω in the process of expectation forming by a given economic agent can be formalised as follows:

Let P be a function defined on $\Omega \times \mathscr{F}$ which takes values in the closed unit interval [0, 1] and which has the properties:

(P1) $P(\omega, .)$ is a probability measure on $(\tilde{\Omega}, \mathscr{F})$ for all $w \in \Omega$,
(P2) $P(., E)$ is a continuous function on Ω for all closed events $E \in \mathscr{F}$.

In other words, P is a continuous Markoff kernel from Ω to $\tilde{\Omega}$. The Markoff kernel P has an obvious interpretation; $P(\omega, E)$ is the (subjective) probability which the economic agent attaches to the future event E when at present he observes ω. (P2) requires that this probability varies only slightly, when the present observable states are almost the same.

Note. In general, the Markoff kernel P will depend not only on the present state ω, but also upon the past history of the world. For instance, not only the present prices but also the past prices in general will influence price expectations. In the extreme case, where an individual's expectations are completely insensitive with respect to the present, P is even independent of ω, and therefore depends only on past observations. This dependence of P upon the past history of the states of the world should always be kept in mind. But as the past is fixed, it does not enter the analysis. What matters are the corrections of expectations due to present observations, which are measured by the dependence of P on ω.

Since the expectations of the decision-maker in general are influenced by his present observations, he does not have a fixed preference ordering on his set of actions $\mathscr{A}$, but rather a family of preference orderings $\lesssim_\omega$ depending on $\omega \in \Omega$. We will always assume that every decision-maker behaves according to the 'expected utility hypothesis' (see (1)). This assumption, therefore, implies that every decision-maker possesses a real-valued measurable utility function u on C, which is unique up to a positive linear transformation, such that for all $\omega \in \Omega$

$$f(\omega, a) = \int_{\tilde{\Omega}} u(a(\tilde{\omega})) P(\omega, d\tilde{\omega}) \tag{1.2}$$

is a utility index for the preference relation $\lesssim_\omega$ on $\mathscr{A}$, i.e.

$$a_1 \lesssim_\omega a_2 \leftrightarrow f(\omega, a_1) \leq f(\omega, a_2).$$

Furthermore, the expected utility hypothesis implies that, given $\omega \in \Omega$, he will maximise his expected utility on the subset $\phi(\omega)$ of all actions a in $\mathscr{A}$ that are feasible under ω. Therefore

$$g(\omega) = \sup \{f(\omega, a) : a \in \phi(\omega)\} \tag{1.3}$$

is his maximal expected utility level, given $\omega \in \Omega$, and

$$\mu(\omega) = \{a \in \phi(\omega) : f(\omega, a) = g(\omega)\} \tag{1.4}$$

is the set of optimal actions with respect to ω.

II. CONTINUITY PROPERTIES

In this section, the continuity properties of the functions f and g, and of the correspondence μ, defined in section I(3) by (1.2), (1.3) and (1.4), are studied.

Proposition 2.1. Assume that the utility function $u : C \to \mathbb{R}$ has the following properties:

u is bounded on C; i.e. there exists $M > 0$, such that $|u(c)| \leq M$ for all $c \in C$. (2.1)

For any sequence (a_n) in $\mathscr{A}$ converging to an $a \in \mathscr{A}$, and for any sequence $(\tilde{\omega}_n)$ in $\tilde{\Omega}$ converging to an $\tilde{\omega} \in \tilde{\Omega}$, one has: $\lim_n u(a_n(\tilde{\omega}_n)) = u(a(\tilde{\omega}))$. (2.2)

Then the function $f : \Omega \times \mathscr{A} \to \mathbb{R}$ defined by (1.2) is continuous.

Remark 2.2. Proposition 2.1 still holds, when the condition (P2) of section I(3) is replaced by the weaker condition

($\overline{\text{P2}}$) For every sequence (ω_n) in Ω converging to $\omega \in \Omega$ and for all closed sets $E \in \tilde{\mathscr{F}}$, one has: $\limsup_n P(\omega_n, E) \leq P(\omega, E)$.

Consider for example the Markoff kernel defined as follows. Let f be a continuous function from Ω into $\tilde{\Omega}$. For every $\omega \in \Omega$ and $E \in \tilde{\mathscr{F}}$, define

$$P(\omega, E) = \begin{cases} 1 & \text{if } f(\omega) \in E \\ 0 & \text{otherwise.} \end{cases}$$

Then P satisfies condition ($\overline{\text{P2}}$), but in general not (P2). It has been shown by Delbaen [9], that if (P2) holds, the assumption (2.2) can be weakened.

Proof of Proposition 2.1. Consider a sequence (ω_n, a_n) in $\Omega \times \mathscr{A}$ converging to (ω_0, a_0) in $\Omega \times \mathscr{A}$. Using the notation $h_n(.) = u(a_n(.))$ and $P_n(.) = P(\omega_n, .)$ for $n = 0, 1 ..$, we have to show

$$\int h_n dP_n \to \int h_0 dP_0. \tag{2.3}$$

For all closed subsets E of $\tilde{\Omega}$ we have by (P2) $\lim_n P_n(E) = P_0(E)$ (resp. $\limsup_n P_n(E) \leq P_0(E)$ by ($\overline{\text{P2}}$)).

Therefore, the sequence of probability measures P_n converges weakly to the probability measure P_0 (see e.g. Billingsley [5], chapter I, theorem 2.1). Furthermore, for every sequence $(\tilde{\omega}_n)$ in $\tilde{\Omega}$ converging to $\tilde{\omega}$ we have by (2.2) that $h_n(\tilde{\omega}_n)$ converges to $h_0(\omega)$; i.e. the sequence of functions (h_n) converges continuously on $\tilde{\Omega}$ to h_0.

Therefore, according to Billingsley ([5], chapter I, theorem 5.5) the sequence of measures $P_n \circ h_n^{-1}$ converges weakly to the measure $P_0 \circ h_0^{-1}$. Since by (2.1) h_0 is bounded, (2.3) follows. Q.E.D.

The continuity of f allows the application of the 'maximum principle' (see Berge ([4], p. 123) or Debreu ([7], 1.8(4))), which yields the following continuity properties of g and μ:

Proposition 2.3. Assume that (2.1) and (2.2) hold. Then if the correspondence ϕ from Ω to $\mathscr{A}$ is continuous and compact-valued, the real function g is continuous on Ω, and the correspondence μ from Ω to $\mathscr{A}$ is upper hemicontinuous and compact-valued.[1]

Remark 2.4. Since according to proposition 2.1 the function $f(\omega, .)$ is continuous, it attains its maximum on compact sets. Therefore, under the assumptions of proposition 2.3, the 'sup' in (1.3) can be replaced by 'max'.

III. SOME REMARKS ON THE TEMPORARY EQUILIBRIUM

What is the justification for calling the decision model, developed in sections I(1) to I(3), the 'general structure' of temporary equilibrium analysis?

The essence of the temporary, or short-run, equilibrium seems to be that what is observable on the spot markets in a given point of time reflects only a small part of the economic activity. Superimposed on the observable behaviour of the economic agents on the spot markets is an invisible net of individual expectations and planning, dating back to the past and reaching to the economic planning horizon of each individual decision-maker. This invisible net links the subsequent spot markets together. In terms of a metaphor of Edgeworth ([10], vol. 3, p. 143), what is observable on the spot markets corresponds to watching the movements of the hands of a clock. But these observable movements are governed by considerable unseen movements of the machinery behind the hands.

But this is exactly the structure of the decision model. The *market behaviour* of each economic agent is described by Part 1.2 of the model, which explains how he reacts to a change in his environment. This environment may be present market prices, present consumption or present investment. The economic significance of proposition 2.3 is, loosely speaking, the assertion that his reactions to a small change in his environment will not be too extreme. This is clearly a

---

[1] For a definition of continuity properties of correspondences see Debreu ([7], 1.8).

basic requirement for the existence of a temporary equilibrium. His *actual decision-making*, however, is described by Part 1.1 of the model, whilst Part 1.3 describes the net of expectations which link these two parts together.

If one is interested only in the existence of an equilibrium on a fixed spot market, it would seem that it is only Part 1.2 which is significant for the analysis, and that one can forget about the underlying expectation and decision-forming structures with all their interdependences. Indeed, this part of the model, due to propositions 2.1 and 2.3, is formally equivalent to the decision model, on which, in Debreu's *Theory of Value* ([7], chapters 3/4), the equilibrium analysis in the case of certainty is based. To return to our metaphor, this part of the model corresponds to the hands of the clock. For example, for the controller of a Walrasian tâtonnement process, this part of the model would seem to be all that he needs to know in order to calculate an equilibrium price system, since it tells him how people will react to a change in their environment. In our metaphor he has only to watch the hands of the clock, without knowing anything about its machinery. However, this is, in general, not quite true. It is true only if the expectations of at least some individuals are not affected too much by the present observable states of the world. This is the purpose of the additional condition (P3) in section VII of this paper. (Compare also Grandmont ([11], 3.8(a)).)

PART II: A TWO-PERIOD MODEL OF AN ECONOMY WITH PRODUCTION AND CAPITAL MARKETS

IV. DESCRIPTION OF THE ECONOMY

As an example of the way in which the general model developed in Part I may be applied to short-run equilibrium analysis, in this part of the paper we will specify the model, in order to study the conditions for the existence of a temporary equilibrium for an economy with production and capital markets operating under price uncertainty.

Consider an economy with a finite number of consumers, producers and commodities, indicated respectively by the finite and disjoint index sets I, J and L.[1] The economy is operating over two periods, called 1 and 2. These two periods may, for instance, be two subsequent Hicksian 'weeks' t and $t+1$ in an infinite sequence of markets

[1] 'Par abus de language' the symbol I (resp. J, L) will be used throughout this paper to denote the index set I and its cardinality $|I| < \infty$.

held on each 'Monday'. Then the restriction to a two-period model means that all economic agents, at the opening of the t-th market, behave as if economic activity would stop at the end of the $t+1$-th week. This is the case considered by Grandmont [11] for an exchange economy where money is the only asset. But the two-period model also permits a more general interpretation. Here period 1 is considered as the 'present'; i.e. the period for the whole length of which contracts can be concluded on the 'spot' markets which are held at its beginning. Period 2 then represents the 'future'; i.e. the time interval from the end of period 1 till the economic planning horizon. In this interpretation, period 2 may be considerably longer than period 1, and its length may be different for different economic agents, varying with their individual planning horizon. If this interpretation is preferred, the economic data of period 2 have to be interpreted as aggregates, on which the individuals base their plans up to the end of their planning horizon.

At the beginning of period 1, commodity and capital markets are opened. All commodities traded on these markets have to be either consumed, or used as production inputs, during the first period. They cannot be stored from one period to the next by consumers. Their only store of value is money or shares of the firms. These assets are traded on the capital markets.

Each consumer and each producer starts at the beginning of period 1 with a given wealth, which for a consumer consists of the market value of his initial commodity endowment, and of his portfolio carried over from the previous period. The wealth of each producer is given by the market value of the output of his production during the past period. It is assumed that producers may also keep a portfolio, for several reasons explained in section VIII. If this is the case, their wealth also comprises the market value of their portfolio. We assume, further, that producers may increase their present wealth by issuing new shares of their firm.

In this paper it is assumed that the economic agents behave as if their preferences and technologies were known to them with certainty. But there is uncertainty about the future commodity and asset prices. Furthermore, consumers are uncertain about their future endowments.

It is assumed that all decision-makers behave as price takers, with respect both to present prices and to their expectations on future prices. This means that we assume that each economic agent has only a 'negligible' influence on the total economic activity. To make this assumption rigorous, we would have to consider a measure space of economic agents (see e.g. Aumann [3] or Hildenbrand [14]), which is beyond the scope of this paper. We assume further, that both consumers and producers act according to the expected utility hypothesis (see section I(1)).

Our aim is to analyse each consumer's and each producer's behaviour on the markets of period 1, and to find conditions ensuring the existence of an equilibrium on these markets.

V. COMMODITY MARKETS

There is a finite set of commodities, denoted by L, which is fixed over time. A commodity bundle available at period t is thus represented by a point in the commodity space $I\!R^L$.

Not all commodities occurring in the economy need to be desired. There may be free commodities, with which the economic agents are satiated, and there may be noxious commodities (e.g. garbage, atomic waste, chemical poisons, smoke), which are joint products of certain production or consumption processes. Adopting Debreu's terminology ([7], 2.6), we call a commodity *scarce*, *free* or *noxious* according to its price being positive, zero or negative. This classification of commodities depends on the equilibrium prices. A given commodity may well be noxious in one period and scarce in another.[1]

Since *a priori* the price of each commodity may be any real number, a commodity price vector p_t at time t is a point of the space $P_t = I\!R^L$.

The commodity markets of period t are held at the beginning of the period (the Hicksian 'Monday'). On these markets each economic agent announces his demand and supply schedule. When an equilibrium price system can be found which equates demand and supply, contracts are made and the markets are closed. Then consumption and production take place during the rest of the period, and the markets are reopened only at the beginning of the next period.

VI. CAPITAL MARKETS

Since we consider a private ownership economy, it is assumed that the market value of each firm belongs to its shareholders. The shares are traded on a stock market at the beginning of each period, in order to allow for a new optimal allocation among the shareholders, according to their expectations about the future development of each firm, and their behaviour towards risk.

Therefore there are as many (risky) assets in the economy as there

---

[1] For instance slag, a joint product of raw iron, used to be a noxious commodity, since its disposal was costly, until becoming a scarce commodity when it came to be used for road construction.

are firms, and both are labelled by the same index set J. It is convenient to normalise the total number of shares of each firm to one. Thus a contract on A_{jt} units of the j-th firm concluded in period t, where A_{jt} may be any non-negative number less than, or equal to one, means to buy or to sell the fraction A_{jt} of the market value of firm j in period $t+1$. Furthermore, it is assumed that there exist a safe asset A_0, called money, yielding no return, and a money market at the beginning of each period. The total amount of units of money available to the economy is a fixed positive number m_0, which does not vary over time. The price per unit of A_0 is per definition always equal to one. Thus a portfolio is characterised by a point $A = (A_1 \ldots A_J, A_0)$ of the asset space

$$M = \{A \in R_+^{J+1} : A_j \leq 1 \text{ for all } j \in J\}.$$

The restriction to non-negative elements means that short sales are not allowed. An asset price vector r_t at time t is a point of the space

$$R_t = \{r_t = (r_{1t} \ldots r_{Jt}, r_{0t}) \in R_+^{J+1} : r_{0t} = 1\}.$$

Here the restriction to non-negative prices means that shareholders have only 'limited liability'; i.e. in the worst case they can lose all their money invested in a given firm, but they do not have to cover losses.

The capital markets are held jointly with the commodity markets at the beginning of each period t. Thus commodity prices p_t and asset prices r_t are determined simultaneously, and the notation $s_t = (p_t, r_t)$ will be used to denote a joint price vector at period t. Furthermore, the assumptions made for the commodity markets in the last paragraph of section V are also valid for the capital markets (no trading out of equilibrium or between market dates).

VII. CONSUMERS

There is a finite set of consumers, denoted by I. Each consumer has to specify a demand and supply schedule for the commodity and asset markets, which are opened at the beginning of period 1. Therefore, for every price system $s_1 = (p_1, r_1)$ he must choose an action, which consists of:

(1) a list of inputs and outputs he is willing to buy or to sell at price s_1 (in short: a consumption plan),
(2) a portfolio he wants to carry over to the next period.

The set of all consumption plans x_{it} which are feasible for consumer i in period t is denoted by X_{it}. Following Debreu [7] the convention is adopted that positive components of X_{it} represent

Temporary Competitive Equilibrium Under Uncertainty

inputs which are consumed by consumer i during period t, and that negative components represent outputs delivered by consumer i during period t. For a detailed discussion of this concept of a consumption set see Debreu ([7], 4.2). We require for all $i \in I$ and $t = 1, 2$:

(X) X_{it} is a compact, convex subset of $\mathbb{R}^L$.

All commodities made available to a given consumer at period t have to be consumed by him during this period. With respect to storage of goods and use of durables by consumers we refer to Debreu ([7], 4.2): 'An individual who buys a house, a car ... for his own use and sells it back later plays two roles: that of a producer who buys and sells houses, cars ... in order to sell their services, and that of a consumer who buys the service, use of that house, of that car ...'. Thus, whereas storage of commodities is excluded for consumers, storage may be technologically feasible for producers (see section VIII).

At the beginning of period 1 the i-th consumer has a fixed preference ordering on the set $C_i = X_{i1} \times X_{i2}$, which is assumed to have the following properties:

(O1) $c^1 \ne c^2 \in C_i$, $c^1 \underset{i}{\sim} c^2$, and $0 < \lambda < 1$ imply $c^1 \underset{i}{\prec} \lambda c^1 + (1-\lambda)c^2$ (strict convexity).

(O2) For every $c^0 \in C_i$ the sets $\{c \in C_i : c \underset{i}{\precsim} c^0\}$ and $\{c \in C_i : c^0 \underset{i}{\precsim} c\}$ are closed in $\mathbb{R}^{2L}$ (continuity).

It is assumed that each consumer $i \in I$, at the beginning of period 1, possesses an initial endowment $e_{i1} = (w_{i1}, A_{i0}) \in X_{i1} \times M_0$ and that the amount of money in the portfolio A_{i0} is positive. Thus for any price system $s_1 \in S_1 = P_1 \times R_1$ one has

$$\inf p_1 X_{i1} < W_i(s_1) = s_1 e_{i1} = p_1 w_{i1} + r_1 A_{i0}. \tag{7.1}$$

Furthermore, each consumer i expects an initial endowment of commodities $w_{i2} \in \mathbb{R}^L$ for period 2. However, w_{i2} is uncertain for him at the beginning of period 1, and it is assumed that he has a probability distribution over $\mathbb{R}^L$, which depends on w_{i1} and his past endowments.

In terms of the decision model of Part I, the behaviour of a given consumer $i \in I$ can then be described as follows (since we consider only one fixed consumer, we will drop the index i in the following).

The environment Ω of the consumer is the set $S_1 = P_1 \times R_1$. The states of the world unknown to him are the prices and his initial endowment in period 2. Thus $\tilde{\Omega}$ is the set $S_2 \times \mathbb{R}^L$. His expectations are given by the Markoff kernel P of section I(3) with the properties

(P1) and (P2). We assume, further, that P has the following properties:

(P3) $\forall\, \epsilon > 0,\ \exists$ compact $K \subset S_2 \times X_2$ such that
$\forall\, \omega \in \Omega : P(\omega, K) \geq 1 - \epsilon$.

The assumption (P3) means, loosely speaking, that his expectations do not 'spread' too widely, and exactly, that his expectations form a *tight* family (see e.g. Billingsley [5], p. 37). Clearly (P3) implies

$$P(\omega, S_2 \times X_2) = 1 \qquad \forall\, \omega \in \Omega. \tag{7.2}$$

This means that the consumer is 'almost sure' that his initial endowment in period 2 will be contained in his consumption set, or expressed more dramatically, starvation is excluded from his forecasts.

The set $\mathcal{A}$ of actions, from which the consumer has to choose, is the set $X_1 \times M_1$, with $M_1 = \{A_1 \in \mathbb{R}_+^{J+1} : A_{1j} \leq 1$ for all $j \in J$, and $A_{10} \geq 1\}$. The correspondence ϕ from S_1 to $\mathcal{A}$ is given by the budget set.

$$\begin{aligned}\phi(s_1) &= \{a \in \mathcal{A} : s_1 a \leq W(s_1) = s_1 e_1\} \\ &= \{(x_1, A_1) \in \mathcal{A} : p_1 x_1 + r_1 A_1 \leq p_1 w_1 + r_1 A_0\}\end{aligned} \tag{7.3}$$

The set of consequences is his intertemporal consumption set $C = X_1 \times X_2$. Assume that the consumer chooses the action $a = (x_1, A_1)$ in period 1, and that $\tilde{\omega} = (s_2, w_2)$ is the state of the world in period 2. Then his wealth in period 2 will be

$$W_2(\tilde{\omega}) = p_2 w_2 + r_2 A_1. \tag{7.4}$$

Since he consumed the commodity bundle x_1 in period 1, he will maximise his preference ordering $\precsim$ over C by choosing, in period 2, the consumption plan

$$x_2(\tilde{\omega}) = \{x_2 \in X_2 : (x_1, x_2)\text{ is } \precsim - \text{maximal in the}$$
$$\text{set } (x_1, y_2) \in C \text{ s.t. } p_2 y_2 \leq W_2(\tilde{\omega})\}. \tag{7.5}$$

This is equivalent to the statement: x_2 is maximal with respect to the spot preference $\precsim_{x_1}$ in the budget set $\{y_2 \in X_2 : p_2 y_2 \leq W_2(\tilde{\omega})\}$, where $\precsim_{x_1}$ is the projection of $\precsim$ on X_2, given x_1. It may well occur that, for some $\tilde{\omega} \in \tilde{\Omega}$, $W_2(\tilde{\omega})$ is so large that $x_2(\tilde{\omega})$ is even $\precsim_{x_1}$ - maximal in X_2. This would mean that, in the specific situation $\tilde{\omega}$, the wealth in period 2 would be high enough in order to derive from it the maximal possible satisfaction. We will, however, assume that our consumer can never be sure that this will be the case in *all* possible situations which may obtain in period 2. Therefore, if he chooses the action $a = (x_1, A_1)$ and if x_2^0 denotes the $\precsim_{x_1}$ - maximal element in X_2', we assume that the Markoff kernel P satisfies the additional condition:

(P4) $\exists\, \delta_a > 0\ \forall \omega \in \Omega : P(\omega, F_a) \geq \delta_a$

with $F_a = \{\tilde{\omega} \in \tilde{\Omega} : p_2 x_2^0 \geq W_2(\tilde{\omega}) + \delta_a\}$.

Note that the probability δ_a may vary with the action a and may approach zero. Thus, when the portfolio A_1 contains more and more assets, the consumer may feel safer and safer that he can achieve his maximal satisfaction in period 2. But (P4) says that he can never be completely sure.

If there exists an element $x_2 \in X_2$ with the property (7.5), then it is uniquely determined by $\tilde{\omega}$ and a, since by (O1) the preference ordering is strictly convex. Since C is compact, for every $w_2 \in X_2$ the existence clearly follows from the continuity of $\precsim$ (O2). Thus each action $a = (x_1, A_1) \in \mathcal{A}$ defines a function from $\tilde{\Omega}$ to C by setting

$$a(\tilde{\omega}) = (x_1, x_2(\tilde{\omega})),$$

where $x_2(\tilde{\omega})$ is defined by (7.5). By (7.2) the function a is defined almost everywhere on $\tilde{\Omega}$, and it is Borel measurable as a consequence of (7.7) (*vide* proof of lemma 7.1).

The expected utility index of the consumer is now given by

$$\begin{aligned} V(s_1; a) &= \int_{\tilde{\Omega}} u(a(\tilde{\omega})) P(s_1, d\tilde{\omega}) \\ &= \int_{S_2 \times \mathbb{R}^L} u(x_1, x_2(A_1, \cdot)) dP(s_1, \cdot) \\ &= V(s_1; x_1, A_1) \end{aligned}$$

By assumption, u is a continuous, concave function on C, which is order preserving with respect to $\precsim$. This means that we assume that the family of preference orderings $(\precsim_{s_1})_{s_1 \in S_1}$ over $\mathcal{A}$ obeys the expected utility hypothesis (see section I(3)) and that our consumer is risk-averse.

If the environment of the consumer in period 1 is given by $s_1 \in S_1$, he will therefore maximise his expected utility $V(s_1; \cdot)$ over the set of actions $\phi(s_1) \subset \mathcal{A}$, which are feasible for him. This is equivalent to solving the program

$$\begin{aligned} \text{Max.} \quad & E_{s_1}[u(x_1, x_2)] \\ \text{S.T.} \quad & p_1 x_1 + r_1 A_1 \leq p_1 w_1 + r_1 A_0 \\ & p_2 x_2 \leq p_2 w_2 + r_2 A_1 \\ & x_t \in X_t \text{ for } t = 1, 2, \ldots \end{aligned} \qquad (7.6)$$

where E_{s_1} denotes his conditional expectation over $\tilde{\Omega}$, given s_1. The solution of (7.6) is given by the correspondence

$$\mu(s_1) = \{(x_1, A_1) \in \mathcal{A} : V(s_1; x_1, A_1) = \max_{a \in \phi(s_1)} V(s_1; a)\}.$$

Thus μ is the consumer's demand correspondence, which is a correspondence from S_1 to $\mathbb{R}^L \times M_1$. His excess demand is thus given by the correspondence,

$$\xi(s_1) = \mu(s_1) - e_1$$

from S_1 to $\mathbb{R}^{L+J+1}$.

This completes the description of the behaviour of a given consumer $i \in I$. We will now study some consequences of this behaviour.

Lemma 7.1. The expected utility index V is continuous on $S_1 \times \mathscr{A}$.

Proof. Consider the sequences (a^n) in $\mathscr{A}$ and $(\tilde{\omega}^n)$ in $\tilde{\Omega}$ converging to $a \in \mathscr{A}$ and $\tilde{\omega} \in \tilde{\Omega}$. We shall show that

$$\lim_n a^n(\tilde{\omega}^n) = a(\tilde{\omega}). \tag{7.7}$$

Clearly $a^n = (x_1^n, A_1^n) \to a = (x_1, A_1)$ implies $x_1^n \to x_1$. Furthermore, $\tilde{\omega}^n = (s_2^n, w_2^n) \to \tilde{\omega} = (s_2, w_2)$ implies

$$\lim_n W_2(\tilde{\omega}^n) = \lim_n (p_2^n w_2^n + r_2^n A_1^n) = W_2(\tilde{\omega}). \tag{7.8}$$

By (7.2) we can assume that $w_2 \in X_2$. Hence we have

$$W_2(\tilde{\omega}) = p_2 w_2 + r_2 A_1 > \inf p_2 X_2 \tag{7.9}$$

Therefore, since C is compact and $\precsim$ is continuous, (7.5), (7.8) and (7.9) imply $\lim_n x_2(\tilde{\omega}^n) = x_2(\tilde{\omega})$, which proves (7.7). Since u is bounded and continuous, the continuity of V thus follows from proposition 2.1.

Lemma 7.2. For each $s_1 \in S_1$ the function $V(s_1; .)$ is concave on $\mathscr{A}$.

Proof. Consider the action $a^0 = \lambda a^1 + (1-\lambda)a^2$, where $a^1, a^2 \in \mathscr{A}$ and $\lambda \in [0,1]$. Since $\mathscr{A}$ is convex, a^0 belongs to $\mathscr{A}$. Fix an $\tilde{\omega} \in \tilde{\Omega}$ and consider the three elements $c^k = a^k(\tilde{\omega})$ in C ($k = 0, 1, 2$). From (7.5) it follows that $\lambda c^1 + (1-\lambda)c^2 \precsim c^0$. Therefore the concavity of u on C implies

$$\lambda u(c^1) + (1-\lambda)u(c^2) \leq u(\lambda c^1 + (1-\lambda)c^2) \leq u(c^0)$$

or equivalently

$$u(a^0(\tilde{\omega})) \geq \lambda(u(a^1(\tilde{\omega})) + (1-\lambda)u(a^2(\tilde{\omega})). \tag{7.10}$$

Since (7.10) holds for all $\tilde{\omega} \in \tilde{\Omega}$, the proposition follows by integrating (7.10) with respect to the measure $P(s_1, .)$.

Proposition 7.3. The correspondence μ is convex-, compact-valued and upper hemicontinuous.

Proof. For every $s_1 \in S_1$ the budget set $\phi(s_1)$ defined by (7.3) is clearly compact, convex and, using (7.1), nonempty. Furthermore, (7.1) implies that ϕ is continuous (see Debreu [7], 4.8 (1)). By lemma 7.1 V is continuous on $S_1 \times \mathscr{A}$, thus, according to proposition 2.3, μ is a compact-valued and upper hemicontinuous correspondence. Since, by lemma 7.2, $V(s_1;.)$ is concave on $\mathscr{A}$ for all s_1, μ is convex-valued.

Proposition 7.4. For any action $a = (x_1, A_1) \in \mathscr{A}$ and any positive real number ρ define the action $a^\rho \in \mathscr{A}$ by $a^\rho = (x_1, A_1^\rho)$ with $A_1^\rho = A_1 + (0 \ldots 0, \rho)$. Then one has, for every $s_1 \in S_1$, $V(s_1, a) < V(s_1, a^\rho)$.

Proof: For given $s_1 \in S_1$ and $\tilde{\omega} = (p_2, r_2, w_2) \in \tilde{\Omega}$ consider the consequences

$$a(\tilde{\omega}) = (x_1, x_2(\tilde{\omega}))$$

and

$$a^\rho(\tilde{\omega}) = (x_1, x_2^\rho(\tilde{\omega})),$$

where $x_2(\tilde{\omega})$ resp. $x_2^\rho(\tilde{\omega})$ are defined by (7.5) with $W_2(\tilde{\omega}) = p_2 w_2 + r_2 A_1$ and $W_2^\rho(\tilde{\omega}) = p_2 w_2 + r_2 A_1^\rho = W_2(\tilde{\omega}) + \rho$. Since $\rho > 0$, one clearly has $a(\tilde{\omega}) \precsim a^\rho(\tilde{\omega})$ or, equivalently, $x_2(\tilde{\omega}) \precsim_{x_1} x_2^\rho(\tilde{\omega})$.
We will show that

$$P_{s_1}[\tilde{\omega} \in \tilde{\Omega} : a(\tilde{\omega}) \prec a^\rho(\tilde{\omega})] > 0 \tag{7.11}$$

Clearly, (7.11) implies $V(s_1, a) > V(s_1, a^\rho)$.
To prove (7.11), assume on the contrary that

$$P_{s_1} - a.e. \text{ on } \tilde{\Omega}, \ x_2(\tilde{\omega}) \ \tilde{x}_1 \ x_2^\rho(\tilde{\omega}). \tag{7.12}$$

Then, since $p_2 x_2(\tilde{\omega}) < W_2^\rho(\tilde{\omega})$ and $x_2(\tilde{\omega})$ is $\precsim_{x_1}$ maximal in $\{x_2 \in x_2 : p_2 x_2 \leq W_2^\rho(\tilde{\omega})\}$, there exists a neighbourhood $U(x_2)$ such that, for all $y_2 \in U$, one has $y_2 \precsim_{x_1} x_2(\tilde{\omega})$. But then, by strict convexity of $\precsim_{x_1}, x_2(\tilde{\omega})$ is $\precsim_{x_1}$ – maximal in X_2.
Hence, since the maximum is unique, (7.12) implies

$$P_{s_1} - a.e. \text{ on } \tilde{\Omega}, \ x_2(\tilde{\omega}) = x_2^\rho(\tilde{\omega}) = x_2^0, \tag{7.13}$$

where x_2^0 is the $\precsim_{x_1}$ – maximal element of X_2. But (7.13) implies

$$P_{s_1}[\tilde{\omega} = (p_2, s_2, w_2) \in \tilde{\Omega} : p_2 x_2^0 \leq W_2(\tilde{\omega}) = p_2 w_2 + r_2 A_1] = 1,$$

which says that, taken the action $a = (x_1, A_1)$ in period 1, the maximum consumption x_2^0 in period 2 is always considered as feasible. But this contradicts (P4).

Corollary. For every $s_1 \in S_1$ the value of the excess demand is zero; i.e. $s_1 z = 0$ for all $z \in \xi(s_1)$.

Proof. Consider $az \in \xi(s_1)$. Thus there exists an action $a = (x_1, A_1) \in \mu(s_1)$ with $z = a - e_1$. Since $a \in \phi(s_1)$, (7.3) implies $s_1 z \leq 0$. Assume $\rho := -s_1 z > 0$. Then the action a^ρ belongs to $\phi(s_1)$. According to the proposition one has $V(s_1, a) < V(s_1, a^\rho)$, in contradiction to the optimality of a. Q.E.D.

The following property of the total excess demand $\xi = \sum_{i \in I} \xi_i$ of all consumers will be crucial for the existence of an equilibrium.

Proposition 7.5. Assume that the initial endowments of all consumers satisfy the condition

$$\sum_{i \in I} e_{i1} \in \text{int} \sum_{i \in I} \mathscr{A}_i. \tag{7.14}$$

Then, if (s^k) is a sequence of prices in S_1 with $\lim_k \|s^k\| = \infty$,[1] for every sequence (z^k) with $z^k \in \xi(s^k)$ one has $\lim_k z_0^k = \infty$ (i.e. the total demand for money tends to infinity).

Proof. Consider the sequence of normalised prices (π^k) with $\pi^k = \dfrac{s^k}{\|s^k\|}$. Since $\|\pi^k\| = 1$ for all k, there exists a convergent subsequence, still denoted by (π^k), converging to a π^0. Now (7.14) implies

$$\sum_{i \in I} \pi^0 e_{i1} > \inf \sum_{i \in I} \pi^0 \mathscr{A}_i = \sum_{i \in I} \inf \pi^0 \mathscr{A}_i.$$

Thus there exists at least one consumer $i \in I$ with

$$W_i(\pi^0) = \pi^0 e_{i1} > \inf \pi^0 \mathscr{A}_i. \tag{7.15}$$

Let P_i be the Markoff kernel of his expectations over $\tilde{\Omega}$. By assumption (P3) this kernel is uniformly tight. Hence by Prohorov's Theorem (see e.g. Billingsley [5], p. 37) the sequence of probability measures $P(s^k, .)$ is relatively weakly compact. Therefore there exists a subsequence of (s^k), still denoted by the same index k, such that the sequence $P(s^k, .)$ converges weakly to the probability measure P_0 on $\tilde{\Omega}$. Consider the expected utility index defined on $\mathscr{A}_i$ by

$$V_0(a) = \int_{\tilde{\Omega}} u_i(a(\tilde{\omega})) P_0(d\tilde{\omega}).$$

Since C_i is compact, the same reasoning as in proposition 2.1 and Lemma 7.1 shows, that for any sequence (a^k) in $\mathscr{A}_i$ converging to an $a^0 \in \mathscr{A}_i$, one has

$$\lim_k V_i(s^k, a^k) = V_0(a^0). \tag{7.16}$$

Assume now that there exists a positive integer N such that $z_0^k \leq N$ for all k. Consider then the sequence $a^k \in \mu_i(s^k)$ ($k = 1 \ldots$) of

[1] $\|\cdot\|$ denotes the Euclidean norm in R^{L+J+1}.

optimal actions of consumer i with respect to s^k. Since C_i is compact and the total demand for money is by assumption bounded, the sequence (a^k) must be bounded. Thus we can again extract a convergent subsequence, still denoted by (a^k), such that $\lim_k a^k = a^0$. For each $k=1,$. a^k belongs to $\phi_i(s^k)$. Therefore one has $s^k a^k \leq s^k e_{i1}$, or equivalently $\pi^k a^k \leq \pi^k e_{i1}$. Thus each a^k is optimal with respect to $V_i(s^k,.)$ in the budget set $\phi_i(\pi^k) = \{a \in \mathcal{A}_i : \pi^k a^k \leq \pi^k e_{i1}\}$. But (7.15) implies that ϕ_i is a continuous correspondence in π^0 (see Debreu [7], 4.8 (1)). Therefore (7.16) and the 'maximum principle' (see Debreu [7], 1.8 (4)) imply that a^0 is optimal in $\phi_i(\pi^0)$ with respect to V_0.

However, the action $\bar{a}^0 = (x^0, \bar{A}^0)$ with $\bar{A}_0{}^0 = N+1$ and $\bar{A}_j{}^0 = A_j{}^0$ for $j \in J$, also belongs to $\phi_i(\pi^0)$, since the price of money is zero in the limit.

Now P_0 is the weak limit of the probability measures $P(s^k,.)$, each of which satisfy the condition (P4). We claim that also P_0 fulfils (P4). Indeed, for any $a \in \mathcal{A}$ the event F_a defined in (P4) is closed. Thus the Portmanteau Theorem (see e.g. Billingsley [5, p. 11]) implies

$$P_0(F_a) \geq \limsup_k P(s^k, F_a) \geq \delta_a.$$

Therefore Proposition 7.4 applies, which proves $V_0(a^0) < V_0(\bar{a}^0)$. But this contradicts the optimality of a^0.

VIII. PRODUCERS

There is a finite set of producers, denoted by J. At the beginning of period 1, each producer chooses a production plan $y = (y_1^-, y_2^+)$, which consists of a non-negative array of inputs for period 1, and a non-negative array of outputs y_2^+, which are available at the beginning of period 2. Thus, following Malinvaud [15], it is assumed that production takes time, and the production plan (y_1^-, y_2^+) represents a transformation of the input y_1^- to the output y_2^+ which is technologically feasible within the first period. The set of all production plans, which are technologically feasible for producer j, is denoted by the subset T_j of $\mathbb{R}_+^{2L}$.

Following Malinvaud [15] and de Montbrial [16] the following assumptions are made:

(T1) T_j is closed and convex.
(T2) $(0, 0) \in T_j$; and $(0, y_2^+) \in T_j$ implies $y_2^+ = 0$.
(T3) For any bounded set $B \in \mathbb{R}_+^L$ the set $\{(y_1^-, y_2^+) \in T_j : y_1^- \in B\}$ is bounded.

The interpretations of these three assumptions are straightforward. Furthermore, if y_1^+ denotes the output of firm j from the previous period, we assume that

(T4) $(y_1^+, y_2^+) \in T_j$ for some $y_2^+ \in \mathbb{R}_+^L$.

(T4) means that the output of the previous period may be used again as an input in period 1 (e.g. may be stored till period 2).

It is useful to have an equivalent description of the technology T_j by means of the set

$$Y_j = \{(y_1, y_2) \in \mathbb{R}^{2L} : y_t = y_t^+ - y_t^- \text{ for } t = 1, 2; y_2^- = 0, (y_1^-, y_2^+) \in T_j\}.$$

This is the concept of a technology used by Debreu [7], where negative components represent inputs, and positive components outputs. Again y_1^+ in the definition of Y_j denotes the initial endowment of the firm, which may be interpreted as the output of the production of the previous period. One can prove the following: If T_j satisfies the conditions (T1), (T2), and (T3), then Y_j is closed, convex, and irreversible (i.e. $Y_j \cap -Y_j = \{0\}$). For a proof see de Montbrial [16]. Also note that (T4) is equivalent to the condition $0 \in Y_{j1}$.

Since production takes time and since there are no forward markets in the economy, each firm, in order to produce, must invest inputs at given market prices, whereas the prices of the outputs are uncertain. Therefore, the production decisions of the producers are decisions under uncertainty. Profit maximisation can no longer be the objective of the firm, since this objective, being undefined, makes no sense. (For a discussion of this problem see e.g. Borch [6], chapter 10). A possible objective for the firm, in this case, could be the maximisation of expected profit. A more general objective would be the maximisation of the expected utility of profit. This objective has been studied for a one-commodity–one-period model by Sandmo [19]. In this paper we will assume that the objective of the firm is to maximise expected utility of future market value, and that producers behave according to the expected utility hypothesis.[1]

We assume, further, that producers may also keep a portfolio from one period to the next, and that they may trade assets and money on the capital markets. The reasons for making this assumption are threefold.

---

[1] We stress the fact that this is a purely behaviouristic assumption, for which at present we have no normative justification. There are at least two other possible objectives for the firm: (1) maximisation of its present market value, and (2) maximisation of its expected future market value. It would be very interesting to investigate the effects of these three different objectives of a firm on the efficiency of the economy.

(1) Formally a firm may own some of its own stock and thus may sell that stock on the market. This introduces the possibility of stock–financing by firms. More specifically, let us assume that a given producer j has been authorised by the shareholders owning his firm in period 0, to increase the capital stock of the firm up to $x\%$ by issuing new shares at market value. The floating date and the actual amount of new shares offered on the market of a given period may be chosen by the producer himself.

This procedure can be described in the framework of this model as follows. The initial endowment of the producer j, $e_{j1} = (y_1^+, A_0)$, contains the portfolio $A_0 = (0 \ldots A_{j0} \ldots 0)$ with $A_{j0} = \alpha(1+\alpha)^{-1}$, where $\alpha = 0.01x \cdot A_{j0}$ represents the 'conditional' capital of firm j. Since the total amount of shares of firm j is normalised to one, the amount of shares owned by the shareholders in period 0 must be equal to $K_{j0} = (1+\alpha)^{-1}$. Assume that in period 1 producer j issues the amount β with $0 \le \beta \le A_{j0}$ of new shares, and thus keeps the amount $A_{j1} = A_{j0} - \beta$ in his portfolio. Then $K_{j1} = K_{j0} + \beta$. Clearly $0 < K_{j1} \le 1$. The market value of firm j in period 2 is formally given by the value of its output plus the value of its portfolio; i.e.

$$M_{j2} = p_2 y_2^+ + r_2 A_1 = p_2 y_2^+ + r_{j2}(A_{j0} - \beta). \qquad (*)$$

But the price r_{j2} of the new shares in period 2 is equal to the market value of the firm in this period. Therefore $r_{j2} = M_{j2}$ and $K_{j0} = 1 - A_{j0}$ imply

$$M_{j2} = \frac{p_2 y_2^+}{K_{j0} + \beta} = \frac{p_2 y_2^+}{K_{j1}}.$$

Thus, formula (*) gives the correct market value of the firm j in period 2, namely the market value of the output per unit of shares actually issued.

Thus the following analysis of producers' behaviour includes, as a special case, the determination of the optimal amount of new shares issued by each producer in each period, under the condition that he behaves as a price taker with respect to the present market value of his firm.

(2) The portfolio of a firm may contain money as a means of transferring value from one period to the next.

(3) The portfolio of a firm may also include shares of other firms. This allows a given producer to reduce the riskiness of his own production by means of diversification.

In terms of our decision model, the behaviour of a given producer j in J can now be described as follows:

The environment Ω of the producer is given by the set $S_1 = P_1 \times R_1$ of present market prices. The unknown states of the world are the elements of the set $\tilde{\Omega} = S_2 = P_2 \times R_2$. Especially r_{j2}, the market value of his own firm, is an element of $\tilde{\Omega}$. The set of actions, from which he has to choose, consists first of his technology T_j; i.e. he has to choose a production plan $(y_1^-, y_2^+) \in T_j$ at the beginning of period 1. We remark, that y_2^+ has also to be chosen before the price vector s_2 becomes known. Furthermore, he has to choose a portfolio A_1, an element of the asset space M_1. Therefore, his set of actions is the space $\mathscr{A}_j = T_j \times M_1$. If his initial endowment is given by $e_{j1} = (y_1^+, A_0)$, the correspondence ϕ_j from S_1 to $\mathscr{A}_j$ is given by his budget set,

$$\phi_j(s_1) = \{a = (y_1^-, y_2^+, A_1) \in \mathscr{A}_j : s_1(y_1^-, A_1) \le s_1 e_{j1}\}$$
$$= \{(y_1^-, y_2^+, A_1) \in T_j \times M_1 : p_1 y_1^- + r_1 A_1 \le p_1 y_1^+ + r_1 A_0\}$$
$$= \{(y, A_1) \in Y_j \times M_1 : r_1 A_1 \le p_1 y_1 + r_1 A_0\}. \tag{8.1}$$

It is assumed that A_{00}, the amount of money in the firm's portfolio, is positive. Hence, for any price system $s_1 \in S_1 = P_1 \times R_1$, it follows from (T4):

$$\inf s_1 (\mathscr{A}_j) := \inf \{s_1(y_1^-, A_1) : (y_1^-, y_2^+, A_1) \in \mathscr{A}_j\}$$
$$= \inf \{p_1 y_1^- + r_1 A_1 : (y_1^-, \cdot, A_1) \in \mathscr{A}_j\}$$
$$\le p_1 y_1^+ > p_1 y_1^+ + r_1 A_0 = s_1 e_{j1}. \tag{8.2}$$

The consequence of an action $a \in \mathscr{A}_j$ will be a certain market value of the firm j in period 2. Thus $C_j = \mathbb{R}$. For each $a \in \mathscr{A}_j$ the mapping $a : S_2 \to C_j$ is defined by

$$a(s_2) = p_2 y_2^+ + r_2 A_1, \tag{8.3}$$

which is the market value of firm j, if the price system s_2 obtains.

Let the expectations of producer j about future prices be described by the Markoff kernel P_j from S_1 to S_2, and his behaviour towards risk by the bounded, continuous, concave and increasing utility function u_j on C_j. His expected utility index will then be

$$V_j(s_1; a) = \int_{S_2} u_j(a(s_2)) P_j(s_1, ds_2)$$
$$= \int_{P_2 \times R_2} u_j(p_2 y_2^+ + r_2 A_1) P_j(s_1, d(p_2 \times r_2))$$
$$= V_j(s_1; y_2^+, A_1).$$

If the environment of producer j in period 1 is given by the price system $s_1 \in S_1$, he will therefore maximise his expected utility index $V_j(s_1; \cdot)$ over the set of actions $\phi_j(s_1) \subset \mathscr{A}_j$, which are feasible to him. This is equivalent to solving the following program:

$$\text{Max. } E_{s_1}[u_j(p_2 y_2^+ + r_2 A_1)]$$

$$\text{S.T. } p_1 y_1^- + r_1 A_1 \leq p_1 y_1^+ + r_1 A_0,$$
$$(y_1^-, y_2^+) \in T_j. \tag{8.4}$$

Here E_{s_1} denotes his conditional expectation over the set S_2, given s_1. Contrary to the consumer's program (7.6), which requires stochastic dynamic programming, for each $s_1 \in S_1$ (8.4) is a standard convex program, which consists of maximising a concave function on a closed convex domain.

The set of solutions of (8.4) for each $s_1 \in S_1$ is given by the correspondence

$$\mu_j(s_1) = \{(y_1^-, y_2^+, A_1) \in \mathscr{A}_j : V_j(s_1; y_2^+, A_1) = \underset{a \in \phi_j(s_1)}{\text{Max}} V_j(s_1; a)\}.$$

Therefore, for each s_1, the demand of producer j is given by

$$\eta_j(s_1) = \{(y_1^-, A_1) : (y_1^-, ., A_1) \in \mu_j(s_1)\}, \tag{8.5}$$

and his excess demand by

$$\xi_j(s_1) = \eta_j(s_1) - e_{j1}. \tag{8.6}$$

Lemma 8.1. The expected utility index V_j is continuous on $S_1 \times \mathscr{A}_j$.

Proof. Clearly $a^n \to a$ and $s_2^n \to s_2$ imply by (8.3) $a^n(s_2^n) \to a(s_2)$. Thus the lemma follows from proposition 2.1.

We omit the proof of

Lemma 8.2. For each $s_1 \in S_1$ the function $V_j(s_1; .)$ is concave on $\mathscr{A}_j$.

Proposition 8.3. If T_j is compact, η_j is a convex-, compact-valued and upper hemicontinuous correspondence from S_1 to $\mathbb{R}_+^L \times M_1$.

Proof. Making use of (8.2), the same arguments as in the proof of proposition 7.3 show that μ_j has the listed properties. But η_j is the projection of μ_j on $\mathbb{R}^{L+J+1}$, and therefore has the same properties.

Proposition 8.4. For all $s_1 \in S_1$ and all $z \in \xi_j(s_1)$, one has $s_1 z = 0$.

Proof. Consider a $z \in \zeta(s_1)$. Then there exists an action $a = (y_1^-, y_2^+, A_1) \in \mu(s_1)$ with $z = (y_1^-, A_1) - (y_1^+, A_0)$. Since $a \in \phi(s_1)$, (8.1) implies $s_1 z = r_1(A_1 - A_0) - p_1 y_1 \leq 0$. Assume that $\rho := -s_1 z > 0$. Then the action $\tilde{a} := (y_2^-, y_2^+, A_1 + (0 \ldots 0, \rho))$ belongs to $\phi(s_1)$ and, for every $s_2 \in S_2$, one has $\tilde{a}(s_2) = a(s_2) + \rho$. Since u is increasing, this clearly implies $V(s_1; \tilde{a}) > V(s_1; a)$. But this contradicts the optimality of a.

IX. MARKET EQUILIBRIUM

We study the problem of the existence of an equilibrium on the commodity and capital markets in period 1. The existence of a market equilibrium will be a test of the logical consistency of the economic model presented in sections IV to VIII.

The economy is completely described by

$$\mathscr{E} = \{(C_i, u_i, P_i, e_{i1}), (T_j, u_j, P_j, e_{j1})\}_{i \in I, \ j \in J}.$$

The first quadruple, characterising consumer i, has been given a precise meaning in section VII, and similarly the second quadruple, characterising producer j, in section VIII. The economy is called *regular*, if the variables of $\mathscr{E}$ satisfy the assumptions made in sections VII and VIII.

Definition 9.1. An equilibrium of the economy $\mathscr{E}$ in period 1 is an $(I+J+1)$-tuple $(a_{i1}^*, \tilde{a}_{j1}^*, s_1^*)$ of points of $\mathbb{R}^L \times \mathbb{R}_+^{J+1}$, such that

(i) $s_1^* = (p_1^* \ldots p_L^*, r_1^* \ldots r_J^*, 1)$
(ii) $a_{i1}^* = (x_{i1}^*, A_{i1}^*) \in \mu_i(s_1^*)$ for every $i \in I$
(iii) $\tilde{a}_{j1}^* = (y_{j1}^{-*}, A_{j1}^*) \in \eta_j(s_1^*)$ for every $j \in J$
(iv) $\sum_{i \in I} a_{i1}^* + \sum_{j \in J} \tilde{a}_{j1}^* = \sum_{k \in I \cup J} e_{k1}.$

Theorem 9.2. If the regular economy $\mathscr{E}$ satisfies the additional condition

$$\sum_{i \in I} e_{i1} \in \text{int} \left(\sum_{i \in I} X_{i1} \times \mathbb{R}_+^{J+1} \right), \tag{9.1}$$

then there exists an equilibrium in period 1.

Proof. (1) Since we have neither monotonicity of preferences, nor free disposal of commodities, any price vector of the set

$$S_1 = P_1 \times R_1 = \{s = (p, r) \in \mathbb{R}^L \times \mathbb{R}_+^{J+1} : r_0 = 1\}$$

may be an equilibrium price system. We note, that in equilibrium, the *absolute* commodity and asset prices are determined. Let (S^k) be an increasing sequence of compact, convex subsets of S_1 with $S_1 = \bigcup_k S^k$. Denote by C^k the cone with vertex 0 generated by S^k, and by Γ^k its polar; i.e. $\Gamma^k = \{z \in \mathbb{R}^{L+J+1} : sz \leq 0 \text{ for all } s \in C^k\}$. By $\mathscr{E}^k$ ($k = 1..$) we denote the truncated economy, where for all $j \in J$ the production sets are replaced by the compact sets $T_j^k = \{y \in T_j : \|y\| \leq k\}$.

(2) For each economy $\mathscr{E}^k$ consider the total excess demand correspondence ξ^k from S_1 to $\mathbb{R}^{L+J+1}$ defined by

$$\xi^k(s_1) = \sum_{h \in I \cup J} \xi_h^k(s_1) = \sum_{i \in I} \mu_i^k(s_1) + \sum_{j \in J} \eta_j^k(s_1) - \sum_{h \in I \cup J} e_{h1}.$$

Without loss of generality, we can restrict ourselves to k's which are large enough that, for every $j \in J$, (T4) holds with T_j replaced by T_j^k.

Temporary Competitive Equilibrium Under Uncertainty

Then ξ^k is well-defined. According to the propositions 7.3 and 8.3, ξ^k is a convex- and compact-valued upper hemicontinuous correspondence. By propositions 7.4 and 8.4 one has, furthermore, $s_1\xi^k(s_1)=0$ for all $s_1 \in S_1$. Therefore, since S^k is compact, $\xi^k(S^k)$ is compact (see e.g. Berge [4], p. 116). Furthermore, C^k is a closed, convex cone with vertex 0, which is not a linear manifold.

Thus, for every $k=1..$, the fundamental lemma of equilibrium theory (see Debreu [8]) implies the existence of an $s^k \in S^k$ such that

$$\Gamma^k \cap \xi^k(s^k) \neq \emptyset. \tag{9.2}$$

This means that there exist two sequences (s^k) and (z^k) with $z^k \in \Gamma^k \cap \xi^k(s^k)$.

(3) Next we will show that the sequences (s^k) and (z^k) are bounded. Denote by Z the range of the sequence (z^k). Since Γ^k, $k=1..$, forms a decreasing sequence of closed cones, containing 0, the asymptotic cone AZ of Z is contained in their intersection (see Debreu [7], 1.9.n). However, one has

$$\Gamma = \bigcap_k \Gamma^k = (\bigcup_k C^k)^0 = S_1^0,$$

where S_1^0 is the polar of S_1. Therefore

$$\Gamma = \{z \in \mathbb{R}^{L+J+1} : sz \leq 0 \text{ for all } s \in S_1\}$$
$$= \{z = (z_c, z_a) \in \mathbb{R}^L \times \mathbb{R}^{J+1} : z_c = 0, z_a \leq 0\}, \tag{9.3}$$

where z_c denotes the excess demand vector for commodities and z_a for assets. But z_a is bounded below by the vector $-\sum_{h \in I \cup J} A_{h0}$. Therefore $AZ = \{0\}$, which proves that the sequence (z^k) is bounded (see Debreu [7], 1.9.(8)). But then the sequence (s^k) must also be bounded, for otherwise one would obtain a contradiction to proposition 7.5.

(4) $z^k \in \xi^k(s^k)$ means that there exists for each $i \in I$ an action $a_i^k \in \mu_i^k(s^k)$, and for each $j \in J$ an element $\bar{a}_j^k \in \eta_j^k(s^k)$ such that

$$z^k = \sum_{i \in I} a_i^k + \sum_{j \in J} \bar{a}_j^k - \sum_{h \in I \cup J} e_{h1}, \tag{9.4}$$

where $\mu_i^k = \mu_i$(resp. η_j^k) denotes the demand correspondences of the agents i(resp. j) in the economy $\mathscr{E}^k$. By assumption (X) for each $i \in I$ the consumption set X_{i1} is bounded. Thus the first sum on the right-hand side of (9.4) is bounded. But the second sum is non-negative by definition of η_j, and the last sum is a constant. Therefore, since the sequence (z^k) is bounded, each of the sequences (a_i^k) and $(\bar{a}_j^k)$ must be bounded. Thus we can extract convergent subsequences, still denoted by the index k, such that

$$\lim_k s^k = s^*, \lim_k a_i^k = a_i^*, \text{ and } \lim_k \bar{a}_j^k = \bar{a}_j^*. \tag{9.5}$$

(5) Choose now k_0 so large that each of the points $\bar{a}_j^*$ ($j \in J$) has norm strictly less than k_0. Since according to propositions 7.3 and 8.3 the correspondences μ_i^k and η_j^k are upper hemicontinuous and compact-valued on S_1, (9.5) implies that, for all $k \geq k_0$, one has

$$a_i^* \in \mu_i(s^*), \text{ and} \qquad (9.6)$$
$$\bar{a}_j^* \in \eta_j^k(s^*). \qquad (9.7)$$

Furthermore $z^k \in \Gamma^k$ for all k implies $z^* \in \cap \ \Gamma^k = S_1^0$. Therefore we have by (9.3) $z_l^* = 0$ for all $l \in L$, and $z_j^* \leq 0$ for all $j \in J$. But $s^*z^* = r^*z_a^* = 0$ and $r_0^* = 1$ imply $z_0^* = 0$. Assume $z_j^* < 0$ for some $j \in J$. Then r_j^* is equal to zero. Thus the action

$$\tilde{a}_j^* = \bar{a}_j^* - (0 \ \ldots \ z_j^* \ \ldots \ 0)$$

is also an element of $\eta_j^k(s^*)$. Therefore the $(I+J+1)$-tuple $(a_i^*, \tilde{a}_j^*, s^*)$ constitutes an equilibrium of the economy $\mathscr{E}^k$ for all $k \geq k_0$.

(6) It remains to show that, for each $j \in J$, $\tilde{a}_j^* \in \eta_j^k(s^*)$ for all $k \geq k_0$ implies $\tilde{a}_j^* \in \eta_j(s^*)$. In the sequel we drop the index j.

By definition of the producers' demand correspondences η^k, $\tilde{a}^* \in \eta^k(s^*)$ means that, for each k, there exists an action a^k with the following properties:

$$a^k = (y_1^-, y_2^k, A_1) \in \mu^k(s^*) \qquad (9.8)$$

and

$$\tilde{a}^* = (y_1^-, A_1). \qquad (9.9)$$

By assumption (T1) and (T3), the set $B = \{y_2^k \in \mathbb{R}^L : (y_1^-, y_2^k) \in T\}$ is compact. Thus we may assume that the sequence (y_2^k) converges to an element $y_2^+ \in B$. We will show that the action $a^* = (y_1^-, y_2^+ A_1)$ belongs to $\mu(s^*)$. Clearly a^* belongs to the budget set $\phi(s^*)$. Assume that there exists an element $a \in \phi(s^*)$ such that $V(s^*, a) > V(s^*, a^*)$. Since the sequence $(a^k)_{k=1}$ converges to a^*, and since V is continuous (Lemma 8.1), this would imply $V(s^*, a) > V(s^*, a^k)$ for all k large enough. But $a \in \phi(s^*)$ also implies $a \in \phi^k(s^*)$ for large enough k. Therefore, for some k, a^k is not optimal, in contradiction to (9.8). Hence $a^* \in \mu(s^*)$, which implies $\tilde{a}^* \in \eta(s^*)$.

This completes the proof that $(a_i^*, \tilde{a}_j^*, s^*)$ constitutes an equilibrium for $\mathscr{E}$.

REFERENCES

[1] K. J. Arrow, *Aspects of the Theory of Risk-Bearing* (Helsinki: Academic Bookstore, 1965).
[2] K. J. Arrow, 'The Role of Securities in the Optimal Allocation of Risk-Bearing', *Rev. Ec. Studies*, vol. XXXI (1964), pp. 91–6.

[3] R. J. Aumann, 'Existence of Competitive Equilibria in Markets with a Continuum of Traders', *Econometrica*, vol. XXXIV (1966), pp. 1–17.
[4] C. Berge, *Espaces topologiques* (2nd edition) (Paris: Dunod, 1966).
[5] P. Billingsley, *Convergence of Probability Measures* (New York: Wiley, 1968).
[6] K. H. Borch, *The Economics of Uncertainty* (Princeton: Princeton University Press, 1968).
[7] G. Debreu, *Theory of Value* (New York: Wiley, 1959).
[8] G. Debreu, 'Market Equilibrium', *Proceedings of the National Academy of Sciences of the USA*, vol. XLII (1956), pp. 876–8.
[9] F. Delbaen, 'Continuity of Expected Utility', chapter 14 *infra*.
[10] F. Y. Edgeworth, *Papers Relating to Political Economy*, vols. I–III (London: Macmillan, 1925).
[11] J.-M. Grandmont, 'On the Short-Run Equilibrium in a Monetary Economy', chapter 12 *supra*.
[12] F. H. Hahn, 'On Some Problems of Proving the Existence of an Equilibrium in a Monetary Economy', in F. H. Hahn and F. P. R. Brechling (eds.), *The Theory of Interest Rates* (London: Macmillan, 1965).
[13] J. R. Hicks, *Value and Capital*, (2nd edition) (Oxford: Clarendon Press, 1946).
[14] W. Hildenbrand, Existence of Equilibria for Economies with Production and a Measure Space of Consumers', *Econometrica*, vol. 38 (1970), pp. 608–623.
[15] E. Malinvaud, 'Capital Accumulation and Efficient Allocation of Resources', *Econometrica*, vol. XXI (1953), pp. 233–68.
[16] T. de Montbrial, 'A Restatement of the Classical Theory of Interest', *Paper prepared for the European Meeting of the Econometric Society* (Barcelona, 1971).
[17] J. von Neumann and O. Morgenstern, *Theory of Games and Economic Behaviour* (3rd edition) (Princeton: Princeton University Press, 1953).
[18] R. Radner, 'Existence of Equilibrium of Plans, Prices and Price Expectations in a Sequence of Markets', *Econometrica*, Vol. XL (1972), pp. 289–303.
[19] A. Sandmo, 'On the Theory of the Competitive Firm under Price Uncertainty', *American Economic Review*, vol. LXI (1971), pp. 65–73.
[20] L. J. Savage, *The Foundations of Statistics* (New York: Wiley, 1954).

14 Continuity of the Expected Utility

F. Delbaen[1]
CORE, LOUVAIN, AND UNIVERSITY OF BRUSSELS

This paper is devoted to proving a more general version of proposition 2.1 of [6]. For any unexplained notion we refer to Dieter Sondermann's paper [6].

Ω will be the environment of the economic agent. We assume that on Ω there is a convergence structure [2] which is locally countable (e.g. Ω can be a metric space). $\tilde{\Omega}$ is the set of unknown future states of the world. $\tilde{\Omega}$ is supposed to be a metric space and $\mathscr{F}$ will be the Borel σ-algebra on $\tilde{\Omega}$. The set C will denote the set of consequences. We assume that on C there is a utility function $u : C \to [-1, +1]$. The set A of acts is a subset of $C^{\tilde{\Omega}}$ and is endowed with a convergence structure which is locally countable (A can be a metric space).

For all $\omega \in \Omega$ there is a probability measure $P(\omega, -)$ defined on $(\tilde{\Omega}, \mathscr{F})$. We assume that

(1) $\forall F \subset \tilde{\Omega}$ F closed, $P_F : \Omega \to \mathbb{R}$, $\omega \to P(\omega, F)$ is a continuous function,
(2) $\forall a \in A$ $u(a(-)) : \tilde{\Omega} \to \mathbb{R}$ is $\mathscr{F}$ measurable,
(3) If $a_n \to a$ in A then $\forall \tilde{\omega} \in \tilde{\Omega}$ $u(a_n(\tilde{\omega})) \to u(a(\tilde{\omega}))$ $f(\omega, a)$ is defined as $\int_{\tilde{\Omega}} u(a(\tilde{\omega})) P(\omega, d\tilde{\omega})$.

Theorem. $f : \Omega \times A \to \mathbb{R}$ is a continuous function.

Proof. Since A and Ω are both locally countable we can work with sequences. So let $a_n \to a$ and $\omega_n \to \omega$. For simplicity we write g_n instead of $u(a_n(.))$ and g instead of $u(a(.))$. The measures $P(\omega_n, .)$ and $P(\omega, -)$ will be denoted by P_n and P resp.

The theorem is then an easy consequence of the following lemma.

Lemma. If $\tilde{\Omega}$ is a metric space, if $\mathscr{F}$ is its Borel σ-algebra, if g_n is a sequence of measurable functions $g_n : \tilde{\Omega} \to [-1, +1]$ such that $g_n \to g$ pointwise, if P_n is a sequence of Borel probabilities such that $P_n(F) \to P(F)$ for all closed sets $F \subset \tilde{\Omega}$ then

$$\int g_n dP_n \to \int g dP.$$

Proof. We recall that by Egoroff's theorem ([4] exercise II-4-4) $\forall \epsilon > 0 \ \exists B \in \mathscr{F}$ such that $P(B) > 1 - \epsilon/3$ and $g_n \to g$ uniformly on B.

[1] I would like to thank Mr Dieter Sondermann for discussion on this topic.

Continuity of the Expected Utility

Since a Borel measure on a metric space is regular with respect to closed sets $\exists G \subset B$ closed such that $P(G) > 1 - \epsilon/3$. We also know (by [5] or [4] exercise II-7-3) : $\exists F$ and F_n such that $P(F) > 1 - \epsilon/3$ and $P(F^n) > 1 - \epsilon/4^n$; and on F (resp. F_n), g (resp. g_n) is continuous. If $M = G \cap F \cap \bigcap_{n \geq 1} F_n$ then $P(M) > 1 - \epsilon$ and on M the sequence of continuous functions g_n tends uniformly to g.

We now note that, restricted to M, the sequence of measures P_n tends weakly to P in the sense of [1] and [5].

It follows that $\exists n_0$ such that, $\forall n \geq n_0$, $|\int_M f dP_n - \int_M g dP| < \epsilon$.
Using the triangle inequality one obtains, for $n \geq n_0$,

$$|\int_{\tilde{\Omega}} g_n dP_n - \int_{\tilde{\Omega}} g dP| \leq$$
$$|\int_{\tilde{\Omega}} g_n dP_n - \int_M g_n dP_n| + |\int_M g_n dP_n - \int_M g dP_n| +$$
$$+ |\int_M g dP_n - \int_M g dP| + |\int_M g dP - \int_{\tilde{\Omega}} g dP|$$
$$\leq P_n(M^c) + \|g_n - g\|_M + \epsilon + P(M^c).$$

Now, let $n_1 \geq n_0$ be such that $\forall n \geq n_1 \|g_n - g\|_M \leq \epsilon$ and $P_n(M^c) < \epsilon$.
Then: $|\int g_n dP_n - \int g dP| \leq 4\epsilon$ and this proves the lemma.

Remark 1. If we suppose that $\forall \omega \in \Omega$ $P(\omega, -)$ is a Radon measure (this is always the case if $\tilde{\Omega}$ is a Borel subset of a Polish space) then (1) can be replaced by (1*) $\forall K \subset \tilde{\Omega}$ K compact $P(-, K) : \Omega \to \mathbb{R}$ is continuous.

Remark 2. If C has a topological structure and if $\forall a \in A : a : \tilde{\Omega} \to C$ is continuous then replacing (3) by (3*) if $a_n \to a$ then $a_n(\tilde{\omega}) \to a(\tilde{\omega})$ $\forall \tilde{\omega} \in \tilde{\Omega}$ yields:

The sequence of induced measures $P_n \cdot a_n^{-1}$ converges weakly to $P \cdot a$ in the sense of [1] and [5]. This in turn implies that f is a continuous function. These references require that C is a metric space but as Tøpsoe has shown in [7] one can also speak of weak convergence in general topological spaces. An easy argument shows that even in this general case

$$P_n \cdot a_n^{-1} \to P \cdot a^{-1}.$$

Remark 3. If u is also dependent on ω and fulfils the assumption: if $\omega_n \to \omega$ and $a_n \to a$ then $\forall \tilde{\omega} \in \tilde{\Omega}$

$$u(a_n(\tilde{\omega}), \omega_n) \to u(a(\tilde{\omega}), \omega),$$

then it still holds that $f(\omega, a) = \int_{\tilde{\Omega}} u(a(\tilde{\omega}), \omega) P(\omega, d\tilde{\omega})$ is a continuous function.

Remark 4. Those familiar with weak compactness arguments can easily see that the lemma can be derived from the results stated in [3].

REFERENCES

[1] P. Billingsley, *Convergence of Probability Measures* (New York: John Wiley, 1969).
[2] H. R. Fischer, 'Limesräume', *Mathematische Annalen*, vol. CXXXVII (1959), pp. 269–303.
[3] A. Grothendieck, 'Sur les applications linéaires faiblement compactes d'espaces du type C(K)', *Canadian Journal of Mathematics*, vol. V (1953), pp. 129–73.
[4] J. Neveu, *Bases mathématiques du calcul des probabilités* (Paris: Masson & Cie, 1964).
[5] K. R. Parthasarathy, *Probability Measures on Metric Spaces* (New York: Academic Press, 1967).
[6] D. Sondermann, 'Temporary Competitive Equilibrium under Uncertainty', chapter 13 *supra*.
[7] F. Tøpsoe, 'Compactness in Spaces of Measures', *Studia Mathematica*, vol. XXXVI (1970), pp. 195–212.